BANKING AND FINANCIAL DEEPENING IN BRAZIL

Banking and Financial Deepening in Brazil

Francis A. Lees
Professor of Economics and Finance
St John's University, New York

James M. Botts
Director
Coopers & Lybrand, São Paulo

and

Rubens Penha Cysne
Professor of Economics
Getulio Vargas Foundation, Rio de Janeiro

Foreword by Roberto Teixeira da Costa
President, Brasilpar Servicos Financeiros (BSF)
São Paulo

St. Martin's Press   New York

First published in the United States of America in 1991

Printed in Great Britain

ISBN 0–312–05776–8

Library of Congress Cataloging-in-Publication Data
Lees, Francis A.
Banking and financial deepening in Brazil/Francis A. Lees and
James M. Botts and Rubens Penha Cysne.
p.   cm.
Includes index.
ISBN 0–312–05776–8
1. Finance—Brazil.   2. Banks and banking—Brazil.   3. Financial
institutions—Brazil.   I. Botts, James M., 1941–   .   II. Cysne,
Rubens Penha.   III.Title.
HG185.B7L43   1991
332.1'0981—dc20
                                                    90–49485
                                                       CIP

To Joaquim Alfredo Mamede Cysne and
Maria Cisanita Penha Cysne

Contents

List of Tables   viii
List of Figures   xii
Foreword   xiii
Acknowledgements   xvi
Postscript   xix

Part I   Economic Policy and Financial Development
1   The Economy of Brazil   3
2   Monetary Correction and Real Interest
    Accounting   10
3   Income and Demand Policies in Brazil   55
4   The Economy in the Eighties and the Debt Crisis   88

Part II   Financial Institutions
5   Historical and Structural Trends in the Brazilian
    Financial System   103
6   Banking Institutions   139
7   Non-Banking Financial Institutions   154

Part III   Financial Market Sectors
8   The Money Market   191
9   The Capital Market: Normalisation and
    Development of Financial Intermediaries   235
10   The Stock Exchanges   279
11   Industrial Finance   314

Part IV   Recent Developments
12   The Debt Conversion Programme   347
13   The Privatisation Programme   364
14   Venture Capital Activities   382

Index   389

List of Tables

1.1	Real growth in GDP, Brazil compared with industrial and developing nations	6
1.2	Comparison of real GDP growth rates, Brazil and other Latin American nations, 1981–6	6
1.3	Gross savings and investment in Brazil	7
1.4	Brazil external debt service	7
2.1	Rents and cost of living indexes at the state of Guanabara (1953 = 100)	14
2.2	Commercial banks' time and demand deposits, balances in Cr$ millions (end of period)	18
2.3	Excess taxed income due to underestimated fiscal depreciation	19
2.4	Monetary correction and inflation indexes (end of period)	24
2.5	Estimates of the consumption function	27
2.6	Inflationary tax, inflationary transfers to commercial banks and total transfers	38
2.7	Data for calculation of the difference between nominal and real interest on the internal net debt	42
2.8	Data for calculation of the difference between nominal and real interest on government external debt	43
2.9	Illusory profits estimates for open corporations, period 1958–64	49
3.1	Economic statistics related to the PAEG plan	63
3.2	Evolution of M_4 – per cent rate of change	70
3.3	Real and operational public deficit	71
3.4	M_4 velocity	72
3.5	Money demand estimates, Equation (3.2) for Brazil: 1947(8)–87	82
3.6	Money demand estimates, Equation (3.3): 1948–87	83
4.1	Average rates of growth of output	89
4.2	Inflation in Brazil, end of period	92
4.3	Real wage indexes	92
4.4	External accounts between 1974 and 1987	95
5.1	Statistical overview of the financial system, 30 June 1987	110
5.2	Sectoral contributions to GDP, 1970–85	122

5.3	Real growth of financial sector vs GDP growth, 1981–7	123
5.4	Financial assets compared with GDP, 1971–87	123
5.5	Average daily 'open market' volume	124
5.6	Evolution of number of financial institutions by category, 1970–87	125
5.7	Evolution of banking system deposits, 1983–7	127
5.8	Evolution of banking system loans to the private sector, 1983–7	128
5.9	Capitalisation of financial institutions, 1983–6	129
5.10	Comparative profitability of selected types of financial institutions, return on average equity: 1983–7	130
5.11	Foreign investment in Brazil's financial system, 31 December 1986	132
5.12	Market share of foreign commercial banks, 31 December 1987	132
7.1	Development of leasing activities, 1982–7	156
7.2	Volume of new issues underwriting on principal stock exchanges	157
7.3	Financial service products: institutional comparisons	160
7.4	Minimum capital requirements for brokerage firms and 'distribuidoras'	167
7.5	Alternative development strategies in the Brazilian financial sector, principal advantages and disadvantages	179
8.1	Percentage shares of non-monetary financial assets	195
8.2	Domestic Federal Government and Central Bank debt	199
8.3	Matrix of Federal Government and Central Bank debt	200
8.4	Central bank repurchase–resale agreements with the money market, 3 August 1987	207
8.5	New facilities for computer transactions in shares, debentures and gold	209
8.6	Information provided by Andima for members	212
8.7	Deposit placing and deposit receiving institutions in the Mercado Interfinanceiro, 31 May 1988	215
8.8	Leading money market interest rates and their significance, 1988	219
8.9	Interest rates: institutional market 22 July 1988	219
8.10	Projected returns on selected instruments, 5 August 1988	219
8.11	Short-term interest rates, mercado interfinanceiro, 1988	221
8.12	Daily trading volume, mercado interfinanceiro and	

	other sectors, August 1988	222
8.13	Average maturities of federal government securities, 1986–8	223
8.14	Comparison of nominal and real returns to investor on three types of mutual funds and seven alternative investments, 1987	228
8.15	Financial instruments tax	229
9.1	Main capital market instruments, 1988	239
9.2	Major capital market financial intermediaries, 1986	256
9.3	Basic structure of closed private pension entities, sponsoring firms, distribution of reserves, and participants	259
9.4	Portfolio of closed pension funds, May 1987, May 1988	264
9.5	Portfolio of open private pension funds, March 1987	266
9.6	Resources of insurance companies, 1982–6	267
9.7	Investment Portfolios of insurance companies, year end 1987	268
9.8	Composition of shareholdings of selected investor groups	269
9.9	Portfolio structure of mutual funds, 1985–6	270
9.10	Investments in mutual funds, 1988	271
9.11	Fund of social participation (FPS) activities in the securities markets, 1984–6	272
9.12	Growth in portfolios of foreign capital investment funds, 1982–6	272
9.13	Selected regional and sectoral fiscal funds	274
10.1	Transactions on the stock exchanges, 1987	281
10.2	Development of investment clubs, 1982–7	285
10.3	Average participation and variability of participation in Bovespa, by type of investor, 1982–6, half-year periods	286
10.4	Distribution of share portfolios among investor groups, 1986–7	288
10.5	Institutional investors main investments, 1986, 1987	289
10.6	Participation of investor groups in trading on the São Paulo stock exchange (percentage of transactions), 1987–8	290
10.7	General summary of public companies	292
10.8	Market capitalisation of companies registered at Bovespa	293
10.9	Share transactions on Brazilian stock market, nominal	

and price adjusted amounts 294
10.10 Stock exchange trading as percentage of national income, 1964–86 295
10.11 New securities issues registered 296
10.12 Comparisons of new debenture issues of non-financial companies, Brazil and selected countries 298
10.13 Comparison of new share issues, Brazil and selected countries 299
10.14 Most actively traded shares, 1986–7 300
10.15 Percentage of total share trading of most traded shares 301
10.16 Comparison of sectoral shares of stock market trading on Rio de Janeiro and São Paulo exchanges 302
10.17 Comparative information: three futures and commodities exchanges in Brazil 308
11.1 Industrial investment and BNDES financing 318
11.2 Balance sheet composition: assets 319
11.3 Balance sheet composition: liabilities and capital 322
11.4 Results from operations 324
11.5 Analysis of profitability of industrial enterprises, 1981–6 326
11.6 Schematic outline of main sources of funds of Brazilian enterprises 328
11.7 Sources of funds of industrial companies 330
11.8 Issue of shares by type of enterprise 331
11.9 Uses of funds of industrial companies 333
11.10 BNDES system: approvals for credits 339
12.1 External debt of Brazil 349
12.2 Estimated effect of special factors in enlarging Brazil's borrowing requirements and external debt 350
12.3 Secondary market price range of Brazilian external debt 351
12.4 Investments inflows and conversions of external credits 354
12.5 Monthly swap auctions: discounts on debt 359
13.1 Cofavi: ownership distribution of capital, growth in sales, balance sheet at 30 April 1988 375
13.2 Caraiba Metais: ownership distribution of capital, growth in sales, balance sheet at 31 Jan. 1988 377
14.1 Brazilian investment and venture capital funds, 1988 385
14.2 Two-tranche capital offering of Equitypar 387

List of Figures

2.1	Credit market	16
2.2	Credit market rationing	17
3.1	Real wage evolution in an inflationary environment	58
3.2	Reduction of wage indexing term and increase of average real wage	60
3.3	The 'average adjustment' methodology	61
5.1	Structure of Brazil's financial system	109
5.2	Structure of typical Brazilian financial conglomerate	112
5.3	Structure of financial conglomerate without a commercial bank affiliation	113
5.4	Proposed structure of Brazil's financial system	120
12.1	Informal conversion of external debt	361
13.1	Electric power sector privatisation model	374

Foreword

The initiative of Professors Lees and Cysne, and of James Botts, to write a book on the Brazilian financial system is commendable. The topic is of utmost importance.

Over the past 25 years Brazilian legislators and monetary authorities have had to cope with high and volatile rates of inflation. In their efforts these authorities have created one of the most complex financial systems of the western world, one possessing a highly sophisticated network of financial intermediaries.

The Brazilian system, basically, was inspired in the concept of specialisation, with different functions assigned to each type of financial intermediary. Over the years the financial system has had to be adapted to the realities of very high inflation rates and persistent problems of monetary expansion. Indexation, fiscal incentives, financial intermediaries, institutional investors (pension funds), stock exchanges, all were important factors contributing to the market development. The respective roles played by each of these was continuously changing, according to the need for trial and error adjustments in response to new conditions. Much in the way of market improvement was gained from experience, and adaptations made from this experience.

Incentives to save, created after the Capital Markets Law of 1965, played an important role in improving the rate of savings during the mid-sixties and the 1970s. The flow of savings into investment helps to explain, among other reasons, why Brazil was able to have one of the fastest growing economies in the developing world over the past quarter-century.

One must remember that the flow of direct foreign investment played a fundamental role in this mobilisation of savings. This was particularly important in the development of the manufacturing sector.

Also the evolution of the financial system was well conceived from the point of view of stimulating Brazilians to cast their votes in favour of national economic development. It was essential that they avoid the temptation to invest elsewhere, a problem of special significance in other parts of Latin America. Owing to the coincidence of unfortunate external events (two oil shocks and the global escalation of interest rates) in the 1970s and early 1980s, the Brazilian financial system found it difficult, if not almost impossible, to maintain the previous rate of economic progress. During the late 1970s and 1980s there was slow adjustment by the Brazilian government to these new realities, associated with an acceleration of the inflationary process. One could say that with these problems Brazil was in the position of seeing all that had been gained in the building of the financial markets placed at risk.

Monetary correction, which had become a fundamental factor on the Brazilian scene as it created incentives to save, later proved to be a perverse mechanism and very difficult to eliminate. It performed well in periods of declining inflation, but when inflation accelerated indexation proved to be responsible for the inertial movement and constant readjustment or realignments of wages and prices. These raised the rate of inflation to incredible levels, reaching almost 1000 per cent (annual rate) in 1988.

Moreover the constant need of the government to issue more and more securities to cover growing public deficits placed the market in the position of being excessively dependent on very short-term developments. This has developed to a point where the whole financial system must carry the portfolio of government securities and refund this portfolio at short-term maturities. The short-term maturities and constant refunding operations tend to overcrowd the financial markets, making impossible the mobilisation of financial resources for longer-term projects which require that source of funding.

Evidently in this environment speculation in financial instruments tends to become a predominant factor in the market. This leaves practically no room for the private sector to raise long-term financial resources. This must be associated with different perceptions of risk between different segments of the private sector. Thus, while the government gives some protection to short-run investors holding indexed assets, basic investment needs may not be fulfilled and long-run growth levels decline. How this vicious circle can be broken is one of the greatest challenges for the government elected in November 1989.

Given the young population and generous disposal of natural resources in Brazil, it is important to remember that this nation is not in a position to lose another decade of economic growth. To resume growth, the financial system must undergo complete reform, so that it can again be a factor in mobilising long-term financial resources for investment. Clearly this is only going to occur when the federal government achieves a dramatic improvement in its financial position, and the internal deficit becomes manageable. The pressures of external debt must be accommodated to prevent Brazil exporting capital. The export of capital has exercised a negative effect on growth in recent years, a critical problem in the case of Brazil's development requirements.

These introductory remarks are expanded upon in fine detail in this excellent work. In Part I the authors deal in great depth with economic policy and the financial development of Brazil. In particular they provide comprehensive information and statistical data about the complex and intriguing monetary correction system, as well as real interest accounting. Also in this part of the volume one finds a well elaborated description of income and demand policies, finishing with an examination of the foreign debt crisis, which is treated with great objectivity.

Parts II and III present an elaborate description of the complex financial system that was created in Brazil. Here it is crucial for the reader to analyse and understand what has taken place over time. Two chapters describe the operation of the capital and money markets, and another supplies excellent information on the stock exchanges of Brazil. Apart from all existing difficulties, the Brazilian stock exchanges are among the best equipped in the emerging markets.

Finally, the book covers recent developments in the financial markets, giving special emphasis to the programmes of debt conversion and privatisation. Potentially, these are of great importance in restoring the high growth of the Brazilian economy. Unfortunately the book was already going into print when the Summer Plan, another effort on the part of President Sarney to avoid hyperinflation, was put into effect (15 January 1989). Unfortunately, it is difficult for any book on Brazil to be updated. This is one of the biggest problems of the country – its propensity for ever-changing conditions!

The preceding is not meant to detract from the merits of this work, which will fill an important place as a reference volume needed to help one understand how Brazil has lived with, and is still fighting, inflation.

ROBERTO TEIXEIRA DA COSTA
President, Brasilpar Servicos Financeiros (BSF), São Paulo

Acknowledgements

The Brazilian financial system is a dynamic and rapidly changing part of the national economy. It reflects some of the basic characteristics of the Brazilian economy, including the high growth orientation, and propensity for detailed regulation. It benefits from the strong entrepreneurial spirit as well as the regional and cultural diversity.

This volume represents two years of intensive effort by the authors, embracing a period in which Brazil had three different finance ministers, adopted a new constitution, and shifted its stabilisation policy approach several times. The dynamics of the situation have made this project challenging, interesting and personally rewarding to the three authors. Coming from different professional backgrounds we hope and expect that this volume has been strengthened by these differences. We have attempted to capture the essential and more lasting aspects of those factors influencing the Brazilian financial system, as well as to depict the current situation as accurately as possible.

This volume is the creation of many minds and voices, too many to be given adequate credit. The following provided a considerable part of this essential assistance. Special thanks go to Roberto Teixeira da Costa for guidance, information and references; and to Mario Henrique Simonsen and Edmar Bacha for valuable suggestions. Also, special thanks must be extended to Dr Riordan Roett, Director of the Center of Brazilian Studies, Johns Hopkins University, for the referrals given to the authors.

Vital information was provided by Jose Breno Bruno Salomão, Superintendente, Rio de Janeiro Stock Exchange (formerly with the National Securities Commission); Bruno Mauricio Ribeiro, Chefe de Divisao, Economics Department, Central Bank, Brasília; Roger Hipskind, Banco Chase Manhattan, Rio de Janeiro; João Luis Mascolo, Diretor de Ensino e Pesquisas, Instituto Brasileiro de Mercado Capitais (IBMEC); Rio de Janeiro; Paulo Mente, President, ABRAPP, São Paulo; Walter Guilherme Piacsek, Director, Banco Safra, São Paulo.

Also Satossi Abe, Chefe de Gabinete, Diretoria de Dívida Públicae Mercado Aberto, Central Bank, Rio de Janeiro; Dr Roberto Faldini, Diretor Financeiro, Metal Leve, São Paulo; Sergio Caruso, Chefe Adjunto de Departamento, Departamento de Operações Com Títulos e Valores Mobiliários, Central Bank, Rio de

Janeiro; Pedro Mader Meloni, Vice President, Banco de Boston, São Paulo; Ilona Beer, Economist, Citicorp, São Paulo; Joao Geraldo Ribeiro Filho, São Paulo Stock Exchange; Afonso Augusto Passos Cardoso, Director Técnico, Bradesco, São Paulo.

Celso Martone, University of São Paulo; Nelson T. Sakaguchi, Director International Banking Group, Noroeste Bank, São Paulo; Vagner Quiterio, Vice President, American Express Bank Ltd., São Paulo; Alvaro Afonso Mendonça, Técnico de Projetos, Bolsa Brasileira de Futuros (BBF), Rio de Janeiro; Luiz Afonso da Silva, Economist, Central Bank, São Paulo; Michael de Sa, Vice President, Citicorp Investment Bank, São Paulo; Carlos Barretto, Director, National Securities Commission, Rio de Janeiro; Paulo Galletta, Executive Secretary, Conselho Federal de Desestatização, Brasília; Elizabeth Schnabl Gonçalves M. Garbayo, Superintendente, Comissão de Valores Mobiliários, Rio de Janeiro; Thomas Henry Carter, US Embassy, Brasília; Francisco Sa Filho, Superintendente, Unibanco, São Paulo; J. Walter Corradi, Diretor, Banco Bandeirantes, São Paulo.

Also Eduardo Suplicy, Fundação Getúlio Vargas, São Paulo; Maria Lucia Orselli, Assessoria Técnica, Commissão Nacional de Bolsas de Valores, Rio de Janeiro; Gay S. Hoar, Financial Attache, US Embassy, Brasília; Antonio Carlos de Vasconcelos Valença, BNDES, Rio de Janeiro; Pedro Alves Vieira Primo, Economics Department, Central Bank, Brasília; Carmen Sylvia Motta Parkinson, Superintendente, National Securities Commission, Rio de Janeiro; Roberto Meire, Assessor da Superintendência de Operações, Rio de Janeiro Stock Exchange; Paul Laase, Economic Affairs, US Embassy, Brasília; Eiiti Sato, University of Brasília.

Also Walter L. Ness, Diretor Superintendente, Instituto Brasileiro de Mercado de Capitais, Rio de Janeiro; Jose Francisco Filho, Instituto Brasileiro de Economia, FGV, Rio de Janeiro; Marco W. Ho, Vice President, Bank of Boston, São Paulo; Arnaldo Pinto, BNDESPAR, Rio de Janeiro; Fernando Spinetti, BNDESPAR, Rio de Janeiro; Dr Roberto Guimaraes, Ministério da Fazenda, Brasília; Luiz T. Forbes, Superintendência Geral, Bolsa Mercantil De Futuros, São Paulo; William Steigelmann, Economics Officer, US Consulate, Rio de Janeiro; Maria Clara Isoldi Whyte, Assesora, National Securities Commission, Rio de Janeiro.

Information and references were provided at early stages of the study by Bruce Juba US Treasury; Dr Nicholas Bruck, The World Bank; James Dinsmoor, Inter-American Development Bank; and

Ray Kennedy, Johns Hopkins University, Center for Latin American Studies.

The following read parts of the manuscript and provided useful suggestions: Professor Sergio Ribeiro da Costa Werlang, Fundação Getulio Vargas; Professor Fernando de Holanda Barbosa, Fundacao Getulio Vargas; Renê de Oliveira Garcia Jr., Corretora Roma SA; Jose Bandeira de Mello Jr., Banco Econômico; Professor Istvan Karoly Kaznar, Fundação Getúlio Vargas; Paulo Sampaio, AN-DIMA, Rio de Janeiro, Flavio Auler, FGV.

Special thanks must be extended to Marco Antonio da Rocha, Executive Director, Fulbright Commission, Brasília; and Marcia Pieredes, Executive Director, Fulbright Comission, Lima, Peru.

Thanks must be extended also to Americo Csengeri Netto, who compiled, analysed, and organised much of the data presented in Chapters 5, 6 and 7.

Most important was the institutional support provided by Fundação Getúlio Vargas, Rio de Janeiro; Coopers & Lybrand, São Paulo; and Fulbright Comission, Washington, DC.

Thanks must be extended to Anaja Cysne Moura Neves for important typing support.

FRANCIS A. LEES
JAMES M. BOTTS
RUBENS PENHA CYSNE

Postscript

Since December 1988 when we completed the basic manuscript of this book a number of events have taken place which should be described. These include (1) the Summer Plan (Plano Verão), (2) suspension of debt-conversion auctions, and (3) continued development of the financial markets.

The Summer plan introduced by President Sarney on 15 January 1989 aimed at controlling inflation, which in 1988 reached a level of 933 per cent, according to official government estimates. The Summer Plan was the third effort under President Sarney to achieve macroeconomic stabilisation, preceded by the ill-fated Cruzado Plan of February 1986, and the Bresser Plan of June 1986. The Summer Plan contained several basic elements: (a) a new currency was introduced, the new Cruzado, corresponding to 1000 old cruzados; (b) a price freeze combined with a standstill on indexation; (c) wages and rents were transformed into new cruzados according to their average purchasing power in the preceding twelve months; and (d) a conversion table (*tablita*) was introduced to adjust (deflate) future payments contracted in old cruzados. This final aspect of the Summer Plan was aimed at neutralising the impact of reduced inflation rates.

The Summer Plan de-indexed the Brazilian economy, abolished monetary correction and abolished the OTN (Treasury bond) as an indexor.

The Summer Plan set out to require that government spend no more than its revenues. Bank reserve requirements were increased up to 80 per cent on demand deposits, and domestic credit expansion was temporarily frozen. While prices were frozen, large price increases were authorised in oil products, and electric power. The Minister of Finance was given authority to realign individual and sectoral prices. Orthodox monetary and fiscal austerity were the core of the Plan.

Finance Minister Mailson da Nóbrega implemented the second stage of the Summer Plan in April 1989 with the return to indexation. The new indexor substitutes a new instrument for the Federal Treasury Bond (OTN). This is the National Treasury Bonus (BTN). Optional adjustment is available in accord with the official dollar exchange rate fluctuations. The BTN does not substitute the OTN for contracts signed before the Summer Plan. These contracts continue and are corrected by the Consumer Price Index (IPC).

For the Summer Plan to be successful, it was necessary that (1) real interest rates be kept at high levels until inflation expectations were reduced, (2) budget cuts be implemented, and (3) there be Congressional approval including support for a reduced expenditure level in the government budget and cutbacks in public sector employment. These requirements were not met, and by May it was becoming clear that the Plan could not work.

In January 1989 the monthly debt conversion auctions were suspended. The year 1988 saw a record amount of conversions of Brazilian external debt into equity investments. This was due to the introduction of a formal conversion programme early in 1988 and a high level of informal conversions. Until the Brazilian authorities resume auctions, informal conversion remains open to investors.

The first discount auction for converting foreign debt into risk capital was held in March 1988, and ten monthly auctions were conducted before the suspension early in 1989. A total of US$1953 million of external debt (already due for repayment) was converted into equity in these auctions. In addition, $845 million in debt was converted according to Circular Letter 1125, conversion without discount (registered with the Central Bank up to 1987). Another $793 million was converted, of debt not yet due for repayment (Circular Letter 1303). Finally, $2.6 billion was converted informally, making an estimated total $6.2 billion in debt conversions in 1988.

Suspension of the monthly auctions was related to a rising level of inflation and concern that liquidity created by debt conversion activity would prevent the Summer Plan from reducing inflation.

During the first half of 1989 the Brazilian stock market experienced a strong expansion, followed by a sharp correction. Between December 1988 and May 1989 average daily turnover on the Brazilian stock exchanges increased fourfold. During May 1989 daily average turnover was 2½ times the average turnover in 1988, and 4½ times that of 1987. By early May 1989 the market value of listed companies was double the year-end 1988 market value (in US dollars).

Illiquidity of a major market speculator triggered a sharp decline in the Brazilian stock market (June 1989). Several stock brokerage houses became insolvent. The leading market indexes lost over 50 per cent of their value in the first half of June. Trading volume contracted sharply, and regulators closed the share options and index futures markets.

The June 1989 market decline should result in stock market reforms that provide an improved market system in the future. Commercial banking and stock brokerage may be separated, regulators may be provided with more substantial resources, and stock market trading rules may be tightened and better enforced.

The face value of a BTN was set at NCz\$ 1.00 (one novo cruzado, which is equivalent to a thousand cruzados) on 1 February 1989. This value is monthly corrected according to the rate of change of the consumer price index (IPC). Some values throughout this book are expressed in OTN, which was abolished with the Summer Plan. The last available value for the OTN is NCz\$ 6.17, on 1 January 1989. The relation between these two means of account depends upon the choice of the price index used to translate the inflation in January 1989. Generally, 1 OTN is taken to be equivalent to a number between 8.5 and 10 BTN.

F.A.L.
J.M.B.
R.P.C.

Part I
Economic Policy and Financial Development

1 The Economy of Brazil

Brazil is the largest nation in Latin America, with over half of the total land mass and approximately half of the population. The economy produces about half of the region's aggregate gross domestic product, and is one of the most diversified economies of the developing world. Close to 60 per cent of merchandise exports consists of industrial products, and these are diversified across many commodity lines.

Brazil has a land area of 3.3 million square miles, bordering all but two South American countries (Chile and Ecuador). Forest resources are extensive, and forest growth covers substantial areas of the country. Agriculture plays a strong role in the economy, despite the fact that industrial production has become a dominant or major contributor to income, employment and exports. Brazil benefits from an extensive river system, with the Amazon alone providing drainage for over half of the nation's land mass. Other large river and tributary systems include the São Francisco in the north-east, the Parana and the Paraguay.

THE ECONOMY

In the last three decades Brazil has changed from an economy highly dependent on agriculture and mining to one based on industry. Industrial growth was achieved through application of an import substitution programme, emphasis on private enterprise which attracted strategic foreign investment, and government support in the financing of infrastructure investment. As a result, in 1986 Brazil was the world's seventh largest steel producer, eighth largest aluminium producer and tenth largest automobile producer.

While the government stresses the role of private enterprise, economic policy has made the government an owner of most public utilities as well as pivotal investor in selected key industries. Energy production, rail transport, telephone and telegraph networks are directly or indirectly controlled by the government. In addition, the government controls some enterprises which might compete with private sector companies. Examples include Banco do Brasil (commercial banking), and principal steel and mining companies. Brazil's

3

largest government-controlled company is Petrobras, which has a legally established monopolistic position in the exploration and production of petroleum in Brazil. The result of these policies is that Brazil has an industrial sector that (in ownership) is divided into three major components: the private national, state enterprise, and foreign controlled sectors.

In 1987 Brazil had a gross domestic product (GDP) of US$325 billion, the largest of any developing nation. During the 1970s GDP had grown at a rate of almost 9 per cent per year. The second oil shock in 1979 and the increased debt burden that followed the sharp escalation in world interest rates (1979–81) brought Brazil's growth rate down to a much lower level. The reduced rate of growth in 1987 (2.9 per cent) reflected increased inflation and a resulting compression in consumer spending power. During the 1980s gross domestic investment in Brazil has been at a low level (18–19 per cent of GDP). This is below investment levels maintained in the 1970s, and much lower than required to achieve sustained economic growth. To achieve satisfactory growth, Brazil requires gross investment levels of between 21 and 25 per cent of GDP. One problem is that the financial mechanism in Brazil has not channelled a sufficient volume of funds into investment. In the past this shortfall has been supplemented by foreign investment funds, foreign loans and government-directed credits. However it is probable that, in the future, the domestic financial system in Brazil will have to provide a larger share of the capital required to support adequate levels of investment.

According to a 1985 National Household Survey, the active work force in Brazil totalled 53.2 million. Of these, 29 per cent were employed in agriculture, forestry and fishing; 22 per cent in the industrial sector (including mining); and 49 per cent in commerce and services, government, and other activities. With some exceptions, unions in Brazil are not politically strong. Nevertheless union pressures for wage increases and for a moratorium on external debt servicing (in 1986–7) have complicated the efforts of the government to combat inflation.

POLITICAL AND ECONOMIC PROGRESS

Brazil is a nation that has achieved much in the twentieth century, in the way of developing its economy, and in modernising its political and social institutions. On the economic side Brazil ranks eighth in the world in ability to produce goods and services, fifth in total population, and twentieth in capturing export markets. In the past two decades the industrial sector has been transformed into a fairly modern and self-sufficient system. Brazil is self-sufficient in manufacturing most of the inputs required for capital goods production (iron and steel, trucks, cement, motors and basic equipment).

On the political side the opening to democracy which took place early in the 1980s is being completed with the adoption of a new constitution. Provision has been made for the first presidential elections to be held under the new constitution. Executive power is vested in the President, who is elected and who appoints ministers of state to preside over various executive departments. The legislature consists of the Senate and Chamber of Deputies. Legislative members are elected directly by the people. The federal government is busy modernising its structure, so that economic decision making and policy can become more responsive to the needs of Brazil as it becomes more integrated into the world economy.

INTERNATIONAL COMPARISONS

Over the past quarter-century Brazil has achieved a high rate of economic growth. This was made necessary by substantial population growth up to the 1970s (2.5 per cent a year). Comparisons of growth in Brazil with that of developing countries and industrial countries are made in Table 1.1. As can be seen, Brazilian economic growth far exceeded that of the industrial market economies, except during the early 1980s. Also the Brazilian growth rate was well ahead of that of the developing nations, except for the same period. The annual growth rates achieved in 1965–73 of 6.8 per cent, and in 1973–80 of 7.9 per cent, permitted Brazil to become one of the largest economies in the world, with a present ranking of eighth in terms of total GDP.

Even during the slower-paced 1980s growth experience in Brazil has compared well with that of other countries. Taking the period 1981–6, we can see in Table 1.2 that Brazilian growth was three times that of the Latin American average, and much higher than the sample of countries shown in the table. Only one country in Latin America – Cuba – achieved a higher growth rate in the period.

Brazil has been able to achieve this successful growth for several reasons. These include a large and diversified territory, which provides Brazil with a diversified agriculture, self-sufficiency in food

Table 1.1   Real growth in GDP, Brazil compared with industrial and
developing nations (annual rates)

	1965–73	1973–80	1981	1982	1983	1984	1985	1986	1987
Developing countries	6.5	5.4	3.4	2.1	2.1	5.1	4.8	4.7	3.9
Industrial market economies	4.5	2.8	1.9	–0.5	2.2	4.6	2.8	2.7	2.9
Brazil	6.8	7.9	–3.1	1.1	–2.8	5.7	8.4	8.0	2.9

Source: World Bank, *World Development Report* 1987 and 1988, p. 16;
Central Bank of Brazil, *Programa Economico*, various issues.

Table 1.2   Comparison of real GDP growth rates, Brazil and other Latin
American nations, 1981–6 (average annual rates)

		Average annual increase (%)
Latin America		1.0
Oil exporting		0.3
Bolivia	–2.4	
Mexico	0.8	
Peru	0.8	
Venezuela	–1.3	
Non-oil exporting		1.4
Argentina	–1.2	
Brazil	3.1	
Chile	0.6	
Colombia	2.9	
Paraguay	2.3	

Source: Mario Henrique Simonsen, *The Developing Country Debt Status*,
Fundação Getúlio Vargas and World Bank, Rio de Janeiro, 1988, p. 23.

production, and an export surplus. A second important factor has
been the enormous forest and mineral deposits, with raw materials
including iron ore, timber, gold, non-ferrous metals and other basic
inputs required to feed a growing industrial base.

A third factor has been the diversified and industrious labour
force. A large part of Brazilian employment is in the informal sector,
which reflects the enterprising spirit of many Brazilians. A fourth
factor has been the ability of Brazil to organise its financial resources

Table 1.3   Gross savings and investment in Brazil (per cent of GDP)

	1965–73	1973–80	1980–85
Gross investment	26.1	26.2	20.4
Gross savings	24.3	21.7	16.9
Balance	– 1.8	– 4.5	– 3.5

Source: World Bank, *World Development Report 1987*, p. 181.

in a manner permitting high levels of saving and investment. As can be noted from Table 1.3, Brazilian gross saving and investment have represented well in excess of 20 per cent of GDP (except in the 1980s). Finally, we should note that Brazil is a country whose people are motivated by a strong entrepreneurial spirit. The Brazilian business sector is managed by an entrepreneurial class that adds immeasurably to overall initiative and productivity.

EXTERNAL DEBT

Brazil is the largest developing country debtor, with an external debt in 1987 of $121 billion. The Brazilian economy has faced a severe constraint as a result of this debt, and of the need to generate a large export surplus to finance the annual debt service payments. In Table 1.4 we present some basic statistics concerning Brazil's debt and debt service payments. As can be seen, despite the debt crisis and freeze in

Table 1.4   Brazil external debt service, US$ millions

	1983	1985	1987
Debt service repayments	8 118	10 672	13 761
Net interest	9 555	9 659	8 792
Total	17 673	20 331	22 553
Gross external debt	93 556	105 125	121 264
International reserves	4 563	11 609	7 458
Exports	21 899	25 639	26 213
Debt service/exports (%)	80.7	79.3	86.0
Net External Debt/Exports (%)	406.4	364.7	434.2

Source: Central Bank of Brazil.

new credits to Brazil, the gross external debt has been increasing at about 6 per cent a year. But, more important, the debt service absorbs a considerable part of export revenues. While Brazil has enjoyed an impressive export growth, and maintained a large trade surplus, the ratio of debt and debt service to exports has crept up year by year.

In February 1987, a moratorium was declared by Brazil on interest paid on external debt, this was maintained until July 1988, when interest payments were resumed. A partial solution to the external debt problem came into being early in 1988, with the debt conversion programme. At the time of writing this programme appeared to be operating successfully. It is described in detail in Chapter 12.

PLAN OF THE BOOK

This volume focuses primarily on Brazil's financial market development, and financial deepening. The financial system, which includes the banks, non-bank financial institutions and financial market sectors, has grown and evolved into a complex system. The financial sector generates over 12 per cent of GDP, and has become an important employer in the labour market. The complexities of the Brazilian financial system are magnified by government regulation, and by repeated changes in government policy.

In Part I we focus on the economics of the financial system, first examining how monetary correction has developed to become a central aspect of financial market activities. Other chapters consider government policy, the Cruzado Plan, and the international debt crisis. In Part II we examine the development and role of Brazil's banks and banking system. Also we consider the role of non-bank institutions in Brazilian financial development, including the corretoras, distribuidoras, investment funds, leasing companies, and venture capital companies.

In Part III we analyse the development of financial market sectors. The money market is considered in the light of the need to deal with high inflation, and in view of the semi-closed foreign exchange market system. Capital market development is viewed in terms of normalisation through development of a legal structure. Secondly, the capital market is considered in terms of the development of financial intermediaries. Part IV considers current developments, including the recent debt conversion programme, and efforts to privatise the industrial sector. A concluding chapter focuses briefly on the outlook for further development of the financial system in Brazil, particularly in the direction of developing venture capital activities.

2 Monetary Correction and Real Interest Accounting

The financial system in Brazil is unique in several respects. In this chapter we focus on one aspect of the Brazilian financial system which gives it a distinct and unique character: monetary correction. Monetary correction was adopted in piecemeal fashion, but now covers most aspects of financial activity.

This chapter considers monetary correction from a number of standpoints, including the implications for the federal budget and budget control, the inflationary redistribution effects favouring banking institutions, and the influence on company finances, given the interaction between inflation and monetary correction.

2.1 INTRODUCTION

Monetary correction is a method used for correcting monetary values when the currency in which claims are denominated has its purchasing power (of a set of goods) changing over time. It is a tool used to reduce the distortions from inflation. Ultimately, it represents an implicit institutional acceptance of the need to dissociate two uses of money: as a means of payment, and as a standard of accounts. Also monetary correction generally is used as a synonym for the difference between nominal and real interest paid on a security. However, when the inflation index differs from the monetary correction index, these amounts are obviously not the same. To differentiate between them, we shall use the distinct terms 'inflationary correction', which takes into consideration the inflation index, and 'monetary correction', based on the monetary correction index. By definition, the difference between nominal and real interest is given by the 'inflationary correction'.

In Brazil the development of monetary correction techniques and legislation began in 1964. The complicated set of rules developed from this date onward reflect a second-best alternative chosen by the country to minimise the costs of inflation. This was done instead of eliminating inflation.

In a certain way, the costly allocation of the nation's scarce resources to create, develop and apply these rules, can be viewed as the price paid for using a fiscal system based more on disguised indirect taxation (inflationary tax) than on explicit direct taxation. As we explain in section 2.3.4, in some years the inflationary tax exceeded 5 per cent of GDP. As a counterpart, two groups have benefited from this perverse method of government financing an excess of expenditures over receipts: the commercial banks, which earn high rates of real interest on the free part of demand deposits, and the accountants and economists, who are paid to create, understand, translate and apply this apparatus.

Monetary correction indexes are set each month at the discretion of the government. As Table 2.4 shows, they have generally been set below the inflation rate. The face value of Indexed Treasury Bonds (BTNs) is the indicator of the monetary correction index.

After a heuristic introduction to the necessity of an institutional apparatus related to monetary correction in countries with inflation, this chapter concentrates solely on the differentiation between nominal and real interest accounting. This problem extends to many important macroeconomic statistics. The first one, studied in sections 2.3.1, 2.3.2, 2.3.3 and 2.3.5, is the controversy about the estimates of public deficits. Since 1982, the operational concept of deficit, which deals with real interest, has been systematically used in Brazil. Many economists, however, continue to doubt that this should be the appropriate figure to use to estimate the disequilibrium in public finance. In these sections, besides presenting some econometric results to serve as empirical background for the question, we try to explain the main lines of the methodology used in these calculations. Some simplified ways to evaluate the difference between nominal and real interest paid on financial assets are also presented.

Section 2.3.4 presents the total amounts of inflationary tax and inflationary transfers of the commercial banks in Brazil since 1947. They are defined as the negative real interest paid by the monetary authorities and the commercial banks, respectively, on the stock of high-powered money and on the excess of demand deposits over reserve requirements of the commercial banks. Added up, they reach, in some years, the amazing figure of almost 9 per cent of GDP.

Section 2.3.6 extends the methodology of real interest accounting to social accounting. The differences are concentrated on the income side. There are two possible distributions of the gross domestic income among the government, households, firms and external sector: one with nominal interest, and the other with real interest accounting. The operational methodology is also introduced. This represents a half-way point between the nominal and real interest methodology.

Finally, section 2.3.7 shows that the use of real interest to calculate the budget deficit of the government or in social accounting can be seen as a simple extension of the profits correction mechanism introduced in Brazil in 1964. Looking from this standpoint, it represents nothing new.

2.2   THE DEMAND FOR MONETARY CORRECTION

In an economy facing high rates of inflation, the continuous loss of real value of the accounting unit leads to the need for compensatory mechanisms which allow for the dissociation between the real and nominal values of the transactions. It is obviously a second-best solution, since it would always be better to live without inflation.

A trivial problem is the one deflating time series for the purpose of comparisons of values situated at different points in time. The method transforms monetary values denominated in currency of (purchasing power of) period j (V_j) into monetary values denominated in currency of period t (V_t) by means of the formula:

$$V_t = V_j (P_t / P_j) \tag{1}$$

P_j and P_t standing for the price level, respectively, at time j and t.

Another crucial problem is to distinguish, in the same period of time (let us say, one year), the nominal interest payment from the real. In periods of inflation, the creditors' real income is less than the nominal one, the opposite applying to the debtors. This distinction is necessary to delineate the appropriate taxation, profits distribution, budgetary forecasts and analysis.

Among the practical problems that arise in the day-to-day life of economic agents, we shall analyse three main categories: (1) those related to the necessary correction of nominal values over time; (2) those concerning the demand and supply of credit and; (3) those concerning the accounting procedures. These last two categories rely on the need for a clear distinction, in the same period of time, between nominal interest and real interest.

2.2.1   Correction of nominal values

Equation (1) tells us that, without price stability, cruzados received at time t are different (in terms of purchasing power) from cruzados received (or paid) at time j. Transactions among economic agents are fundamentally based on purchasing power, rather than on nominal values. Consequently, it would be reasonable to expect that automatic corrections based on Equation (1) were endogenously incorporated in contracts and agreements concluded between economic agents. This is the popular escalator clause mechanism, which proves its usefulness whenever the same transaction has its money payment specified in at least two different points in time. Among the best-known examples are the penalties incurred by debtors in the case of delaying a previously agreed payment and the setting of different types of income (such as wages or rents) to be received at different points in time.

Although it may seem trivial, many years of inflation-induced arbitrary transfers from creditors to debtors ocurred before this institutional apparatus of monetary correction was legally established in Brazil. For example, with respect to tax liabilities, only in 1964 was debt correction introduced. The very high rates of inflation existing in those years (51.2 per cent in 1962, 81.3 per cent in 1963 and 91.9 per cent in 1964) made it highly profitable to delay payments to the government. Law 4357 stipulated that fiscal debts should be corrected according to indexes to be established by the Planning Ministry. Moreover any fines and penalties associated with delayed payments were to be calculated over the corrected values.

Before 1964, wages were generally corrected on a yearly basis, informally, taking into consideration past inflation. The methodology introduced by Laws 54018 (of 14 July 1964) and 54228 (of 1 September 1964) established the first official rules for fixing wages in Brazil. The details of this are analysed in the next chapter. As concerns rents, the situation until 1964 was really a dramatic one. Between 1950 and 1964, rents were systematically corrected below inflation. This led to a decrease in the real income of real estate owners, a sharp increase in the initial prices of the new rents, and a decrease in investments in the sector, aggravating the housing shortage. Table 2.1 contrasts movement in the rent cost index with the General Price Index during the period 1953–1968. One can observe the sharp deterioriation of the terms of trade against the landlords until 1964,

Table 2.1   Rents and cost of living indexes at the state of Guanabara
(1953 = 100)

Year	Rent index (A)	Cost of living index (B)	A/B
1953	100	100	1.000
1954	120	122	0.984
1955	137	151	0.907
1956	160	182	0.879
1957	191	212	0.901
1958	223	243	0.918
1959	267	338	0.790
1960	317	437	0.725
1961	372	583	0.638
1962	509	884	0.576
1963	774	1507	0.514
1964	1169	2889	0.405
1965	2313	4787	0.483
1966	4050	6764	0.599
1967	6213	8824	0.704
1968	8426	1 0766	0.783

Source: Chacel, Simonsen and Wald (1976), original source: Getulio Vargas
Foundation.

and the inversion of this trend as of this date, when escalator clauses
were introduced and became generalised.

The classical stabilisation mechanism, by means of which high rates
of inflation lead to a migration of tax payers from lower levels to the
higher levels of income tax brackets was not important in Brazil.
First, with the high rates of inflation after 1961, these brackets of
income were fixed in terms of minimum wages, which were periodically revised (otherwise, the taxation would become unbearable for
those situated in the lower-income brackets). Second, indirect taxes
always represented the largest share of taxation, and the direct taxes
on firms were more important than the same taxes on individuals.
Beginning with Law 4506 (1965) income brackets became indexed.
Nowadays they are adjusted annually according to a coefficient
established at the discretion of the Ministry of Finance, which is
generally a measure of the inflation that ocurred in the period.

2.2.2 Demand and suppy of credit

A natural solution to unanticipated devaluation of the figures set in loan agreements due to inflation would be a floating interest rate. This interest rate would reflect the costs of attracting money to financial institutions and should vary in proportion to inflation. As is well known, however, this mechanism does not work in high-inflation environments, for one simple reason: if the interest is not accrued to the principal (by this we mean, if net current receipts exactly match interest payments leaving unchanged the nominal value of the net debt), the higher the inflation, the higher will be the fall of the real value of the debt or credit. This subject is discussed in section 2.3.1. Such a situation can lead to acute problems of insolvency. If we take, for instance, 100 per cent a year inflation, the complete payment of the nominal interest accruing on the principal will reduce the real value of the net debt to one-half. In other words, in one year, the debtor would have been obliged to pay off half of the real value of the net debt. A feasible alternative would be the floating of the real rate of interest. The nominal periodical payments would be corrected by some price index, and a real and variable interest rate would accrue over this amount.

In Brazil, there was no room for these procedures up to 1964. Law 23501, enacted in 27 November 1933, prohibited the use of any means of account other than cruzeiros. This made it illegal monetarily to correct contracted or agreed values (taking into consideration the exchange rate devaluation or the variation of the domestic price index in the period). At the same time, Law 22626, of 7 April 1933, prohibited the charging of nominal interest rates above 12 per cent a year (a similar measure has just been introduced in the new constitution, but, this time, concerning the real rate).

With these two Laws in force interest rates in Brazil had a ceiling of 12 per cent a year. Given the escalation of inflation from 1957 onward, the natural consequence was a decline of the real interest rate and an excess demand for credit. Suddenly it became very cheap to borrow: good for borrowers, but bad for lenders. Three artifices to increase the effective price of loans were in general use by lenders at this time. The first was the widespread use of banking comissions. The second was constituted by off-the-record payments. The third, and more important, was the requirement of maintaining a minimum stipulated cash deposit relative to the loan taken out.

In practice, this last trick means that the financial institution

Figure 2.1   Credit market

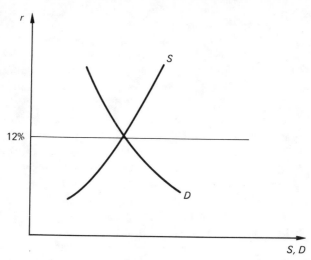

actually lends only a fraction of what is stipulated in the contract. By this procedure, a 12 per cent a year loan of ten cruzeiros followed by the requirement of five cruzeiros as average balance in cash turned out to be equivalent to a 24 per cent a year cost of the loan. Yet, these artifices were not enough to deal with the interest ceiling problem. Figure 2.1 helps to explain what happens to the credit market on such an occasion. We admit that both borrowers and lenders have no money illusion and that, consequently, both the supply of funds (S) and the demand for credit (D) are functions of the real expected interest rate ($\bar{r}-\bar{\pi}^e$). $\bar{\pi}^e$ stands for the logarithm expected rate of inflation and $\bar{r}$ for the logarithm nominal interest rate.[1] For the sake of simplicity, we admit that expected inflation is equal to the actual rate of inflation ($\bar{\pi} = \bar{\pi}^e$).

We depart from an initial short-run equilibrium, shown in Figure 2.1. With the rise of inflation (and, consequently, of the expected inflation) the two curves shift upwards (since both S and D are functions of $\bar{r} - \bar{\pi}^e$) leading to an excess demand for credit given by $D' - S'$, as shown in Figure 2.2. The natural consequence of the interest ceiling is an arbitrary income transfer against those with limited access to the market. Since the minimum between demand and supply must prevail, the statistics of the supplied credit must

Figure 2.2   Credit market rationing

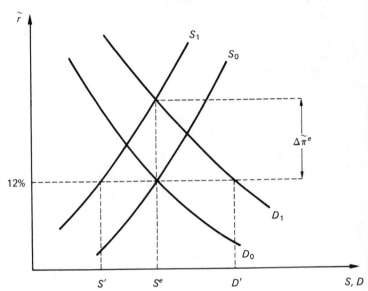

show a sharp decline (from S^e to S'). In fact, they do. Table 2.2 shows that the time deposit share in M_2 (M_1 plus time deposits) declined from 24 per cent in 1951 to 4.0 per cent in 1965. As of this date, a small recovery, due to the introduction of monetary correction, can be observed. Concerning debentures, the situation was the same. Despite the premium and the short maturity at which they were sold, their proportion to GDP fell steadily between 1956 and 1964.

Behind all these hindrances to the efficient working of the financial markets and, consequently, to capital formation and economic development, was the law making it illegal to transform cruzeiros of one period into cruzeiros of another. In other words, it was impossible to use escalator clauses in contracts and agreements. These obstacles were finally removed after 1964. On 17 July 1964, Law 4357 allowed the government to issue bonds with escalator clauses. This was a first step towards a generalised indexation of other assets, including saving accounts, mortgages, labour funds (FGTS) and so on.

Table 2.2   Commercial banks' time and demand deposits balances in Cr$ millions (end of period)

Year	Deposits in cruzeiros				General wholesale price index (1953=100)	Deposits in constant cruzeiros	
	Demand Deposits (1)	Time Deposits (2)	Total (3)	Percentage (2) in (3)		demand deposits	time deposits
1951	52.2	16.9	69.1	24.4	82.5	63.3	20.5
1952	60.3	16.9	72.2	23.4	90.4	66.7	18.7
1953	71.2	17.7	88.9	19.9	113.2	62.9	15.6
1954	84.9	20.4	105.3	19.3	140.3	60.5	14.5
1955	102.4	19.8	122.2	16.2	153.5	66.7	12.9
1956	126.6	21.1	147.7	14.3	192.9	65.6	10.9
1957	176.1	24.3	200.4	12.1	199.4	88.3	12.2
1958	216.1	25.8	241.9	10.6	255.0	84.7	10.1
1959	321.6	30.8	352.4	8.7	347.1	92.7	8.9
1960	438.2	47.4	485.6	9.8	460.8	95.1	10.3
1961	610.8	55.2	666.0	8.3	691.6	88.3	8.0
1962	1 037.7	56.3	1 094.0	5.1	1 037.0	100.0	5.4
1963	1 703.9	89.4	1 793.3	5.0	1 886.0	90.3	4.7
1964	3 069.6	148.3	3 217.9	4.6	3 645.0	84.2	4.1
1965	5 799.7	241.7	6 041.4	4.0	4 676.0	124.0	5.2
1966	6 390.0	696.0	7 086.0	9.8	6 413.0	99.6	10.9
1967	9 622.0	533.5	10 155.5	5.3	7 881.0	122.1	6.8
1968	13 483.8	918.5	14 403.30	6.4	9 854.0	136.9	9.3

Source: Chacel, Simonsen and Wald (1976), original source: Central Bank of Brazil.

2.2.3   Accounting procedures

Finally let us turn our attention to the accounting problems which arise as a result of inflation. We focus on them for the remainder of this chapter. With respect to the enterprise sector, they are twofold. First, the net financial assets generate a flow of income (nominal interest) whose main part (the inflationary correction) is only to keep constant its real value over time. If this income is incorporated into the profit calculations, there will be an overestimation of this figure, leading the firm to pay more taxes and distribute more dividends to shareholders than it should. As a consequence, other things constant, the real value of the firms assets will decrease at the end of the period.

Data available for the period 1958–64 show that these illusory profits were responsible for over 50 per cent of the profits of corporations. These figures will be presented in section 2.3.7. To avoid such problems the correct procedure would be to distinguish the nominal from the real interest, and only incorporate the latter in profits. In Brazil, the figures calculated under this methodology are called 'lucros corrigidos' (corrected profits). We will get back to this matter in section 2.3.7.

The need to distinguish between nominal and real profits is the same when a firm or an individual sells a capital good. Should the difference between the selling and buying price be interpreted as a profit, the effective tax burden would be higher than it should, since part of this difference can be attributed to inflationary correction of the physical asset price.

Another problem for business firms which exists when there is inflation (and this problem is not recognised by the laws) is the overpayment of taxes due to the underestimation of the allowed fiscal depreciation of physical assets. The point is that, with prices steadily rising, the replacement values of the physical assets are higher than the historical ones. If this fact is not legally recognised, the fiscal depreciation of physical assets, calculated in terms of the historical values, will be systematically underestimated. To illustrate this, let us take a firm which has acquired a Cz$100 capital good, whose useful life is supposed to be four years. If we work with an inflation rate of 100 per cent a year the corrected depreciation and the depreciation based on the historical value of the capital good would be, in current cruzados, as indicated in Table 2.3. As can be seen, the underestimation of the amount to be subtracted from the gross income (per-

Table 2.3   Excess taxed income due to underestimated fiscal depreciation

Year	Corrected value of the capital good at average prices of the year	Corrected depreciation	Allowed depreciation	Excess taxed income (corrected – allowed depreciation)
1	150	37.5	25	12.5
2	300	75	25	50
3	600	150	25	125
4	1.200	300	25	275
Total	–	562.5	100	462.5

mitted depreciation amount) to obtain the taxable income systematically leads to overtaxation. This problem was first recognized by Law 4357, of 1 July 1964, which allowed for the use of monetarily corrected depreciation values.

Another reason for careful discrimination between nominal and real interest arises in the construction of the flow of funds and social accounting statistics. If there is no money illusion, the figures of the budget deficit calculated with real interest can eventually be more appropriate than the other ones. The same thing happens in social accounting. This will be the main subject of section 2.3.1 and 2.3.6.

2.3   THE REAL INTEREST ACCOUNTING METHODOLOGY

2.3.1   Controversy over different concepts of the public deficit

A striking problem emerged during the negotiations initiated between Brasil and The International Monetary Fund (IMF) representatives at the end of 1982. The IMF maintained that Brazilian negotiators should calculate the budget figures in accordance with the agreed forecast of inflation. The problem is that these forecasts were systematically underestimated. The indexation rules existing at that time made the economy much less sensitive to aggregate demand control than would normally be expected. Consequently, interest paid on the public debt was systematically underestimated. In sum, every time the inflation rate was higher than predicted, interest expenditures of the government paid on public debt were also higher and, as a result, so was the budget deficit.

This problem partially explains why the IMF, which generally negotiates one 'Letter of Commitment' a year with countries which seek its financial aid, found it necessary to analyse four proposed agreements in 1983 and three in 1984, during negotiations with the Brazilian authorities. At this time the Brazilian representative at the IMF suggested that the budget forecasts should deal only with real interest paid on the debt, since the part of interest payments due to inflation would always be beyond the control of the government. The suggestion was not easily or promptly accepted by the Fund technicians (or even by the majority of Brazilian economists). They argued that nominal interest expenses were to be matched exactly like all other expenses: by tax collection, printing of money, or expansion of the public net debt. Thus it would be nonsense to try to construct a deficit figure leaving aside these amounts.

Six years later, in 1988, the real interest approach to the calculus of budget figures seems to be accepted as common sense. In Brazil, the 'operational deficit' (which will be defined later) is the statistic connected to fiscal policy management divulged by the government. In the Mexican stabilisation plan of 1988, aggregate demand monitoring was based on what is termed 'primary deficit', which goes beyond Brazilian methodology, also excluding the real interest payments from recorded government expenditures. As a general rule, the same kind of procedure has been used to describe the fiscal accounts of many countries facing high rates of inflation.

Our main purpose here will be to analyse the possible theoretical bases behind these (previously unusual) procedures. We begin by remembering a trivial fact already mentioned in section 2.2: in inflationary environments, if the interest on net debts is not accrued to the principal, the higher the inflation rate, the more quickly the real value of the debt will decline. As a general rule, if the nominal deficit is equal to zero and inflation to π, the real amortisation of the principal will be equal to a fraction $\pi/(1 + \pi)$ of the initial real net debt.[2] As can easily be seen, in this case the amortisation of the real value of the net debt is an increasing function of inflation.

Put another way, this reasoning means that high nominal government deficits in high-inflation countries should be seen as a natural consequence of the fact that debtors cannot clear up their real debts, given such high rates,[3] and, even if they could, there is no economic reason why amortisation should be kept proportional to inflation, as in the case of a zero (or any other fixed number) nominal deficit target.

This simple arithmetic shows that, in countries where inflation is high and unstable, it becomes very difficult to try to monitor aggregate demand by forecasting nominal budget deficit figures. The two possible alternatives are (1) to fully eliminate any interest receipts or payments from the budget calculations; and (2) to work only with real interest rates.

Another point to be noted is that, contrary to the arguments presented by IMF members, interest payments are not exactly equivalent to wage, dividend or rental payments. The reason is an accounting one: only financial assets systematically lose their value in inflationary environments. This does not mean that wages, for example, are not affected by inflation, but that the possible losses or gains arising from inflation are not systematic, since they are continuously readjusted over time. In other words, it makes no sense, for instance, for a firm to compare total wage payments with total interest payments, in order to evaluate the relative shares in production costs. Indeed, included in the nominal interest payments is the real amortisation of the firm's liabilities, which has nothing to do with production costs.

If inflation is 100 per cent a year, and the real interest rate zero, a Cz$100 debt will be responsible for Cz$100 interest payments, but the real value of this debt will be reduced to a half at the end of the period: should one want to compare relative shares in production costs, real interest should replace nominal interest. This is equivalent to working with nominal interest and crediting the current account of the economic agent with the real amortisation of the respective debt. This distinction between interest and other remunerations led to the differentiated treatment given to interest in the corporate profits evaluation. The operational deficit concept can be seen as a simple extension of this accounting asymmetry.

Of course, the construction of any statistic will be more or less appropriate depending on its intended uses. Let us assume that the main purpose of the budget deficit calculations is to relate these to the control of aggregate demand. As we know, interest receipts and payments affect aggregate demand by means of the changes they impose on the net income of the private sector. Consequently what we have to ask is: what kind of net income of the private sector should be considered – the one calculated with nominal interest or real interest? In a first approach to this question, wholly based on the possibility of there existing money illusion, the answer would be the first, if economic agents decide about their consumption levels taking into consideration the whole amount of interest they get from holding public debt; and the second, if they recognised that a part of these earnings is only a nominal restitution of the real value of the debt that was lost owing to inflation. In other words, if there existed money illusion, the nominal deficit would also be the important one to determine private consumption; the other way around, if the household sector of the economy were free of confusion between nominal and real values, they would consider as income only the real interest received (or paid) on the net government debt. This constitutes the case for real interest accounting.

This last point is equivalent to the supposition that the marginal propensity to consume over inflationary correction is equal to zero. Other things constant, at the maturity date of the government securities the roll-over of the debt would not call for any increase in the real interest rate. In a 200 per cent inflation environment, for example, people would recognise that the first two cruzados interest paid on each cruzado invested in Treasury Securities, at the beginning of the period, should not be taken as real income, and in this way, should not affect their consumption levels.

According to some analysts, the possibility of there existing money illusion would tell us only one part of the story. They argue that even in the absence of money illusion the nominal deficit would also be appropriate to measure the government budget disequilibrium. The argument is that an increase of inflation (and, consequently, of the nominal deficit) leads to an increase of the risk to keep securities issued by the government. The consequence would be an increase of the real interest paid on the debt or a flight to physical assets, fostering aggregate demand.

It is really possible that this might occur, mainly when inflation rises beyond a certain level. The risk premium would translate the probability of a disguised (via monetary correction indexes) or explicit (possibly partial) moratorium on the domestic debt. With the same real interest paid on the debt, this would lead to a correlation between the increase of the nominal deficit and aggregate demand (due to the hedge with physical assets). However, it must be well understood that although this correlation may exist, this point has no direct link with our previous discussion of measuring the deficit with nominal or real interest. The possible increase of demand owing to the increase of inflation is not a direct consequence of the increase of the nominal deficit, but of the increase of uncertainty (it must be kept in mind that almost the whole debt has to be financed in a daily basis due to repurchase agreements). Our conclusion is that the question of using nominal or real interest on the public deficit estimates is entirely a question of there existing or not money illusion.

Before presenting some empirical estimates concerning this last question, we would like to stress that the monetary correction indexes have systematically lied behind inflation in the recent past. Table 2.4 displays this point, by presenting the 1972–87 series of monetary correction indexes (which are used to index financial assets, but not wages and rents) vis a vis two alternative inflation indexes.

Thus, a disguised and continuous moratorium on the public debt (which extends to other income transfers from creditors to debtors in

Table 2.4   Monetary correction and inflation indexes (end of period rate of change)

	1972	1973	1974	1975	1976	1977	1978	1979	1980	1981	1982	1983	1984	1985	1986	1987
Monetary																
Correction (M)	15.3	12.8	33.3	24.2	37.2	30.1	36.2	47.2	50.8	95.6	97.8	156.6	215.3	219.4	50.7	391.5
Inflation π_1																
(IGP-DI)	15.7	15.5	34.5	29.4	46.3	38.8	40.8	77.2	110.2	95.2	99.7	211.0	223.8	235.1	65.0	415.8
Inflation π_2																
(IPA-DI)	15.9	15.3	29.1	29.3	44.9	35.5	43.0	80.1	121.3	94.3	97.7	234.0	223.6	225.7	62.6	407.2
$\alpha_1 = \dfrac{M}{\pi_2}$	0.97	0.83	0.96	0.82	0.80	0.77	0.89	0.61	0.46	1.00	0.98	0.74	0.96	0.93	0.78	0.94
$\alpha_1 = \dfrac{M}{\pi_2}$	0.96	0.84	1.14	0.82	0.83	0.85	0.84	0.59	0.42	1.01	1.00	0.66	0.96	0.95	0.81	0.96

Source: *Revista Conjuntura Econômica*, April, 1988.

the private sector) has been possible due to the discretionary power of the Ministry of Finance to set the monetary correction indexes. Of late, with the sharp increase of inflation, monetary correction indexes have behaved well, being set equal to the previous monthly inflation rate. This procedure makes monetary correction share a very important characteristic with all lagged indexation schemes: real earnings increase when inflation is falling and decrease when inflation is rising. Actually, it can very easily be shown that, under lagged indexation, the increase of inflation between two periods is exactly equal (when logarithmic rates are used) to the decrease of the real value of an indexed security. If inflation jumps from 10 per cent a month to 20 per cent a month (or from 20 to 30), the real value of an indexed asset will have decreased to around 90 per cent of its initial value at the end of the period (this is to say that if the *ex ante* agreed real interest was 0 per cent, the actual real interest will be around minus 10 per cent).

Given the hypothesis of money illusion, the choice between the use of nominal or real interest figures in the calculations of the budget deficit is a purely empirical question. In each economy, at each period in time, the task is to determine if the possible confusion between nominal and real interest makes aggregate demand a positive function of inflationary correction. Two possible kinds of tests are: (1) to obtain estimates of the consumption function of the private sector taking as one of the explanatory variables the inflationary correction on the government internal debt, and (2) to accompany the roll-over process of the debt, to determine if higher real interest rates are demanded by savers when the nominal value of the debt increases.

In Brazil, no serious attempt has been made up to now to evaluate what definition of public deficit is more relevant in fine tuning control over aggregate demand. After the introduction of the 'operational deficit' concept (which works with real interest) in 1982, this statistic has been systematically used, not only in academic and theoretical discussions, but also in negotiations with international organisations such as the IMF and the World Bank. The nominal deficit figures are also divulged by the Central Bank, but have scarcely been referred to in economic discussions.

A simple correlation exercise shows us that the marginal propensity to consume over the difference between nominal and real interest, if different from zero, could not be very high. Indeed after 1982 inflation rates more than doubled and, with this, the inflationary correction of the government debt received by the private sector.

Nevertheless, private savings increased as a percentage of GNP in the years 1983, 1984 and 1985 (from 13.5 per cent in 1983 to 19.4 per cent in 1984 and 25.9 per cent in 1985).

In order to provide empirical evidence for this question, we present here some econometric exercises, where the consumption function is taken as the endogenous variable and the GDP and the monetary correction on the internal (federal, state and local government) debt as the explanatory variables. We work with data available for the period 1970–1986. Because of lags, definitions of variables (using variations) and the use of econometric methods other than ordinary least squares,[4] the number of observations range from 13 to 15. To avoid multicolinearity, all variables are used in constant cruzados.

The basic equation to be estimated is given by:

$$C = a + bY_D + cICI \qquad (2)$$

where C = consumption,
    Y_D = disposable income of the private sector
    ICI = inflationary correction on the internal debt

The ICI variable was obtained taking into consideration the inflation in each period, rather than the correction indexes arbitrarily set by the government. The disposable income of the private sector was calculated subtracting from the gross national product (GNP) government net receipts (taxes minus subsidies and transfers (except interest)) and the inflationary tax. The nominal interest on the public debt received by the private sector was not included. Other technical details concerning the calculations are presented in the appendix to this chapter.

Table 2.5 displays the main results. Theoretically, b should be positive, and range between zero and one. Were there money illusion, coefficient a should be strictly positive. One can observe in all equations that it is statistically impossible to neglect the hypothesis that aggregate consumption does not depend on monetary correction. This result provides an empirical support for the use of real interest in fiscal accounting.[5]

2.3.2   The methodology behind the public deficit estimates

The developments here presented derive from Simonsen and Cysne (1987). Our main purpose is to define the real and operational

Table 2.5   Estimates of the consumption function

Variables / Equations	Constant	Y_t	Y_{t-1}	ICI_t	ICI_{t-1}	Dummy	Method	IV	R^2	DW	Range	Number of observations
1	$9.4 \cdot 10^4$ (0.14)	0.85 (23.17)	—	0.093 (0.61)	—	—	OLSQ	—	0.988	1.48	1971/85	15
2	$6.9 \cdot 10^5$ (0.81)	0.802 (14.33)	—	0.01 (0.059)	—	$4.5 \cdot 10^5$ (1.11)	OLSQ	—	0.989	1.94	1971/85	15
3	$3.1 \cdot 10^6$ (3.24)	—	0.734 (13.23)	0.312 (1.243)	—	—	OLSQ	—	0.966	1.87	1971/85	15
4	$-5.2 \cdot 10^5$ (−0.56)	0.882 (17.65)	—	0.022 (0.116)	—	—	IV	Y_{t-1}	0.983	1.51	1972/85	14
5	$11.3 \cdot 10^3$ ($9.1 \cdot 10^{-3}$)	0.845 (11.03)	—	−0.035 (−0.166)	—	$2.9 \cdot 10^5$ (0.589)	IV	ICI_{t-1} Y_{t-1}	0.984	1.81	1972/85	14
6	$3.7 \cdot 10^6$ (3.10)	—	0.71 (10.02)	—	0.39 (0.94)	—	OLSQ	—	0.950	2.07	1972/85	14

Notes: (1) Endogenous Variable = C_t.
(2) IV = Instrumental Variables.
(3) DW = Durbin-Watson statistic.
(4) The number below the estimates of the coefficients stands for the t – statistics.
(5) The Dummy Variable assumes values 0 for 1970–5, 1 for 1975–80 and 2 for 1980–5.

concepts of public deficits under two different assumptions. The first considers capital gains or losses due to real exchange valuations or depreciations. The second does not take capital gains and losses into consideration.

We start with the deficit financing equation:

$$D_g = I_g + G - GNR = \Delta V \tag{3}$$

where D_g = public (government) deficit
     I_g = government investment
     G = government consumption (excluding interest payments and receipts)
   GNR = government net receipts (direct and indirect taxes + other current receipts − transfers − subsidies − other current expenditures)

The terms 'other current expenditures' and 'other current receipts' include the interest paid and received on the external debt, as well as profits and rents. Interest related to the internal debt is included in the item 'Transfers'. ΔV = net increase of government liabilities.

We subdivide V into three different parts: V_1, bought by the Central Bank; V_2, bought by the remaining domestic economic agents and EK acquired by non-residents (we admit, with no loss in generality, that this part of the debt (K) is entirely dollar denominated). E stands for the nominal cruzado/dollar exchange rate. The Central Bank balance sheet is supposed to be given by:

Central Bank Simplified Balance Sheet

Assets	Liabilities
International Reserves (*Res*) Net loans to the Government (V_1) Net loans to the private sector (L)	Monetary Base (*B*)

As a result we have, from Equation (3):

$$D_g = \Delta V_1 + \Delta V_2 + \Delta EK = \Delta B + \Delta V_2 - \Delta Res - \Delta L + \Delta EK,$$

making $F = V_2 - Res - L$,

$$D_g = \Delta B + \Delta F + \Delta EK \tag{4}$$

This is the classical equation that relates the budget deficit to money and net debt creation. All of this is aimed at correctly qualifying the definition of the domestic net debt (F) that should be used in it. It must be equal to the net increase of public debt in the hands of the public minus the net assets of the Central Bank against the private and external sector of the economy.

There is nothing new with Equation (4). It simply shows that an excess of expenditures over receipts must correspond to an increase of net liabilities. D_g corresponds to the nominal deficit, and the right member to the net nominal increase of the government liabilities.

The adjustments to be made in order to pass from the nominal to the real interest rate estimate of the public deficit lie entirely in the term *GNR*. The items 'transfers', 'other current receipts' and 'other current expenditures' should be properly modified. The basic operation to be carried out is to transform nominal interest into real by means of the following operation:

Real[6] receipts = nominal receipts minus nominal interest received plus nominal interest paid minus real interest paid plus real interest received.

The symmetric calculations apply for the expenditures:

Real expenditures = nominal expenditures minus nominal interest paid plus nominal interest received minus real interest received plus real interest paid.

Following these procedures, the term 'real transfers' will differ from the nominal one by the exclusion of the inflationary correction paid on the net government debt. The real figures of 'other current receipts' and 'other current expenditures' will include the inflationary tax, which represent the real interest earned by the Central Bank (here, consolidated with the public sector) stock of high-powered money. All these corrections are automatically transferred to the government net receipts, saving and deficit, originating the real concepts of these derived variables.

Finally, profits of government enterprises should be corrected, excluding the possible monetary correction earnings on their net financial assets (this procedure will be further detailed in section 2.3.7).

To calculate these differences between nominal and real interest rates, we work with the right side of Equation (3). This amount (which we denote by *NR*) will be given, at prices of an arbitrary period *j*, by

$$NR_j = P_j \int_0^1 \frac{B + F + EK}{P} \frac{dP}{Pdt} \, dt \tag{5}$$

We decompose this total into three parts, all of them denominated in prices of periods *j*:

$$II_j = P_j \int_0^1 \frac{B}{P} \frac{dP}{Pdt} \, dt \tag{6}$$

$$ICI_j = P_j \int_0^1 \frac{F}{P} \frac{dP}{Pdt} \, dt \tag{7}$$

and

$$MCE_j = P_j \int_0^1 \frac{EK}{P} \frac{dP}{Pdt} \, dt \tag{8}$$

where P = price index and

$$NR_j = II_j + ICI_j + MCE_j \tag{5'}$$

The first term in the second member of (5'), *II*, is the inflationary tax. The other two, *ICI* and *MCE*, stand for, respectively, the inflationary correction on the domestic net debt and on the external debt.

Equation (5) implicitly admits that *B*, *F* and *EK* can be expressed as continuous functions of time. Approximations to these calculations can be carried out in two ways. The first is to work with summations, instead of integrals, taking the average monthly values of each considered variable. The second, a rough simplification of this tedious calculation, can be accomplished by means of some hypotheses concerning the time path of *B*, *F*, *Q*, *E*, *K* and the instantaneous inflation rate $(1/P)\,(dP/dt)$. Before displaying each one of these possibilities, we shall define:

(a) The real deficit (D'_{gr}) = nominal deficit $- (II + ICI + MCE)$
(b) The operational deficit (D'_{go}) = nominal deficit $- (ICI + MCE)$
    = real deficit + II.

The concept of real deficit extends the discrimination between nominal and real interest to the total amount of government net liabilities. The operational concept excludes the monetary base from this total. There being no money illusion, the real concept (as against the operational one) is a better statistic to represent the role of the government in determining aggregate demand. Indeed, the higher the inflationary tax, the lower will be the disposable income of the private sector[7] and, consequently, private consumption. At the same time, the lower will be the real deficit, in accordance with the fall of aggregate demand. The operational concept, on the other hand, is a useful concept when one needs to determine the disequilibrium of public finance. In fact this statistic presents the excess of real expenditures over real receipts before the inflationary tax has been added as a current real receipt.[8]

It is interesting to show that the tautology which makes the budget deficit equal to the increase of the net public debt remains valid even in the real accounting. Indeed, if Z stands for $F + B + EK$, the real deficit (D_{gr}) between time t and $t + dt$ will be given by:

$$dD'_{gr} = dZ - Z(dP/P)$$

At prices of period j,

$$dD'_{grj} = P_j \left(\frac{dZ}{P} - \frac{Z}{P} \frac{dP}{P} \right) = P_j D\left(\frac{Z}{P} \right) \qquad (8')$$

Integrating between periods 0 and 1,

$$D'_{grj} = P_j \left(\frac{B_1}{P_1} - \frac{B_0}{P_0} + \frac{F_1}{P_1} - \frac{F_0}{P_0} + \frac{E_1 K_1}{P_1} - \frac{E_0 K_0}{P_0} \right) \qquad (9)$$

Equation (9) tells us that the real deficit can be measured in term of the increase, during the time period considered, of the real values of the monetary base, of the domestic net debt and of the government external debt.

It is sometimes useful to decompose the definition presented here of the real external deficit as the sum of two components:

$$D'_{grj} = D_{grj} + CL_j \qquad (10)$$

The first, D_{grj}, is the concept of deficit which does not incorporate the capital gains or losses due to real exchange rate changes. To obtain it, the correction from nominal to real interest with respect to the share of government debt denominated in foreign currency must be carried out taking into consideration the external, rather than the internal, inflation. The result must be translated to cruzados at the given exchange rate. Thus, between time t and $t + dt$, if Q stands for the external price level, and simplifying, $B + F = 0$,

$$dD_{gr} = E\,(dK - KdQ/Q) \tag{11}$$

Since, with respect to the external debt,

$$dD'_{gr} = K\,dE + EdK - (EK)\frac{dP}{P}$$

we get, from this expression and (11),

$$dD'_{gr} - dD_{gr} = EK\left(\frac{dE}{E} + \frac{dQ}{Q} - \frac{dP}{P}\right) = EK\,\frac{d(EQ/P)}{EQ/P}$$

In currency of period j,

$$dD'_{grj} - dD_{gr} = P_j\,\frac{EK}{P}\,\frac{d(EQ/P)}{EQ/P}$$

Integrating between periods 0 and 1, we get Equation (12),

$$D'_{grj} = D_{grj} + CL_j,$$

where

$$CL_j = P_j \int_0^1 \frac{EK}{P}\,\frac{d(EQ/P)}{(EQ/P)dt}\,dt \tag{12}$$

CL_j transates the increase of the real deficit (D'_{grj}) due to real exchange rate devaluations.

The value of the narrower concept of real deficit D_{gr} can be found using Equations (9), (10) and (12). Alternatively, since the distinction between D_{gr} and D'_{gr} relies solely on the part of the government debt denominated in foreign currency:

$$D_{grj} = P_j \left(\frac{B_1}{P_1} - \frac{B_0}{P_0} + \frac{F_1}{P_1} - \frac{F_0}{P_0} \right) + P_j \int_0^1 \frac{E}{P} \frac{dK}{dt} \, dt$$

$$- P_j \int_0^1 \frac{EK}{PQ} \frac{dQ}{dt} dt \tag{13}$$

In the above expression, which follows directly from Equations (11) and (9), the first integral in the second member stands for a possible definition of the nominal external deficit, and the second for the difference between nominal and real interest (taking into consideration the foreign inflation).[9] It is sometimes reasonable to admit that the nominal exchange rate depreciation equals internal inflation (E/P = constant), and that the logarithmic external inflation rate is kept unchanged during the period under consideration (($1/Q$) (dQ/dt) = π^*). In this case, we get the useful expression derived from (13) (which we shall use in section 2.3.5 to calculate the real deficit figures prevailing between 1983 and 1987):

$$D_{grj} = P_j \left(\frac{B_1}{P_1} - \frac{B_0}{P_0} \right) + P_j \left(\frac{F_1}{P_1} - \frac{F_0}{P_0} \right) + E_j (K_1 - K_0)$$

$$- E_j \bar{K} \pi^* \tag{13a}$$

$\bar{K}$ standing for the average value of the foreign debt during the year.

What we have shown is that there are two possible concepts for the real deficit, taking into consideration the treatment to liabilities denominated in foreign currencies. The first, D_{gr}, given by (11), is solely due to the real increase of these obligations. The second concept, D'_{gr}, which we shall call 'extended deficit', adds to D_{gr} the capital gains and losses due to real exchange rate appreciations or depreciations (CL).

The inclusion or not of capital gains and losses in the deficit concept depends upon the use which will be made of this variable. The extended version presents what is called a 'consistency property', which means that the deficit figure is always equal to the increase of net borrowing requirements. But one must have in mind that any increase in the extended public deficit figures due to real exchange rate changes does not lead to additional nominal borrowing requirements. In other words, it does not generate a lending operation. The increase in the real borrowing requirements is automatic, since the cruzado value of the net government external debt is automatically increased after a real exchange depreciation.

For this reason, and also because the increase in the real value of the public debt originated from real depreciation of the exchange rate is not supposed to affect aggregate demand (since the external debt is in the hands of non-residents), the non-extended definition is the one we shall use for macroeconomic purposes. The use of the extended concept in periods when there is a sharp real exchange appreciation can be very misleading. With the capital gains, public deficit figures can remain constant, while aggregate demand is given a strong stimulus by government expenditures.

Another observation must be made, this time with respect to the inflationary tax definition which we have been using. If we denote by II' the total revenue from money creation:

$$II'_j = P_j \int_0^1 \frac{dB}{Pdt}\, dt$$

Since $\dfrac{dB}{P} = \dfrac{B}{P}\dfrac{dP}{P} + d\left(\dfrac{B}{P}\right)$, it is clear that

$$II'_j = II_j + P_j \left(\frac{B_1}{P_1} - \frac{B_0}{P_0} \right) \tag{14}$$

In other words, the total revenue arising from money creation is equal to the inflationary tax (II) plus the real seignorage gain which takes place.

Given the definition of the operational deficit, it follows from (9) that:

$$D'_{goj} = P_j \left(\frac{F_1}{P_1} - \frac{F_0}{P_0} \right) + P_j \left(\frac{E_1 K_1}{P_1} - \frac{E_0 K_0}{P_0} \right)$$

$$+ P_j \left(\frac{B_1}{P_1} - \frac{B_0}{P_0} \right) + II_j$$

or, given (14),

$$D'_{goj} = P_j \left(\frac{F_1}{P_1} - \frac{F_0}{P_0} \right) + P_j \left(\frac{E_1 K_1}{P_1} - \frac{E_0 K_0}{P_0} \right) + II'_j$$

The non-extended concept of operational deficit can be directly obtained from D_{grj}, by adding the inflationary tax:

$$D_{goj} = D_{grj} + II$$

where D_{grj} is given by (13) or, if E/P and π^* remain constant in the time period considered, by (13a).

2.3.3 Some simplified expressions for the evaluation of the difference between nominal and real interest (NR)

In this section we develop some analytical expressions that might be of help in obtaining estimates of the variables previously mentioned (II, ICI and MCE). We shall deal with three different possibilities, all expressions following from (6), (7) and (8). To simplify, variable X stands for B, F or EK.

(a) The nominal value of the considered net liability is kept constant over the period ($X = \bar{X}$).

$$NR_j = (P_j/P_1)\, \bar{X}\pi \tag{15}$$

(b) The real value of the considered net liability is kept constant over the time period considered.

$$NR_j = \tilde{\pi}X_j \tag{16}$$

where $\tilde{\pi} = ln\,(1 + \pi) = $ logarithmic inflation rate.

(c) The instantaneous rate of growth of the real value of the net liability (a) and of the inflation rate ($\tilde{\pi}_i$) are kept constant over time. This means

$$\frac{X}{P} = \frac{X_0}{P_0}\, e^{at} \qquad a = \text{constant}$$

$$\frac{1}{P}\frac{dP}{dt} = \tilde{\pi}_i \qquad \tilde{\pi}_i = \text{constant}$$

In this case,

$$NR_j = (P_j/P_0)\, X_0\, \tilde{\pi}\, (e^a - 1)/a \tag{17}$$

To illustrate the use of these expressions, we shall present some examples:

1. We use expression (15) to calculate the amount of inflationary tax paid by an economic agent who keeps Cz$100 in cash (currency) during a month when the rate of inflation was 15 per cent:

$$NR_0 = 100 \cdot \pi/(1 + \pi) = Cz\$_0 \ 13.04$$

or, in currency of the end of the month,

$$NR_1 = 100 \cdot \pi = Cz\$_1 \ 15.00$$

2. Equation (16) is used to evaluate inflationary tax when the economic agent begins the month with Cz$100 but increases this amount continually in order to keep constant, at each point in time, the purchasing power of his cash balances:

$$NR_0 = X_0 \ \tilde{\pi} = Cz\$_0 \ (100 \cdot ln \ 1.15) = Cz\$_0 \ 13.98$$

or, in currency at the end of the period,

$$NR_1 = Cz\$_1 \ 16.07$$

As one should expect, the amount of inflationary tax is higher than in example (1), since the average cash balances during the month are also higher.

2.3.4   Inflationary tax and inflationary transfers to commercial banks

By definition, inflationary tax is the amount of real interest earned by the monetary authorities on the stock of high-powered money. Since this liability of the monetary authorities pays zero nominal interest, the real interest earned in each point in time is equal to the monetary base (B) times the inflation rate.

An extension of this concept to the commercial banks is the inflationary transfer to commercial banks (IT). In each point in time, if M_1 stands for the means of payment, it is given by $(M_1 - B) \ \pi$. Since $M_1 - B$ is also equal to the difference between commercial banks sight deposits and total reserve requirements, IT can be seen as the real interest earned by the banks on demand deposits minus the real interest on total reserve requirements which they pay to the monetary authorities. In other words, it is equal to the real interest earned by the commercial banks on the net quantity of money they create $(M_1 - B)$.

From the above exposition it follows that, by adding the inflationary tax (II) to the inflationary transfers to commercial banks (IT), one can get the total amount of real interest paid by the non-banking system to the banking system due to inflation.[10] We shall denominate total inflationary transfers (TIT):

$$TIT = II + IT = B\pi + (M_1 - B)\,\pi = M_1\,\pi$$

TIT is equal, in each point in time, to M_1 times the rate of inflation. This equation tells us that the non-banking system, by holding an asset which pays zero nominal interest (M_1) in an inflationary environment, is actually paying real interest to the banking system. These payments are subdivided into two categories: payments to the monetary authorities (in Brazil, they should include Central Bank and Banco do Brasil) and payments to the remainder of the banking system, the commercial banks (we define commercial bank as a financial institution allowed to receive demand deposits).

Table 2.6 presents the value of II, IT and TIT as a percentage of GDP and also in 1987 dollars. The figures range from 1947 up to 1987. Other technical details are presented in the appendix to this chapter.

Some preliminary comments about the raw data must be made, before we go through these results. For the years 1986 and 1987, the new concept of monetary base (taking Banco do Brasil as a commercial bank) was used.[11] This explains the relative increase of the rate IT/II starting in 1986. Because of this change in the definition of B (which became narrower), the numbers in each series II and IT should only be compared between 1947 and 1985. The means of payment definition was also changed as of March 1986. Demand deposits in the 'Caixas Econômicas' and 'Banco Nacional de Crédito Cooperativo' were added to the old concept. This constitutes an autonomous motive for increase of the total transfers figures (TIT) we are calculating, as of this date. With this kept in mind, TIT can be compared in the whole series.

The following remarks derive from Table 2.6.

1. In constant dollars of 1987, the year 1987 appears as the one in which the total transfers from the non-banking system were the highest (approximately 23.8 billion dollars). This was also the year

Table 2.6 Inflationary tax (II), inflationary transfers to commercial banks (IT) and total transfers (TIT = II + IT)

Year	Inflation (%)	II/GDP (%)	IT/GDP (%)	TIT/GDP (%)	II	IT	TIT
47	2.6	0.40	0.20	0.60	0.10	0.05	0.15
48	8.2	1.13	0.55	1.68	0.29	0.14	0.44
49	12.4	1.56	0.85	2.41	0.44	0.24	0.69
50	12.4	1.56	1.05	2.62	0.47	0.31	0.78
51	12.0	1.46	1.00	2.46	0.46	0.32	0.78
52	13.1	1.53	1.10	2.63	0.51	0.37	0.87
53	20.7	2.33	1.62	3.95	0.81	0.56	1.37
54	25.3	2.44	1.84	4.28	0.91	0.69	1.60
55	12.6	1.26	0.94	2.20	0.49	0.37	0.86
56	24.3	2.15	1.70	3.85	0.88	0.70	1.58
57	7.0	0.69	0.52	1.21	0.30	0.23	0.53
58	24.1	2.27	1.86	4.14	1.09	0.90	1.99
59	39.4	2.97	2.45	5.42	1.55	1.28	2.82
60	30.6	2.34	2.12	4.47	1.30	1.18	2.47
61	47.7	3.54	2.84	6.38	2.09	1.68	3.77
62	51.4	3.76	2.86	6.62	2.34	1.78	4.12
63	81.3	5.04	3.44	8.48	3.22	2.20	5.42
64	91.9	5.23	3.39	8.62	3.44	2.23	5.67
65	34.5	2.50	1.74	4.24	1.71	1.18	2.89
66	38.2	2.74	1.91	4.66	1.99	1.39	3.38
67	24.9	1.85	1.26	3.11	1.38	0.94	2.32
68	25.5	1.85	1.44	3.29	1.54	1.20	2.74
69	20.1	1.44	1.24	2.69	1.32	1.13	2.45
70	19.3	1.33	1.27	2.60	1.30	1.24	2.54
71	19.5	1.26	1.26	2.52	1.37	1.37	2.74
72	15.7	1.01	1.01	2.02	1.26	1.25	2.51

Year							
73	15.5	0.95	1.16	2.11	1.43	1.75	3.18
74	34.5	1.91	2.25	4.15	3.27	3.86	7.13
75	29.4	1.43	1.95	3.38	2.71	3.69	6.39
76	46.3	1.87	2.49	4.36	4.05	5.40	9.44
77	38.8	1.70	1.66	3.36	3.95	3.87	7.81
78	40.8	1.79	1.59	3.38	4.36	3.89	8.25
79	77.2	2.82	2.32	5.14	7.46	6.12	13.58
80	110.2	3.04	2.63	5.67	8.39	7.27	15.66
81	95.2	2.25	2.01	4.27	5.80	5.19	10.99
82	99.7	2.20	2.01	4.21	5.65	5.16	10.81
83	211.0	2.97	2.30	5.27	7.35	5.68	13.03
84	223.8	2.23	1.60	3.83	5.65	4.05	9.70
85	235.1	2.11	1.53	3.64	5.94	4.32	10.27
86	65.0	1.17	1.62	2.79	3.48	4.81	8.29
87	415.8	3.53	4.05	7.58	11.07	12.71	23.78

Notes: (1) The GDP figure used for 1987 was a preliminary one.
(2) The last three columns present figures in constant dollars of 1987.
(3) For 1986 and 1987 the new concept of monetary based was used.

when inflation achieved its record (415.8 per cent). From this total, around 11 billion dollars (3.53 per cent of GDP) represented transfers to the Central Bank, and 12.71 billion dollars (4.05 per cent of GDP), transfers to the commercial banks.[12]

2. As a percentage of GDP, the highest value of the total transfers (TIT) happened in 1964 (8.62 per cent of GDP). From this total, 5.23 per cent of GDP were transferred to the monetary authorities and 3.39 per cent of GDP to the commercial banks.

3. Between 1947 and 1985, the inflationary tax (II) and transfers to commercial banks (IT) reached a maximum in 1980, in constant dollars, or 1964 (II) and 1963 (TI), as a percentage of GDP. The high values of IT and II in the years 1963 and 1964, in spite of the relatively low inflation then existing (relative to the levels which occurred in the eighties) reflect the increase in the income velocity of money as of 1964. Financial innovations (defined as anything which leads to a decrease in the cost of shifting funds from M_1 to interest bearing assets) played an important role in this process of reducing the equilibrium value of real balances as a percentage of GDP.

4. After the fifties the period of lowest inflationary transfers to the banking system as a percentage of GDP occurred in the years 1969–73 (popularly known as the 'Miracle Years', when the real GDP grew at rates above 10 per cent a year). The reason can be found in the very low rates of inflation in these years, mostly due to the positive supply shocks, relative monetary stability and real product outburst.

5. During the period 1980–6, the average inflation rate of the three last years (1983–5) was rather more than double that of the level prevailing during 1980–2. However the inflationary tax collected by the government remained almost the same. The total transfers, on the average, declined with the rise of inflation. This was surely corroborated by the financial innovations which ocurred in the period.

6. The average value of the inflationary tax as a percentage of GDP after 1960 was 2.4.

2.3.5   Approximate estimates of the difference between nominal and operational deficit

We now use Equation (17) to evaluate the difference between nominal and real interest paid by the government on its net internal debt. Following the hypotheses considered previously, where this expression was obtained, the real value of the internal debt is admitted to follow the trajectory:

$$\frac{F(t)}{P(t)} = \frac{F_0}{P_0} e^{bt} \qquad 0 \le t \le 1$$

and the price level to be given by:

$$P(t) = P_0 e^{\bar{\pi}t}$$

We work with the data available in the *Brazil Economic Program*, volume 16, published by the Central Bank of Brazil in March, 1988. The necessary data for the calculations are presented in Table 2.7. From these data we get

$$\bar{\pi} = 1.538$$

$$b = 0.234$$

$$\bar{P}_{87} = \text{average price index in 1987} = P(0) \left(\frac{e^{\bar{\pi}} - 1}{\bar{\pi}} \right) = 290.7$$

Using Equation (17),

$$ICI_{\overline{87}} = (\bar{P}_{87}/P_{Dec\,86}) \cdot F_{Dec\,86} \cdot \bar{\pi} \cdot \left(\frac{e^b - 1}{b} \right)$$

As a percentage of GDP, we have

$$ICI/GDP = 0.29$$

The difference between the nominal and operational concepts includes not only the inflationary correction on the internal debt, but also that on the external one. Therefore, to get the appropriate number related to this difference, we should repeat the same calculations taking into consideration also the external debt. Since the latter corresponds to 56.1 per cent of the total government debt, we would find the approximate estimates of the total difference between nominal and real interest to be about 66 per cent of GDP.

If we work with the concept of deficit which does not include . capital gains or losses due to real exchange rate changes (D_{go}, instead of D'_{go}), the calculations with respect to the dollar denominated debt

Table 2.7   Data for calculation of the difference between nominal and real interest on the internal net debt

	1986	1987
Net internal debt (F) (Cz\$ millions)	868 114	5 111 950
Price level (P) (consumer price index) March/86 = 100)	122.3	569.8
GDP (Cz\$ Millions)	3 681 145	12 305 048

Notes: (1) Monetary unities expressed in Cz\$ millions.
        (2) The internal debt figure is evaluated at the end of period.

would become totally different. The inflation to be considered would be that taking place overseas, rather than the domestic one. Let us provide an approximation to this total. The amount to be added to the previous estimate would be given by:

$$NR_e = P_j \int_0^1 \frac{EK}{P} \frac{dQ}{Qdt} \ dt \tag{18}$$

We suppose that the real exchange rate $(\theta = EQ/P)$, the real external debt and the instantaneous external inflation are given by

$$\theta(t) = \theta_0 \, e^{dt}$$

$$\frac{K}{Q} = \frac{K_0}{Q_0} \, e^{ct}, \qquad c + d \neq 0$$

and $\frac{dlnQ}{dt} = \pi^*$. According to these hypotheses,

$$NR_{ej} = (P_j/P_0) \, E_0 K_0 \pi^* \, ((e^{c+d} - 1)/(c + d)) \tag{19}$$

The data used (*Brazil Economic Program*) are shown in Table 2.8. From these, we get:

$$c. = 0.06$$

$$\pi^* = 0.044$$

Table 2.8   Data for calculation of the difference between nominal and
real interest on government external debt

	1986	1987
External net government debt (US$ millions)	81 807	90 733
External price index	111	116
Domestic price index	122.3	569.8
Nominal exchange rate (Cz$/US$)	14.6	67.9
Real exchange rate index	100	104.3

Note: All data reflect end of period (31 December) positions.
Source: Central Bank of Brazil, *Brazil Economic Program*, vol. 16, March
1988.

From these, we obtain:

$$d = 0.042; c = 0.06; \pi^* = 0.044$$

$$P_j/P_0 = P_{\overline{87}}/P_0 = 2.38$$

From these data, it follows that

$$NR_e/PIB = 0.0107$$

This figure means that approximately 1 per cent of GDP was paid
by the government to its external creditors only to replace the loss of
value of the foreign debt due to external inflation.

The use of monetary correction indexes to carry out the estimates
between nominal and real interest can lead to sharp miscalculations.
Inflation indexes are obviously the most appropriate, since the asset
purchasing power of interest in this respect is better measured in
terms of goods, rather than in BTNs.

Disadvantages of the simplified calculations here presented are
obviously the arbitrary hypotheses related to the time path of the
relevant variables. The more appropriate formula, with summations,
(which was used with monthly data to evaluate the difference between nominal and real interest necessary to the regressions presented in section 2.3.1) can be found in the appendix to this chapter.
A comparison with the numbers here presented is not possible, since
in the former case (of section 2.3.1) we worked with a narrower
concept of government debt. Data for the larger concept, used in this
section, are not available for the period before 1982.

2.3.6   Extension to social accounting

Let us take the two basic identities of social accounting:

$$C + S_p + GNR + RLE = Y = C + I + G + H \qquad (20)$$

where C = private consumption
   S_p = gross private saving (firms and households)
   GNR = government net receipts
   RLE = net transfer of income abroad
   Y = gross domestic product
   I = gross investment
   G = government consumption
   H = net transfer of resources abroad

The first equation equals the income to GDP, and, the second, the GDP to the ex-post demand. The values of C, I, G or H are the same, under the nominal or real interest criteria. The components of demand are not accountingly affected by the deterioration of the purchasing power of the financial assets. As suggested by the United Nations operational surplus methodology of the social accounts, the debt side of the production account should include no receipt of payments of interest. Therefore, under the production view (as against the income view), there is no reason to distinguish between nominal and real interest. The terms C, I, G and H are equal under the two methodologies.

With respect to the foreign currency denominated liabilities, the correction between nominal and real interest must be made by using Equation (18), rather than (8), since it is a common practice in social accounting not to include capital gains or losses.

Equation (20) can be written in three different ways. Using the sub-indexes o and r to denote, respectively, operational and real, and leaving it blank in the case of the nominal concept, we have:

$$C + S_p + GNR + RLE = C + S_{pr} + GNR_r + RLE_r = C + S_{po}$$

$$+ GNR_o + RLE_o = Y \qquad (21)$$

This is to say that the total sum of the different parcels of income is the same (and equal to GDP measured at market prices) under any accounting system. What really changes, from one case to the other, is the distribution among the parts. As we previously mentioned, in periods of inflation the real net income of the debtors is higher than the nominal one, the opposite happening to the creditors.

To begin with, let us take a closed economy where the government presents a net positive debt, and restrict ourselves to the nominal and real accounting, leaving the operational one aside for a moment. From (21) we have:

$$S_p + GNR = S_{pr} + GNR_r = Y \qquad (22)$$

which allows us to conclude that

$$GNR_r - GNR = S_p - S_{pr} \qquad (23)$$

This equation tells us that the excess of the real concept of GNR over the nominal one (which is equal to the excess of the nominal government deficit over the real one) is equal to the difference between the nominal and the real concepts of the private gross savings. While one sector experiences a net earnings increase with the change in methodology, the other experiences a decrease.

Subtracting the inflationary tax from both sides of the above equation, we get its operational counterpart:

$$GNR_o - GNR = S_p - S_{po} \qquad (24)$$

Since the inflationary tax is supposed to be positive, the difference between the operational and nominal concepts of government net receipts (and, consequently of government nominal and operational deficits) is lower than in the real case.

The difference between the operational and real concepts is due only to the inflationary tax (*II*). At currency of the same period, we have:

$$S_{gr} - S_{go} = GNR_r - GNR_o = D_{go} - D_{gr} = S_{po} - S_{pr} = II \qquad (25)$$

(S_g = government savings).

Opening the economy makes it necessary to introduce three different concepts of the net transfer of income abroad into the discussion. We remember that the change from nominal to real interest must take into consideration the loss of purchasing power of the currency in which the specific asset or liability is denominated. Consequently, following our simplifying hypothesis introduced in section 2.3.2, which assumed all net liabilities in the hands of non-residents to be dollar denominated, the operational and real values of *RLE* will coincide (since this assumption implies that all the stock of high-powered money is in the hands of residents). It can then be written

$$S_{pr} + GNR_r = S_{po} + GNR_o \qquad (25a)$$

In the case where the external (dollar) inflation may be considered null, it can still be written

$$S_{pr} + GNR_r = S_p + GNR \qquad (25b)$$

since the nominal and real values of RLE will be the same.

From Equations (20) and (21) we also conclude that the other generally utilised national accounts identities:

$$S_g + S_p + S_e = I \qquad (26)$$

$$D_g = S_p - I_p + S_e \qquad (27)$$

(where S_e stands for the external savings) are all valid under the operational and real criteria:

$$S_{go} + S_{po} + S_{eo} = I \qquad (26a)$$

$$S_{gr} + S_{pr} + S_{er} = I \qquad (26b)$$

$$D_{go} = S_{po} - I_p + S_{eo} \qquad (27a)$$

$$D_{gr} = S_{pr} - I_p + S_{er} \qquad (27b)$$

These extensions provide a useful tool to deal with the social account statistics. As was argued before, if there is no money illusion, the figures calculated with real interest should be more appropriate. Moreover, if one wishes to have an idea of the real values of the social aggregates without extending the distinction between nominal and real interest to the monetary base, the operational concept should be used.

2.3.7   Extension to correction of corporate profits[13]

In a country where there is inflation, at least two reasons make it necessary to distinguish between the nominal and inflation corrected profits: first, the dividends distribution and, second, taxation. In the absence of this mechanism, a firm with positive net financial assets will show illusory profits, since a part of its interest income only aims at replacing the loss of value of these financial assets due to inflation. If this fact is not recognised in the related tax legislation, the higher the inflation, the more quickly the real value of the firms financial assets will decline, owing to an overvaluation of the profits to be taxed and distributed to the shareholders.

In order to make this point clear, let us take a firm whose simplified balance sheet in cruzados is given, at the beginning of the year, by:

$$t = 0$$

Assets	*Liabilities*
Financial assets $Cz\$_0$ 10	Net worth $Cz\$_0$ 10

We suppose, to simplify, that the *ad valorem* tax on the gross profits is 35 per cent, and that there are no retained profits. If the inflation rate is 100 per cent a year and the real interest rate equal to zero, the firm's balance at the end of period, before and after tax and dividends distribution will be:

$t = 1$ Before		$t = 1$ After	
Assets	Liabilities	Assets	Liabilities
Financial Assets $Cz\$_1$ 10 Cash $Cz\$_1$ 10	Net worth $Cz\$_1$ 20	Financial Assets $Cz\$_1$ 10	Net worth $Cz\$_1$ 10

The last balance, written with cruzados of period zero, would be, according to (1):

$t = 1$

Balance After Tax and Profits Distribution
(in cruzados of period 0)

Assets	Liabilities
Financial assets Cz$_0$ 5	Net worth Cz$_0$ 5

Comparing this balance with the first one, one can notice that, if the Cz$_0$ 10 of monetary correction are considered for taxation and profits distribution, the real assets of the firm will have declined by one-half at the end of the period. This happened because the Cz$3.5 paid to the government and the remaining Cz$6.5 distributed to the shareholders were not real income, but only an amount paid by the debtor to the firm to keep unchanged the real value (purchasing power) of the debt. Taxation in this case actually happens to be a capital levy, rather than an income tax. In the same way, what the firm is distributing to its shareholders is not current profit, but part of its net patrimony.

What the real interest accounting actually does is to recognise this fact, allowing for the correction, in the profits calculation, of the earned interest which is only due to the loss of purchasing power of the currency in which the financial assets are denominated. In the previous examples, taxes and profit distribution would be zero, since this was also the real profit of the firm. Of course, if the firm had positive financial liabilities, instead of assets, then the opposite would occur (as it would in the case of positive net assets and deflation). The non-corrected profits would be lower than the corrected figures, leading to an undervaluation of taxation and profits distribution.

This problem was very important in Brazil up to 1964, when Law 4357 (enacted in 17 July 1964) first recognised the necessity of distinguishing between nominal and real interest rates. Table 2.9 presents some relevant data. The importance of the distinction between nominal and corrected profits becomes evident. Illusory profits ranged between 52.1 per cent and 74 per cent of total profits of open corporations between 1958 and 1964.

To avoid a sizeable loss of receipts due to the sudden recognition of the illusory profits, Law 4357 only allowed for a partial correction of

Table 2.9 Illusory profits estimates for open corporations, period 1958–64

	1958	1959	1960	1961	1962	1963	1964
(A) Number of firms	6 818	7 104	5 587	6 441	6 882	6 998	7 915
(B) Financial net assets at the beginning of period (in millions of cruzeiros)	112 876	156 876	163 873	201 279	298 284	404 639	712 357
(C) Inflation rate	127.9	36.1	32.8	50.1	50.3	81.9	93.3
(D) Illusory profits	31 493	56 474	53 750	100 838	150 037	331 399	664 629
(E) Total profits (in millions of cruzeiros)	58 399	84 936	102 849	168 287	288 193	447 975	1 140 187
(F) Percentage D/E	53.9	66.5	52.3	59.9	52.1	74.0	58.3

Notes: The calculus of item (E) implicity admits that: (a) The net financial assets related to item (b) are kept constant in nominal terms during the whole year; (b) The total profits presented in item (c) are denominated in currency of the end of the period. Under these circumstances, Equation (15) can be used.

balances. Three Decree Laws were enacted concerning this matter after 1964: Decree Law 62 (1967), Decree-Law 401 (30 December 1968), and Decree Law 417 (1969). Each of these provided mechanisms to avoid overtaxation on financial earnings.

The profits correction was last regulated by Decree Law 1758, enacted in 1976. In order to understand it, let us take the simplified balance sheet of a firm:

Assets	*Liabilities*
A Physical assets	
B Net financial assets denominated in domestic currency	W Net worth
C Net financial assets denominated in foreign currency	

The so-called 'corrected profits' are obtained from the nominal profits by the following steps:

1. Monetary correction is added to the physical assets (since their overvaluation due to inflation is not included in the nominal profits).
2. Exchange rate correction is added to the net assets denominated in foreign currency.
3. Monetary correction is subtracted from the net worth.

It must be observed that, since $W = A + B + C$: (a) with respect to the domestic currency denominated financial assets, this procedure is equivalent to transforming nominal into real interest (since the net result of these proceedings, with respect to B, is the deduction of monetary correction); (b) with respect to the foreign currency denominated financial assets, the real interest mentioned above incorporates the excess of exchange devaluation over the domestic inflation. This is a capital gain for the firm, which should certainly be considered in terms of taxation and profits distribution. Item (b) suggests that, if we define the real profits taking into consideration, with respect to the external liquid assets, the foreign inflation, the corrected profits should be equal to the real profits plus the capital gains and losses due to real exchange rate appreciations or depreciations.[14] This is the practice. Given our previous developments,

Nominal profits – real profits =

$$P_j \int_0^1 \frac{B}{P^2} \frac{dP}{dt} \, dt + P_j \int_0^1 \frac{EC}{PQ} \frac{dQ}{dt} \, dt$$

On the other hand, following the three steps of profit correction:

Corrected profits – nominal profits =

$$P_j \int_0^1 \frac{C}{P} \frac{dE}{dt} \, dt + P_j \int_0^1 \frac{A-W}{P^2} \frac{dP}{dt} \, dt$$

Since $A - W = - (B + EC)$

Corrected profits – real profits =

$$P_j \int_0^1 \frac{EC}{P} \left(\frac{1}{E} \frac{dE}{dt} + \frac{1}{Q} \frac{dQ}{dt} - \frac{1}{P} \frac{dP}{dt} \right) dt = P_j \int_0^1 \frac{EC}{P\theta} \frac{d\theta}{dt} \, dt$$

where $\theta = \dfrac{EQ}{P}$ stands for the real exchange rate, and

$$P_j \int_0^1 \frac{EC}{P\theta} \frac{d\theta}{dt} \, dt$$

represents the capital gain or loss of the firm due to real exchange rate variations.

APPENDIX

1. Section 2.3.1 Evaluation of the difference between nominal and real interest on the net internal public debt, at prices of period $j(NR_j)$. Formula used:

$$NR_j = P_j \sum_{t=1}^{12} \frac{F_t + F_{t-1}}{P_t + P_{t-1}} \frac{P_t - P_{t-1}}{P_{t-1}} \tag{A.1}$$

P_j = Arithmetic average price level of year j ($IGP - DI$)
F_t = Total internal government (federal, state and local) debt, relative to month t (end of period)
P_t = Price index relative to month $t(IGP - DI)$

$(F_t + F_{t-1})/(P_t + P_{t-1})$ = Average debt balance/average price level, in each month

$(P_t + P_{t-1})/P_{t-1}$ = Monthly inflation

This formula presents an approximation of the actual difference between nominal and real interest (which does not depend on the monetary correction index).

2. Section 2.3.4 Evaluation of the inflationary tax (II_j) and inflationary transfers to commercial banks (IT_j) at prices of period j.

$$II_j = P_j \sum_{t=1}^{12} \frac{B_t + B_{t-1}}{P_t + P_{t-1}} \; \frac{P_t - P_{t-1}}{P_t} \tag{A.2}$$

$$IT_j = P_j \sum_{t=1}^{12} \frac{(M_t - B_t)+(M_{t-1} - B_{t-1})}{P_t + P_{t-1}} \; \frac{P_t - P_{t-1}}{P_t} \tag{A.3}$$

P_j = Arithmetic average price level of year $j(IGP - DI)$
B_t = Stock of high-powered money at the end of month t
M_t = Stock of means of payment (M_1) at the end of month t
P_t = Price level ($IGP - DI$) in month t

From the equations which define the relation between the real interest rate (r) and nominal interest (i):

$$(1 + r)(1 + \pi) = (1 + i) \tag{A.4}$$

Since M and B pay zero nominal interest, the real interest paid can be calculated putting i = 0 in (A.4):

$$r + \pi + r\pi = 0 \rightarrow r = \frac{-\pi}{1 + \pi}$$

The real interest received by the banking system on M_1 or B is then given by

$$-r = \pi/(1 + \pi) = \frac{P_t - P_{t-1}}{P_t}$$

Thus nominal interest paid − real interest paid = real interest received = $\bar{B}.(P_t - P_{t-1})/P_t$ in the case of the monetary authorities, or $(M_1 - B) (P_t - P_{t-1})/P_t$ in the case of the commercial banks. $\bar{B}$ and $(M_1 - B)$ represent, respectively, the monthly average balance of high powered money, and demand deposits in the commercial banks minus total reserve requirements. In (A.2) and (A.3), they are approximated by $(B_t + B_{t-1})/2$ and $(M_t + M_{t-1})/2$. An arithmetic average is also used to approximate the average price level during the month.

Some additional calculations using the monthly averages of the daily balances of B and $M-B$ were also used for the period 1982–7. This option is surely more appropriate (because of the sharp balance variations of both B

and M that there can be at the last day of the month), but the necessary data is not available for the period 1947–82. Anyway, the results of these data did not show substantive variations, when compared with the ones here presented.

    Source of data: Fundação Getulio Vargas, *Conjuntura Econômica*, and ARIES Project; Central Bank of Brazil, several publications.

NOTES

1. We work with logarithmic rates of inflation and interest defined as $\tilde{\pi} = ln(1 + \pi)$ and $\tilde{r} = ln(1+r)$ where π and r are the popular rates. This artifice transforms operations with composed interest into operations with simple (logarithmic) interest. By this procudere, $\tilde{r}-\tilde{\pi}^e$ is not an approximation, but an exact value of the real expected rate of inflation.
2. If F_t stands for the nominal debt the real amortisation between period zero and one at prices of period zero will be equal to $F_0-(F_0/(1+\pi)) = F_0\pi/(1+\pi)$.
3. With an inflation rate of more than 200 per cent a year, for example, as presented by Brazil in the period 1983–5, real amortisation of the net debt with a zero nominal deficit would be over two-thirds of the net debt in each year.
4. Owing to the well known problem of simultaneity related to the estimation of the consumption function, we also present some results based on two-stage least squares.
5. It must be emphasised that this result is very intuitive. Otherwise, how could the government have afforded domestically to finance the major part (67 per cent) of its (nominal) deficit, around 30 per cent of GDP, with almost zero average real interest rates, as happened in 1987?
6. 'Real' and 'nominal' here refer to calculated with real or nominal interest. It has not the usual meaning of deflating time series.
7. Calculated according to the real interest methodology. See section 2.3.1.
8. It must be observed that, while in the nominal interest accounting it is totally meaningless to add the inflationary tax (in the way here defined, which does not include the real seignorage) as a current receipt, in the real interest accounting it is a common proceeding.
9. Remember that we have made in (11), to simplify the notation, $B+F = 0$. Without this assumption, the integration with respect to $B+F$ follows exactly as in the other case, presented in (9).
10. We use the word 'payment' despite the fact that the inflationary transfers do not generate a payment in the strict sense of the word. This is a distinction between the inflationary tax and all other taxes: it does not generate a withdrawing operation; income is transferred to the government in real terms, rather than in nominal (monetary) terms. It can be imagined, if one desires, that economic agents receive the necessary amount of money from the government to keep constant the real value of their cash balances and, in a tax payment operation (now in the strict

sense of 'payment') return this money to the government as a tax (we are obviously consolidating the Central Bank with the government, a common praxis in the analysis of Brazilian economy).

11. Data on the old concept of monetary base is not available as of March 1986.

12. We are only referring to the real interest earned on B (in the case of the monetary authorities) and $M_1 - B$ (in the case of the commercial banks). Other compensatory gains and losses due to inflation or taxation (in the case of the commercial banks) may exist, but are not considered here. In short, we are working with a gross type of income, rather than a net concept.

13. We suppose in this section that monetary correction indexes are equal to inflation indexes. But one should keep in mind that the profits correction mechanism assured by the laws is based on the monetary correction indexes.

14. This result was first disclosed by Simonsen, and is presented in Simonsen and Cysne (1987).

REFERENCES

CENTRAL BANK OF BRAZIL *Brazil Economic Program*, volume 16, March 1988, and other issues.

CHACEL, SIMONSEN and WALD, *A Correção Monetária*, (Rio de Janeiro: APEC Editora S.A., 1976).

FUNDAÇÃO GETULIO VARGAS, *Conjuntura Econômica*, several Issues.

SIMONSEN, MARIO H. and RUBENS P. CYSNE, *As Contas Nacionais*, published by Simposium Consultoria e Serviços Técnicos Ltda, 1987.

3 Income and Demand Policies in Brazil

3.1 INTRODUCTION

This chapter is divided into four main sections. In section 3.2 are presented three different ways to correct the continuous loss of purchasing power of wages in an inflationary environment. We concentrate our attention on the two mechanisms that have been used in Brazil: The 'peak adjustment' and the 'average adjustment'. In the former case, wages are corrected, taking into consideration only past inflation. In the latter, future inflation must be forecast to permit the calculation of the nominal wage adjustment necessary to keep its purchasing power at the previous prevailing value. These different methodologies lead to completely different situations with respect to combating inflation, and are a key step in understanding the inflationary process in Brazil. The 'peak adjustment' is generally referred to in the literature as lagged (backward-looking) indexation. The 'average adjustment' is better defined as an incomes policy than as a method of indexing wages. It also is referred to as 'forward-looking indexation'.

The 'average adjustment', which presents an additional degree of freedom for policy makers trying to combat inflation, was the basic tool used to bring yearly inflation down from 91.9 per cent to 24.9 per cent in the period 1964–7 (under the PAEG Plan). This was the only successful attempt to combat high rates of inflation (for Brazilian standards, high rates should be defined as above 40 per cent a year) in Brazil. The extent to which inflation was reduced finds no parallel in the economic history of the country. A second attempt to use the 'average adjustment' methodology, this time in order to stabilise the 226 per cent average inflation rates prevailing between 1983 and 1985, was given by the Cruzado Plan, launched on 28 February 1986. However lack of adequate demand controls led to disaster. Section 3.3 is dedicated to the description and comparison of these two attempts at price stabilisation (PAEG and Cruzado Plans).

Section 3.4 concentrates on the complicated institutional relationships between the Federal Treasury, Central Bank of Brazil and Banco do Brasil, which has led to the existence of two different budgets: the monetary budget and the fiscal budget. The former is related to the forecast and approved (by the National Monetary Council) operating targets of the Central Bank and Banco do Brasil. Monetary (M_1) expansion is predetermined, and the assets and liabilities of these institutions are carefully analysed, in order to make the high-powered money expansion compatible with the forecast evolution of the banking multiplier and the previously determined expansion rate of M_1 (currency plus demand deposits). The fiscal budget is the official one, and the only one subject to approval of the Congress. It has not been representative of the government budgetary disequilibrium, however, since many of the expenses of the federal government are carried out by Banco do Brasil or the Central Bank, and directly financed by changes in money supply.

Finally, section 3.5 concentrates on the consequences for money demand arising from the continuous process of financial innovations. The econometric estimates presented allow us to evaluate the magnitude of the autonomous decline in the demand for real cash balances, which was around 6 per cent a year from 1964. Particularly, if the purpose is to evaluate the role of monetary policy in affecting aggregate demand, this instability of money demand makes it necessary to analyse the changes taking place in other much broader monetary aggregates.

3.2   INCOME POLICIES

Roughly speaking, there are three main ways to correct the continuous loss of purchasing power of wages due to inflation. The first, instantaneous indexing, is more easily described by textbooks than applied in practice. Here, wages are corrected continuously, and their real value is kept constant over time. Its approximation in the real world is given by the trigger point methodology: when accumulated inflation since the last readjustment reaches a certain limit, say x per cent, wages are automatically multiplied by $1 + x/100$. The lower the value of x stipulated in the wage agreements, the lower will be the variation of real wages.

The main disadvantage of this process, which has been used already in Italy and Belgium, relies on the fact that the average purchasing power of labour remuneration in an economy should not be considered an exogenous constant. Indeed, in periods of adverse supply shocks, such as real exchange rate devaluations, losses of

crops, increase of indirect taxes, decreases of subsidies or deterioration in the terms of trade, full employment real wages are naturally
supposed to decline. The same thing would happen in the case of
sharp increases of real interest or capital remuneration. If the given
escalator mechanism does not recognise this fact, as would be the
case under the trigger point mechanism with low values of inflation to
determine the nominal correction of wages, the economy becomes
subjected to high unemployment rates.

The technical solution to this problem would be the use of inflation
indexes which filter out large and unexpected price level shifts due to
supply shocks. But this is not an easy task to achieve. First, spillover
effects make it technically complicated to evaluate the effect of
supply shocks on the price index. For example, it is hard to say to
what extent a loss of production in one (orange) crop has affected the
price of another (apples). Second, it is not easy for an employee to
understand why his wage is being adjusted at a rate below the
inflation rate, because of something the economists refer to as 'supply
shocks'. They do have some reason, since positive supply shocks
generally do not lead to wage corrections higher than inflation rates.
All of these problems explain why this methodology was put aside in
the aforementioned countries. Overall results were not positive.

We turn now to the second, and by far the most popular instrument
used in Brazil to replace purchasing power of wages over time, the
so-called 'peak adjustment' method. The difference between this
method and the previously mentioned 'trigger point' one relies on the
timing of adjustment. In the 'peak adjustment' case, these dates are
determined exogenously and settled *ex ante*. The timing is set arbitrarily: for instance, every six months or every twelve months may be
the intervals at which wages are revised. In the case of the trigger
point methodology, these dates are not previously agreed upon, but
endogenously determined by the prevailing rate of inflation. If it was
stipulated that wages were to be adjusted each time the price level
increases, for instance, by 10 per cent, the adjustment will be quarterly if quarterly inflation is 10 per cent, or yearly, if yearly inflation is
10 per cent.

An important difference derives from this fact. Under the trigger
point methodology, if W_p stands for the real wage just after the
adjustment date (which we call the 'peak wage'), the lowest value the
wages can reach before the next adjustment is given by $W_p/(1+\pi)$,
where π represents the rate of inflation which triggers the new
nominal wage revision. If it was previously settled that wages would

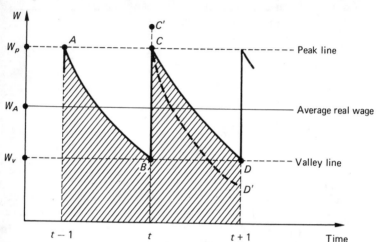

Figure 3.1   Real wage evolution in an inflationary environment

be revised each time inflation reached 10 per cent, the lowest value of real wages (valley wage, W_v) would represent a fraction 10/11 of the peak value. With a uniform rate of inflation, the average wage would be around 95.4 per cent of the value existing just after the last adjustment.

Under the 'peak adjustment' methodology, average and valley real wages are a decreasing function of the rate of inflation occurring between the two pre-settled dates of adjustment. As in the previous case the valley real wage (W_v) is a fraction $1/(1+\pi)$ of the peak real wage. But now the inflation rate in the denominator is indeterminate, not of a fixed value. It can be 1, 100 or 1000 per cent, depending upon the inflation index between the two adjustment dates. Figure 3.1, which presents the evolution of real wages over time, helps to understand this issue.

At date $t-1$, real wages were brought to the peak. As time goes on, nominal wages are held constant (up to time t), but prices are continuously rising. This leads to a fall of the purchasing power of wages over time, translated by the line AB. At time t, real wages reach their lowest value (W_v), but are subsequently adjusted to the peak (point C in the figure). This adjustment is made by multiplying the nominal wages by $(1 + \pi)$, where π is the inflation rate which occurred between dates $t-1$ and t.

The average purchasing power of wages between dates $t-1$ and t is proportional to the dashed area below line *AB*. We show in the appendix to this chapter that, if the rate of inflation is constant over the time period considered, the average real wage (W_A) will be related to the value (W_p) by the formula:

$$W_A = W_p \cdot \frac{\pi}{(1+\pi) \ln (1+\pi)} \tag{1}$$

where π stands for the inflation which occurred between the dates of wage negotiations. Thus, if wages are adjusted once a year and yearly inflation is 40 per cent, their average purchasing power will be around 85 per cent of that existing at the day when they were adjusted.

Equation (1) leads to the following conclusions regarding the characteristics of the peak adjustment:

(a) the higher the inflation rate, the lower will be the average-peak ratio (APR) W_A/W_p;
(b) given the inflation rate and the term of wage negotiations (and, consequently, APR), the higher we bring peak real wages on the adjustment date, the higher will be their average purchasing power;
(c) given a certain rate of prices increase, the shorter the period of time between wage adjustments, the higher will be APR.

Equation (1) represents a simple tautology, which, under certain hypotheses, defines the average value of real wages. We will see in the next section how this formula had its status changed in some economic analyses in Brazil, from a tautology to a theory of inflation, leading to the disastrous cruzado stabilisation plan in 1986.

All these three facts can be easily understood by examining Figure 3.1 between periods t and $t + 1$. Line *CD* presents a similar evolution of real wages as existed between periods $t-1$ and t. It would be the actual one, should the time scheduling of wage adjustments, the inflation rate and the peak wage repeat those of the previous period. Line *CD'* shows what would happen to real wages if inflation were somewhat higher than that existing between periods $t-1$ and t. Real wages would fall more quickly and their valley value would be lower. Also the average real wage would decline relative to the last period.

Point *C'* illustrates a possible adjustment above the peak value. It becomes clear that, given the rate of inflation, the average real wage would be higher in this case than if the adjustment had established as a target the peak value W_p.

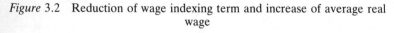

Figure 3.2   Reduction of wage indexing term and increase of average real wage

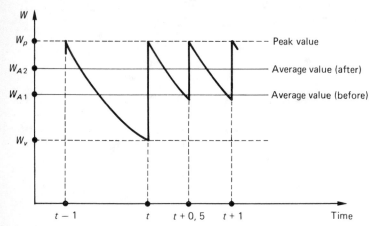

Finally, in Figure 3.2, we display the third property of the 'peak adjustment' methodology: given the rate of inflation, the average peak ratio (*APR*) is a decreasing function of the wage indexing term. With a yearly inflation rate of 40 per cent, for instance, average real wages will correspond to 84.9 per cent of the peak value if the indexing term is annual, but 92.0 per cent of the peak value if the indexing term is half-yearly.[1]

As can be seen, the 'peak adjustment' methodology operates as a severe barrier to any sudden stabilisation of inflation. Let us take the Brazilian case, for instance, in 1985. The annual inflation rate was 235.1 per cent and wage negotiations were half-yearly. This is to say that average wages represented about 75 per cent of the peak value. Consequently, a sudden drop of the inflation rate to zero would mean that, after all wages had been adjusted according to the previous peak, there would be a 33 per cent increase of real wages. This is clearly impossible in the short run, and means that there is no possibility for such a stabilisation measure to be effective without a change of income policy.

The solution to this problem, which we call the 'average-peak dilemma', is given by the use of the third method of wage adjustments we are going to present here: the adjustment by the average ('average adjustment'). The main difference is that the correction of nominal wages is not directed towards the recomposition of its peak purchasing power, but carried out in order to keep unchanged its

Figure 3.3 The 'average adjustment' methodology

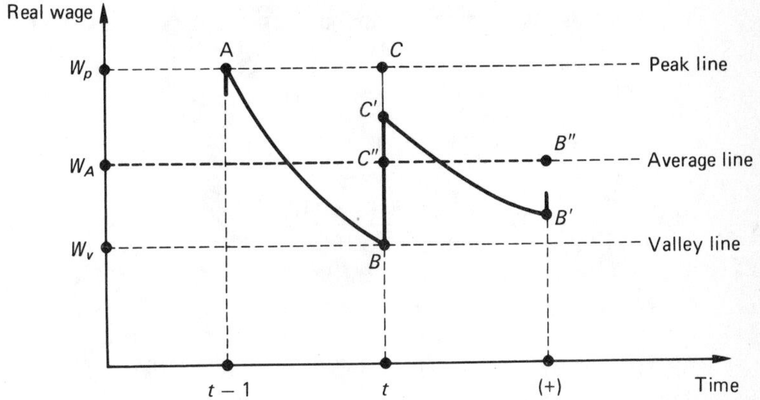

prevailing average real value in the next period.[2] Figure 3.3 illustrates this methodology.

Following the peak methodology approach, as we have previously seen, real wages would be brought to point C at time t. This would also be the adjustment following the 'average methodology', if the inflation expected to take place between time t and $t + 1$ were equal to that between time $t-1$ and time t. Indeed this would make the expected average value of real wage between dates t and $t + 1$ equal to the previous actual level.

But if the objective is to initiate a stabilisation plan, expected inflation for period $t(\pi_t^e)$ will surely be lower than the previous inflation (π_{t-1}). Consequently real wages should be brought to a point below C, which we illustrate in the figure by C'. If the actual inflation really declines as forecast, average real wages will remain the same. In the case when expected inflation for the next period is zero, nominal adjustments must bring real wages to point C''. Their trajectory in this case would be given by line $C''-B''$, which repeats the average real wage of period $t-1$. These points are formalised in the appendix to this chapter. Equation (1) is taken as the basis for formal explanations.

Although it represents a solution to the *APR* dilemma, the above described methodology presents a technical challenge: the forecast of future inflation. If actual inflation prevailing as of time t is higher than that predicted (used to correct wages), average real wages will turn out to be lower than in the previous period. A possible way to overcome this difficulty is to base the wage adjustment to be carried out at date $t + 1$ on the average value that would have prevailed had inflation been correctly forecast, and not on that actually existing. This was done in Brazil between 1968 and 1979.

3.3   TWO ATTEMPTS AT STABILISATION

The solution of the average-peak dilemma by means of an income policy centred on the 'average adjustment' methodology was introduced on two occasions in Brazil. In the first, during the 'Plano de Estabilização do Governo Castello Branco' (PAEG), it was also accompanied by demand restrictions, and led to great success in terms of stabilising inflation. This happened between 1964 and 1966, when inflation fell from 91.9 to 38.2 per cent a year. However the second attempt was a complete disaster. It happened in 1986, with the so-called 'Cruzado Plan'. The income policy was correct, but, as we shall see further in this section, the easy monetary–fiscal policy destroyed all possibilities of achieving any success. Only a few months after the beginning of the Plan, all the efforts at stabilisation had failed irreversibly.

Table 3.1 presents some statistics related to the PAEG plan. As can be observed from the data, in 1964–6 both monetary and fiscal policy were relatively tight. The discrepancy between the inflation rate and monetary policy in 1965 can be explained by the decrease in income velocity of money which accompanies such stabilisation programmes. Inflation in the first quarter of 1964 reached 25 per cent, which means, by extrapolation, a 144 per cent yearly rate. From this point of view, the 91.9 per cent rate of inflation at the end of 1964 demonstrated that the plan introduced after March was a step in the right direction.

Two important facts which helped to tame inflation in 1965 were the excellent agricultural crop and use of the 'average adjustment' mechanism to correct minimum wages in February. Had the peak adjustment methodology been used, minimum wages would have been multiplied by 2.09. With the adjustment aimed at keeping the average real purchasing power equal to the preceding period, minimum wages were increased by only 57 per cent. In July 1965, forward-looking indexation was extended to all wage negotiations carried out under federal government influence.

The most common criticism made about the PAEG Plan was that

Table 3.1   Economic statistics related to the PAEG plan

	1964	1965	1966
Public deficit as % of GDP	4.0	1.6	1.1
Monetary (M₁) expansion (%)	84.6	76.5	15.8
Inflation (%) (IGP-DI)	91.9	34.5	38.2
GDP growth (%)	2.6	2.1	5.4
Agricultural sector growth (%)	– 1.3	20.1	–14.6

Sources: Conjuntura Econômica, November, 1972; Zerkowsky and Velloso (1982) for the national account statistics.

stabilisation was achieved through the decline of real wages. Projected inflation, which was used to correct nominal wages, was systematically set below actual inflation, leading to a continuous decline (in 1965, 1966 and 1967) of average purchasing power of wages-paid labour. The situation persisted up to 1968, when the wage adjustment law was modified. This criticism applies, not because of the fall in real wages, but because of the fall in labour income as a percentage of GDP (measured by Langoni, 1970, p. 163). Indeed, as we have already mentioned and formally display in the appendix, the decline in real wages was to be expected as a natural consequence of the real exchange rate devaluation, reduction of subsidies, and correction of the prices of public utilities which took place at this time. However this is not to imply a decrease in the labour share of GDP. This decline shows that the burden of stabilisation was really biased against employees. An active policy of increased taxation on capital revenues and decreased taxation on labour income should have been used to achieve a better sharing of the burdens of adjustment between the two factors of production.

We should not analyse the PAEG plan only as an anti-inflation-oriented programme. Following the inheritance of a very undesirable economic situation, the economic policy of the second semester of 1964 actually set down the basis for the period of high economic growth rates which commenced in 1968. In the period just prior to the introduction of the PAEG Plan the economic situation was chaotic. Inflation rates, besides being high, were repressed by the many price controls then in operation. The fiscal system was technically inconsistent. This added to the problem of many distortions caused by inflation, such as illusory profits taxation, underestimation of depreciation values and deliberate delays in making payments by taxpayers. Instead of being applied over value added, sometimes taxation fell upon the final value of the product (as was the case of the 'Imposto de Vendas e Consignações'). Nor was the balance of payments situation very comfortable. An overvalued exchange rate, coupled with the absence of external credit, let to systematic deficits. The financial market obviously could not survive in an environment where nominal interest rates were restricted to 12 per cent, with inflation over 90 per cent a year. The consequence was a narrowing process of financial intermediation, where only privileged investors could get loans (highly subsidised) from official institutions.

Among the important achievements attained between 1964 and 1967 can be mentioned the following (see Simonsen and Campos, 1974):

1. The development of the monetary correction mechanism, which, as we saw in Chapter 2, became an indispensable tool to foster private saving and correct various distortions arising from inflation.
2. The improvement of the external accounts, represented by the current account surpluses in 1964, 1965 and 1966, as well as by renewal of the country's ready access to funds borrowed in the international financial markets.
3. The improvement of the fiscal system. The 'Imposto Sobre Vendas e Consignações', which fell on the final value of production, was replaced by the 'Imposto de Circulação de Mercadorias', which was based on value added. Moreover illusory profits taxation was abolished and monetarily corrected values of the firm's physical assets began to be used in the determination of depreciation values. Fiscal debts postponed by taxpayers were now being monetarily corrected and some non-functional taxes (as the 'imposto do selo') were abolished.
4. The creation of the 'Fundo de Garantia de Tempo de Serviço' (FGTS), a labour indemnification system managed by the recently created 'Banco Nacional da Habitação' (BNH). Besides fostering private savings, this mechanism injected a new dynamism into the labour force. It provided revenues equal to 8 per cent of the labour expenses of the firms and could be withdrawn if workers lost their job.
5. The creation of the 'Sistema Financeiro da Habitação' (SFH), whose main institution was the BNH. Its main purpose was to finance the development of the housing sector. Assets and liab-

ilities of all institutions affiliated in the SFH were subjected to monetary correction. FGTS reserves were included among the SFH's liabilities.
6. The creation of the Bancos de Investimento and FINAME, the former making available long-term credit to investors and the latter dedicated to financing the purchasing of national capital goods.

The other attempt at stabilisation of inflation based on the 'average adjustment' as a solution to the 'average-peak dilemma' was the Cruzado Plan, initiated on 28 February 1986. Contrary to the monetary–fiscal discipline observed between 1964 and 1967, the Cruzado Plan was followed by an easy demand policy, which undermined any possibility of success. Moreover real wages were not brought to the average (which should have been the case, since expected inflation was equal to zero), but subjected to an increase of 8 per cent (and 15 per cent in the case of minimum wages).

This lack of attention on the demand side was due to technical errors as well as political reasons. On the technical side, the accounts related to public expenditures were not clear enough to allow the necessary estimates of disequilibrium in the public finances. As ex-Planning Minister Delfim Netto once mentioned, 'the current annualized public deficit was zero at the first moment, under calculation one month later, less than two per cent of GDP after three months, and more than five per cent of GDP when it could not be hidden anymore'. Furthermore, the increase of real tax receipts due to the fall of inflation (Oliveira–Tanzi effect) was overestimated. The fiscal reform carried out three months before the plan was introduced reduced the lags between the generating factors and effective tax receipts by the government, at least in the case of household income tax.

Besides the lack of reliable public deficit estimates, which really made it difficult to manage aggregate demand, there seems to have been a real bias in the overall conception of the plan. The difficulties associated with the supply side of inflation were overemphasised, and the demand side was relegated to second place. With the continuous failure to tame inflation by means of monetary–fiscal policy (between 1979 and 1986), it was somewhat out of fashion, among the Brazilian economists who were about to become policy makers, to present orthodox solutions for the problem of inflation. What the administrators of economic policy seem to have forgotten was that, although this concentration upon eliminating inflationary inertia was justifiable before the beginning of the plan, when the economy was wholly indexed, it became dangerously misleading after indexation came to a halt. As a Brazilian economist once said, there is 'nothing better than a team of monetarists in the government to make unorthodox proposals reasonable, and nothing more appropriate than a team of unorthodox economists in the government to justify orthodox recommendations'.

A measure of this bias can be observed in the theory of 'inertial inflation', the term the parents of the Cruzado Plan employed in describing Brazilian inflation prevailing at the end of 1985.[3] Inertial inflation is a term that was in fashion during 1986 among Brazilian economists. By this definition, inflation of period t was wholly explained by inflation of period $t-1$. This would be a result of independent actions of economic agents, who would try to protect their relative shares of income by increasing prices and wages, until they reached their maximum prior purchasing power. Formally, the theory of inertial inflation can be described as a change of status of Equation (1), which is changed from a simple tautology into a theory of inflation, by means of the three following hypotheses:

$H1$: wages are always readjusted to the maximum purchasing power previously reached;
$H2$: the average-peak ratio W_A/W_p is a constant;
$H3$: the period of time between nominal adjustments can be controlled by the government and is kept constant.

Given these three hypotheses, it follows directly from (1), since $APR_t = APR_{t-1}$, that $\pi_t = \pi_{t-1}$.[4] This means that inflation repeats itself as a consequence of the average-peak dilemma. Of course the main problem of such a theory of inflation relies on the assumption that wages are always adjusted to the peak ($H1$), which eliminates the mechanism by means of which controls over aggregate demand play an important role in the process. We will come back to this point.

In the context here presented, inertial inflation can be defined as the rate of inflation which (in an economy where revenues are readjusted at distinct and pre-established dates aiming at the highest purchasing power previously reached) keeps constant the average-peak ratio. In other words, it is the inflation rate that brings real wages to their previous average value.

Before carefully analysing the validity of the three hypotheses behind this 'theory of inflation', it is of interest to explore this apparatus, given by (1) and *H*1, *H*2, *H*3. First of all, the inflation rate will cease to repeat itself each period if any one of the three hypotheses *H*1, *H*2, *H*3 fails to apply. To begin with, let us take an economy with yearly revenue adjustments and a 40 per cent annual inflation rate. From (1), we get $APR = 0.85$. If nothing occurs, that is, if *H*1, *H*2 and *H*3 remain valid in the next period, this inflation rate will repeat itself to keep $APR = 0.85$. Let us develop some variations around the theme. First, in item *a*, we will admit both H1 and H2 to hold, but not H3. The period of time between wage adjustments is supposed to change from one year to a half year. Second, in item *b*, we admit H1 and H3 to hold, but not H2. The average/peak ratio is admitted to decline owing to supply shocks. Both examples lead to different values of the (endogenously determined) inflation rate, which can be made compatible with the Brazilian case.

(a) The adjustment term is reduced from twelve (yearly) to six months. With this change, since the inflation rate π in (1) represents the rate of change of prices between the adjustment it follows, if H1 and H2 are true, the annual inflation will turn out to be half-yearly. This means that yearly inflation will rise from 40 per cent to 96 per cent $(((1.4)^2-1) \times 100$ per cent$)$. This example fits well with the evolution of Brazilian inflation in the eighties. Between 1974 and 1979, inflation was around 40 per cent a year, having jumped to 101.4 per cent between 1980 and 1982. In November 1979, incidentally, wage adjustments turned from annual to half-yearly, which means that the increase of inflation rates was at a level necessary to keep unchanged the average-peak ratio. This fact corroborates hypotheses H1 and H2 (H1 was enforced by the backward-looking indexation).

(b) Owing to supply shocks (exchange rate devaluations, indirect tax increases, loss of crops and so on), the average-peak ratio changes from 0.84 to 0.76, with half-yearly adjustments. Making $APR = 0.76$ in (1), we get $\pi = 80$ per cent per semester or, equivalently, 223 per cent per year. Again, and on purpose, we used in the example some numbers that make equation (1) able to get along with the evolution of Brazilian inflation. After three years (1980 to 1982) with a rate around 100 per cent per year, inflation increased to average 223 per cent between 1983 and 1986. Two important factors in this process were the agricultural shock in 1982 and the real exchange rate devaluation of 1983. Referring to the model we are dealing with, the rise of inflation would be explained as necessary to allow the fall of real wages resulting from the adverse supply shocks. Since *APR* turned from 0.84 to 0.76, the *ex post* explanation of inflation is that real wages had to fall about 9.5 percentage points. Inflation in this case would be a consequence of supply shocks, coupled with a lagged indexation system. Of course, money supply is implicitly considered to be passive.[5]

These two examples show that a theory of inflation based on equation (1) and on a flexible version of hypotheses H1, H2 and H3 can be useful as a complementary tool to understand inflation in an economy subjected to lagged indexation and an accommodative monetary–fiscal policy. However, as a theory which predicts that inflation of period t will exactly repeat inflation of period $t-1$ (inertial inflation), it is extremely poor. The derivation of this proposition from (1) demands that hypotheses H1, H2 and H3 are entirely and always verified, obviously an overstatement.

The main problem of the 'inertial inflation' theory is that it relies on the assumption that nominal adjustments are always made in order to bring real wages to the previous peak of purchasing power. This supposition eliminates the channels by means of which demand controls affect the path of inflation. Indeed, if the economy is subjected to a huge recession and future monetary policy is supposed to continue tight, it is meaningless to expect that all real wages will always be brought to the previous peak. Even in an economy subjected to lagged indexation, the amplitude of this mechanism is not total. A part of the economy (including new contracts) is always free to translate revised expectations and unemployment into lower demands for nominal remunerations.

Lagged indexation mechanisms surely give more support to the 'peak adjustment' hypothesis (H1), which, as we saw, constitutes an essential condition for the theory of inertial inflation. Lopes (1986) argued that indexation was not necessary for H1 to hold. He used Tobin's (1981) criticism of rational expectations models, later formalised by Simonsen (1987), to present an alternative theoretical background for the 'peak adjustment' hypothesis. Tobin's criticism was based on the disassociation between each economic agent's rationality and overall rationality. Following this argument, Lopes argued that each economic agent could act in a manner dissociated from others, increasing their nominal income (the role of demand was not discussed adequately in the process) in order to replace the previous peak of purchasing power. The reasoning for this attitude would be the equivalent behaviour he would expect others to follow.

Lopes (1983) explicitly recognised that demand policy could affect the path of inflation. However, following his Phillips curve estimates, the product gap cost to be paid made this option inadvisable. What was not sufficiently taken into consideration in the Cruzado strategy, though, is that, after the beginning of the Plan and the end of indexation, the sensitivity of the economy to demand management was much higher than before.

Contrary to the necessary emphasis on the monetary–fiscal policy side, the period during the Cruzado Plan was characterised by comprehensive and obligatory price controls. The main objective was not to combat inflation through its symptoms, but to provide the economy with a centralised signalling of the expected behaviour of other economic agents with respect to price setting. Prices were to be controlled for a short period of time (around three months). However, things happened differently. After the first four months, it was not possible to achieve a market equilibrium with the frozen price level and higher income, and a system of price-premia and black markets appeared. The initial objective of using a price freeze as a way to avoid the dissociation between individual and general behaviour had given place to a desperate attempt to hide the near collapse of the Cruzado Plan strategy.

The price freeze turned out to be an unfortunate device during the Cruzado Plan, first, because its signalling function did not work. It was useless to announce that prices would remain frozen and, at the same time, conduct an easy fiscal and monetary policy. Inconsistency is not compatible with credibility. And credibility is a necessary condition for acting as an orchestra conductor. Second, the price freeze led to a disastrous disregard of demand controls. Inflation seemed to be under control and there was no political support, in the six months after 28 February 1986, for laying off government employees or cutting off other public expenditures. A price freeze was conceived to avoid the hard process of learning by doing which characterises most stabilisation plans. Had the Cruzado Plan shifted the emphasis on this mechanism to demand controls, things could have happened in a completely different way. A short recession could

Table 3.2   Evolution of M_4 – per cent rate of change

03/86	04/86	05/86	06/86	07/86	08/86	09/86	10/86
12.2	1.1	2.8	3.3	0.3	5.2	5.5	3.4
11/86	12/86	01/87	02/87	Accumulated Feb. 86/Feb. 87			
2.0	5.0	5.3	16.3	82.2%			

Source: Central Bank of Brazil, *Brazil Economic Program*.

have led, as had happened between 1964 and 1966, to a future period of relative price stability and growth. 'Who everything wants, everything loses.'

Tables 3.2 and 3.3 present the statistics related to the monetary-fiscal policy during the plan. Owing to the changes of income velocity of M_1 resulting from the fall and rise of inflation in the period 1985–7, as well as the continuous autonomous shift of the money demand function due to financial innovations (see section 3.5), we work with the broader monetary concept M_4. This is equal to M_1 plus saving accounts, certificates of deposits and outstanding government debt. To a certain extent, it gives a measure of the total credit provided by the private financial system of the economy.

Real public deficit figures were calculated from Equation (13a) of Chapter 2:

$$D_{grj} = P_j \left(\frac{B_1}{P_1} - \frac{B_0}{P_0} \right) + P_j \left(\frac{F_1}{P_1} - \frac{F_0}{P_0} \right) + E_j (K_1 - K_0) - E_j \check{K} \pi^*$$

where:

$$DI = P_j \left(\frac{B_1}{P_1} - \frac{B_0}{P_0} \right) + P_j \left(\frac{F_1}{P_1} - \frac{F_0}{P_0} \right)$$

represents the part of the real deficit financed by private savings, and $DE = E_j(K_1 - K_0) - E_j \check{K} \pi^*$ the remaining part financed by non-residents.

As shown in Chapter 2, this formula allows the calculation of the public deficit with real interest, including the inflationary tax as a real current account receipt of the public sector (since the Central Bank is consolidated to the government, and the monetary base is included in the consolidated domestic debt F).[6] Consequently, to allow comparisons with the operational deficit figures provided by the Central Bank

Table 3.3   Real and operational public deficit (percentages)

	1984	1985	1986	1987
(1) DI/GDP	3.9	2.6	0.5	2.73
(2) DE/GDP	0.44	2.32	5.29	1.57
(3) DE/DI+DE)	0.11	0.47	0.90	0.36
(4) D_{gr}/GDP (%)	4.34	4.92	5.79	4.30
(5) IT/GDP (%)	2.23	2.11	1.17	3.53
(6) D_g0/GDP (%)	6.57	7.03	6.96	7.83
(7) D_g0-BACEN/GDP	2.7	4.3	3.6	5.5

Notes: (1) Original source of data: Getulio Vargas Foundation, *Revista Conjuntura Econômica*; IBGE, 'Contas Nacionais do Brasil', mimeo, 21 June 1988; Central Bank, *Brazil Economic Program*.
(2) Inflationary tax values were obtained from Chapter 2.
(3) The discrepancies between the numbers presented here and those provided by the Central Bank are due to the different methodologies used in each case.
(4) World Bank (1987) and Toledo (1986) are other examples of the operational public deficit estimates considerably higher than the official numbers presented by Central Bank, shown in line (7).

$(D_{g0}$ – Bacen) we must add the inflationary tax (II) to the real deficit given by Equation (2.13a). We denote the numbers calculated under this methodology by D_{g0} (operational public deficit). $\bar{K}$ was approximated by the simple arithmetic average of K at the beginning and at the end of the period.

Beginning with Table 3.2, it can be seen that the expansion of M_4 was basically incompatible with the zero inflation target assumed by architects of the Cruzado Plan. The long-run stability of M_4 velocity (see Table 3.4) pointed out a high correlation between this aggregate and the nominal national product.[7] In accordance with this empirical observation, the rate of expansion of M_4 should have been kept very close to zero, through the control of the consolidated Treasury's and Central Bank's liabilities.

Table 3.3 reflects a disequilibrium in public finance in 1986 much higher than that presented by official estimates. The numbers here calculated show an operational deficit of 6.96 per cent of GDP, as against the 3.6 per cent presented by the Central Bank. From this amount, 90 per cent (5.29 per cent of GDP) was externally financed. The external financing is closely associated with the deterioration of the commercial balance which occurred in this year. Exports were controlled and imports largely used to support the artificial price

Table 3.4 M_4 velocity

Period		M_4 velocity
1980		4.4
1981		4.2
1982		3.7
1983		4.0
1984		3.9
1985		3.4
1986	Jan/Mar	3.4
	Apr/Jun	3.4
	Jul/Sep	3.3
	Oct/Dec	3.3
1987	Jan/Mar	3.2
	Apr/Jun	3.4
	Jul/Sep	3.6
	Oct/Dec	3.7
1988	Jan/Mar	3.7
1988	Apr/May	3.9

Source: Central Bank of Brazil, *Brazil Economic Program.*

controls. The contribution of external savings to minimise the *ex ante* excess demand translates into the sharp increase in the current account deficit, which, in constant dollars of 1987, averaged 327 million dollars in 1984, 1985 and 1987, as against 4.6 billion dollars in 1986.

The process of continued borrowing in foreign currency by the government can also be observed in Table 3.3. Between 1984 and 1986, the part of the real deficit externally financed jumped, as a percentage of GDP, from 0.44 per cent in 1984, to 2.32 per cent in 1985 and to 5.29 per cent in 1986. In 1987 the process was reversed, with only 36 per cent of the government's budget deficit being externally financed (this represented 1.57 per cent of GDP).

The evaluation of the real deficit is also useful, since this is the concept most correlated with *ex ante* aggregate demand. Indeed, when inflationary tax falls, the operational deficit remains unchanged, but the real deficit increases. The same thing happens with aggregate demand, since the available real income of the private sector (calculated with real interest) increases. In this way, the fact that the real deficit was bigger in 1986 than in any other year helps to explain the outbursts of consumption which occurred in this year. Besides the increase of real wages,[8] the fall of the real inflationary transfers from the private sector to the monetary authorities was one of the factors behind this fact.

The preceding discussion presents the reasons for the failure of the Cruzado Plan. Fundamentals were not taken into account as they should have been. Policy makers were too ambitious in establishing economic goals. In their own words, architects of the Cruzado Plan stated that it should 'allow a growth like Japan's with an inflation rate like Switzerland's'. Moreover the plan should be able to reverse the effects of previous 'unfair' economic policies carried out in Brazil.[9] Finally, it should serve as a lesson to the Argentinians, who were regarded as facing an unnecessary recession with their Austral Plan. The Cruzado Plan should demonstrate that it was possible to tame inflation with no recession.

The financial intermediation process in Brazil was in many aspects influenced by the Cruzado Plan. The Brazilian banking system, as shown in Chapter 2, has been rewarded with considerable real transfers from the non-banking system, owing to the high rates of inflation. Following the economic principle by means of which marginal costs can be increased up to the limit where they reach marginal receipts, many banking agencies operated under circumstances that would not be profitable with zero inflation. The agencies operated in remote geographical areas with excess employees, or operated in extremely competitive environments. In the first months after the beginning of the Plan, when it was still believed (with prices frozen) that zero inflation was a feasible target, analysts expected the closing of some agencies and temporary difficulties experienced by certain banks. These developments really did take place, but below the levels forecast. This is because the government itself was also unprepared to live without an inflation tax. In the very near future economic conditions would return to their previous state. Inflation would return to its old level; providing the banks and the government easy access to inflationary transfers and to inflationary tax.[10]

Just after the introduction of the Cruzado Plan, the stock exchanges experienced a sharp expansion. Expectations about future profits were most optimistic. Real interest rates were forecast to be kept very low, which reinforced the initial enthusiasm. At the same time, real estate prices advanced, for the same reasons. Many microfirms emerged with easy credit and there was an outburst of aggregate demand. However when the failure of the Plan became clear the situation was completely reversed. Stock prices fell more rapidly than profits. The dollar price of real estate also fell sharply. Many micro-firms became insolvent. Fortunately for them, they were granted a partial debt amnesty by the new constitution. This amnesty represented a heavy financial burden to the government, since most of the loans were provided by Banco do Brasil. Private banks were also hurt (the total amount of loans was 0.8 per cent of GDP).

With the sharp decline in inflation associated with the Cruzado Plan, the deposits at 'Caderneta de Poupança', the most popular savings account in Brazil, declined at an alarming rate. Since this indexed asset pays a constant real interest rate, despite the rate of inflation, some analysts agreed that these withdrawals constituted clear evidence of 'money illusion'. One could find many people at this time who were worried about the decline in monetary correction credited to their savings accounts. Previously, 15 per cent monthly inflation generated fifteen cruzados for every 100 cruzados of deposits. Some people interpreted this as a real gain, rather than a simple replacement of the purchasing power of the investment. It is interesting that, according to the econometric estimates presented in Chapter 2, money illusion, if it existed, was not a significant factor on the whole. As time goes on, those who spend their monetary correction revenues realise that what they are really doing is depleting their accumulated capital. Another reason, completely independent of money illusion, can explain the large withdrawals from saving accounts. While the real rate of interest was kept unchanged (6 per cent a year on savings deposits), the real interest paid by another asset, M_1, was increased considerably with the decline in inflation. Consequently there was a portfolio reallocation based on the change of relative (real) returns.

With respect to the dollar black market, the situation developed much as in the case of the Austral Plan in Argentina (16 June 1985). Just before the plan was launched, the premium on the official market reached a peak, suddenly falling after new measures were announced and understood by the population. In Argentina, high (domestic) real interest rates perpetuated this situation for some months; on some occasions, the official dollar quotation was even higher than the market quotation. In Brazil, on the other hand, the black market premium soon began to reflect an increasing suspicion concerning the success of the Cruzado Plan. Instead of increasing the real interest rate and correcting the disequilibrium in public finances, nothing was effectively done by the government to improve the situation.

3.4 THE INTERDEPENDENCE OF MONETARY AND FISCAL POLICY

In the forty-one year period December 1946 to December 1987, M_1 increased by a factor of 23 582 766 times, which means an average increase of 51.29 per cent a year. An easy conclusion to reach from these numbers is that the Brazilian monetary system seems to have a natural propensity toward high growth of the money supply. This can be attributed to a very simple reason: money issue has always been under the control of the Executive. As noted from Table 2.6, the use of an inflationary tax as a tool to generate real current receipts has been the usual procedure, from one administration to another. This kind of tax is particularly attractive to policy makers, for two reasons: first, it is indirect, being paid by those who hold cash balances during a given period; second, it is an invisible tax which the average person cannot be aware of. Unlike taxes generally levied by governments and collected in the form of a physical transfer of money, the inflation tax is not accompanied by payment or transfer of money.

Until 1965, there was no Central Bank in Brazil. Monetary regulations were under the responsibility of SUMOC (Superintendência da Moeda e do Crédito). Legal currency was issued by the Federal Treasury, at the request of Banco do Brasil. The Central Bank of Brazil was created in 1965. The usual functions ascribed to central banks were delegated to this institution: providing a physical money supply, acting as a banker for banks, and as a fiscal agent of the Treasury, and providing for the custody and register of international reserves. While the new Central Bank assumed the external appearance of other central banks, relevant things did not change. The Executive branch of the government retained most of its former authority in matters relating to money and credit creation. The printing of money remained under the control (now indirect) of the Minister of Finance. Indeed most relevant decisions regarding monetary and foreign exchange matters have been taken, since 1965, by the National Monetary Council (Conselho Monetário Nacional, CMN) which is chaired by the Minister of Finance. There is, even nowadays, no independence of the Central Bank from the Executive. Directors of this institution can be changed at any moment, at the discretion of the President of the Republic. Their terms are not pre-established, which makes them subject to political pressures.

An important complication to Central Bank credit control has been posed by the so called 'movement account'.[11] This facility allowed Banco do Brasil to withdraw monetary resources at the Central Bank, paying a nominal interest rate of 1 per cent a year. In effect, this made Banco do Brasil a second Central Bank, since its active operations were not limited to its available resources, but to the limits settled by the National Monetary Council. The following illustration reflects how Banco do Brasil operations actually gener-ated a simultaneous increase in the stock of high-powered money (the monetary base).

Banco do Brasil		Central Bank	
Assets	Liabilities	Assets	Liabilities
△ Loans	△ Movement account	△ Movement account	△ Monetary base

In effect, new loans provided by Banco do Brasil to the private sector led to a drawing of funds from the movement account and, conse-quently, to an expansion of the monetary base.

Due to Banco do Brasil's automatic access to monetary resources provided by the Central Bank, the balance sheets of these two institutions have been presented as consolidated, under the desig-nation 'monetary authorities balance sheet'. In theory, Banco do Brasil could use this rediscount facility only up to the limits pre-determined by the CMN. Until 1979, excesses were penalised with heavy rediscount rates. From 1979 on these penalties were practically abolished. This situation lasted until March 1986, when policy mak-ers tried to eliminate the role of Banco do Brasil as a Central Bank by extinguishing the 'movement account' and creating the 'supply ac-count'. The difference between the two is that, in the second case, the monetary transfers from Central Bank to Banco do Brasil should be subjected to the approval of the Secretary of the Treasury. Since the institutional basis which determines the relationship between the Treasury, Banco Central and Banco do Brasil were not effectively modified, the change has been purely semantic. Invariably the Sec-retary of the Treasury has not denied approval to most of Banco do Brasil (BB) expenditures. This is because this institution is a strong political force; and because Banco do Brasil continued conducting operations (established in prior agreements which were not modified) of interest to the Executive. It should be noted that these operations are largely dissociated from normal commercial bank operations.

While many things remained the same, in practice (starting March

1986) Banco do Brasil is no longer officially classified as a monetary authority. The demand deposits in Banco do Brasil, which previously were counted as part of the stock of high-powered money, are now considered to be part of commercial bank sight deposits, and are not counted in the monetary base. The Brazilian banking multiplier and high-powered money series must be analysed with care. Starting in March 1986, the latter decreased and the former increased. The series organised under the new methodology were published, starting in December 1982. Although Banco do Brasil is now treated as any other commercial bank, its function as a development bank and as the government's bank remains practically unchanged. An indication that changes were purely semantic is provided by the real value of the transfers from the Central Bank to Banco do Brasil. They did not decrease after March 1986. In the twelve-month period before March 1986, the transfers from Central Bank to Banco do Brasil averaged (in billions of cruzados with February 1988 purchasing power) CZ$153.247. In the 23-month period to February 1988 these transfers averaged CZ$201.075 billion (February 1988 purchasing power). This is the best proof that the change of Banco do Brazil's status was purely cosmetic.

The National Monetary Council (CMN), the decision-making organ related to monetary and foreign exchange policy, is composed of five ministers of state, eight chairmen of federal financial institutions (including the Banco do Brasil and the Central Bank), and by a fixed number of private advisors. As previously mentioned, the Council is chaired by the Minister of Finance. The CMN is responsible for the so-called monetary budget, which refers to the several ceilings applied to aggregate monetary expansion. Among the ceilings included in the monetary budget are the maximum yearly expansion rate of the monetary base, means of payment, and Banco do Brasil assets.

In addition to the fiscal budget, the evaluation of Brazilian fiscal policy is complicated by the existence of two additional budgets: the 'monetary budget', which we have just referred to, and the 'state enterprises budget', which establishes ceilings for state enterprises' net financial borrowings. The coexistence of the fiscal and monetary budget provided a way of transforming large budget deficits into official surpluses. Indeed many operations of the federal government were included among the assets and liabilities of the monetary authorities, often creating large current deficits, financed by increases in money supply. Since these deficits, arising from subsidised credits and transfers, were not included in the fiscal budget submitted to the Congress, an official surplus could emerge.

One large government expense not included in the fiscal budget was the payment of interest on the public deficit. Since 1971, following the 'Lei Complementar número 12', the Central Bank was allowed to issue federal government debt. It was a counterpart of the many operations of the federal government carried out by the monetary authorities. Interest paid on the debt was also under the responsibility of the monetary authorities, and was not included in the fiscal budget.

Beginning in March 1986, many measures have been introduced to simplify the complicated relations involving the Federal Treasury, Central Bank and Banco do Brasil. The first we have already described, that was to classify Banco do Brasil as a commercial bank, rather than a monetary authority. Another group of resolutions aimed at including in the fiscal budget all current expenditures of the federal government carried out by the Central Bank. The purpose was to make fully transparent to the taxpayers, represented by the Congress, the destination of taxes paid. Central Bank power to issue debt in the name of the government was removed. In addition the cost of the federal government debt service was assigned to the Treasury Secretary (Secretaria do Tesouro). For this purpose, the LBC (Letra do Banco Central, Central Bank short-term liability) is being replaced by the LFT (Letra Financeira do Tesouro) as concerns open-market operations. An important difference between LBC and LFT is that interest paid on LFT is to be included in the fiscal budget, since it is issued by the Treasury. The Central Bank continues to act as a dealer for the Treasury. It remains to be seen if this increased transparency will result in increased budgetary efficiency by the federal government.

Another institutional change to occur, as of 1989, is the use of escalator clauses in the fiscal budget. Practically, the means of account in this budget will be the BTN, rather than the cruzado. This procedure may be unavoidable, if one wants the fiscal budget approved by the Congress to be representative of actual expenses. Indeed, with a 15–20 per cent monthly inflation, the use of figures denominated in cruzados would be subject to severe changes. Monetary correction applied to federal government securities would make the monthly budget expenses subject to large upward revisions. On a cumulative basis these revisions in the budget could inflate the budget deficit to a high percentage of GDP. Evidence of the need to index the budget is given by the recent past (1986–7), when the figures initially determined for the budget turned out to be totally inadequate relative to actual needs.

3.4.1 The changes with the new constitution

The new Brazilian constitution, enacted in 5 October 1988, is characterised in many aspects by an increase of the power of the Congress. As it relates to our previous discussion, three budgets will be examined by the Congress: the fiscal budget, the state enterprises budget and the social security budget. Additionally, the Congress will be responsible for setting limits related to money printing and also to the consolidated government debt.

New expenditures can be created by the Congress, provided that the respective resources are explicitly indicated. Central Bank is prohibited to finance the government directly or indirectly. In a very much criticized decision, the new constitution set a ceiling on real interest rates of 12 per cent a year.

It remains to be seen how these two measures will be made compatible with the present budget deficit, which amounts to around 6 per cent of GDP. At the time of writing, the 12 per cent limit was not yet in practice. Further ordinary regulations were expected to determine the details and sanctions related to this unusual constitutional principle.

3.5 FINANCIAL INNOVATIONS AND MONEY DEMAND

As defined in the previous chapter, we define 'financial innovation' as anything which decreases the cost of converting assets from money (M_1) into interest-bearing assets. Among these financial innovations one can cite as examples the popularisation of public applications into government assets (overnight or longer periods) since the beginning of the eighties, the reduction of the minimum term of deposit in 'caderneta de poupança' in 1984, and the introduction of the 'contas remuneradas' (remunerated accounts) in 1988. The remunerated account allows the bank customer to obtain daily remuneration on his sight deposits (based on overnight interest rates). Technically, daily remuneration does not accrue on the sight deposit, but on overnight applications in LBC (Central Bank Bills) or LFT (Treasury Bills). However commercial banks provide for daily transfers of these funds at the close of the business day. Consequently they are treated as overnight applications, but for practical purposes function as demand deposits.

Before the Cruzado Plan, when inflation reached 235 per cent in the twelve-month period before December 1985, transfers from sight deposits to one day or one week applications were already becoming a widespread practice. They required only a telephone call to the bank officer. The higher the amount of transfer, the higher the interest rate paid on the funds. Thus an application of ten million cruzeiros could enjoy a return for one day of 90 per cent of the overnight rate (the remaining 10 per cent accruing to the financial institution). At the same time, an application of five million cruzeiros for a one day application could enjoy a return of 80 per cent of the overnight rate. These hypothetical numbers provide an indication of how each bank could determine rules for negotiating for these funds under the limits imposed by the relevant Central Bank regulations.

At the end of 1987, with a yearly inflation rate over 415 per cent, the practice of shifting funds from sight deposits to one-day government assets was automated in many banks. This new financial innovation was called 'contas remuneradas' (remunerated accounts). The excess of funds over a certain limit (established by each bank) was regularly and daily transferred for depositors to LBC or LFT. The Central Bank was the loser in this case, since it could not earn the high real interest rates on commercial bank reserve requirements (which decreased in the operation, owing to the accounting of sight deposits as LBC purchases). The inflationary tax which had been accruing to the Central Bank was now shared with deposit customers of the bank in what in effect was a zero sum game.

All of these defensive manoeuvres reflect an attempt on the part of economic agents to escape from the heavy burden of high negative real interest rates associated with holding money assets (M_1). Since M_1 pays no nominal interest, the real interest paid by firms and citizens to hold this asset is an increasing function of the rate of inflation.[12]

In 1987, for instance, when inflation was 415.8 per cent the real interest paid by those who held money was 80.61 per cent a year. To make this point clear, let us take an economic agent who held one thousand cruzados during 1987. It follows that he could buy one hundred units of a certain good with a unit price of ten cruzados. At the end of the year, though, if the price of this good rose according to the rate of inflation, it will cost Cz$51.58, and he will only be able to buy 19 (100 000/5158) of them. The remaining 81 are real gains of the banking system. This loss (81 out of 100) reflects the 80.61 per cent a year real interest paid by holders of money balances.[13]

Financial innovations tend to increase in use with the escalation of nominal interest rates, the opportunity cost of holding money. This means that, *ceteris paribus*, monetary policy becomes less effective when the purpose is to use higher interest rates to control economic activity. Indeed a reduction of real cash balances also leads to an autonomous fall of money demand. Theoretically it can be argued that the *LM* curve (which represents the combination of income and interest rates which equilibrates demand and supply in the money market) becomes more elastic (less steep) when the economy tends to present quicker responses (financial innovations) to increases in nominal interest rates. This point suggests strongly that application of tight monetary policy in Brazil (as in the eighties) is much weaker in its effectiveness than a similar policy would have been had it been implemented in the sixties.

In order to examine the interest and income elasticities of money demand in Brazil, as well as to measure the possible autonomous fall of money demand due to financial innovations, we estimated some regressions for the period 1947–87. The five equations presented in Table 3.5 display the values of the estimates for the basic equation:

$$m - p = a_0 + a_1 y + a_2 \pi + a_3 t \tag{2}$$

where $m - p$ = logarithm of real cash balances
y = real product index
π = logarithmic inflation rate
t = year − 1964 (tendency variable)

We work with the inflation rate replacing the nominal interest variable, owing to the lack of a reliable series for this latter variable in Brazil. In many periods interest was controlled, making the recorded values highly artificial. The tendency variable used in estimations (4) and (5) tried to capture the process of financial innovations which occurred after 1964.

All estimates present the signs predicted by theory. Moreover t-statistics do not allow us to neglect any one of the explanatory variables. Given the way we defined the inflation rate $(1n(P_t/P_{t-1}))$ in Equation (2), the interest elasticity of money demand is not constant, but equal, in each year, to a fraction $(\pi/(1+\pi))$ of the coefficient 'a_2'

Table 3.5   Money demand estimates, Equation (2) for Brazil: 1947(8)–87

Estimates \ Coefficients	a_0	a_1	a_2	a_3	Method	$\bar{R}^2$	DW
1	4.8	0.79	−1.07				
	(42.7)	(21.5)	(−11.4)	—	OLSQ	0.92	1.1
2	4.8	0.79	−1.07		IV		
	(40.4)	(20.9)	(−11.4)	—	$Y_{-1}\, \pi_{-1}$	0.92	1.07
3	4.6	0.83	−1.15		CO		
	(23.8)	(13.9)	(−9.1)	—	$\varrho = 0.47$	0.94	1.77
4	2.8	1.6	−0.84	−0.06			
	(4.3)	(5.8)	(−7.5)	(−3.06)	OLSQ	0.93	1.4
5	3.0	1.6	−0.93	−0.05	CO		
	(3.6)	(4.3)	(−6.8)	(−2.11)	$\varrho = 0.324$	0.94	1.81

Notes: (1) OLSQ = Ordinary least squares.
　　　　　(2) IV   = Instrumental variables procedure.
　　　　　(3) CO   = Cochrane Orcutt procedure.
　　　　　(4) The numbers in parenthesis display the *t*-statistics.
　　　　　(5) $\bar{R}^2$ = Adjusted R^2 coefficient.
　　　　　(6) DW   = Durbin-Watson statistic.

Instrumental variables were used in (2) because the rational expectations hypothesis for the expected inflation rates make the residual of Equation (2) correlated with the explaining variables.
Cochrane Orcutt method was used in (3) and (5) in an attempt to minimise the serial correlation of the residuals.
Average annual date were used for both P (price level) and M_1. The new concept of M_1 (including demand deposits at the Caixas Econômicas and BNCC) was used as of December 1982.
Source of original data: Central Bank of Brazil, *Boletim Mensal* and Getúlio Vargas Foundation, *Revista Conjuntura Econômica*.

presented in Table 3.5. These estimates can be interpreted, then, as upper limits of the absolute value of the interest elasticities. They range, as can be observed in Table 3.5, from 0.84 to 1.15. The income elasticity, on the other hand, ranges from 0.79 to 1.6, depending upon the equation considered.

The possibility that money demand was particularly affected by financial innovations that took place after 1964 cannot be rejected in terms of the trend variable. Besides being significant at the 5 per cent confidence level, it follows the predicted negative sign.

In order to measure this autonomous decline in money demand as a response to financial innovations we re-estimated Equation (2) with first differences:

$$z_t - \pi_t = b_0 + b_1 n_t + b_2 (\pi_t - \pi_{t-1}) + b_3 DU_3 + b_4 DU_4 + b_5 DU_5 \quad (3)$$

where z_t $= m_t - m_{t-1}$ = monetary expansion
π_τ $= p_t - p_{t-1}$ = logarithmic inflation rate
n_t $= y_t - y_{t-1}$ = real product rate of growth
DU_3 = dummy variable for the period 1979–87[14]
DU_4 = dummy variable for 1986
DU_5 = dummy variable for 1987

The underlying hypothesis is that financial innovations shift the demand function according to a trend component plus a random walk. This would explain the poor Durbin-Watson statistic presented in Table 3.5, as well as the low income elasticities relative to estimations (1), (2) and (3). The absence of a third variable non-orthogonal to the others would lead to a bias of the estimated coefficients. Particularly in the case of the income variable, the income elasticity would be underestimated.

Table 3.6   Money demand estimates, equation (3): (1948–87)

Estimates \ Coefficients	b_0	b_1	b_2	b_3	b_4	b_5	Method	$\bar{R}^2$	DW
6	−0.059 (−1.32)	1.78 (2.96)	−1.24 (−6.76)	—	—	—	OLSQ	0.62	2.16
7	−0.059 (−1.79)	1.55 (3.75)	−0.69 (−4.47)	−0.09 (−2.09)	0.81 (7.18)	—	OLSQ	0.84	1.64
8	−0.057 (−2.22)	1.50 (4.69)	−0.54 (−4.52)	−0.06 (−2.0)	0.83 (9.51)	−0.36 (−4.91)	OLSQ	0.91	2.12

Notes: Dummies D_4 and D_5 are used, owing to the institutional changes during and just after the Cruzado Plan in 1986.

The results based on equation (3) are displayed in Table 3.6. All these equations present the signs as theoretically predicted. The adjusted R^2 coefficient seems very reasonable for first difference estimates, especially in (8). The improvement of the Durbin-Watson statistic corroborates our previous hypothesis of the autonomous stochastic shift of the money demand function. The coefficient b_0 translates into an autonomous decline in money demand of 5.9–6 per cent a year. Remember that b_0 represents logarithmic rates of growth. Under the hypothesis here presented this is explained by the continuous development of the money market and appearance of financial innovations. The significance of the coefficient b_3 does not allow us to neglect that this process becomes accelerated as a result of the increase of inflation of 1979. Indeed, this was the period when open market operations became more popular and feasible to most economic agents.

What these results show is that the understanding of monetary policy making in Brazil, mainly in the last eight years, has to be undertaken in connection with the continuous shifts of money demand. In turn these shifts of money demand are in part due to the development of the financial market. This has led to the need for economists to consider using broader concepts of money than M_1 in evaluating the effects of monetary policy and other factors in the demand for financial assets.

APPENDIX

(a) Let S stand for the nominal wage and $P(t)$ for the price level at time t. If the instantaneous inflation rate is constant over time, and equal to $\tilde{\pi}$, the average real wage (W_A) between time 0 and 1 will be given by:

$$W_A = \int_0^1 W_p \, e^{-\tilde{\pi}t} dt \tag{A.1}$$

where W_p represents the value of the real wage just after the last adjustment has been made. Since W_p and $\tilde{\pi}$ are constants, integrating (A.1) we get:

$$W_a = W_p \frac{1 - e^{-\tilde{\pi}}}{\tilde{\pi}} \tag{A.2}$$

Instantaneous inflation rate $(\tilde{\pi})$ relates to the periodical rate π by the expression:

$$\tilde{\pi} = 1n(1 + \pi) \tag{A.3}$$

Substituting (A.3) into (A.2), we got the expression used in this chapter:

$$W_A = W_p \frac{\pi}{(1+\pi) \, 1n(1+\pi)} \tag{A.4}$$

(b) If the purpose is to depart from a given average real wage to get the 'peak' value W_p based on an expected rate of inflation π^e, this formula leads to:

$$W_p = \frac{W_A (1+\pi^e) \, 1n \, (1+\pi^e)}{\pi^e} \quad \text{if} \quad \pi^e \neq 0$$

or

$$W_p = W_A \qquad\qquad \text{if} \qquad \pi^e = 0$$

(c) To show the negative correlation between full employment real wages and supply shocks, we depart from the labour demand equation for a competitive economy:

$$\frac{S}{P} = f'\ (N) \qquad f'' < 0 \tag{A.5}$$

where S   = nominal wage
           P   = implicit GNP deflator
           $f'\ (N)$= Marginal productivity of labour
           N   = labour force

We have the consumer price index (Q) to be given by:

$$Q = (EP^*)^\alpha\ (P)^{1-\alpha}\ (1+t) \tag{A.6}$$

where P^* = price index of imported goods
           E = nominal exchange rate
           α = share of income spent on the imported good
           t = indirect tax applicable to both the domestic and the imported good.

Making Θ represent the real exchange rate, expression (A.5) can read:

$$Q = \Theta_\alpha\ P(1+t) \tag{A.7}$$

Using (A.7) and (A.5),

$$\frac{S}{Q} = \frac{f'\ (N)}{\Theta^\alpha\ (1+t)}$$

If we define supply shocks as consisting of either a real exchange rate devaluation, an increase of indirect taxes, or a decrease in the marginal productivity of labour, the immediate conclusion is that supply shocks lead to a fall in the full employment real wage. This is shown in the diagram overleaf.

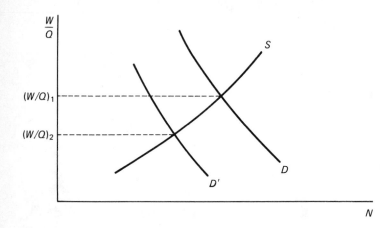

NOTES

1. If yearly inflation is 40 per cent and uniform, half-yearly inflation will be 18.32 per cent. Entering this number in (1) results in $W_A = 0.920\ W_p$.
2. A productivity gain can also be added to the prior average, as it was for example, in the case of Brazil between 1965 and 1967, when this additional adjustment was fixed by the government.
3. See, for instance, Lopes (1986).
4. We should remember that APR is a strictly decreasing function of π.
5. Actually both upward shifts in inflation described in items *a* and *b* were preceded by an increase in the rate of monetary expansion in the previous half-year. In the 1979–80 turn, the wage policy change in November 1979 only ratified the new annual 100 per cent inflation already operating since August (making it impossible to return to the old 40 per cent a year level). In the 1982–3 period, monetary expansion in the second half of 1982 (due to the elections) must also be included, besides the supply shocks in a lagged indexed economy, among the relevant determinants of the new 220 per cent annual level of inflation prevailing up to 1986.
6. See Chapter 2.
7. Of course this high correlation is in part due to the fact that most assets included in M_4 are indexed. However, this does not imply non-controllability.
8. As shown in Table 4.3, average real wages increased by around 19 per cent between 1985 and 1986.
9. This was said by the Labour Minister in a Conference held in São Paulo some time after the start of the plan.
10. Inflation moved to even higher levels.

11. Effective March 1986, these have been called 'supply account' or 'Conta de Suprimento'.
12. If π stands for the inflation rate during period Δt, the real interest paid by all those holding M_1 during this period is given by $\pi/(1+\pi)$. Indeed, if i stands for the nominal interest and r for the real interest paid on M_1, we have, following the definition of real interest rate, $1+r=(1+i)/(1+\pi)$. Making $i = 0$ in this expression, we get $r = -\pi/(1+\pi)$, which means that M_1 pays negative real interest or, put in another way, whoever holds money pays $\pi/(1+\pi)$ to the banking system.
13. We assume indivisibility of the good, and have therefore rounded 80.61 to 81.
14. Dummy variables for period t assume value 1 for period t and zero in the other years.

REFERENCES

BANCO CENTRAL DO BRASIL, *Brasil Programa Econômico*, Março de 1987 e Março de 1988.
WORLD BANK, *A Macroeconomic Evaluation of the Cruzado Plan*, a World Bank case study, 1987.
CYSNE, RUBENS P., *Política Macroeconômica no Brasil: 1964–1966 e 1980–84*, publicado pela Lonsango Distribuidora de Títulos e Valores Mobiliários, Rio de Janeiro, 1985.
LANGONI, C. G., 'A Study in Economic Growth: The Brazilian Case', dissertação de Doutoramento, Universidade de Chicago, 1970.
LOPES, FRANCISCO L. P., *Choque Heterodoxo – Combate à Inflação e Reforma Monetária* (Rio de Janeiro: Editora Campus, 1986).
LOPES, FRANCISCO L. P., INFLAÇÃO E NíVEL DE ATIVIDADE NO BRASIL, Programa Nacional de Pesquisa Econômica, Série Fac-Símile no. 2, 1983.
SIMONSEN, MÁRIO HENRIQUE, 'Rational Expectations, Income Policies and Game Theory', *Revista Brasileira de Econometria*, 1987.
SIMONSEN, MÁRIO H. and R. O. CAMPOS, *A Nova Economia Brasileira*, (Rio de Janeiro: José Olympio Editora, 1974).
TOBIN, J., 'Diagnosing Inflation: A Taxonomy', *Academic Press Development in an Inflationary World* (New York: Academic Press, 1981).
TOLEDO, JOAQUIM CIRNE DE, 'Estimação do Déficit Público e do Imposto Inflacionário', mimeo, USP, São Paulo, maio de 1986.
ZERKOWSKY, R. M. and VELLOSO, M. A. 'Seis Décadas de Economia Brasileira Através do PIB' *Revista Brasileira de Economia*, 36 (1932) 331–8.

4 The Economy in the Eighties and the Debt Crisis

4.1 THE BRAZILIAN ECONOMY IN THE EIGHTIES

In terms of economic development, the eighties have proved fruitless to Brazil. Table 4.1 compares the average rate of growth of real GDP with previous periods. Sectoral data related to industrial and agricultural product are also included. One can easily observe, from lines (1), (2) and (3), the sharp deterioration of product rates of growth in the eighties. Growth of industrial product, which averaged 7.0 per cent in the sixties and 9.4 per cent in the seventies, was reduced to an average increase of 1.4 per cent between 1980 and 1988. At the same time, the average annual increase in agricultural production declined from 4.2 per cent in the last two decades (2.9 per cent in the sixties and 5.5 per cent in the seventies) to 2.6 per cent in the eighties. Following this trend, real GDP growth displayed a very poor average rate of increase of 2.3 per cent per year. This is quite low when compared to the 5.9 per cent in the sixties or the 8.7 per cent in the seventies. If we take a longer period for purpose of comparisons, the conclusion remains the same. Brazilian GDP growth averaged 6.2 per cent between 1920 and 1980, and 7.1 per cent between 1950 and 1980.

Two basic reasons can explain this reversal in growth trend: (1) the mismanagement of economic policy starting in the second half of 1979; and (2) the sudden reduction of voluntary external financing to the perennial current account deficit of the Brazilian balance of payments.[1] This last point will be analysed in the next section. We concentrate our attention here on the conduct of macroeconomic policy in the eighties.

Given the second oil shock and the increase in external interest rates in 1979, it became evident that the country should review its strategy of aiming for 7 per cent growth of real GDP at the cost of external borrowing. This had been the choice taken in 1974, after the first oil shock. The economy grew 7 per cent a year in 1974–9, at the cost of huge current account deficits in the balance of payments.

Table 4.1   Average rates of growth of output (%)

Period	GDP	Industrial product	Agricultural product
(1) 1960–70	5.9	7.0	2.9
(2) 1970–80	8.7	9.4	5.5
(3) 1980–88*	2.3	1.4	2.6
(4) 1981	–3.1	–5.5	5.8
(5) 1982	1.1	0.6	–2.5
(6) 1983	–2.8	–6.7	2.2
(7) 1984	5.7	6.1	3.1
(8) 1985	8.4	8.9	8.8
(9) 1986	8.0	12.2	–7.2
(10) 1987	2.9	0.2	14.3
(11) 1988*	–0.9	–2.9	1.5

* = Predicted
Sources: (1) Industrial and agricultural product, up to 1980: Zerkowsky and Velloso (1982); from 1981 to 1987: *Conjuntura Economica*.
(2) Real GDP up to 1969: Zerkowsky and Velloso (1982); from 1970 to 1987: IBGE, *National Accounts and Population* (1988).
(3) Forecasts for 1988: IPEA–INPES, *Boletim Conjuntural* (July, 1988).

Macroeconomic administration carried out between March 1979 (when the new government took office) and August 1979 was based exclusively on the need to tighten monetary and fiscal policy. It was thought that this, together with a real exchange rate devaluation, should allow the necessary increase in non-oil net exports. However the idea of decreased rates of growth, even if only for a short period, did not find enough political support. Finance Minister Mario Henrique Simonsen resigned and in his place Delfim Netto introduced a set of unorthodox measures whose main result was to increase the yearly inflation rate from the 38.4 per cent level in the period 1974–8 to 76.9 per cent in 1979.

The predominant idea of the new administration was that inflation should be combated through accelerated growth. Money supply was expanded rapidly with the argument that enlarged credit to the agricultural sector would provide the necessary increase in production to dampen the elevation of prices. Needless to say, the proposition was completely belied by the facts: first, because the abundant credit to agriculture reflected more on the price of land than on production; second, because of the concomitant increase of aggregate demand. Coupled with lagged indexaton, this was an additional and powerful fuel to inflation.

The surge in demand and the quick upward adjustment of administered prices after the ministerial change, referred to as corrective
inflation, were immediately reflected in the monthly inflation rates.
The annualised rate of monetary base expansion, which had been
44.8 per cent up to the end of July, was increased to 158.7 per cent
from 31 July to the end of December. At the same time, annualised
inflation jumped from 56.9 per cent between December 1978 and
July 1979 to 109.2 per cent in the last five months of the year (or,
equivalently, to 104.3 per cent between July and November).

These new levels of inflation were ratified by the change in the
term of wage adjustments in November. Nominal revisions turned
from annual to half-yearly, keeping the average peak ratio practically
unchanged (see Chapter 3), but making impossible the return of
inflation to the earlier 38.4 per cent a year level (1974–9). Indeed
inflation rates between 1980 and 1982 were, on average, very close to
the new annualised level in effect between the end of July and
December 1979: 101.4 per cent a year. Except during the artificial
decline in inflation which occurred during the Cruzado Plan, the
situation has worsened steadily. The 40 per cent yearly inflation level
remains a dream to Brazilians.

The upward shift of inflation made the shortening of the term of
wage adjustments politically unavoidable. However the change of
income policy irreversibly determined a new floor for inflation rates
of around 100 per cent a year. Indeed a decline to the previous 40 per
cent a year level would mean an increase of about 9 per cent of the
average real wages. And this was not compatible with the economic
conditions at that time. In addition, the new wage policy included
some aspects of unorthodox economic policy. Besides the automatic
correction provided by indexation, a further free negotiated real
increase, labelled 'productivity gain', was superimposed on the nominal adjustment. Moreover a 10 per cent half-yearly bonus incident
on the wage correction indexes was granted to all salaries up to three
minimum wages. This method of wage adjustment had two effects:
(1) it tended to narrow wage differentials; and (2) this narrowing
process was an increasing function of the rate of inflation.

On 7 December 1979 the rate on dollars set by the Central Bank
was increased by 30 per cent. A real exchange devaluation was really
necessary, but was not effectively achieved through this measure. Its
real impact was largely reduced, owing to the withdrawal of export
subsidies and import prior deposits. Moreover, in the next year
(1980), exchange rate devaluation (60 per cent) failed to keep pace

with domestic inflation (110.2 per cent). In, short, the exchange rate change carried out in December provided no price incentives to increase exports or decrease imports. It was at best an interruption of an eleven-year tradition of crawling-pegs, fostering inflation and expectations about future devaluations. Autonomous capital inflows were dramatically reduced as of December 1979, as a result of the fear that new maxi-devaluations could occur. To encourage voluntary net borrowing from overseas, an artificial interest rate increase was achieved through domestic credit rationing. This was introduced in April 1980, and lasted, with some modifications, until June 1983.

In January 1980, the government decided that a strong psychological measure was necessary to reverse the upsurge in inflationary expectations taking place since August of the previous year. Price controls were introduced and subsidies increased. A heroic measure was the announcement that monetary correction and exchange devaluations would be limited to, respectively, 45 per cent and 40 per cent, during the whole year in course. The measure was completely incompatible with the evolution of aggregate demand and the indexing of the economy. As one should expect, its only consequences were the appreciation of the real exchange rate and a strong capital flight from indexed bonds to non-indexed securities and to the purchasing of durable consumption goods.

The new trend of inflation as of 1979 can be seen in Table 4.2. Apart from the first upward shift of inflation which occurred in the second half of 1979, another must be investigated: the one from 101.6 per cent (between 1980 and 1982) to 223.2 per cent between 1983 and 1985. The explanation usually found for this second surge is of inflation is based on the effect of supply shocks in a backward-looking indexed economy. As exemplified in section 2 of Chapter 3, the 101.6 per cent average yearly inflation between 1980 and 1982 meant an average-peak ratio, under half-yearly adjustments, around .84 per cent. On the other hand, the 223.2 per cent average yearly inflation between December 1982 and December 1985 reflected an average peak ratio for real wages around .76 per cent. Consequently, an *ex post* explanation for the rise in inflation can be obtained by saying that, because of the supply shocks which occurred in 1982 and 1983, real wages had to fall 9.5 per cent ((76/84)–1) × 100 per cent).

Real wages did decline between 1980–2 and 1983–5, not by 9.5 per cent, but by around 22 per cent. Table 4.3 presents the real wage indexes for the period 1975–1987. This discrepancy can be reconciled with the average-peak apparatus presented in Chapter 3 if one

Table 4.2   Inflation in Brazil, end of period

Years	Inflation rate	Years	Inflation rate
1960–70	41.6	1983	211.0
1970–80	40.3	1984	223.8
1980–87	172.6	1985	235.1
1981	95.2	1986	65.0
1982	99.7	1987	415.8

Source: *Conjuntura Econômica.*

Table 4.3   Real wage indexes

Year	Real wage index
1975	86
1976	94
1977	99
1978	111
1979	117
1980	114
1981	106
1982	109
1983	90.6
1984	78.6
1985	88.4
1986	105
1987	100

Notes: Original sources of data: FIESP for monthly wage indexes, and Getulio Vargas Foundation for monthly price index. Annual indexes were obtained from monthly indexes by simple arithmetic average.

remembers that the six different wage policies in effect between 1983 and 1985 did not provide for a full replacement of the previous purchasing power of wages. This only happened with incomes up to three minimum wages. Other ranges were subject to a correction, of around 95 per cent, 80 per cent or 50 per cent of inflation, depending upon the Decree Law in term and upon the different ranges of real wages (denominated in minimum wages). Following Decree-Law 2065, for example, which was in effect between October 1983 and October 1984, the percentage of inflation correction granted by law was 100 per cent for incomes up to three times minimum wages, 80 per cent between 3 and 7 minimum wages, 60 per cent between 7 and

15 minimum wages and only 50 per cent of inflation for incomes higher than 15 minimum wages. Of course these corrections were cumulative, as in the case of income taxes. So, if the minimum wage stood at one cruzeiro and a worker had a wage of 7 cruzeiros at the beginning of the period, he would have his income corrected to 13.2 cruzados ($7 + 3 \times 1 + 4 \times 0.8 \times 1$) if the inflation rate had been a 100 per cent in the period.

The supply shocks can be translated by the Zero rate of growth of the agricultural sector in 1982 and 1983 (see Table 4.1) as well as by the effective real exchange rate devaluation (around 27 per cent) which took place between these two years. One point is missing in this reasoning: demand management does not enter the analysis, which implicitly means that money supply is supposed to be passive, accommodating the price jump solely explained by supply shocks in a backward-indexed economy. However, if one observes the monthly rates of monetary expansion since 1982, one important fact provides an additional explanation for the change of inflation level starting in 1983: the sharp increase of the monetary expansion rates in the second semester of 1982.[2] Between December 1981 (end of period) and June 1982, M_1 and the monetary base expanded, respectively, by 13.7 per cent and 22 per cent. In a further six-month period, starting at the end of June, these rates increased to, respectively, 47.7 per cent and 53.8 per cent. These data reflect a huge incentive to inflation arising from the demand side, which must be considered when analysing this inflation.

After experiencing three years of inflation rates around 223 per cent, the Cruzado Plan was introduced in 28 February 1986. The details of this plan, as well as the reasons for its complete failure, have already been presented in a previous chapter. After a twelve-month period, starting with the launching of the plan, when the inflation rate was reduced to 46.3 per cent at the cost of artificial price controls and a complete depletion of the international reserves held by the Central Bank. Yearly inflation finally reached 1038 per cent in 1988.

This whole story provides the basis for understanding one of the causes of Brazilian stagnation in the eighties. Mismanagement of economic policy started in the second semester of 1979 and has been present in the country up to the present. First, there was an unortho-dox economic policy in 1979–80. Second, there was non-recognition of the weak response of inflation to (sometimes) restrictive demand policies in an economy facing supply shocks and backward-looking indexation. Third, there was the appearance of theories of inflation biased against demand controls, leading to the disastrous Cruzado Plan. Fourth, there was the weak attempt to revive a price freeze strategy in 1987 (the so-called Bresser Plan) without solving the huge public deficit problem. Later there was the 'política de feijão com arroz' (rice with beans politics), whose main promise of gradually reducing inflation through demand controls was a complete failure. Finally, the disastrous 'Summer Plan', introduced on 15 February 1989, which was only able to reduce inflation (due to artificial price controls) during three months.

Although the cut in the budget deficit remains as a necessary condition to combat inflation, the same problem that occurred between 1979 and 1985 arose in 1988: the existence of a backward-looking indexation system severely dampening the fall of inflation. The solution, of course, would be to use a mix of tight demand policy and forward-looking indexation. However, the Cruzado, Bresser and Summer Plan highly discredited income policies, making a concomitant demand and supply approach to inflation a distant first best solution to the problem.

4.2 THE DEBT CRISIS

The sequence of economic policy errors is not the only explanation for the stagnation of Brazilian per capita income since 1980. As in the case of other indebted countries in South America, Brazil was deeply affected by the second oil shock and by the increase in international interest rates, which commenced in 1979. At times economic policy makers must recognise that it is necessary to allow the economy to slow down before it can resume its growth path. In Brazil this would have meant a tight demand policy followed by a real exchange rate devaluation (year 1979). If this course had been taken, the effect of the external shocks would have been much reduced.

The deterioration of the external accounts between 1979 and 1982 can be considered by examining data in Table 4.4. All monetary figures are presented in dollars of 1987. Column (1) shows the value of the imports of oil and derivatives. Columns (2) and (3) decompose the current account of the balance of payments into two parts. The first, which we call H (net resource transfers abroad) represents the commercial balance surplus plus the non-factor services surplus. It is supposed to be the most controllable one, since interest, royalties

Table 4.4   External accounts between 1974 and 1987

Year	(1) Imports of oil and derivatives	(2) H	(3) RLE	(4) T=(RLE-H)	(5) Res	(6) Net Debt	(7) Res/Imp	(8) Net debt Exp
1974–8	5757	−6432	4013	10445	11454	43244	0.55	2.5
1978	6162	−3522	6744	10266	17610	59175	0.87	3.2
1979	8396	−6081	7935	14016	12695	60174	0.51	3.0
1980	11272	−6056	8607	14663	7880	65644	0.30	2.8
1981	11543	−1050	11257	12307	7851	69701	0.34	2.8
1982	10411	−1922	14856	16778	4050	83642	0.21	4.0
1983	8309	4980	11926	6946	4643	90412	0.29	4.1
1984	6812	11747	11702	−45	11890	89320	0.46	3.3
1985	5674	11459	11699	240	11608	93199	0.88	3.6
1986	3101	7283	11879	4596	11608	107090	0.48	4.6
1987	4123	9861	10648	787	7458	116932	0.29	4.5

Notes: (1) Original source of data: Central Bank of Brazil and International Financial Statistics (IFS).

(2) Columns 1 to 6 are presented in constant million dollars of 1987. Average wholesale price index of the United States was used as deflator.

(3) International reserves are presented in a gross concept, including some non-liquid assets, and not providing for the subtraction of short-term liabilities. Actual international liquidity immediately available for the country was considerably (on average, 3 to 5 billion dollars) shorter.

(4) Exports used to derive the net debt/exports indicator (column 8) do not include exports of non-factor services.

(5) H = Commercial balance, plus international travels, plus transports, plus insurance, plus governmental accounts, plus other non-factor services surplus.

(6) RLE = −(interests plus royalties plus rents plus wages plus other factor services plus unrequited transfers) surplus.

and profits payments are not included. The second part of the current account is given by what we have already called in Chapter 2 *RLE* (net income transfers abroad). It represents the interest, royalties, profits, labour remuneration and unrequited transfers surplus, but with a changed sign. It follows that the current account deficit (T), presented in column (3), can be given by $T = RLE - H$. Total reserves positions are shown in column (5), within a broad concept of international liquidity. The availability of international means of payment should be seen as around three to five billion dollars below these numbers. Column (6) presents the extended version of the net debt (debt minus reserves), which includes registered as well as non-registered debt. Finally, columns (7) and (8) display some usual indicators of the status of the external accounts.

The empirical background for our thesis that the stagnation of Brazilian economy in the eighties must also be attributed to external shocks is easily derived from Table 4.4. The total value of imports of oil and derivatives was about 100 per cent higher in 1980–2, when compared with the five-year period after the first oil shock (1974–8). Although the relative increase in the international price of oil was less in 1979 compared with that in 1973–4, the absolute change was much higher in the more recent period.

At the same time, interest rates soared from an average 7 per cent per year in the period 1975–7 to 9.2 per cent in 1978 and 12.6 per cent in 1979. In 1980, the annualised LIBOR and prime rate reached, respectively, 14 per cent and 21.5 per cent. These facts are reflected in the term *RLE*, which mainly consists of interest payments. As shown in column (3), net income transfers abroad increased around 200 per cent (in real terms) between 1981 and 1987, when compared with the period 1974–8. At that time, net debt was still around US$43.2 billion (of 1987 purchasing power), and the interest rates much lower.

The result of these two factors was the sharp increase in the current account deficit, from an average US$10.4 billion (of 1987 purchasing power) in 1974–8 to around US$14.4 billion (of 1987 purchasing power) in 1979–82. The increase would have been higher if there had not been a concomitant increase of the non-oil commercial balance surplus, beginning in 1981.

External shocks have affected the rate of growth of GDP in two ways. Using a short-run perspective, income-dampening policies were largely used between 1981 and 1983 to reduce imports. The US$5.0 billion (1987 purchasing power) increase of net resource transfer in 1981 was achieved by means of negative growth (−3.1 per cent), the first negative growth of GDP in Brazilian history. A second decline occurred in 1983, and was also an important element in achieving an additional US$6.9 billion (1987 purchasing power) increase of net resource transfer. Between 1981 and 1983 Brazil's per capita income fell 11 per cent. Most of this can be attributed to a compression of income needed to dampen imports. Taking a long-run perspective, we must emphasise the sharp decrease since 1982 in the use of external savings to foster Brazilian development. As a percentage of GNP, the participation of external savings in Brazilian capital formation declined from 6.1 per cent in 1982 to around 0.7 per cent in the period 1985–7.

Column (5) points to the continuous loss of reserves as of December 1978. At that time the Central Bank held US$17.6 billion (1987 purchasing power) of international liquidity (see note (3) below Table 4.4). This was reduced gradually to US$12.7 billion in 1979, US$7.9 in 1980, US$7.8 billion in 1981, and US$4.0 billion in 1982 (all 1987 purchasing power). One can see from column (3) that the drop in reserves between 1978 and 1979 is not very different from the increase in the current account deficit. The current account deficit remained practically the same in 1980, leading to a continued fall of reserves. The comparison of columns (4) and (5) between 1979 and 1980 displays a fixed level of external financing of around US$9.5 billion per year.

Looking at columns (2) and (3) one can see a radical change in the composition of the current account deficit in the period 1980–1. Net resource transfers abroad were sharply reduced but, at the same time, the net income transfers abroad were increased by almost the same amount. Goods exports increased from US$22.9 billion (1987 purchasing power) to US$26.7 billion, while interest payments jumped from US$7.23 billion to US$10.49 billion.

This improvement in the controllable part of the current account deficit (H) can be attributed to the radical change in economic policy in January 1981. The measures which had been seen as indispensable by the previous economic administration in the first half-year of 1979, finally arrived, but with one and a half crucial years of delay. Interest controls were abolished, monetary policy was tightened,[3] exchange rate mini-devaluations were accelerated and many export subsidies and import duties restored. The price to be paid for the US$5.0 billion (1987 purchasing power) urgently needed improvement in the non-interest current account was a 5.5 per cent decline in industrial production and a 3.1 per cent decline in real GDP.

The external liquidity crisis was temporarily put off, at the cost of a sharp recession and short-term borrowing. Overseas branches of Brazilian banks were used to attain extended credit for the country. Final disruption came in late 1982, when the Mexican moratorium put a stop to new voluntary lending to indebted nations, including Brazil. As a further complication, Brazil's commercial credits against some countries suddenly became illiquid. Reserves were almost completely depleted. Official statistics reflected reserves which would be enough for barely two and a half months of imports (column 7). In November 1982, the application for an IMF-supported adjustment programme had been made unavoidable.

Brazilian reaction to the external crisis as of 1983 was remarkable. The current account deficit was reduced sharply, from US$16.8 billion (1987 purchasing power) to a small surplus in 1984. Except for the unusual Cruzado Plan experience, this equilibrium has been maintained up to 1988. Net resource transfers abroad have almost exactly met the necessary interest, royalty, labour remuneration, and profit remittance payments to non-residents. The US$13.3 billion (1987 purchasing power) trade surplus in 1983, which far exceeded the IMF targets, was a result of three factors: the 29.4 per cent real exchange rate devaluation which occurred after 1982, the economic growth in OECD countries, and the outcome of an outward-oriented industrial policy set down in the seventies. Brazil was now able to export what it previously imported: capital and petrochemical goods, paper and pulp, steel products and so on. In spite of the 17 per cent appreciation of the real exchange which occurred in the period 1984–7, the mega-surpluses of the commercial balance have been kept, up to the present time, permitting near equilibrium of the current account.

NOTES

1. In the 41-year period 1947–87, only in eight years has Brazil presented a current account surplus in the balance of payments. This was in 1950, 1953, 1955, 1956, 1964, 1965, 1966 and 1984.
2. The elections which were going to be held in November of that year generated large amounts of election-oriented credits and current expenditures. This was supported by expansion of the monetary base.
3. The M_1 expansion rate was reduced from 58.4 per cent in the six-month period before January 1981 to 37.9 per cent in the next half-year period.

REFERENCES

FUNDAÇÃO GETULIO VARGAS, *Conjuntura Econômica*, several issues.
IBGE (Instituto Brasileiro de Geografia e Estatística), *Contas Nacionais e População* (National Accounts and Population), 1988.

IPEA/INPES, *Boletim Conjuntural*, July 1988.
SIMONSEN, M. H. 'Inflation And Inflationary Policies in Brazil', mimeo, EPGE-FGV, 1980.
SIMONSEN, M. H., 'Foreign Capital and Economic Growth: The Brazilian Case Study', in R. Dornbusch and Leslie Helmers (eds), *The Open Economy* Banco Mundial, 1987.
ZERKOWSKI, R. M. and M. A. VELLOSO, 'Seis Décadas de Economia Brasileira Através do PIB,' *Revista Brasileira de Economia*, 1982.

Part II
Financial Institutions

5 Historical and Structural Trends in the Brazilian Financial System

5.1 INTRODUCTION

Two recent events of a legal nature are expected to exert a significant impact on the structure and functioning of Brazil's financial system. One is the new Brazilian constitution which was promulgated on 5 October 1988. Chapter IV (specifically, Article 198) sets forth certain legal guidelines for a banking reform law which is to be enacted by Congress. The other is Central Bank Resolution 1.524, dated 21 September 1988, establishing the bases for a multiple bank system of financial institution organisation, modelled essentially along Mexican lines and having been developed with support from the World Bank.

In this chapter, we will first summarise the essential objectives of these two documents in order to orient the reader with respect to the directions which organisational and structural changes appear to be assuming. We shall then trace the qualitative aspects of the development of Brazil's financial system, ending with a more detailed discussion of the changes introduced by the constitution and Resolution 1.524. The purpose of this approach is twofold: to provide background information for a more thorough understanding as to why these changes are taking place, and to demonstrate the structural outlines of the financial system as it at present exists, keeping in mind that the newly instituted legal changes have not been in force long enough to affect them directly.

Having examined the qualitative aspects of structural developments, we will analyse the quantitative evolution of Brazil's financial system, demonstrating not only its own dramatic growth over the years but also the extent to which it has contributed to the country's economic development. This section will also provide statistical information on foreign ownership of Brazilian financial institutions. In the final section of this chapter, and keeping in mind the present organisational structure of Brazil's financial system, we will review some of its most distinctive features – those which both fascinate and frequently complicate understanding on the part of all but the most seasoned observers.

Throughout this chapter and the two which succeed it, we hope to communicate to the reader the rapidity and dynamism which characterise the development and organisational structure of Brazil's financial system. We also wish to emphasise that these characteristics are likely to remain as permanent features of the system in the years ahead.

5.2 SUMMARY OF OBJECTIVES OF CHAPTER IV OF THE BRAZILIAN CONSTITUTION AND CENTRAL BANK RESOLUTION 1.524

The fundamental objective of the constitution is to require Congress to enact a new banking law which would have the status of complementary legislation, that is, ranking above all other types of law in the Brazilian legal hierarchy. This new legislation would replace Law 4.595/64, certain provisions of Law 4.131/62, and other relevant laws, decrees and resolutions. The constitution has determined that it must address the following issues:

- foreign ownership of shares in Brazilian financial institutions;
- the conversion of credit co-operatives into banks;
- the involvement of banking institutions in unrelated activities, such as insurance;
- the intransferability and non-negotiability of financial institution charters.

A draft complementary law was submitted to Congress shortly after the constitution came into effect, but has not yet been processed. The Senate alone can pass the law as, according to constitutional provisions, approval by the Chamber of Deputies is not required.

Central Bank Resolution 1.524 and accompanying regulations contain the following essential elements:

1. They provide for the merger of largely similar banking functions, hitherto separated legally, in accordance with institutional specialisation, into a single institution defined as a *Multibank*. The Multibank would thus replace the conglomerate concept as far as commercial banks, investment banks, savings and loan companies,

consumer finance companies, and development banks are concerned. (See Chapters 6 and 7 for a description of these types of institutions.) Brokerage firms, 'distribuidoras,' and leasing companies will continue to function as separate institutions, either independently or as part of a conglomerate. The merger/incorporation provisions are optional.

2. They support and promote the concept of capitalisation as a principal criterion for bank ownership and management and are in line with the constitution's requirement that financial institution charters are no longer negotiable in a free market but are obtainable from the Central Bank without charge as long as capitalisation and reputation requirements are met.

3. They expand the possibilities for ownership and operation of a number of individual banking units. This is accomplished by liberalising ownership qualifications at the institutional level; for example, brokerage houses and 'distribuidoras' not affiliated through ownership with a financial conglomerate are entitled to file for charters to establish Multibanks. Many such petitions have already been approved by the Central Bank. By liberalising market entry requirements, the Central Bank has effectively eliminated the point system established by Resolution 1.060 in 1985 (but functioning in practice prior to that time), which resulted in severely restricting the expansion of the number of market participants.

4. They permit, at least until enactment of the complementary law, foreign shareholdings in Multibanks in accordance with Articles 50 and 51 of Law 4.131/62, that is, up to 30 per cent of voting capital subject to reciprocity from the country of domicile of the foreign investor. Thus, a foreign bank which owned 50 per cent of the capital stock of an investment bank ($33 \frac{1}{3}$ per cent of voting shares and $66 \frac{2}{3}$ per cent of preferred shares) affiliated through ownership with conglomerate which filed for approval of a Multibank, would inherit the right to own up to 30 per cent of the voting stock of all the institutions incorporated into the new Multibank, including the commercial bank, to which foreign access has hitherto been severely restricted.

Further information on the Multibank concept and its implications will be provided after our analysis of the development of Brazil's financial institution structure up to the present time.

5.3   QUALITATIVE ANALYSIS OF THE DEVELOPMENT OF BRAZIL'S FINANCIAL SYSTEM STRUCTURE

An observer of Brazil's financial system three to four decades ago would hardly recognise it today. Then, the country's depositors had access to around 400 individual commercial banking units. Some of these had a few branches in their respective regions, but none was organised on a national scale, with the exception of Banco do Brasil. Smaller, remote communities were likely not to have any of their own banking services. The atomised structure of commercial banks prevailing at that time was about the only option available to people in need of banking services. Very few other types of financial institutions existed. The incentive to create new banks lay to a large extent in high rates of inflation (though not as high in nominal terms as in the 1980s) and negative real interest rates. These phenomena made it attractive for many entrepreneurs to create new banks, locate them on appreciating property, and mobilise sight deposits for lending. Investments in banking overhead were tiny in comparison with today's requirements. Operations and processing functions were performed largely by hand, and the small daily volume of transactions was commensurate with banks' processing capabilities.

During the succeeding two decades, several factors contributed to the evolution of this regionalised and largely antiquated financial structure into one which at present consists of a large array of theoretically specialised institutions and, in the banking area, is dominated by a relatively few conglomerates which are national in scope and modern by international standards. The impetus for structural change has arisen primarily from the following factors:

1. The enactment of a banking reform law (Law 4.595) and the capital markets law (Law 4.728) in the mid-1960s. These laws helped to set in motion the processes of bank concentration and diversification of institutional categories and products.
2. The growing importance, primarily in the 1970s, of foreign capital and export surpluses in Brazil's economic and financial development. Small banks, acting alone, would not be able, from a credit-worthiness viewpoint, to tap the growing supply of foreign funding available to finance investments, working capital and foreign trade.
3. Inflation ebbed during the latter part of the 1960s and the early 1970s, thus reducing the incentive to establish new banks for

marshalling sight deposits. Declining inflation also contributed to development of the capital markets.

4. The monetary authorities, following on the establishment of the Central Bank of Brazil in 1965, strongly encouraged bank ownership concentration in the private sector, resulting in the decline of private commercial banks from 328 in 1964 to 76 in mid-1987.

5. Brazil's rapid economic growth and investment boom during the 1970s encouraged modernisation of the financial system, requiring financial institutions to invest heavily in data-processing equipment in order to handle the rapidly increasing volume of transactions.

6. The economic development process became a nation-wide phenomenon, and the financial industry was obliged to follow. Branch network expansion proved to be more economical from both social and private viewpoints than the opening of new banks, and the consolidated institutional basis for supporting such expansion was rapidly being formed. Thus once largely regional banks became national banks, with large branch networks throughout the country.

7. Competition intensified between the declining number of separately owned banks, making it difficult for smaller banks to survive in a nation-wide banking context. Competition arising from the growing number of non-bank financial institutions contributed as well to the diminishing number of banks.

8. The breadth of financial products increasingly being demanded expanded to such an extent that small banks were not in a position to invest in the expertise, system and administrative structure needed to deliver them.

9. Brazil's Companies Law, enacted in 1976, promoted the consolidation of banking conglomerates through formalising the 'group' concept. By facilitating the transfer of assets and liabilities between companies related by ownership under a legally constituted holding company umbrella, the 'group' notion of organisation resulted in the development of today's typical banking conglomerate structure. Under this structure, a commercial bank, for example, can act as the holding company for a series of other financial institutions, such as an investment bank, 'distribuidora', brokerage firm, insurance company, savings and loan company, trading company, leasing company, consumer finance company, and so forth. In many financial groups, tiered holding company structures are also utilised.

5.3.1 Brazil's financial institution structure in the 1980s

Figure 5.1 presents the financial institution structure that has evolved over the past three decades. The complex web of institutions which exists today stands in sharp contrast to the relatively simple structure of commercial banks, consumer finance companies and savings banks which prevailed prior to the 1960s.[1] The number of separate institutions and branch offices in each category is shown in Table 5.1.

Figure 5.2 shows the structure of a typical financial conglomerate as exists at the present time. A conglomerate, also referred to as a 'financial group' or 'financial supermarket', consists both of institutions which will be included in the Multibank form of organisation and of those which will remain outside it. As Figure 5.2 reveals, the business/product-oriented structure prevailing in the private financial sector crosses the theoretical regulatory boundaries shown in Figure 5.1. The combined regulatory and market events which produced this phenomenon serve as the basis for the Multibank form which is coming into effect.

According to present regulatory practice, the Central Bank, under the direction of the National Monetary Council (which is the supreme regulatory body), supervises the entire system, while the Securities Commission (CVM) and the insurance regulators (principally SUSEP, Private Insurance Superintendency) exercise supervisory responsibility for their respective areas of competence. Over the years, the specific functions of each organ have been reasonably well defined in order to minimise overlapping and to promote co-operate efforts.

It is important to note the close interrelationship between investment banks, 'distribuidoras' and brokerage firms. In a large conglomerate, they may actually have separate roles to play with varying degrees of operational integration. However, many of their principal products are more similar to each other than to those of other institutions in a conglomerate. Because of this, and since investment banks can engage at the same time in most of the same types of business as commercial banks, different variants of conglomerate organisation have evolved in response to market circumstances. In Figure 5.3 we show the structure of a conglomerate headed by an investment bank without commercial bank affiliation.

There is yet another form of organisation, whereby a small commercial bank exists in the same group as the structure shown in

Figure 5.1 Structure of Brazil's financial system

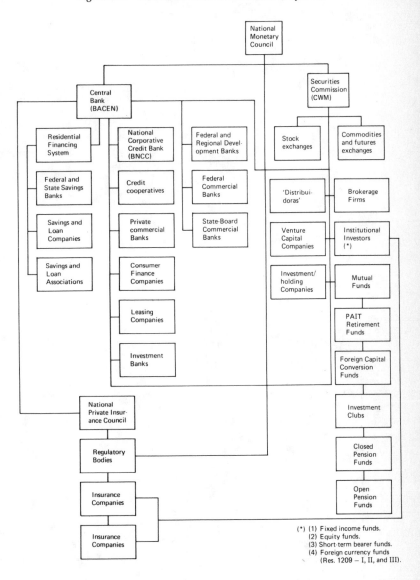

Source: Coopers & Lybrand financial consulting department, São Paulo, Brazil.

Table 5.1   Statistical overview of the financial system, 30 June 1987

Type of institution	Number of charters or licenses	Number of operating entities	Number of branch or other offices
Commercial banks	105	102	21 050
Federal (a)	5	5	4365
State	24	24	4577
Private, national	57	55	12 037
Private, foreign	19	18	71
Savings banks (state and federal)	5	5	3084
Investment banks	41	39	142
Consumer finance companies	112	111	488
Federal development banks (b)	2	2	41
Regional development banks	13	13	17
Saving and loan companies	79	74	606
Savings and loan associations	2	2	2
'Distribuidoras'	417	403	927
Brokerage firms	274	266	160
Stock exchanges	9	9	—
Futures and commodities exchanges	3	3	—
Credit co-operatives	579	579	—
Mutual funds (c)	328	328	—
Open pension funds	116	113	—
Closed pension funds	281	164	—

'Capitalisation' companies	18	6	—
Leasing companies	56	56	125
Insurance companies	97	96	1857

(a) Banco do Nordeste do Brasil, Banco do Brasil S.A., Banco da Amazônia S.A., Banco de Roraima S.A. and Banco Meridional S.A. Although the federal government also owns a controlling interest in Banco de Brasília S.A., this bank is operationally considered as a state bank.

(b) Banco Nacional de Crédito Cooperativo (BNCC) and Banco Nacional de Desenvolvimento Econômico e Social (BNDES).

(c) Includes fixed-income funds, equity funds, short-term bearer funds, PAIT retirement funds, and foreign currency-funded portfolios under DL 1.401. Other foreign currency-sourced mutual funds and investment portfolios are not included herein, owing to their having been established in late 1987 or in 1988.

Most of the data above have been supplied by the Central Bank of Brazil, supplemented by that of professional associations. The figures are valid as of 30 June 1987, excepting commercial banks and savings and loan associations 31 December 1986 data) as well as open pension funds, for which only 1985 figures are available.

Table compiled by Américo Czengeri Netto.

Figure 5.2   Structure of typical Brazilian financial conglomerate

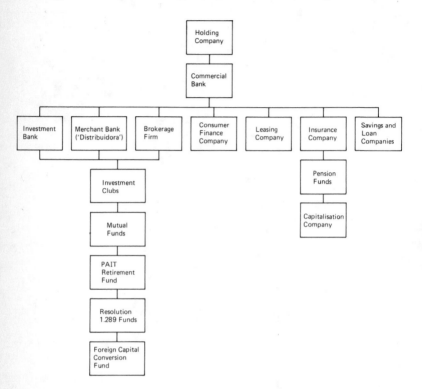

Source: Coopers & Lybrand financial consulting department, São Paulo, Brazil.

Figure 5.3. In some cases, this arrangement results from a foreign investment in a non-commercial banking institution in the group. Since until the present time new foreign investment in Brazilian commercial banks has not been permitted (except in the case of special reciprocity arrangements with certain countries), some groups have elected to concentrate business development in their investment banks or other institutions with foreign participation and operate their commercial banks under a separate shareholding structure, normally with a relatively small asset base.

Still other smaller conglomerate forms exist, headed by a consumer finance company or other type of institution. Some of these smaller groups exercise influence in the market out of proportion to their financial statement figures. This observation is particularly applicable

Figure 5.3 Structure of financial conglomerate without a commercial bank affiliation

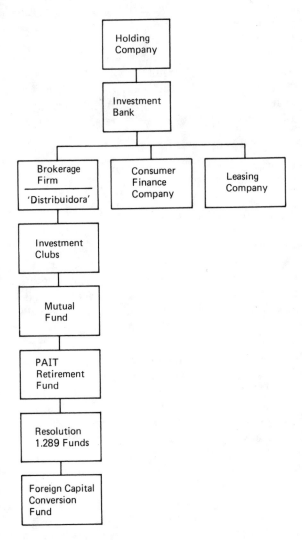

Source: Coopers & Lybrand financial consulting department, São Paulo, Brazil.

to securities trading and underwriting and trading on Brazil's rapidly growing commodities and futures exchanges.

To summarise, as a result of structural developments and the erosion of functional/product barriers, competition between financial institutions has actually been enhanced, despite the concentration of commercial bank ownership. At the same time, the overall structure has become too unwieldy, with too great a multiplicity of institutional categories, with entry into certain fields of financial activity too severely limited by laws and regulations.

This is, in essence, the background for understanding the new Multibank structure in the process of being implemented, as well as its advantages from many viewpoints and its likely future evolution.

5.4 EVOLVING STRUCTURAL CHANGES IN THE BRAZILIAN FINANCIAL SYSTEM

5.4.1 Financial institution charters

A charter to own and operate a financial institution is simply a letter from the Central Bank of Brazil to the petitioning party authorising it to conduct business as a particular type of financial institution subject to stipulated conditions and valid for an undetermined period of time. The charter in and of itself has no intrinsic value, and in accordance with Chapter IV of the new constitution is no longer negotiable in the market-place.

What gave rise to previous negotiability was the creation of scarcity of new institutions by the Central Bank, which first promoted the reduction of the number of financial organisations, particularly in the areas of banking, leasing and insurance, and then reinforced this step with the point system promulgated by Resolution 1.060. This system assigned a certain number of points to each category of financial institution but limited the total number of points available to a specifically stipulated amount. Within this global limit there could of course be manoeuvring, whereby, for example, the points resulting from ownership (through point acquisition in the market or otherwise) of three consumer finance company licences could be converted into ownership of an investment bank, or, theoretically, a commercial bank licence. However the aggregate number of points could not be increased. Moreover specific limits were set on certain types of financial institutions, whether by fiat or by Central Bank discretion, thus making conversion into those types impossible, regardless of the point count involved.

The point system has effectively been eliminated in favour of a free entry concept stipulated in the constitution. Under this concept, approval to operate a financial institution can be based only on capitalisation, experience of ownership and management, and their general reputation in the market.[2] The Multibank system introduced by the Central Bank reinforces the free entry concept. Excepted from the general elimination is a reported total of about 900 points, mostly related to commercial bank branches (which were also included in the point system) which were not yet being utilised in October 1988, when the constitution came into effect. The parties which possess these points have until April of 1989 to submit petitions to the Central Bank for institutional or branch approvals. The points in any event cannot legally be negotiated or transferred to another party.

As an addendum to the foregoing material, it must be pointed out that insurance company charters have traditionally been subject to a separate processing system and thus were outside the purview of the pointing mechanism. The same is true of brokerage firms, which are acquired through the purchase of a seat on the stock exchange in the city where the firm is to be located. Although Central Bank approval is required, brokerage firms were not assigned points. This process for acquiring a brokerage firm, which also requires approval by the Securities Commission (CVM), is not likely to be altered.

Finally, the question of converting credit co-operatives into commercial or mutiple banks will remain an open issue until the complementary legislation required by the constitution is enacted by the Brazilian Senate. It seems fairly clear, however, that the constitutionally-ordained criteria regarding capitalisation and ownership qualifications will take precedence in Central Bank processing of petitions to own and operate such institutions. As of this date, some 100 co-operatives have at least indicated interest in converting into banks. However no action has been taken by the Central Bank, and there are signs that many such co-operatives would not be able to meet minimum capital or net worth requirements. Chapter 5 provides a description of credit co-operatives and their functions.

5.4.2 Multiple banks

We have summarised some of the most important principles related to Multiple Bank organisation earlier in this chapter. We will now proceed to supply further information relative thereto.

Under Resolution 1.524, four categories of financial institutions at present affiliated within a conglomerate structure can be converted into 'carteiras' (departments) of a single Multibank organisation. This conversion is entirely optional, but it is understood that at least two departments must be formed in order for an institution to be considered a Multibank. The four categories, as stated earlier, are: commercial bank, investment bank, savings and loan company, and consumer credit company. The conversion of these institutions into departments of a single organisation may be accomplished by merger, incorporation, spin-off or other legal processes in accordance with the criterion of suitability for the conglomerate from the viewpoint of its shareholding structure. The conversion process results in the issue by the Central Bank of a Multibank charter and the cancellation of charters previously granted relative to the institutions which become departments of the Multibank.

A fifth category of 'carteira' concerns development banking. However a development banking department cannot coexist in the same Multibank structure as an investment bank, and in any event the formation of Multibanks embracing development banking activities is reserved to the public sector. In this respect, Resolution 1.524 does not alter the present situation but simply permits state and regional development banks to convert into Multibanks, either directly or in the case of states, through the state-owned commercial bank.

Perhaps the most significant aspect of Resolution 1.524 is its opening access to Multibank ownership by independent financial institutions, brokerage firms, 'distribuidoras', and financial institutions 'not subject to ownership by the same group of shareholders'. Such organisations may petition the Central Bank for approval of a Multibank licence, subject to their agreement to establish one separate financial institution, such as a commercial bank, which would embrace the other 'carteiras' (minimum of two) within the Multibank structure. The petitioner must also agree to meet the minimum capital requirements as set forth in Resolution 1.524.

Institutions which are being organised as Multibanks must meet two further requirements. First of all, they must promise to participate in the deposit insurance system, when it becomes effective (at present there is no mechanism for establishing or regulating deposit insurance). Secondly, each 'carteira' must adhere to the regulations in force for the institutional category to which it would pertain if it were operating as a separate legal entity. Thus an investment banking department of a Multibank must abide by the regulations relative to investment banks as separate institutions. Excepted from this general requirement are minimum net worth levels and operating limits, which are subject to separate treatment (see below).

As of 7 December 1988, about 200 petitions have reportedly been filed with the Central Bank, requesting permission to organise Multibanks. According to reports published by the Central Bank, 69 such petitions have been approved. The authorised petitions were submitted by commercial and investment banks, 'distribuidoras', brokerage firms and consumer finance companies. About half of the approved petitions had been filed by the latter three types of institutions.

5.4.3 Principal operating limits of multibanks

Aggregate deposit and foreign currency borrowing liabilities of Multibanks may not exceed 15 times net worth. Excluded from this leverage limitation are commitments to repurchase government securities, borrowings contracted for on-lending purposes, and interbank deposits, all of which are subject to specific leverage controls. In addition, foreign exchange transactions, repurchase commitments, and interbank borrowings remain subject in all aspects to specific regulations governing these types of business.

The Multibank's total 'permanent' investment portfolio plus holdings of fixed assets (that is, bank premises, furniture, fixtures and equipment) cannot exceed 90 per cent of net worth.

5.4.4 Minimum net worth/capital requirements

A Multibank must have a minimum net worth of specific amounts based on the types of 'carteiras' which it elects to incorporate into its structure. These amounts are stipulated in OTN (National Treasury Obligation) values and are shown below in their approximate US dollar equivalents:

1. Commercial banking department   US$9 600 000
2. Investment banking department   US$9 600 000
3. Savings and loan department   US$4 800 000
4. Consumer finance department   US$2 800 000
5. Commercial banking department arising from a
   commercial bank under foreign majority
   ownership   US$19 200 000

The minimum capital requirement for a savings and loan department has been established on a regional basis (see Chapter 6 for a description of the regional organisation of Brazil's savings and loan companies). Thus, a Multibank incorporating, for example, savings and loan companies established in three regions would be required to maintain a minimum net worth of $14 000 000 in order to operate a savings and loan department. There are additional capital requirements for establishing branches as well as for conducting foreign exchange business. A forex licence to operate in one office carries a minimum capital requirement of US$3.6 million plus US$1.2 million for each additional foreign exchange branch.

In the case of existing financial conglomerates which elect to adopt the Multibank structure, 50 per cent of the minimum net worth requirements must be fulfilled by the date on which Central Bank authorisation is obtained. The remainder of the requirement can be complied with over a period of up to five years, at the discretion of the Central Bank. However, in the case of Multibanks being formed by the creation of new institutions (as opposed to the conversion of existing institutions into departments), the minimum capital requirement must be met in its entirety by the date on which the Central Bank issues its charter.

More liberal capitalisation provisions are allowed in the case of Multibanks established in relatively underdeveloped regions, such as the north-east.

5.4.5 Foreign participation in the multibank system

Apart from the special minimum capital requirement related to foreign-owned commercial banks as discussed above, Resolution 1.524 (Chapter II, paragraphs 1 and 2) stipulates that:

1. Except in cases of overriding national interest and special reciprocity agreements, foreign participation in financial institutions must comply with Articles 50 and 51 of Law 4.131/62 [the contents of which were described earlier in this chapter].
2. Existing foreign participations are frozen at their present levels.

With respect to the second provision, it is understood that the Central Bank is following a policy of freezing the aggregate foreign participation in financial institutions as a whole but may permit shifting of positions to take place within this limit. Parties interested in exploring this matter further should be aware of three important aspects: (1) Central Bank policy is subject to change at any time; (2) in any event, each foreign shareholding petition is considered on a case-by-case basis; and (3) foreign participation in the Brazilian financial system is an issue which must be addressed by the Senate in its deliberation on the complementary banking law, which would replace existing ordinary law governing foreign shareholdings.

Until this law is passed, the Central Bank apparently exercises a certain amount of leeway in its treatment of petitions involving foreign participation in the financial system. On the other hand, the nationalist political leanings which the Brazilian legislative organs have generally demonstrated so far suggest that it would be imprudent at this time to expect that the issue of foreign participation will be treated with increased liberalism in the foreseeable future.

5.4.6 Structural evolution of Brazil's financial system

The Multibank structure is a significant step forward in tidying up the legal relationship between financial products and institutional categories. A further step would seem plausible with respect to the categories not embraced by the Multibank concept. In an earlier proposal circulated by the Central Bank such a step was clearly foreseen. This proposal envisaged a financial system consisting of two major segments: (1) the banking system; and (2) the capital markets, insurance and leasing system. The structure which would result from adoption of this proposal is suggested in Figure 5.4. However the necessary legislation and regulations have not been enacted.

The structure set forth in Figure 5.4 could have important implications for foreign financial institutions interested in investing in Brazil. At the present time, a petition to the Central Bank by a foreign bank for a new participation in a financial institution within the second segment described above would probably not be approved, except in special circumstances. Let us suppose, however, that the complementary banking law concerns itself only with the first segment, that is, banking institutions. If this were to occur, the result might be to open up discretionary opportunities for investment in a second segment institution. It is of course impossible to predict the precise legal outcome of the constitution's guidelines. We only wish to suggest that interested potential investors should follow legislative and regulatory developments closely in order to identify specific opportunities which might develop.

Figure 5.4 Proposed structure of Brazil's financial system

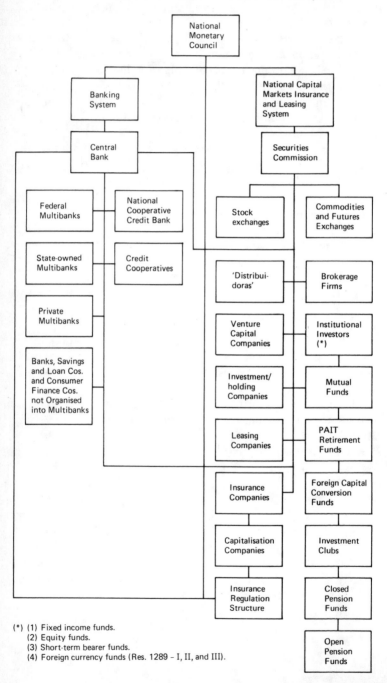

(*) (1) Fixed income funds.
 (2) Equity funds.
 (3) Short-term bearer funds.
 (4) Foreign currency funds (Res. 1289 – I, II, and III).

5.4.7 Concluding comment

As a result of the enhanced importance assumed by the legislative branch relative to the executive branch of government in the new constitution, it is likely that the formerly free rein accorded to the National Monetary Council, the Central Bank, and the CVM, essentially to enact banking laws as well as supervise their enforcement, will be circumscribed. The separation of authorities in practice is not yet clear. None the less the evolution of roles of the two branches as regards financial institution activities is a matter which requires close attention by the interested observer.

5.5 QUANTITATIVE ANALYSIS OF TRENDS IN THE BRAZILIAN FINANCIAL SECTOR

Finance is a big business in Brazil. Its bigness can be measured by the substantial share its revenues represent in total GDP – about 12 per cent in 1987 – the large number of different types of financial institutions conducting business, the number of financial institution branch and sales offices, employment in finance, and the breadth of financial products offered to the public. In this section, we will demonstrate statistically how important finance has become to Brazil over the years and what quantitative trends characterise its development at the present time.

5.5.1 Contribution of the financial sector to GDP

The financial sector contribution to GDP of 12 per cent in 1985 contrasts sharply with the 6 per cent share in 1970. In Table 5.2 we demonstrate how the financial industry has grown in comparison with the rest of the economy between 1970 and 1985. These figures, published by IBGE (Brazilian Statistics Institute), are reinforced by Central Bank figures comparing GDP and financial sector growth rates in the 1980s. Table 5.3.

5.5.2 Expansion of financial assets

Rapid growth of the financial sector has been accompanied by commensurate expansion of financial assets in the hands of the public. The ratio of average financial assets to GDP is shown in Table 5.4 for the period 1971 to 1987.

The size of the market for government securities funded by re-

Table 5.2   Sectoral Contributions to GDP, 1970–85

Sector	% Sectoral Share of GDP															
	1970	1971	1972	1973	1974	1975	1976	1977	1978	1979	1980	1981	1982	1983	1984	1985
SERVICES	52.5	52.1	51.7	50.7	50.4	51.3	51.0	50.6	52.5	52.3	51.8	54.4	56.0	56.9	55.4	55.8
Commercial	16.4	16.4	16.6	16.7	16.9	16.5	15.6	15.0	14.8	14.4	14.5	13.8	13.7	13.4	13.3	12.9
Transportation	3.7	3.6	3.5	3.3	3.5	3.4	3.7	3.6	3.8	3.9	3.6	3.8	4.2	3.8	3.8	3.7
Communications	0.6	0.6	0.7	0.8	0.7	0.8	0.7	0.9	0.9	0.9	0.8	0.9	1.0	1.0	0.9	0.9
FINANCIAL INSTITUTIONS	6.0	6.1	5.9	5.7	6.1	6.9	7.4	7.6	8.6	8.3	7.9	10.2	10.5	11.6	11.0	11.4
Public Sector	9.2	9.0	8.7	8.1	7.3	7.9	7.6	6.9	7.2	7.1	6.3	6.4	6.8	6.5	5.5	6.6
Rent	9.3	8.8	8.3	7.6	7.2	7.0	6.5	6.5	6.6	6.5	6.7	7.5	7.9	8.6	8.8	8.3
Other services	7.3	7.6	8.0	8.5	8.7	8.8	9.5	10.1	10.6	11.2	12.0	11.8	11.9	12.0	12.1	12.0
OTHER SECTORS	47.5	47.9	48.3	49.3	49.6	48.7	49.0	49.4	47.5	47.7	48.2	45.6	44.0	43.1	44.6	44.2
TOTAL	100.0	100.0	100.0	100.0	100.0	100.0	100.0	100.0	100.0	100.0	100.0	100.0	100.0	100.0	100.0	100.0

Source: IBGE, Central Bank of Brazil.
Table compiled by Américo Csengeri Netto.

Table 5.3   Real growth of financial sector vs GDP growth, 1981–7

Year	% growth GDP	% growth financial sector
1981	–3.4	6.6
1982	0.9	4.2
1983	–2.5	5.6
1984	5.7	7.7
1985	8.3	10.0
1986	8.2	7.2
1987	2.9	3.5

Source: IBGE, Central Bank of Brazil.
Table compiled by Américo Csengeri Netto.

Table 5.4   Financial assets compared with GDP, 1971–87 (millions US dollars)

Year	Average financial assets	GDP	Ratio of financial assets to GDP (%)
1971	14 632	48 975	29.9
1972	19 849	58 490	33.9
1973	29 537	79 504	37.2
1974	36 717	104 374	35.2
1975	44 109	121 818	36.2
1976	52 281	151 101	34.6
1977	58 126	173 250	33.6
1978	67 854	197 761	34.3
1979	75 328	220 902	34.1
1980	63 265	231 132	27.4
1981	73 257	261 214	28.0
1982	90 751	260 816	34.8
1983	74 312	204 284	36.4
1984	76 061	211 171	36.0
1985	76 696	225 974	33.9
1986	100 075	270 046	37.1
1987	94 311	307 076	30.7

Source: Central Bank of Brazil, *Conjuntura Econômica*.
Table compiled by Américo Csengeri Netto.

purchase commitments is estimated by market participants to be of the order of US$40 billion on a daily volume basis. The actual dimensions of this market are difficult to present on a historical basis, for strict, on-balance sheet disclosure requirements were not set

Table 5.5   Average daily 'open market' volume (billions of US dollars)

December 1986	19.9
January 1987	17.4
February	19.8
March	20.3
April	23.9
May	23.3
June	21.6
July	22.7
August	25.2
September	29.0
October	28.3
November	34.3
December	36.2

Table compiled by Américo Csengeri Netto.

down until 1986. ANDIMA (National Association of Open Market Dealers) figures for end-1986 and 1987 are shown in Table 5.5. Increasing volume throughout the year was due to increasing domestic indebtedness of the federal government, declining portfolio spreads urging more rapid turnover, more liberal leverage requirements, and the entry of new institutions into the market. The expansion of financial assets is a natural outgrowth of rapid economic development, high rates of savings and investment, and the creation of a structure of financial institutions and products capable of translating favorable economic phenomena into meaningful financial realities. The fact that Brazil's savings and investment rates in the 1980s have been about 20 per cent lower than those prevailing in the 1970s (investment has averaged 18 per cent of GDP in the 1980s, as compared with 21 per cent in the 1970s) suggests that even further efforts will be devoted to stimulating the interest of surplus funds sectors in investments in financial instruments.

5.5.3   Diversification of Brazil's institutional structure

The historical diversification of Brazil's institutional structure is demonstrated in Table 5.6, which traces the number of each category of financial institutions from 1970 to 1987. Of particular note is the proliferation of institutions engaged in capital market-related activities: investment banks, 'distribuidoras', mutual funds, and brokerage firms. This evolution is symptomatic of the erosion of functional

Table 5.6 Evolution of number of financial institutions by category

	1970	1971	1972	1973	1974	1975	1976	1977	1978	1979	1980	1981	1982	1983	1984	1985	1986	1987
Commercial banks	178	155	128	115	109	106	106	107	107	108	111	111	114	113	111	107	103	103
Federal	4	4	4	4	4	4	4	4	4	4	4	4	4	4	4	5	5	5
State	24	24	24	24	24	24	23	23	23	23	23	23	23	24	24	24	24	24
Private	142	119	92	79	72	69	69	70	68	68	67	67	69	66	64	60	57	56
Foreign	8	8	8	8	9	9	10	10	13	13	17	17	18	19	19	18	19	18
Federal and state savings banks	6	6	6	6	6	6	6	6	6	5	5	5	5	5	5	5	5	5
Investment banks	30	40	44	45	41	40	39	39	39	39	39	39	39	39	39	38	41	44
Consumer finance companies	214	170	157	152	150	142	135	126	119	118	115	115	115	114	112	113	112	112
Federal development banks	3	3	3	3	3	3	3	3	3	3	3	3	3	3	2	2	2	2
Regional development banks	10	10	10	10	11	12	12	13	13	13	13	13	13	13	13	13	13	13
Savings and loan associations	32	34	34	36	36	36	36	36	36	36	36	35	25	22	12	10	2	2
Saving and loan companies	44	45	46	44	46	42	40	40	40	45	53	56	64	76	74	75	79	70
'Distribuidoras'	573	572	568	569	567	552	527	509	477	468	461	440	434	426	411	408	412	434
Brokerage firms	404	421	417	414	396	380	362	327	290	265	271	262	255	259	266	273	275	477
Stock exchanges	16	16	16	16	17	16	15	15	12	10	9	9	9	9	9	9	9	9
Insurance companies	157	157	144	110	100	98	96	96	95	95	95	95	95	96	96	98	97	N/A
Credit co-operatives	N.A.	N.A.	N.A.	324	329	334	349	360	367	383	403	453	481	530	558	579	583	579
Leasing companies	—	—	—	—	4	51	55	56	57	57	57	56	56	56	56	56	56	56

Sources: Central Bank of Brazil, 'Brasil Financeira 73–74' (BANAS), *Gazeta Mercantil*.

barriers, comparative sectoral profit opportunities, and the interest of the authorities in promoting the development of longer-term sources of financing.

What this table does not show is the increasing sophistication on the part of many types of institutions, particularly commercial banks and capital markets institutions. Such sophistication becomes noticeable to the on-the-spot observer in terms of product breadth, product quality, personnel preparedness at certain levels, and the ever-increasing use of advanced data-processing techniques.

5.5.4 Expansion of deposits and loans

Additional financial industry growth indicators are shown in Table 5.7, relative to the expansion of total deposits of the banking system since 1983, and Table 5.8, which shows loan growth during the same period. These tables emphasise the difficulties in distinguishing clearly between banking and non-banking institutions under the present system. Private consumer finance and savings and loan companies, which in many countries might be treated outside the banking system, compete vigorously with private commercial and investment banks as well as government-owned financial institutions for deposit and lending business. The tables also reveal, perhaps more ominously, the increasing share of the market being taken by institutions owned by federal and state governments. The figures suggest the formation of a secular trend in favour of the public sector. However the retraction of private banks from lending in 1987 may make it premature to assess accurately the tendency of public vs. private sector competition in the years ahead.

5.5.5 Capitalisation of financial institutions

Capitalisation of most types of financial institutions has been commensurate with the growth of deposits and loans (see Table 5.9). The high degree of equity relative to deposit liabilities in most Brazilian financial institutions is due to both their profitability and the capital adequacy concerns manifested by the monetary authorities. However many commercial banks in both public and private sectors are thought to be under-capitalised in relation to fixed assets, and the authorities are attempting to apply an 80 per cent (ratio of fixed assets to net worth) yardstick. The accumulation of fixed assets in commercial banks has been due primarily to three factors: (1) expan-

Table 5.7 Evolution of banking system deposits[1], 1983–7 (millions of US dollars)

	1983 Amount	1983 % Market share	1984 Amount	1984 % Market share	1985 Amount	1985 % Market share	1986 Amount	1986 % Market share	1987 Amount	1987 % Market share	Average annual growth rate
PUBLIC SECTOR BANKS											
Banco do Brasil	1 637	4.2	1 632	3.9	2 594	5.7	6 386	8.6	5 885	11.0	37.7
Federal and state-owned commercial banks	2 626	6.7	2 797	6.6	4 231	9.3	8 332	11.2	3 254	6.1	5.5
Federal savings bank	7 295	18.5	7 990	18.9	6 772	14.9	10 175	13.7	11 212	21.0	11.3
State savings banks	2 787	7.1	2 739	6.4	2 941	6.5	3 654	4.9	3 791	7.2	8.0
BNCC	22	0.1	9	0.1	11	0.1	29	0.1	15	0.0	−9.1
Regional development banks	944	2.4	927	2.1	1 089	2.4	1 265	1.7	865	1.6	−2.2
SUB-TOTAL	15 311	39.0	16 094	38.0	17 638	38.9	29 841	40.2	25 022	46.9	13.1
PRIVATE INSTITUTIONS											
Commercial banks	7 768	19.7	9 354	22.0	11 078	24.4	27 191	36.6	11 468	21.5	10.2
Investment banks	4 280	10.8	4 535	10.7	3 799	8.4	4 363	5.9	3 423	6.4	5.4
Savings and loan companies and associations	8 788	22.3	9 318	22.0	9 673	21.3	9 724	13.1	12 184	22.8	8.5
Consumer finance companies	3 252	8.2	3 083	7.3	3 130	6.9	3 103	4.2	1 294	2.4	−20.6
SUB-TOTAL	24 088	61.0	26 290	62.0	27 680	61.1	44 381	59.8	28 369	53.1	4.2
GENERAL TOTAL	39 399	100.0	42 384	100.0	45 318	100.0	74 222	100.0	53 391	100.0	7.9

[1] Includes sight, time and savings deposits and bills exchange.
Source: Central Bank of Brazil.
Table compiled by Américo Csengeri Netto.

Table 5.8 Evolution of banking system loans to the private sector, 1983–7 (millions of US dollars)

	1983		1984		1985		1986		1987	
	Amount	% Market share	Amount	% Market share	Amount	% Market share	Amount	% Market share	Amount	% Market share
PUBLIC SECTOR BANKS										
Banco do Brasil	7 359	13.3	5 034	9.9	6 033	11.0	12 320	14.6	11 416	17.6
Federal and state-owned commercial banks	3 628	6.5	3 016	5.9	3 355	6.1	6 161	7.3	3 495	5.4
BNDES	1 288	2.3	1 312	2.6	1 279	2.3	1 603	1.9	2 454	3.8
Federal savings bank	9 436	17.1	8 022	15.7	10 086	18.4	14 986	17.8	12 774	19.6
State savings banks	2 758	5.0	2 450	4.8	2 354	4.5	2 999	3.6	2 804	4.3
Other institutions	2 802	5.1	2 989	5.9	3 777	6.9	4 839	5.7	3 852	5.9
SUB-TOTAL	27 271	49.3	22 823	44.8	26 884	49.0	42 908	50.9	36 795	56.6
PRIVATE INSTITUTIONS										
Commercial banks	9 141	16.5	10 570	20.7	11 523	21.1	22 960	27.2	15 326	23.5
Investment banks	4 735	8.6	5 144	10.1	4 677	8.6	7 293	8.7	4 567	7.0
Consumer finance companies	5 336	9.6	5 226	10.3	5 186	9.5	4 362	5.2	2 842	4.4
Savings and loan companies	8 858	16.0	7 179	14.1	6 478	11.8	6 765	8.0	5 511	8.5
SUB-TOTAL	28 070	50.7	28 119	55.2	27 864	51.0	41 380	49.1	28 246	43.4
GENERAL TOTAL	55 341	100.0	50 942	100.0	54 748	100.0	84 288	100.0	65 041	100.0

Source: Central Bank of Brazil.
Table compiled by Américo Csengeri Netto.

Table 5.9   Capitalisation of financial institutions, 1983–6 (millions of US dollars)

	1983	*1984*	*1985*	*1986*
Banco do Brasil	4 465	2 596	3 535	4 332
Commercial banks	4 063	4 397	4 962	6 780
Investment banks	1 125	1 261	1 345	1 720
Consumer finance companies	636	700	730	1 009
Federal savings bank	1 075	1 190	1 121	1 921
State savings banks	111	101	122	150
Savings and loan companies	718	735	713	830[1]
Regional development banks	380	299	380	501
BNCC	37	28	58	69
Leasing companies	218	289	278	380
Insurance companies	1 148	1 254	1 602	1 950[1]
TOTAL	13 976	12 850	14 846	19 642

[1] Estimate.
Source: Central Bank of Brazil.

sion of branch networks in the 1970s and early 1980s, (2) substantial investments in data processing systems and equipment, and (3) commercial banks developing a holding company role within their respective conglomerates, resulting in the acquisition of shares in subsidiary companies and financial institutions.

5.5.6 Profitability of financial institutions

The profitability of financial institutions is more difficult to measure reliably. Each conglomerate has its own policies relative to booking of income and costs in subsidiary institutions. Monetary restatement and equity method accounting make comparisons of financial institution profitability hazardous, as does the influence of fiscal consider-ations in judgements regarding statement presentation. Data services in both public and private sectors do not apply uniform criteria for calculating profitability and normally do not reveal clearly the meth-odologies employed. We have thus chosen to construct our own analysis (see Table 5.10) showing the rate of return on average equity for a sample of the largest financial institutions in each of five categories (private commercial banks, investment banks, consumer finance companies, brokerage firms, and 'distribuidoras'), size being measured by shareholders' equity. Other methodological factors are explained in footnotes to Table 5.10.

Table 5.10 Comparative profitability of selected types of financial institutions[1], return on average equity: 1983–7

	Private commercial banks[2] %	Private investment banks[3] %	Consumer finance companies[4] %	'Distribuidoras'[5] %	Brokerage firms[6] %
1983	30.4	28.2	17.0	55.6	47.2
1984	22.2	21.9	13.5	34.8	35.8
1985	29.4	24.1	16.6	27.2	41.6
1986	21.3	21.3	14.3	12.9	14.9
1987	22.0	15.1	6.8	14.5	24.1

[1] Net profits after tax and monetary restatement as a percentage of average equity (sum of year-end equity for current and previous years divided by 2). Weighted average exchange rate for each year was employed.
[2] Sample consisting of Bradesco, Itaú, Unibanco, Real, Nacional, Bamerindus, Safra, Francês e Brasileiro, Econômico and Mercantil de São Paulo.
[3] Sample consisting of Bradesco, Real, Unibanco, Itaú, Safra, Multiplic, Bozano Simonsen, BCN, Garantia and Credibanco.
[4] Sample: Bradesco, Itaú, Real, Finasa, Bamerindus, Sinal, Noroeste, HM, Mappin, Unibanco, General Motors, Pão de Açucar.
[5] Sample of 15 largest institutions in each category. Sample contains changes in names each year, due to volatility in rankings.
[6] Sample of 15 largest brokerage firms.
Sources: Central Bank of Brazil, *Exame*, *Balanço Financeiro*, *Revista Bancária Brasileira*.

One should beware of concluding from the statistics presented that 'distribuidoras' and brokerage firms are subject to secularly declining profitability. Both kinds of companies were deleteriously affected by the sharp fall-off in stock market activities from mid-1986 to the end of 1987, as well as by steadily declining spreads on government securities portfolios funded in the 'open market'. As a general rule, such types of institutions are more profitable than others, owing to their relatively small staff requirements and their ability to shift product emphasis rapidly.

5.5.7 Foreign ownership of financial institutions

As shown in Table 5.11 below, foreign shareholdings in Brazil's financial institutions are modest when considered as a percentage of total financial institution capitalization. Foreign controlled commercial banks tend to occupy relatively small market shares in traditional product areas. Their combined share of sight deposits, for example, is tiny, owing primarily to branching restrictions, and they must rely largely on purchased funds and foreign currency borrowings to fund their traditional lending activities. Table 5.12 below illustrates the minor market share corresponding to Brazil's foreign-owned commercial banks.

5.5.8 Comment on institutional size vs. profitability in a competitive environment

There is no firm yardstick to suggest that the largest Brazilian banking institutions are also the most profitable ones. In fact, smaller institutions with relatively small branch networks have often proved to be more profitable in terms of rate of return on shareholders equity than the larger banks. Figures published by *Gazeta Mercantil* on 9 April 1988, show that 15 mostly small banks were Brazil's most profitable in 1987. These banks were Banco da Amazônia, Deutsche Bank, Induscred, Sumitomo, Hispano Americano, Bank of Boston, BBI, Banfort, Banco de la Provincia de Buenos Aires, Banco Financial Português, LIBUR, Banco do Nordeste do Brasil, Banco Industrial e Comercial, Lloyds Bank, and Banco Mercantil de Crédito. The explanation for the high rate of profitability of many of Brazil's smallest banks may lie in product specialisation, low automated systems requirements, and a high ratio of deposits per branch with low personnel/deposit implications.

Table 5.11   Foreign investment in Brazil's financial system, 31 December 1986 (millions of US dollars)

	A *Foreign capital*	B *Total capital*	*A:B*
Commercial banks	772.4	11 112.0	7.0%
Investment banks	257.7	1 720.0	15.0%
Other institutions	98.6	4 868.0	2.0%
TOTAL	1 128.7	17 700.0	6.4%

Source: Central Bank of Brazil.

Table 5.12   Market share of foreign commercial banks, 31 December 1987

	Public sector banks %	*Private Brazilian banks* %	*Foreign banks*[1] %	*Total*
Credit transactions	44.4%	45.5%	10.1%	100
Fixed interest securities	8.4%	84.2%	7.4%	100
Sight deposits	39.6%	59.5%	0.9%	100
Time deposits	14.7%	71.4%	13.9%	100

[1] Subsidiaries and branches.
Source: Central Bank of Brazil.

There has been concern among observers during the past two decades about the future feasibility of medium-sized banks, which have faced, and continue to face, the spectre of substantial investments if they wish to become larger or gradual reversion to smaller bank status. Even worse, they could face extinction, as was the fate of Auxiliar and Comind, which are highly illustrative examples of financial conglomerates that unsuccessfuly chose the first route. From the viewpoints of profitability, security and survival, many bankers believe that it is preferable to retain existing market shares and search for special market niches involving a selected list of clients which will, it is hoped, expand their banking needs and at the same time remain loyal. Still others believe that the development of new products and/or the introduction of improvements in existing ones will compensate for perceived competitive inadequacies.

The adoption of appropriate banking strategies will become increasingly urgent if existing institutions are to be sufficiently strong to face substantially increased competition resulting from the large number of multiple banks being formed through the creation of new institutions, the possible strengthening of credit co-operatives, and the outcome of the current process of strengthening state-owned banks.

5.6 DISTINCTIVE FEATURES OF THE BRAZILIAN FINANCIAL SYSTEM

It would seem fitting as a conclusion to this chapter to devote some time to enumerating a few of the principal factors which are peculiar to the Brazilian financial system and which set it apart from systems existing in many other Latin American countries and in other parts of the world. Since the banking reform process is still ongoing and will soon involve changes which can not presently be accurately predicted, the material in this conclusion will be based on the present structure of the Brazilian financial system (i.e., as summarized in Figure 1).

5.6.1 The influence of the regulatory authorities

The National Monetary Council and its implementing agency, the Central Bank of Brazil, exert far-reaching power over both the shaping of the financial system and its day-to-day activities. Since 1965, the Central Bank has published over 5000 resolutions, circulars and circular letters, not to mention both public and internal instructions and other documents concerning the most minute aspects of financial institution administration. Much of this material is centralised in the MNI (Manual of Rules and Instructions) and the standardised charts of accounts and accounting rules and procedures issued for each type of financial institution. Efforts are under way by the Central Bank, acting in co-operation with Ibracon (Brazilian Institute of Accountancy), to streamline the regulatory system and both simplify and consolidate accounting rules. The result of these efforts is a new consolidated chart of accounts (COSIF), which is applicable to the four types of institutions which would compose the new multibank structure.

Much of the Central Bank's power in financial matters rests on its dominant position in the financial markets (securities trading, foreign exchange) as well as its ability to grant and retract charters for ownership of financial institutions. The charter to own and operate a financial institution has normally been the result of a lengthy bureaucratic process, involving not only the institution itself but also specific segments of the business it intends to conduct, for which specific approvals are required. Charter cancellation has generally been accompanied by Central Bank intervention and extrajudicial liquidation of the institution involved. In such situations, the statutorily elected 'directors' of the intervened institution are personally responsible with their own assets for payment of obligations to creditors, and the assets are freed up only after such obligations have been satisfactorily retired. The personal responsibility of directors is objective and thus independent of the subjective question of their guilt or innocence in any civil wrongdoings.

5.6.2   The influence of inflation

The impact of inflation on financial institution development has been substantial and pervasive. A few examples may help to illustrate some of its most important ramifications:

1. Long-term funding sources are practically non-existent (see below). Most funding has carried a term of a maximum 180 days, and at the present time terms does not normally exceed 60 days.
2. Commercial bank profits are at present being derived disproportionately from float, sight deposits and, increasingly, services.
3. Huge numbers of small cheques burden the clearing system, as depositors avoid holding large amounts of cash. It is estimated that Brazil clears 7 billion cheques a year, 95 per cent of which are cleared in 24 hours. By comparison, American Express processes on a worldwide basis 28 million items a month, about the same number of cheques cleared in a single day in Brazil.

- Inflation obfuscates the real profitability which extensive branch networks would have in the event of monetary stability.
- Central Bank attempts to use monetary policies and controls to restrain inflation introduce elements of extreme complexity into the system and result in very frequent changes in the 'rules of the game'. This is particularly true with respect to such important parameters as indexing of monetary instruments, reserve requirements, and portfolio composition requirements.
- Monetary policy, in turn, is made more difficult by the high level of

domestic federal government indebtedness. Attempts to push interest rates upwards and soak up excess liquidity also increase debt servicing requirements, thus worsening the government's deficit. While this phenomenon also exists in such countries as the United States, it becomes much more difficult to control in a hyper-inflationary environment.

• Inflation also contributes to foreign exchange market/domestic market distortions which give rise to artificially profitable products (oftentimes referred to as 'financial engineering' products) that are readily offered by many types of financial institutions to their clients. Since market conditions which favor such products are not normally of an enduring nature, the real profitability of financial institutions normally can not be assessed over a long period of time due to the distortions occasioned by opportunism. It is believed that in 1988 the foreign exchange departments of commercial and investment banks were obtaining a large share of their profits from charging commissions on the repayment of Resolution 63 loans in cruzados ('informal conversions') rather than continuing foreign exchange and trade financing transactions.

• Inflation has contributed to making the Brazilian financial market a noticeably dynamic one, in which short-term profits take precedence over longer-term vision in the tailoring of financial institutions and the formulation of business plans.

5.6.3 Near absence of long-term financing sources

Since inflation implies a transfer of real resources from the private sector to the government, it is not surprising that a large share of scarce long-term funding has been provided by the public sector, acting principally through the National Bank for Economic and Social Development (BNDES), Banco do Brasil, and other institutions owned by the state and federal governments. The role of BNDES in industrial finance is discussed in Chapter 11.

Another important source of long-term finance over the years has been foreign currency denominated, involving either direct loans from overseas lenders to Brazilian borrowers (Law 4.131) or on-lending by local banks using funds they borrowed from abroad (Resolution 63). Other sources of long-term funding have been:

• Issues of corporate debentures and shares on the Brazilian stock exchanges. Securities underwriting exceeded US$1 billion in 1986 and amounted to about $500 million in 1987. This is discussed in detail in Chapter 9.

- Issues of mortgage and real estate notes by savings and loan entities. These instruments fell out of use during the 1970s but are being developed again at the present time.

- Loans for the construction and sale of residential housing units made under the Residential Financing System (SFH), funded primarily by savings accounts held by private depositors with federal, state and private savings institutions. Such accounts are not in themselves considered as long-term, but continued expansion of the aggregate stock of savings suggests that they are suitable for funding long-term lending activities (the present stock of savings accounts is about $24 billion).

- Lease and lease-back transactions, the funding for much of which is provided from foreign currency borrowings contracted by leasing companies.

- 'Capitalisation' securities issued by 'capitalisation' companies. Such securities generally have terms of from five to ten years and attract depositors because of their ability to earn cash prizes equal to several times the amount of their deposits in twice weekly lottery-type drawings. 'Capitalisation' securities have been successfully employed for several decades by the Silvio Santos Group and are now being offered by Nacional, Bamerindus and Bradesco. The funds derived from the issue of such securities have typically been used for real estate-related projects as well as for the general pool of funds of the conglomerate which controls the issuing company.

5.6.4 Institutional specialisation vs. functional homogenisation

By law, the nearly thirty different types of financial institutions and institutional investors in Brazil are intended to be specialised, and to a certain extent they still are. However, as discussed in section 2, a variety of forces, laws and regulations has made fiction of the degree of specialisation originally intended by the banking reform and capital markets legislation of the 1960s. From the foreign investor's viewpoint, the most important factor in making investment decisions regarding Brazil is to identify the products it wishes to develop and then select the institutional structure which is most convenient for delivering them. The often-heard maxim that a 'distribuidora' can do just about everything that an investment bank can, albeit more inexpensively, and that an investment bank is tantamount to a commercial bank, is not at all far from the truth.

The complex structure to which institutional/product homogenisation has given rise is being streamlined by the banking reform process, particularly with respect to the formation of multiple banks. For the time being, however, structural complexity continues to prevail in Brazil, posing intricate decision-making issues for foreign investors.

It is useful to illustrate the similarity of commercial bank and investment bank business activities (later on, the activities of 'distribuidoras', investment banks, and brokerage firms will be compared). It will be recalled that, under the multiple bank structure, the two types of banks can optionally become departments of a single banking institution.

	Commercial banks	*Investment banks*
Checking accounts	Permitted	Not permitted
Access to clearing system	Permitted	Not permitted
Other current accounts	Permitted	Permitted
Forex services	Permitted	Permitted
Rural credit	Permitted	Permitted, not required
Personal loans	Permitted	Not permitted
Corporate lending	Permitted	Permitted
On-lending of foreign funds	Permitted	Permitted
On-lending of government funds	Permitted	Permitted
Securities custody	Permitted	Permitted
Trading in government securities	Permitted	Permitted
Corporate securities underwriting	Not permitted	Permitted
Administration of mutual funds	Not permitted	Permitted
Guarantees of foreign currency obligations	Restricted	Permitted
Trading in gold	Permitted	Permitted

5.7 CONCLUDING COMMENT

We have reviewed to the extent permitted by the purview of this book the structural development of Brazil's financial system, the special structural changes expected to be achieved through different banking reform measures, the quantitative development of Brazil's financial system, and offered a description of some its principal peculiarities. We have also attempted to establish certain bases for assessing likely future structural trends and to provide information of special interest to potential foreign investors.

In the following two chapters we will provide a description of the banking system and non-banking institutions, respectively, as they exist and conduct business at the present time.

NOTES

1. The Financial Consultancy Department of Coopers & Lybrand, São Paulo, Brazil.
2. 'Multiple Banks and the National Financial Restructuring,' article published in 'Gazeta Mercantil' on November 18, 1988, by Walter Douglas Stuber, a partner in the Mattos Filho e Suchodolski law firm in São Paulo. Much of the material contained in this part of the chapter is derived at least partially from the succinct but comprehensive presentation made by Dr. Stuber.

6 Banking Institutions

6.1 INTRODUCTION

The objective of this chapter is to introduce the reader to Brazil's banking institutions by means of a description of the different categories presently recognised by the authorities as being banks or conducting business which is essentially that of a bank. It is important to keep in mind the material contained in Chapter 5 with respect to Multibanks, as many of the institutional types described herein can optionally become converted into departments of a single banking institution.

6.2 DEFINITION OF BANKING INSTITUTIONS

Banks are defined for purposes of this chapter to include all types of financial institutions the principal activity of which is to attract funds from the general or restricted public for the primary purpose of lending them to qualified borrowers. Under this definition, consumer finance and savings and loan companies are considered as banks even though their official nomenclature does not specifically mention the word 'bank'. Brazilian financial practice also appears to be tending towards the treatment of credit co-operatives as banks, because they obtain funds from the public, albeit restricted to co-operative members, for the purpose of making largely agri-business-related loans to these members.

The definition of banking institutions also embraces development banks because of the importance of their lending activities, even though these institutions do not specifically attract public funds. Moreover state and regional development banks (that is, owned by individual state governments or the combined governments of states located in a geographical region) are entitled under Resolution 1.524 to convert into Multibanks, composed of commercial banking, consumer finance and savings and loan departments, but excluding investment banking.

Brazil's banking authorities utilise different systems for categorising banks, for example, by size, by number and location of branches, and by ownership. The most useful classification for our purposes at

139

this time concerns ownership, whereby banks are divided into four groups:

1. Public sector banks (or 'official banks'), including state and federal government ownership.
2. Banks owned by private Brazilian residents (individuals or companies).
3. Banks controlled by private Brazilian residents but with significant foreign minority participation.
4. Banks under the majority control of foreigners.

This classification method may be subject to alterations as experience is gained with the new Multibank system of organisation.

6.3   DESCRIPTION OF BRAZIL'S BANKING INSTITUTIONS

6.3.1   The business and products of commercial banks

It was originally intended that commercial banks would engage in business activities normally ascribed to this type of institution: that is, the attraction of sight and time deposits for purposes of short-term lending. However, owing to broadened public demand for increasingly sophisticated products and the need to maximise institutional capabilities for supplying them, commercial banks have greatly expanded their role within the financial system. This process has been abetted by the development of the nation-wide banking conglomerate structure and the resulting economic power which has accrued to the principal banking organisations. At the same time, the product capabilities of investment banks have also expanded dramatically and, except for the prohibition on sight deposits and participation in the clearing system, there is little of importance that an investment bank cannot do in comparison with a commercial bank.

  In the case of commercial banks, it is probably more instructive to enumerate the activities they are constrained from conducting:[1]

- underwriting of securities;
- administration of mutual funds;
- guarantee foreign loans under Law 4.131 (except with approval of the Federal Senate);
- direct participation on the stock and futures exchanges;
- direct trading in commodities, except for physical gold;

- creation of acceptances, except as related to foreign trade;
- acceptance of savings accounts;
- insurance activities, except for the performance of collection services.

It is worthwhile noting that, since most commercial banks lie at the apex of large conglomerates embracing institutions which can in fact perform the functions outlined above, their original restrictive intent is not at present very meaningful.

6.3.2 Commercial banks owned by the federal government[2]

Six Brazilian commercial banks are majority owned by the federal government, together accounting for over 40 per cent of total commercial bank deposits at December 31, 1987. These banks are: Banco do Brasil (BB), Banco da Amazônia (BASA), Banco de Roraima, Banco de Brasília, Banco Meridional, and Banco do Nordeste do Brasil (BNB).

Banco do Brasil (BB)

Banco do Brasil is by far the largest and most important commercial bank controlled by the federal government. With nearly 2500 branches throughout Brazil and 46 banking offices overseas, BB conducts a complete commercial banking business (including some of the restricted areas listed above, such as foreign loan guarantees) and at the same time performs policy execution functions in critical areas, such as rural credit. The latter type of activity derives from BB's having been Brazil's central bank until 1965 and the gradual nature of the process of transferring its central banking functions to the Central Bank of Brazil. Banco do Brasil now ranks among the 60 largest banks in the world, its position having fallen from one of the 20 largest in the early 1980s.

BB competes vigorously with private sector and state-owned banks for domestic banking business and derives significant benefits from its being the only clearing bank. It accounts for over half of total banking system sight deposits as well as commercial bank operating profits. For 1987, it reported an operating profit of more than 50 per cent of shareholders' equity. Although BB is under the majority ownership of the federal government, its common and preferred shares are actively traded on Brazil's stock exchanges and are considered 'blue chip'.

BB has also expanded its activities into sectors traditionally reserved for private and some state-owned banks. In 1987, it was authorised to open savings accounts under the name of 'caderneta rural' (rural savings account), the proceeds of deposits being designed to fund rural lending activities. The success of this type of savings account was instantaneous, with deposits rising to about US$2 billion by the end of the year. On the other hand, BB does not have a savings and loan company, which may have important implications relative to the multi-bank structure being contemplated under present banking reform proposals.

Apart from savings accounts, BB has been authorised to establish a consumer finance company and can administer certain types of mutual funds. It also has a credit card agreement with Visa. BB has not so far been authorised to open an investment bank or participate directly in underwriting activities.

While gradually diminishing its role in acting as a monetary authority, BB, because of its extensive branch system and other factors, still exercises responsibility for:

1. Acting as domestic and foreign paying and receiving agent of the federal government.
2. Implementing agricultural minimum price policies and in general playing a pre-eminent role in the implementation of the rural credit programme.
3. Granting guarantees on behalf of the federal government.
4. Providing financial services to the federal government and acting as depository of excess funds generated by federal government entities and enterprises.
5. Operating Brazil's extensive clearing house system and receiving sight deposits from financial institutions. (Brazilian banks are not permitted to maintain sight deposits accounts with each other, although they can acquire each other's time deposit paper.)
6. Executing Brazil's foreign trade policy, providing working capital financing on better-than-market terms to exporters, and financing specific export sales transactions under the FINEX program. The latter two functions are executed both directly by CACEX (Carteira de Comércio Exterior) and also through co-operation with the banking system. CACEX is a department within BB which wields considerable power through its exclusive prerogative over the issue of import and export licences, its role in export and

exporter financing, and its international and domestic promotion of Brazilian trade.

Until 1986, BB shared responsibility for monetary policy execution with the Central Bank. BB's role was derived from its access to Ministry of Finance funds on deposit with the Central Bank without the need for prior approval. On being denied such access in 1986, BB was deprived of what it perceived to be a significant contributor to its profits. However, the Bank was compensated by being permitted to engage in new types of activities, such as accepting rural savings deposits.

Banco do Nordeste do Brasil (BNB)

As implied by its name, the Bank provides banking and financial services in Brazil's north-east. BNB acts as both commercial and development bank, thus being able to attract customer deposits and at the same time obtaining resources from fiscal incentive pro-grammes, government contributions, foreign currency financings, official relending programmes, and international lending agencies. BNB is the financial agent for SUDENE (Superintendency for the Development of the North-east). A hybrid institution, BNB is hier-archically subordinated to the Ministry of the Interior (though super-vised and regulated by the Central Bank), and its primary objective is to promote economic development.

BNB's resource base received an important stimulus by its being allowed, along with Banco do Brasil, to attract savings deposits through the rural savings account mechanism.

Banco de Roraima and Banco da Amazônia

Also subject to the Interior Ministry's jurisdiction, these two feder-ally owned banks perform hybrid banking functions similar to those of BNB, limited of course to their respective geographical regions.

Banco de Brasília

Banco de Brasília (formerly Banco Regional de Brasília) is owned by the federal government because of its location in the Federal District. However it functions largely in the same manner as the state-owned commercial banks.

Banco Meridional

This bank, which ranked as Brazil's nineteenth largest in total deposits at the end of 1987, is the successor to Banco Sul Brasileiro, which failed in 1985 and was taken over and administered by the Central Bank. Banco Meridional is a full service commercial banking conglomerate with about 356 branches located in most parts of Brazil. Its conglomerate includes an investment bank, a leasing company, a brokerage firm and 'distribuidora'.

6.3.3   Banco Nacional de Crédito Cooperativo (BNCC)

As its name implies, BNCC (National Co-operative Credit Bank) performs an agricultural development function and does not operate *per se* in most commercial banking areas. An arm of the Ministry of Agriculture, BNCC was established to promote the development of credit co-operatives, principally in rural areas, through the provision of subsidized credit. Funding is derived from loans by international lending agencies and foreign banks, foreign aid programmes, deposits placed by member co-operatives, reinvested profits, and federal budgetary appropriations. BNCC also operates in foreign exchange and trade financing, and was authorised, along with BB and BNB, to raise savings deposits through the rural savings programme.

6.3.4   Development banking – federal government

The principal development bank in Brazil is BNDES (National Bank for Economic and Social Development), which under the jurisdiction of the federal Planning Secretariat, is primarily responsible for granting medium- and long-term loans to Brazilian companies for purposes of financing the expansion of plant, machinery and equipment produced in Brazil. Its lending activities are accompanied by a substantial volume of equity investments, which in recent years have been sold to the public through offerings on the stock exchanges.

The main sources of funding arise from federal budgetary resources, loans from foreign commercial banks, international lending agency loans, foreign aid programs, and reinvested profits. BNDES lends its resources directly to end borrowers in the private and public sectors but also sponsors numerous specific on-lending programs using commercial and investment banks, savings banks, and regional development banks as agents.

BNDES also administers the Social Investment Fund (Finsocial), which mobilises resources from a levy on corporate sales revenue to provide financial support to social assistance programmes in the areas of basic foodstuffs, health, education, housing and small-scale farming activities.

A potentially very important role may be played by BNDES in Brazil's privatisation programme, which it is developing in co-ordination with the Planning Secretariat. BNDES owns majority and minority shareholdings in companies which qualify for privatisation. Its subsidiary, BNDESPAR, which has already been a lead manager or co-lead manager of important securities issues, would play a critical role in selling off shares which are at present owned by BNDES or other organs of the government to the public at large.

6.3.5 Regional and state development banks

There are 13 regional or state development banks in Brazil. Wealthier or larger states have established their own development banks to provide financial support to economic activities primarily of interest to the state, notably in the areas of industrial and agricultural infrastructure. Development banks, besides making medium- and long-term loans, also conduct leasing and lease-back transactions, on-lend foreign currency and government funds under special programmes, make equity investments, and underwrite securities issues.

The principal source of funds available to state and regional development banks consists of budgetary appropriations, customer time deposits, foreign currency borrowings from private and official sources, reinvested profits, and their own capital issues.

Regional development banks have resulted from the pooling of resources by neighbouring states with the objective of financing projects which are of regional scope rather than of interest to a single state.

6.3.6 Commercial banks

Brazil's 105 chartered commercial banks include not only the six federally-owned institutions described above but also the 24 state-owned banks, 19 foreign banks, and 56 private Brazilian-owned banks (including those with minority foreign shareholders). Although they have different sources of ownership, commercial banks operate in a largely similar fashion, the principal differences being:

- Not all state-owned banks are organised as financial conglomerates. This type of organisation is limited mainly to the banks owned by the largest states (such as São Paulo, Rio Grande do Sul and Rio de Janeiro).
- Foreign commercial banks are generally not permitted to expand their domestic branch networks, which are effectively frozen at present levels. However, one foreign bank may sell branches to another one. These restrictions are not generally applied to locally owned banks with minority foreign shareholders. Most foreign banks have established a conglomerate form of organisation.
- State-owned banks generally enjoy a monopoly over the performance of financial services for state governments and governmental entities, including their deposits and the management of surplus funds.

The product/business activity areas in which commercial banks are normally not permitted to operate were delineated above. Among the products which they are entitled to offer are the following:

- Foreign exchange financing, including loans to exporters and importers.
- Other foreign exchange services, such as remittances and collections.
- Discounts of trade bills and notes receivable.
- Provision of short-term loans (normally, up to 180 days).
- Provision of rural credit financing.
- Acting as agent for on-lending of government and foreign currency funds.
- Performing a full service treasury function, including the issue of repurchase commitments as a funding mechanism.
- Acceptance of sight and time deposits from the public and inter-bank time deposit certificates.
- Performance of traditional commercial banking services, such as payment and transfer orders, issue of traveller's cheques, collections, correspondent services, payment and receipt services, intermediation in auctions of treasury bills, issue of local currency and foreign trade-related guarantees, opening of letters of credit, custody of documents and securities, and rental of safe deposit facilities.
- Collection of taxes, payments and receipts on behalf of both private and public sector entities.

The asset- and liability-generating activities of commercial banks are subject to strict operating limits which are enforced by the Central Bank. Apart from the general leverage limit of 15 times equity, we shall not enumerate these limits because of their changeability and the scope of this work.

As of this writing, bank lending activity is in the midst of a stagnation process resulting from a variety of factors, including low loan demand on the part of borrowers deemed creditworthy and the slowdown in investment financed by indebtedness. On the other hand, commercial banks are generating profits through their treasury activities and, in particular, by emphasising services which generate float and other forms of 'free' funding. The banks' ability to develop large volumes of float is a consequence of the very significant strides taken in Brazil in the past 20 years to streamline check processing and make the inter-bank payments systems respond adequately to the prevailing inflationary environment. Certain facts are notably illustrative of the achievements of Brazil's banking system in this area:

1. The number of cheques cleared in 1980 was 5.4 million per business day, or 30 times the volume in 1960.
2. The number of cheques cleared in 1987 is estimated at 28 million per day, or about 7 billion per year. For comparison purposes, one of the world's largest financial services companies processes 28 million items in a month.
3. About 95 per cent of all checks are cleared in 24 hours. (On 9 December the monetary authorities announced that clearing within the same city would take place on a 'same day' basis. Rules were also set down to speed up clearings of checks involving two different locations.)

Fundamental causes of this situation are Brazil's high rate of inflation and the public's preference for avoiding carrying large amounts of cash. However, it has been made possible by the conscious policy of Brazil's larger banking conglomerates to develop sophisticated, increasingly automated payments and money transfer systems for their corporate and individual clientele. Indeed, one of the most salient trends in Brazilian commercial banking today is the emphasis on services rather than asset-based lending, and the result is a dramatic increase in the share of total profits occupied by service income. It is obvious that the institutions with the largest national coverage in terms of banking offices and automated teller machines and with the resources required for investing in advanced data-processing systems have benefited most substantially from the general trend toward service-oriented banking. The implications of this fact in terms of concentration and competition issues are coming under increasing public scrutiny and underlie the mounting pressures for promoting competition through the authorisation of new commercial banks.

6.3.7 Investment banks

Law 4.728 of 1966 created investment banks to act as suppliers of medium- and long-term finance and to promote the development of Brazil's capital markets. Today, the actual business conducted by Brazil's investment banks is substantially different in scope from that foreseen in the original enabling legislation.

Organisationally, investment banks can be divided into three categories:

1. Those forming an integral part of financial conglomerates with a commercial bank as the central institution. In these cases, the investment bank acts largely as a department of the conglomerate, although its separate legal identity is, for the present, retained.
2. Those acting as principal institution in a conglomerate which includes a relatively small commercial bank with only a few banking offices.
3. Those which act as the central institution for their own respective conglomerates without a commercial bank affiliation. Typically, these conglomerates include a brokerage firm and/or 'distribuidora', leasing company, and consumer finance company.

The distinction between product lines offered by investment banks and commercial banks has become so blurred that, operationally speaking, it is difficult for most observers to note significant differences. Investment banks can not accept checking accounts, participate directly in the documentary clearing system, develop an extensive branch system, or leverage themselves to the same extent as commercial banks. On the other hand, investment banks are permitted to underwrite corporate share issues and guarantee foreign loans, which are off-limits to commercial banks.

An important measure assisting investment banks was the Central Bank decision in 1986 to permit them to offer a complete range of foreign exchange services, an area denied to such banks since 1966.

With the ability to engage in all types of foreign exchange transactions, conducting a lending business largely identical to that of a
commercial bank, and with similar minimum capital requirements,
investment banks have understandably become one of the most
popular vehicles for new investment in Brazil's financial system.

6.3.8 Savings institutions

Brazil's savings institutions are organised into a nation-wide system
designed primarily to attract individual savings accounts and utilise
the proceeds therefrom for financing the construction and sale of
residential housing. Known commonly as the SFH (Residential
Financing System), the savings and loan structure is guided operationally by the Federal Savings Bank (Caixa Econômica Federal:
CEF) subject to regulation and supervision by the Central Bank. In
the mid-1980s, the CEF absorbed the activities of the National
Housing Bank (BNH), which ceased to exist.

Complementing the CEF are 79 licensed private savings and loan
companies, most of which form part of financial conglomerates, four
state savings banks, and savings and loan associations. These associations have practically gone out of business and thus will not be
treated in this work.

Federal Savings Bank (CEF)

The CEF is jurisdictionally responsible to the Ministry of Urban
Development and the Environment and is the principal agent responsible for administration of residential housing loans under the SFH
programme. This function involves both direct financing of the construction and sale of housing units and the refinancing of state and
private agents under various types of specific purpose programmes.
The function of regulating, supervising, and establishing important
policies for all SFH agents is exercised by the Central Bank of Brazil.

The principal source of funding for the CEF consists of customer
checking and savings accounts, in addition to public issues of mortgage certificates. Recently, the CEF was authorised by the Central
Bank to fund its treasury activities through the issue of repurchase
commitments. Additional sources of funds are made available to the
CEF through its administration of the various national lotteries. It
also manages the FGTS (Job Tenure Guarantee Fund), a function it
inherited when it absorbed the National Housing Bank.

State savings banks

There are four state savings banks, one each for the states of São Paulo, Goiás, Minas Gerais and Rio Grande do Sul. Their activities and sources of funds follow patterns similar to those of CEF. The states are the respective controlling shareholders of their savings banks. Deposits obtained by these institutions are insured by the federal government up to an amount of approximately US$27 000.

Savings and loan companies

Operating since 1966, following on the establishment of the National Housing Bank, savings and loan companies (known in Brazil as 'sociedades de crédito imobiliário') attract large individuals' savings accounts which are insured up to the same limit as that applicable to state savings bank accounts. Resources are applied to the development, construction, purchase and sale of residential housing units. Savings and loan companies are also permitted to make working capital financing available to producers of construction equipment and building materials.

Brazil's savings and loan system is divided into eleven geographical regions, and companies headquartered in one region are not permitted to conduct business in another region unless they own a savings and loan company located therein.

Most savings and loan companies pertain to financial conglomerates. Owing to the competition of savings accounts with other types of investment instruments (such as bank time deposits, consumer finance company bills of exchange, government securities, and various types of mutual funds), it is at present envisaged that savings and loan companies will be merged into the multi-bank structure. Under this arrangement, savings and loan companies would lose their specific legal identities and function, as they already are in practice, departments of the multi-bank.

Savings accounts typically account for over 50 per cent of banking system deposits and are particularly popular among small savers. They earn 6 per cent a year interest: over monetary correction.

In addition they are subject to fiscal incentives up to a limited amount saved. Their widespread popularity makes them relatively immune from significant changes in regulations, and the yield they generate frequently serves as the benchmark for establishing yields on competing instruments. Savings account redemptions can be effected at any time, although if made between monthly anniversary dates the withdrawer does not receive monetary correction for the period between the most recent anniversary date and the date of withdrawal.

Credit co-operatives

Credit co-operatives are private institutions designed to provide credit and other services to their associate members. Organised as associations of individuals and acting as financial institutions under the purview of the Central Bank, Brazil's credit co-operatives are of three basic types:

1. Mutual credit co-operatives, formed by individuals belonging to the same profession and having the same employer. The activities of these co-operatives must be for the benefit only of their members and within limits established by the Central Bank of Brazil.
2. Popular credit co-operatives, the members and activities of which are confined to a single geographical area. Such co-operatives in practice serve as a pool of funds for small personal loans.
3. Rural credit co-operatives, with membership composed of both individuals and agri-business companies and designed generally to provide loans for agricultural, fishing or mining activities. The type of credit extended follows the ground rules established by the Central Bank's rural credit regulations. Co-operatives raise funds through capital contributions, members' deposits, and loans from the National Co-operative Credit Bank (BNCC) and other official institutions.

In 31 December 1986, credit co-operatives had nearly 750 000 members, which indicates the widespread appeal they enjoy, particularly in rural areas. Many of them act as agents for raising 'rural savings accounts' which become part of the funding base of BNCC.

A fundamental issue in banking reform has arisen due to the interest of co-operatives in being entitled to convert into commercial banks. The effect of converting over 500 small credit co-operatives into banks would be a reversion to the old atomised, regionalised banking structure which proved to be inadequate for financial development in an increasingly sophisticated environment. On the other hand, the agri-business sector exercises considerable political influence, and its own perception is that the demise of certain subsidies in the production and pricing areas as well as reduced credit availability from the banking sector must be offset by cheaper credit form financial agents which are specialised in agriculture. The Constitutional Assembly has ordained that a complementary law (which ranks just below the constitution itself in terms of legal authority) be passed, once the constitution is finally approved, permitting credit co-operatives the option of becoming banks. However, because of the opposition of powerful forces, the exact nature of the conversion provisions cannot at present be defined.

Consumer finance companies

While not strictly banks, consumer finance companies, like banks, are engaged in raising funds from the public for purposes of lending. The instrument used by these companies for funding their activities is the bill of exchange ('letra de câmbio'), which from an operational viewpoint is practically identical to a negotiable time deposit certificate, although there are minor legal differences between the two instruments. The bill of exchange is probably the oldest investment instrument in Brazil.

Consumer finance companies have been in existence longer than most other financial institutions, except commercial banks. For years their principal activity was to add their name to trade bills, thus making them readily negotiable and thus suitable for financing consumer purchases. As the companies evolved, they issued bills of exchange in their own name.

With the passage of Law 4.595, finance companies were empowered to act in substantially the same fashion as investment banks are today. However, under Law 4.728, which created the investment bank concept in 1966, capital market and industrial lending functions were transferred to investment banks. Finance companies were consequentially limited to providing consumer loans, although they would still act as on-lending agents for BNDES (FINAME programme for financing the purchase of Brazilian-made equipment is an example).

Consumer finance companies offer basically two products: direct consumer financing for general purposes for the acquisition of products, and indirect financing, whereby the seller becomes effectively co-obligor. Consumer finance companies can also provide certain types of working capital financing to companies in addition to their role as on-lending agents of BNDES funds under specific programmes.

From the structural viewpoint, consumer finance companies generally fall into one of three categories: (1) those integrated into financial conglomerates; (2) those which are wholly independent; and (3) those which are owned by commercial or industrial groups. Many of the largest consumer finance companies form part of this latter category. As discussed in Chapter 4, companies which already have an ownership affiliation with a financial conglomerate can optionally become departments within the Multibank which it creates. Independent consumer finance companies (that is, those falling into the second and third categories above) can petition the Central Bank to create their own multiple banks.

The share of finance company bills in aggregate financial assets declined from a high of 12.6 per cent to under 2 per cent in very recent times. This trend reflects a decrease of lending activities in the consumer finance area as well as the channelling of personal lending through commercial banking entities. During the same period, finance company loans as a percentage of aggregate banking system loans fell from 10 per cent to around 5 per cent. These trends have probably been more heavily influenced by government anti-inflationary regulations strictly limiting financing terms than by purely economic phenomena.

NOTES

1. *Manual of Rules and Instructions* (MNI), issued by the Central Bank.
2. The Central Bank publishes semi-annually a compendium of financial institutions, providing data such as address, ownership, capital, branches, and other relevant information. Much of the material contained herein has been derived from the said publication, which is entitled '*Sistema Financeiro Nacional: Dados Estatísticos e Gerais*' (National Financial System: General and Statistical Data).

An important source of information for this chapter was:
Coopers & Lybrand, *Profile of Banking and Finance in Brazil*, May 1986.

7 Non-Banking Financial Institutions

7.1 DESCRIPTION OF PRINCIPAL NON-BANKING FINANCIAL INSTITUTIONS

The non-banking institution segment of the financial industry offers considerable potential for long-term growth as well as short-term profits. This segment generally is involved in developing and intermediating longer term sources of finance for rapidly growing corporations, as well as in managing wealth. In accordance with the evolving multi-bank concept, this segment would be separate from the banking system and would include institutions involved in capital markets, insurance, investments and possibly leasing. (Reference should be made to Table 7.5 and related material in Chapter 5.)

Institutions which are active in this segment are normally open to foreign investment (except in the area of insurance, where new foreign investment presently is not being authorised). New foreign investment in certain types of activity is given unofficial encouragement by the authorities. Moreover whatever restrictions might ensue from the constitutional process on foreign investment in the banking sector are less likely to affect the capital market segment significantly.

Certain types of capital market-related institutions are discussed elsewhere in this book and will thus be examined only cursorily in this section. Here we focus primarily on a description of the following types of entities:

- leasing companies;
- brokerage firms and 'distribuidoras';
- domestic currency mutual funds;
- foreign currency mutual funds;
- investment/holding companies;
- venture capital companies;
- PAIT funds;
- insurance companies and pension funds;
- National Development Fund;
- non-financial institutions active in financial intermediation.

Having completed the descriptive section, we will examine the product and institutional opportunities available to foreign investors, turning our attention thereafter to a brief overview of the experience of joint ventures between local and foreign partners in Brazilian financial institutions.

It is useful to keep in mind that, in most cases in this segment of financial market activity, the institution is practically synonymous with the products it offers. Exceptions to this include brokerage firms and 'distribuidoras', which can and do engage in a wide variety of financial business activities. Moreover the products in this segment of the market change rapidly, depending on customer demand, changes in government regulations, and the responsiveness of market participants. It is in this general area of what is often referred to as 'investment banking', 'merchant banking', 'banco de negócios' (a term comparable to 'banque d'affaires' in French), or 'financial engineering' that new products or variations on existing ones are constantly appearing. Therefore, it is the area which offers perhaps the greatest scope for the development of new products and the deepening of existing ones.

7.1.1 Leasing companies

Leasing companies were authorised to operate in Brazil in 1975 under Law 6.099, which was enacted in late 1974. At mid-year 1988 56 leasing companies were conducting business. These companies offer different types of leasing and lease-back services to clients, including the sub-leasing of equipment imported from abroad. Leasing companies are entitled to have foreign shareholders with up to 33⅓ per cent of voting capital and 50 per cent of total capital. However some leasing company charters confer 100 per cent ownership rights to foreign interests, their having been issued prior to the extension of the foreign ownership limitations to leasing companies. A majority of Brazil's leasing companies form part of financial conglomerates. The principal professional association is ABEL, the Brazilian Association of Leasing Companies.

Since Brazil declared a moratorium on the repayment of principal on external debt to foreign banks in 1982, leasing company activities have been deleteriously affected, owing to the difficulties in obtaining new sources of foreign currency funding on a scale which prevailed in earlier years. In Table 7.1, we show the development of outstanding contracts and new leasing business since 1982.

Table 7.1   Development of leasing activities, 1982–7[1] (US$ millions)

Year	Assets under lease	% change over previous period	New contracts	% change
1982	2 635	–	1 526	–
1983	1 706	(35.3)	687	(55.0)
1984	1 719	0.8	857	24.7
1985	2 028	18.0	1 302	51.9
1986	2 697	33.0	1 576	21.0
1987	2 400*	(11.0)	1 000*	(36.5)

* Estimates.
Source: ABEL.

During the mid-1980s, leasing companies made substantial debenture issues through Brazilian stock exchanges, enabling them to supplement foreign currency resources and thus return to earlier growth rates. However, new debenture activity declined significantly from 1986 onwards, thus effectively depriving leasing companies of an important source of local currency funding and liability diversification possibilities.

Leasing companies must have a minimum net worth of about US$4 million, which can be leveraged up to 12 times with debt obligations. Central Bank Resolution 980 froze the number of leasing company licences at the level then in existence.

The all-important fiscal treatment of leasing and lease-back transactions is dealt with in both Law 6.099 (12 September 1974) and Law 7.132 (26 October 1983).

7.1.2   Stock exchanges

There are at present nine stock exchanges existing in Brazil, the principal exchanges being those of Rio de Janeiro and São Paulo, where over 95 per cent of total trading is concentrated. There is also a small over-the-counter market ('mercado de balção'). Stock exchanges are organised as non-profit civil associations and are responsible for providing securities trading locations, publishing information on transactions, creating and supervising trading mechanisms, establishing and enforcing standards of ethical behavior, and providing clearing and custodian facilities.

Except for a spurt of activity in 1970–1, Brazil's stock exchanges

Table 7.2   Volume of new issues underwriting on principal stock exchanges[2] (US$ millions)

	1983	1984	1985	1986	1987
Shares	253	591	653	1 090	334
Debentures	784	423	210	128	20
TOTAL	1 037	1 014	863	1 218	354

Source: Central Bank of Brazil.

have not until recent years been important centres of financial activity. However the diversification and growth of institutional sources of funding have helped to promote the liquidity of secondary trading and volume of new issues (primary market) on the stock exchanges.

The volume of securities underwriting has evolved as shown in TABLE 7.2. It is estimated that securities underwritings in 1988 will approach or perhaps surpass levels achieved in the 1983–86 period. Securities trading volume declined in 1987 relative to previous years. Total BOVESPA trading volume fell from US$17.7 billion in 1986 to $5.9 billion in 1987, while trading on the Rio exchange, which totalled $11 billion in 1986, was recorded at only $4 billion the following year. Average daily trading volumes on the two exchanges have ranged from $21 800 000 in 1980 to a high, so far, of $118 million in 1986. Average daily volume on the two leading exchanges in first half 1988 was in the neighborhood of $40 to $80 million. On 30 April 1988 the total capitalisation of listed companies was US$28 billion.

The monthly auctions where foreign debt can be converted into local equity generally are carried out at the São Paulo and Rio de Janeiro Stock Exchanges. These auctions determine the value in Brazil of debt obligations acquired overseas by parties interested in direct investments in Brazil. The value of these obligations, that is, face value less a discount set at the auctions, determines simultaneously the amount of funds to be received from the Central Bank by the investor and the amount which can be registered as foreign capital (and, thus, the basis for future repatriation and dividend remittances). Debt/equity conversions generally are expected to contribute to the development of stock market activity over the longer run.

7.1.3   Commodities and futures exchanges

There are three commodities and futures exchanges in Brazil offering an increasingly wide range of trading products to an expanding body of interested investors. The oldest is the São Paulo Commodities Exchange (BMSP), which has been operating since the last century, traditionally concentrating its activities in coffee contracts but more recently expanding beyond commodities into financial futures of different types. The Brazilian Futures Exchange (BBF) was opened in Rio de Janeiro in 1985, and the Mercantile and Futures Exchange (BMF) was opened in São Paulo in 1986. The three exchanges operate in a largely self-regulated environment and are responsible for developing their own trading products.

The BMSP offers spot and futures contracts in gold, coffee, cattle, soy beans, corn and poultry. The BBF and BMF tend to be more active in interest rate, inflation index, stock exchange index, and exchange rate futures contracts as well as in spot and future gold trading. Total trading registered on the BMF alone in 1987 was over US$6 billion, reflecting the increasing importance of hedging products to investors.[3]

Exchange membership rules vary according to each exchange, but full membership rights are normally reserved for brokerage firms or officially registered individual brokers. Each exchange maintains its own clearing system. These exchanges are discussed in somewhat greater detail in Chapter 10.

7.1.4   Brokerage firms and 'distribuidoras'

The legally authorised activities and product areas of these two types of institution are so nearly alike that they will be treated herein under the same heading. The types of business they conduct in actual practice are also practically identical, although most institutions tend to specialise or develop market niches in specific areas.

Brokerage firms have been in existence in Brazil since the formation of stock markets, and 275 of these operate in the Brazilian markets today. 'Distribuidoras', of which there are over 400, were created by the Capital Markets Law (Law 4.728), the implementing regulations being Central Bank Resolution 48 of 10 March 1967, and Resolution 76 of 22 November 1967.

The principal difference between the two types of institution is that brokerage firms, but not 'distribuidoras', are entitled to acquire seats on stock and commodities/futures exchanges. A stock exchange seat constitutes a licence to operate. There are no further chartering requirements, although Central Bank prior approval must be granted before the firm can operate. The cost of a seat on the BOVESPA is (circa 1988) approximately US$900 000.

Both types of firms perform largely financial intermediation, and in some cases cash management, services. Many brokerage houses have charters limiting them to foreign exchange and/or commodities brokerage. The meaning of 'intermediation' in the Brazilian context is broad, and in practice the more active 'distribuidoras' and broker-age firms apply as liberal an interpretation as possible to the products they offer to their clients.

In Table 7.3 we compare the product opportunities offered by both types of institutions with those of investment banks. The product areas available to financial intermediation companies acting as invest-ment or holding companies ('bancos de negócios') are also com-pared. This presentation is keyed to 'distribuidoras', brokerage firms and intermediation companies and thus does not focus in detail on the commercial banking functions of investment banks.

The table highlights the conclusion of many observers that 'distri-buidoras' and brokerage firms, given the hybrid nature of their activities, can do just about anything an investment bank can do, except in strictly commercial banking areas. Not having responsi-bilities in these areas can, on the other hand, be a significant advan-tage in terms of minimising overheads and regulatory requirements, and maximising the capacity to respond flexibly to new opportunities in a highly dynamic market.

The Central Bank at present distinguishes between 'distribuidoras'/ brokerage firms in accordance with their minimum capital endow-ments, establishing four levels of capitalisation in order to ensure that product risk is supported by adequate equity. In Table 7.4, we show the minimum capital at present required for the principal types of products of brokerage firms and 'distribuidoras' (these regulations are applicable to firms headquartered in São Paulo and Rio de Janeiro).

7.1.5 Domestic currency mutual funds

There are three types of mutual funds operating in Brazil, all of them organised on an open-end basis:

Table 7.3 Financial service products: institutional comparisons[4]

Product or activity	Type of institution	Investment bank (3)	Brokerage firm (corretora)	Securities dealer (distribuidora)	General purpose or holding company
Minimum capital	(1) (2)	1.2 million OTN without a foreign exchange licence. 1.6 million OTN with a forex licence.	Ranges from 40 000 to 400 000 OTN in São Paulo and Rio de Janeiro, depending on business activities to be conducted.	Same as for brokerage firm.	No specific minimum capital requirement.
Foreign ownership limitations		Foreign shareholding cannot exceed 33 1/3% of voting stock or 50% of total capital.	Same as for investment bank.	Same as for investment bank.	None.
Fixed asset limits		100% of equity.	100% of equity.	100% of equity.	No limit.
Branching possibilities		Limit of 6 branch offices subject to special capital allocation.	Limit of 10 offices apart from head office. Separate allocation of 10% of the required minimum capital for each office. Corretora must in principle acquire seat on stock exchange of the city where an office is located.	Limit of 10 offices apart from the head office but with separate allocation of 10% of minimum capital for each office.	No limit.

ASSET MANAGEMENT

Portfolios

Fixed income mutual funds.	Permitted.	Permitted.	Permitted.	Not permitted.
Equity mutual fund.	Permitted.	Permitted.	Permitted.	Not permitted.
Private portfolio (includes client current account balances not accessed by checks and management of investment clubs).	Permitted.	Permitted.	Permitted.	Not prohibited but not practised.
Margin account financing.	Credit transactions with individuals not permitted to investment banks.	Permitted up to 5 times equity.	Permitted up to 5 times equity.	Not permitted.
Management of PAIT private retirement funds and/or other types of pension-type funds.	Permitted.	Permitted.	Permitted.	Not permitted.
Brokerage commodities Spot and futures contracts on São Paulo Commodities Exchange (cattle, gold, coffee,	Investment banks are not admitted by the exchanges to full membership.	Brokerage firms are admitted by the exchanges to full membership.	'Distribuidoras' not admitted by exchanges to full membership.	Not admitted by exchanges to full membership.

continued

Table 7.3 continued

Product or activity / Type of institution	Investment bank (3)	Brokerage firm (corretora)	Securities dealer (distribuidora)	General purpose or holding company
soybeans, cattle, cocoa and other commodities).				
Ownership of seats on stock and futures exchanges.	Not permitted.	Permitted.	Not permitted.	Not permitted.
Brokerage on the stock markets.	Not permitted.	Permitted.	Permitted under contract with brokerage firm.	Not permitted.
Brokerage on the futures markets.	Not directly permitted.	Permitted.	Permitted under contract with brokerage house.	Not permitted.
Ownership of seats on futures markets. Mercantile and Futures Exchange – BMF (São Paulo): Spot, futures and options contracts in gold; stock exchange index futures; OTN futures; interest rate futures.	Normally operates on futures exchanges through affiliated corretora.	Ownership of full membership seats permitted.	Cannot own full membership seats but can have full services through contract with a corretora.	Not permitted to transact on exchanges, except as investor acting through a corretora.

TREASURY (4)

Repo government fixed income securities.	Permitted with specific allocation of capital (minimum of 100 000 OTN).	Permitted with unrestricted clientele for firms with minimum equity of 100 000 OTN, up to limit of 30 times equity. Permitted with equity of 50 000 OTN, but clientele is restricted to financial institutions.	Same as for brokerage firms.	This is a function restricted to financial institutions within the framework established by Resolution 1.088.
Repo private fixed income securities.	Permitted assuming adequate capital allocation. Ceiling of 3 times equity.	Permitted for firms with minimum equity of 100 000 OTN, up to limit of 3 times equity.	Same as for brokerage firms.	Restricted to financial institutions in accordance with Resolution 1.088.
Portfolio trading.	Authorised without specific minimum capital requirement.	Authorised without specific minimum capital requirement.	Authorised without specific minimum capital requirement.	Not permitted.
Financial institution paper.	Not practised by investment banks acting on their own.	Authorised without specific minimum capital requirement.	Authorised without specific minimum capital requirement.	Not permitted.
Own portfolio.	Permitted.	Permitted.	Permitted.	Permitted.
Brazilian Futures Exchange – BBF (Rio de Janeiro). Foreign exchange hedges; stock index futures; OTN futures.	(See above)	(See above)	(See above)	(See above)

continued

Table 7.3 continued

Product or activity	Type of institution	Investment bank (3)	Brokerage firm (corretora)	Securities dealer (distribuidora)	General purpose or holding company
MERCHANT BANKING					
Debentures underwriting.		Authorised and practised.	Authorised and practised as regards publicly issued debentures.	Authorised and practised as regards publicly issued debentures.	Permitted to invest surplus cash in debentures.
Equity underwriting.		Authorised and practised.	Authorised and practised.	Authorised and practised, although 'distribuidoras' do not act as lead managers.	Not permitted.
Conversion mutual fund.	(5)	Management of fund permitted.	Management of fund permitted.	Management of fund permitted.	Not permitted to manage fund.
Investment company.		Not regulated.	Not regulated.	Not regulated.	This type of company can be legally structured to operate as both a holding and investment company.
Other financial intermediation.		Permitted.	Permitted.	Permitted.	Permitted.
COMMERCIAL BANKING					
Loans and guarantees		Complete corporate lending capability for	Not permitted except as indicated above.	Not permitted except as indicated above.	Not technically permitted except as

	minimum term of 60 days. Generally complete loan guarantee capability, in both local and foreign currencies.		regards related companies.	Not permitted.
Deposits and funding	May accept deposits accessed by cheque and for minimum term of 60 days. Investment banks have access to all important government relending facilities and foreign financing sources, exclusive of residential financing funds.	Not permitted except as indicated above.	Not permitted except as indicated above.	Not permitted.
Foreign exchange	Complete foreign exchange trading and financing capability as long as investment bank does not form part of a financial group in which a commercial bank has a forex licence.	Intermediation capability only.	Intermediation capability conducted under contract with a brokerage firm.	Not permitted.

continued

Table 7.3 continued

Product or activity	Type of institution	Investment bank (3)	Brokerage firm (corretora)	Securities dealer (distribuidora)	General purpose or holding company

Notes:

(1) The minimum capital requirement herein is stated in terms of OTN, which at the average official US dollar/cruzado exchange rate is worth about US$7.75. However, for purposes of meeting minimum requirements, the Central Bank of Brazil uses a formula for calculating OTN values and for actual payment of capital which considerably reduces the dollar equivalent of the cruzados eventually paid in.

(2) As used herein, 'equity' refers to net worth in accordance with the Central Bank formula. Basically, this formula is the sum of paid in capital, free reserves and retained earnings.

(3) When examining the functions of investment banks, it should be recalled that virtually all such banks either form part of a financial conglomerate or are the leading institution in their own conglomerates. In both cases, investment banks have their own affiliated brokerage firms and 'distribuidoras' and can thus use them to offer a full range of brokerage and merchant banking services, including those which the banks cannot offer on their own.

(4) A financial conglomerate can select only one of its institutions (commercial or investment bank, brokerage firm or 'distribuidora') to act as sole trader in the government securities market, funding its positions with short-term repurchase commitments. When the commercial bank or investment bank is so designated, the conglomerate's subsidiary brokerage firm or 'distribuidora' may also trade on a repo basis, but only with respect to the obligations of the affiliated commercial or investment bank.

(5) Conversion mutual funds or, more correctly, Foreign Capital Conversion Funds, were created conceptually in Resolution 1.460 which also provided for debt/equity conversions on a more liberal basis than in Resolution 1.416. Resolution 1.460 alludes to the fact that Foreign Capital Conversion Funds would be similar in structure, procedure, supervision and other factors to the three kinds of foreign currency mutual fund-type portfolios provided for in Resolution 1.289. However the regulations go no further in specifically regulating Foreign Capital Conversion Funds. Central Bank approval has been given to Bank of Boston, Chase Manhattan and other institutions to establish such funds, but their activity to date is non-existent. It is generally believed that further regulation will be required in order to render such funds operational.

One fact is clear: neither 1.289 nor 1.460 funds may acquire more than 5 per cent of the voting control or 20 per cent of the total capital of companies in which they invest.

Table 7.4   Minimum capital requirements for brokerage firms and 'distribuidoras'

Capital	Tranche number	Product capabilities
40 000 OTN (about $320 000)	1	Intermediation in general. All other pertinent activities except those specified below.
50 000 OTN (about $400 000)	2	Management of mutual funds (except short-term bearer funds) and registered investment clubs. Issue of repurchase commitments to fund own fixed-interest securities portfolio. Subject to the terms of 'Article 8'.*
100 000 OTN (about $800 000)	3	Securities custody. Issue of repurchase commitments under both Articles 7 and 8.*
400 000 OTN (about $3.2 million)	4	Management of short-term bearer mutual funds.

* Articles 7 and 8 of Central Bank Resolution 1.088 refer to the types of clients to which repurchase commitments may be issued. Article 7 permits their issue to an unrestricted clientele, whereas under Article 8 such commitments can be undertaken only with financial institutions.
Notes
(1) Activities such as investments in corporate shares and securities underwriting which are not specifically referred to above or proscribed in other regulations are permitted for firms registered under all tranches.
(2) It is of importance to note that this tranching system enables newly organised 'distribuidoras' and brokerage firms to gauge their product development stages to capitalisation capabilities, earnings, and staff endowments.

- fixed income funds;
- equity funds;
- short-term bearer funds.

All three types of funds may be managed by investment banks, 'distribuidoras' and brokerage firms. Mutual funds are subject to joint supervision and regulation by the Securities Commission (CVM) and the Central Bank, although the latter focuses primarily on portfolio composition and other general policy matters.

Fixed income funds

Fixed income funds actually came into existence during the early 1980s without benefit of specific enabling legislation or regulations. They thus represent an important example of the Central Bank's accompanying the market rather than leading it.

The funds raise money from the public (both individuals and corporations) and develop portfolios consisting of federal, state and municipal obligations, bank time deposits, bills of exchange, corporate debentures, real estate bills, mortgage bills, and interest rate futures contracts. In practice, the Central Bank regulates closely the portfolio composition of fixed income fund portfolios in accordance with the needs of macroeconomic policy as they change from time to time. Strict limitations are also applied to investments in paper issued by related institutions.

Fixed income funds were established beginning in 1984, and by 1985 their aggregate net assets had attained US$2 billion. At this stage, the funds were an indispensable factor in the development of the corporate debentures market. The decline in debentures activity in later years contributed to the decline in the net asset value of fixed income funds to $897 million in 1987.

Central Bank Resolution 1.286 of 20 March 1987 governs the activities of fixed income funds. Quotaholders' earnings from these funds are not subject to income taxation.

Equity funds

Equity funds mobilise public resources (from both individuals and corporations) for investment in publicly listed corporate shares. They are also entitled to investment in government obligations and shares traded in the over-the-counter market. Portfolio composition rules are subject to alteration by the Central Bank from time to time.

Some fund management institutions offer alternatives to investors based on the risk/return component of their portfolios. At the height of the 1985–6 stock market boom, net asset values of mutual funds climbed to over US$2 billion. However, as stock market activity fell off dramatically after May 1986, equity fund net asset values declined, and quotaholders withdrew their funds. The aggregate net asset value of equity fund (1988) is in the neighborhood of $600 to 700 million.

The activities of local currency equity funds are governed by Central Bank Resolution 1.280 of 20 March 1987.

Short-term bearer funds

Short-term bearer funds were authorised by Central Bank Resolution 1.199 of 10 October 1986, and are designed to attract resources from investors who wish for tax reasons to remain anonymous. Bearer fund accounts are identified only by a secret number divulged only to quotaholders. They, in turn, are not required to disclose to the tax authorities either income earned from the fund or the value of their holdings therein. Bearer funds are authorised to invest in federal and state government securities, repurchase commitments issued by financial institutions with terms of up to 28 days, bills of exchange, and time deposits. At the present time, they must allocate 80 per cent of their portfolios to investments in government securities.

Bearer funds have enjoyed widespread public appeal, their net assets presently approaching the $5 billion level, even though they only began operating in late 1986.

7.1.6 Foreign currency mutual funds

This terminology is generally applied to entities which derive resources from acquisitions by foreigners of shares in the funds, which in turn invest in publicly traded corporate shares. There are three types of diversified portfolio mechanisms involving investments of 'new money' (in addition to the Foreign Capital Conversion Funds, which are treated separately herein):

- Foreign Capital Investment Company ('Sociedade de Investimento – Capital Estrangeiro');
- Foreign Capital Investment Fund ('Fundo de Investimento – Capital Estrangeiro');
- Managed Securities Portfolios ('Carteiras de Títulos e Valores Mobiliários').

These three vehicles are governed by Resolution 1.289 of 20 March 1987, and are jointly regulated by the CVM and the Central Bank.

Although in terms of legal organisation each vehicle is different, operationally they have the following characteristics in common:

- All three vehicles must be administered by a Brazilian investment bank, 'distribuidora', or brokerage firm.
- Qualified agents may be contracted overseas for the purpose of raising capital resources.

- Portfolio composition rules are the same for all three entities.
- All are restricted from investing in more than 5 per cent of the voting capital or 20 per cent of total capital of a company. Moreover their investment in a single company may not exceed 10 per cent of the total portfolio.
- Repatriation of foreign capital invested may take place within 90 days of the date of investment. This is accomplished through a simple quota or share redemption process.
- Restricted activities include the receipt of deposits, acquisition of fixed assets, borrowing or lending money, rediscounting, guaranteeing of third party obligations, pledging of assets in portfolio, acquisition of quotas in other managed portfolios or funds, transacting in publicly-listed securities outside of stock exchange sessions, or trading in the shares of companies which are negotiated only over-the-counter. Strict rules have also been established to avoid transactions involving related parties.
- Foreign Capital Investment Funds are specifically required to invest at least 70 per cent of their portfolios in public-listed shares and are authorised to enter into foreign exchange and stock exchange index futures and options contracts.
- These three vehicles are commonly referred to as 'new money funds', as their funding is derived from the investment of foreign resources not related to Brazil's debt rescheduling negotiations.

In 1988, there were 22 such vehicles in operation (including Foreign Capital Conversion Funds), with aggregate net asset values approaching the $200 million level.

Foreign Capital Conversion Funds

Foreign Capital Conversion Funds were created by Resolution 1.460 as a vehicle for channelling resources arising from foreign debt conversions into equity investments in Brazilian corporate securities. In 1988 a large number of these funds was registered with the Central Bank and the CVM, but only a few of them were operational. Only a small part of the funds released through monthly auctions for debt conversion have been directed into these funds. This topic is discussed in greater detail in Chapters 12 and 14.

Resolution 1.460 stipulates that Foreign Capital Conversion Funds are to be governed by Chapter II of Resolution 1.289 (the section dealing with Foreign Capital Investment Funds) the difference between the two being essentially the source of funding. However, under the terms of Chapter II, foreign investments may be repatriated in 90 days, whereas repatriation of hard currency funds invested in Foreign Capital Conversion Funds must remain in Brazil for 12 years although overseas trading in positions may take place at an earlier date. Conversion funds are subject to less favourable tax treatment than 'new money' funds.

7.1.7 Investment/holding companies

A new type of diversified portfolio has been created under the orientation of Central Bank Circular 1.339 of 28 July 1988. Basically, this circular establishes that:

- The investment companies may have foreign as well as local investors. Foreign investment may be effected via the conversion of foreign debt into equity.
- Said companies must not conduct business activities which would be confused with those of foreign currency mutual funds.
- Their share purchases must be conducted in the primary securities market and be of the nature of a permanent investment.
- Said companies, which would operate in the same fashion as holding companies, may not acquire voting control of Brazilian corporations.
- They are entitled to use the secondary market for taking public the corporations in which they have made primary market investments.

This type of investment vehicle might become attractive to the majority of foreign bank investors which are discouraged from setting up purely foreign currency mutual funds owing to their portfolio composition restrictions and the requirement that only publicly traded corporate securities may be acquired. This type of fund is discussed further in Chapter 14.

7.1.8 Venture capital companies

Venture capital companies were authorised by Central Bank Resolution 1.184 of 4 September 1986. The objective of these companies is to invest their own resources in the shares of unlisted small- and medium-sized Brazilian companies. Venture capital companies may not invest in financial institutions, companies engaged in real estate activities, importers, warehousers, advertising agencies, and most types of professional service companies.

Resolution 1.184 provided for fiscal incentives to companies receiving venture capital investments. These incentives include the right to exclude profits and dividends paid to venture capitalists from their own taxable income. Statistics on venture capital companies and their activities are not available. Venture capital activity is discussed further in Chapter 14.

7.1.9 PAIT funds

Created by Decree Law 2.292 of 21 November 1986, and with implementation provisions established in Decree 93.989 of 30 January 1987, PAIT (Patrimônio Individual do Trabalhador) funds are intended to serve as a tax-deductible savings and investment plan for workers in general. They can be established by both individuals and companies interested in providing additional benefits to their employees. The tax incentive provisions are fully applicable as long as invested funds are not withdrawn before 10 years.

PAIT funds are subject to most of the same rules and regulations as equity mutual funds and can be administered by investment banks, 'distribuidoras' and brokerage firms. Under present regulations, PAIT funds need only invest 10 per cent of their portfolios in government securities, the remainder being available for investments in shares.

7.1.10 'Capitalisation' companies

These companies, generally organised as separate entities within financial conglomerates, issue 'capitalisation' securities to the general public. Such securities, which can have terms of as long as 10 years, yield normally below market rates but attract a large volume of savings due to special awards which can be earned in periodic lottery-type drawings. One of the oldest types of financial institution in Brazil, capitalisation companies have specialised in developing real estate projects. In effect, however, they act today as funding vehicles for the general purpose needs of the respective conglomerates with which they are affiliated.

7.1.11 Insurance companies

Brazil has 97 insurance companies, of which just under half are affiliated with financial conglomerates, while six are wholly foreign-owned, and another 14 have minority foreign shareholders. Insurance companies are considered as financial institutions by the National Monetary Council and the Central Bank. This attitude is justified by:

- The role of these monetary authorities in regulating the composition of investment portfolios and the utilisation of technical reserves. As of the time of this writing, insurance companies are required to invest a minimum of 25 per cent and a maximum of 50 per cent of their free technical reserves in publicly traded corporate securities and are thus an important source of funds for the share markets.
- The linkage of insurance and financial products, such as credit insurance, the investment of reserves, the financing of insurance premiums by the banking system, and the insurance of fixed and other assets acquired with bank financing.

When a financial conglomerate includes an insurance company, the opportunities for synergies and cross-selling are significant.

The Brazilian Reinsurance Institute (IRB) exercises a monopoly over domestic and foreign reinsurance activities. The National Private Insurance Council sets policy and guidelines for insurance company operations, while the Superintendency of Private Insurance (SUSEP) enforces the Council's policies and supervises the utilisation of technical reserves. Supervisory authority in general is shared by the National Monetary Council and Central Bank with the insurance authorities. Most insurance companies are owned by private capital.

7.1.12 Pension funds

Established under Law 6.435 of 1977 and Decree Law 81.402 of 1978, Brazilian pension funds are largely follow the pattern of those of the United States, and are intended to complement the retirement pension activities of the Social Security System. Pension funds may be created with the prior approval of the Ministry of Finance, and their activities are regulated by SUSEP.

According to existing law, pension funds may be closed or open. Closed funds are by definition non-profit making and are restricted to the employees of a single company or related group of companies. Open pension funds may be organised either as corporations or non-profit foundations. Insurance companies may operate pension funds, as long as special technical reserves and provisions are set aside to guarantee their obligations. Investment banks, brokerage firms, and 'distribuidoras' are also entitled to manage pension funds.

The aggregate portfolio value of closed pension funds at the end of March 1988, was over US$7 billion, while that of open pension funds was reported to be $139 million at the end of 1987. Both types of funds are significant investors in publicly traded corporate securities. Their portfolio composition is regulated by the National Monetary Council acting through the Central Bank.

7.1.13   National Development Fund

The National Development Fund (FND) was created by Decree Law 2.288 of 23 July 1986, and regulated by Law 93.538, dated 6 November 1986, its objective being to invest in priority projects in the public and private sectors. Operated under the responsibility of Banco do Brasil, its sources of funds consist primarily of a 'compulsory loan' of 28 per cent on the consumption of petrol and combustible alcohol, 30 per cent of the investments of public sector closed pension funds, and the issue of FND debt securities. By 1990, quotas in the FND will be distributed to vehicle fuel consumers in proportion to their estimated consumption.

FND's portfolio may be composed of shares acquired directly, loans, or securities issued by the government or government banks. BNDES, Banco do Nordeste do Brasil, and Banco da Amazônia may act as financial agents of FND.

In 1986, FND raised US$1 billion in resources, having access at that time to the now extinct compulsory loans on motor car purchases and foreign travel. Funds raised in 1987 totalled approximately $2 billion. At 31 March 1988, 59 per cent of FND resources had been invested in Siderbrás (the government-owned steel sector holding company) and Eletrobrás (the public sector electrical utilities holding company). An additional 33 per cent had been invested in BNDES projects. The composition of FND's portfolio is published periodically in Brazilian newspapers and magazines.

7.1.14   Factoring companies

Factoring companies, of which some 50 out of 200 are active in Brazil, are not legally defined as financial institutions. The Federal Appeals Court ruled in 1986 that factoring is a commercial rather than financial activity. With an aggregate monthly business volume estimated at about US$12 million (but reported by some observers to be three or four times this amount), factoring companies apply their own capital and borrowed funds in the non-recourse purchase of customer accounts and notes receivable. Their principal clients are small- and medium-sized companies, operating particularly in the areas of graphic arts, manufacture of clothing and textiles, and commerce and services in general.

7.1.15 Non-financial institutions active in the financial markets

Large-scale financial activity in Brazil is not limited to duly registered financial institutions. Frequent and important participants in the arranging of intermediation of oftentimes large financial transactions include:

- consulting firms, including those related to some of the 'big 8' auditing firms;
- law offices;
- merchant banking companies;
- foreign bank representative offices;
- individual brokers.

The diversity of sources of financial intermediation in Brazil contributes to the well-known dynamism, resiliency, and responsiveness of the country's financial markets.

7.2 PRODUCT OPPORTUNITIES FOR FOREIGN INVESTORS IN BRAZIL

7.2.1 General orientation for a foreign investor's financial product interest in Brazil

A foreign bank may be primarily, but not exclusively, interested in developing the following types of products in Brazil as particular areas of specialisation:

- merchant banking;
- corporate finance;
- trade finance;
- government securities dealing and trading;

- corporate securities dealing and trading;
- private wealth management (Brazilian assets).

Presumably the investor would have an international client base with affiliations in Brazil to which these products would be delivered, and the products would bear a direct relationship to its international synergy potential. They could also be related to the investor's interest in administering its Brazilian exposure in an efficient and profitable manner.

7.2.2   Product definition in the Brazilian context

Merchant banking

In the Brazilian environment, merchant banking would probably be defined to include debt/equity conversions of various types for the investor's account and that of third parties, mergers and acquisitions (M&A) business, the intermediation of currency swaps, and intermediation of other attractive types of business involving a cross-border element. If the investor chose to establish an investment/holding company as defined in the first section of this chapter or participate with other investors in such a company, it could also offer interim or structured financing products in which it would take part with its own funds. Such transactions would amount to merchant banking in accordance with its traditional definition.

Corporate finance

Corporate finance could be defined to include arranging financing for corporate customers. In this case, vehicles such as 'distribuidoras' or even a foreign bank representative office would be adequate. However, if the interest of the foreign bank lies in providing direct loan financing to its Brazilian customers, it would require a shareholding participation in a banking institution.

Trade finance

Trade finance, like corporate finance, can be efficiently developed on an intermediation basis through a representative office, 'banco de negócios', 'distribuidora', or a brokerage house. Direct funding of trade finance activities would require the foreign investor to be a shareholder in a commercial or investment bank. Brokerage firms and 'distribuidoras' (acting through brokerage firms) can intermediate foreign exchange contracts between banks and exporters/ importers. However this activity is dominated by a few brokerage firms, which act to discourage entry. Moreover transactions spreads are low, creating the need to develop a large volume, which is difficult without a captive clientele.

Securities dealing and trading

This area of activity could embrace the following types of products:

1. Investing in government and financial institution paper, funded with overnight repurchase commitments issued to clients. This type of business can be conducted by commercial and investment banks, brokerage firms, and 'distribuidoras' (the Federal Savings Bank was also authorised in 1988 to conduct this activity). Government securities might also include exchange indexed bonds, which were authorised in July 1988, and could serve as a hedge for the foreign investor's capital.
2. Investing in any type of security using the institution's own capital. This activity can be performed by any type of company.
3. Executing client orders on the stock and commodities/futures exchanges and underwriting of corporate securities. The development of this business must be through a brokerage firm or 'distribuidora', although investment/holding companies (organised under Central Bank Circular 1.339) and investment banks can execute underwritings.
4. Management of mutual funds, for which an investment bank, brokerage firm or 'distribuidora' is required.
5. Management of private foreign currency portfolios under Resolution 1.289.
6. Management of private portfolios (see below), which any person or firm authorised by the Securities Commission can conduct.

Private wealth management

The concept of private wealth management is relatively new to Brazil and is likely to grow very rapidly in the coming years. The wide and increasing range of investment options and the growing level of financial assets make portfolio management for relatively well-to-do individuals and cash-surplus companies a mutually advantageous product, as long as clients are adequately serviced and their resources professionally and profitably managed. As stated above, any individual or company can engage in wealth management, subject to approval by the Securities Commission. However a banking vehicle would be required in order to make loans available to 'blue-chip' clients, and a brokerage firm or 'distribuidora' would be needed to provide margin financing.

7.2.3   Comparison of alternative vehicles

We have reviewed certain products which are generally of greatest interest to foreign investors and will now relate them to institutional vehicle options with accompanying review of advantages and disadvantages.

As a prologue, mention should be made of the relatively intense activity on the part of both foreign and local investors in the financial community to establish investment banks with foreign shareholding partners. This activity is due in part to expected, and possibly unfavourable, changes in rules regarding foreign investment in the Brazilian financial system. It is also due to possible alterations in the pointing system, authorisation process, stricter minimum capital rules in the future, and to the present availability of charter points at a historically reasonable price (negotiated in the free market, an investment bank charter can be obtained for around $3 to $4 million as opposed to $6.5 million in the recent past).

This increase in the number of investment banks, most of them in search of developing the same kinds of merchant banking-type of business, will increase competition, which is already intense owing to the activities of 'bancos de negócios', foreign bank representative offices, 'distribuidoras', brokerage firms and other intermediaries.

7.2.4   Advantages and disadvantages of the principal types of vehicles for foreign investors

In Table 7.5 we present a succinct and inexhaustive review of institutional/product options of primary interest to foreign investors. All of the options presented in Table 7.5 must be checked against evolving banking reform legislation, and are in any event subject to prior approval by the monetary authorities. Subsequently we will close the chapter with comments on different structures embracing foreign shareholders and the past experience in Brazil of foreign/local joint ventures or other partnership arrangements.

Table 7.5 Alternative development strategies in the Brazilian financial sector, principal advantages and disadvantages[5]

Strategy	Advantages	Disadvantages	Comments
• Acquisition of shareholding in existing conglomerate.	• Immediate market position. • Immediate earnings stream. • May be most acceptable alternative for debt/equity conversion. • Investment in related business. • Affords business diversification opportunities in, theoretically, several different product areas simultaneously.	• Ineffective management control possibilities. • Minimal control over profit accounting and distribution. • Market perception that most 'marriages' between local conglomerates and foreign banks have been unsuccessful. • Object of acquisition may not have competitive strength to survive a rapidly changing environment over the long term.	• See discussion of passive vs. active roles below. • Some principal disadvantages of acquisition can be avoided, depending, on what each party expects from the association.
• Acquisition of shareholding in start-up investment bank.	• Enables development of conglomerate and its business and strategic plans on cooperative basis between principal shareholders. • Agreement on product and operating plans facilitated, thus enhancing flexibility in response to changing market. • 'Goodwill' cost of entry	• Investment in staff and training. • Assumptions of overheads in other areas. • Same inadequate control over profits and profit distribution. • Market image and earnings stream would have to be developed.	• Several pre-operational investment banks are seeking foreign partners.

continued

Table 7.5 continued

Strategy	Advantages	Disadvantages	Comments
	presently declining.	• Greater competitive uncertainty than in other strategies.	
• Relative to the above: Passive foreign investor role.	• Moderate management and staff commitment. • Opportunity for leveraging relationship to attract own business. • Synergies for overall organisation of the foreign investor depending on skill of management committed.	• Absence of effective control over any important aspect of conglomerate management. • Generally unfavourable past experience.	• In any association arrangement. It is vital that the parties know and state clearly to each other what they wish to achieve, jointly and separately, from the association. Normally, this is not done.
Active foreign investor role	• Enhanced opportunities for developing business and synergies. • Opportunity for influencing activities in order to meet competitive challenges. • Enhanced but incomplete opportunities for control over profits and accounting.	• Difficulty in negotiating and administering management contract, whether on institutional, functional or product basis. • Experience of all attempts in this area has been largely (though not entirely) unsuccessful.	• Brazillian Companies Law, by affording inadequate protection to shareholders with less than voting control, is a natural impediment to the success of any minority acquisition.
• Acquisition of own license or authorisation to operate:	• Capability to develop own business from outset. • Ability to establish own business and synergy plan.	• Earnings stream will require at least one year to develop in all cases and possibly longer in an	• There is a separate set of arguments for and against these 3 types of institutions. Such

Investment bank Brokerage firm 'Distribuidora'		

- Local partners would to have to be identified with investment in place within 4 years. In many cases, foreign banks select silent partners from the fields of commerce and industry.
- In the case of the latter two institutions, minimum capital requirements are small to conduct basic types of business.
- Minimum capital is structured by the Central Bank in such a way as to permit step-by-step development instead of entering into a large number of product areas at the outset.
- Investment would probably be 'grandfathered' in event of nationalistic measures *vis-à-vis* foreign bank shareholdings.

- investment bank.
- Significant Foreign investor involvement in staffing, training, and management time.
- Detailed knowledge of certain markets and products required for senior management and staff.
- Central Bank approval may be delayed or not granted, in view of constitutional develoments.

- arguments are treated generically in this summary.
- The principal advantage of all three types of institutions is a function of control, management, and immediate, firm presence in the market. Such presence is not institutionalised in the case of representative office.
- To summarise:
  - An investment bank permits doing most types of banking business and 'merchant banking'.
  - A brokerage firm or 'distribuidora' affords most of the important product capabilities as an investment bank but with less capital and staff/management involvement.

continued

Table 7.5 continued

Strategy	Advantages	Disadvantages	Comments
• Broadening of the representative office function to emphasise 'merchant banking' and corporate finance products. Two variants: Expansion of an existing representative office. If acquisition is made, station a representative in the entity acquired or give foreign investor's director the responsibility for business development.	• Complements acquisition by adding product dimension which may not exist. • Enables development of foreign investor synergies and market opportunities independently from local partners. • Offers two business referral points: the foreign investor directly or the group in which it has made an investment. • Basing in acquired institution may suggest low overheads. • Staff and management commitments relatively small. • Basing in acquired institution may broaden range of contacts and sources of new business and market opportunities.	• Business referral agreement required to avoid 'crossed wires' if representation function is combined with acquisition. In this event, there may be conflicts of interest if the foreign investor's director is also business development representative. May be preferable to keep the two function (and corresponding remuneration) separate. • Product and operating limits and aspiration of acquired entity may interfere with referrals thereto. Entity acquired may have unsatisfactory referral/image promotion capability in product areas of interest to the foreign investor.	• Many of the 'disadvantages' cited are in the nature of problems which can arise in the event appropriate written understandings are not clarified with local partners. • There are presently very profitable business opportunities in the Brazilian market in which a foreign investor may wish to intensify its development separately from any of the other alternatives herein considered. This approach could be adopted immediately on the investor's own initiative.
• Institutionalisation of 'merchant banking' corporate finance	• Can be established within existing office structure, thus minimising overheads.	• Cannot manage mutual funds or Foreign Capital Conversion Funds, although	• There are several successful models for an active holding/investment

		company, among them, International Capital Corporation of American Express and Atlantic Capital Corporation, which has no foreign bank affiliation.
representation function by the incorporation of a holding/investment company, which might form part of an investor's global merchant banking network.	it can manage private portfolios in Brazil. • Does not provide direct access to important segments of the market, such as those involving securities, futures and commodities trading. • Substantiates presence in Brazil through specialised institution. • Earnings stream can be immediate, depending on products chosen and dynamism in placing them. • Acts as vehicle for investments under debt/equity programme or otherwise. • Image can be high or low profile at option SecPac. • Not subject to Central Bank regulation. • Affords capability to offer many products of interest to SecPac without costs and regulatory requirements relative to financial institutions. • Could form part of SecPac Latin American 'merchant banking' structure.	
• Establishment of a 'distribuidora' (or brokerage firm) with a specialised market niche (e.g. intermediation and	• Brazil's gold market is growing rapidly (trading averaging an estimated $60 million daily) but with few specialised participants.	• Disadvantages are the same as for any 'distribuidora' in terms of SecPac's commitment and need for control.	• This type of institution could be developed by SecPac (with local partners) separately from other acquisition

continued

Table 7.5 continued

Strategy	Advantages	Disadvantages	Comments
positioning in gold).	• Brazil's position of free world's 5th largest gold producer with over 70 tons of annual production suggests increasing importance of gold in financial sector activity. • Gold increasingly popular as investment instrument. Also used by Central Bank for certain types of remittances. • Bearer gold funds as investment vehicle for individuals and corporations being considered by Central Bank. Nominative gold funds already exist. • Due to thinness of real competition, specialised trading in gold is highly profitable. Little probability of crowding-out effect in the short run. • Vehicle can develop other financial products as appropriate.		alternatives, owing to the specialised nature of the business to be conducted. • The presentation herein assumes specialisation only in gold, owing to its 'related business' qualities and thus probable greater interest on the part of SecPac. • A separate study would be required to assess properly the feasibility of a specialised 'distribuidora' in view of a developeing market and SecPac synergies.

- Establishment of a holding company under Central Bank Circular 1–339 to make debt/equity conversion and other investments, which would be managed by a separate company. Holding company capital would be supplied by the foreign investor and/or other banks, and portfolio would be diversified like that of mutual fund but without composition restrictions imposed on such funds.
- The foreign investor could invest in its own vehicle or in a holding/investment company being formed with the capital of various foreign banks.
- The company would have a closed-end structure.

- Diversified risk.
- Risk dilution through participation of eventual partners in investments.
- Possibility for enchancement of return on funds permanently committed to Brazil.
- Portfolio could consist of relatively short-term investments outside the stock markets and not simply long-term venture or investment capital projects.

- If conversion funds are used, investor is locked in technically for 12 years, but may be able to negotiate shares overseas.
- May optimalise utilisation of conversion funds.
- Does not interfere with other investment plans of interest to the foreign investor.

- If the foreign investor acquires shares along with other banks in a holding company being formed, interest in control over investment decisions may not be satisfied by board membership and other protections.
- Discretionary authority of management company, in the event of minority participation, may be unsatisfactory.

- EquityPar has a structure identical to the one presented herein but with an operating philosophy oriented towards long-term investments. Risk diversification possibilities are thus relatively fewer.

7.2.5 Structures for foreign/local partnerships

There are several cases of foreign association with local financial institutions, and each situation is structured to serve the interests of the respective parties rather than to conform to established norms. The principal object of foreign shareholdings is the investment bank vehicle. However, major international institutions have invested in 'distribuidoras', brokerage firms and Circular 1.339 investment/holding companies.

Shareholdings vary significantly as to participation in capital and corresponding influence over management. Listed below are some of the most common types of arrangements:

• Small minority participations of several foreign banks in an investment bank forming part of a financial conglomerate (for example, Unibanco and Bradesco). The foreign shareholders exercise practically no management influence.
• 50/50 joint venture between foreign and local partners with strong foreign management.
• 50/50 joint venture with management of specific business and product areas divided between foreign and local partners.
• 50/50 joint venture in an investment bank which heads a sub-conglomerate of institutions in which foreign shareholding (direct or indirect) is permitted, such as consumer finance companies, leasing companies, savings and loan companies, and so forth.

The management contract can be constructed effectively to accord a strong management role to foreign partners interested in developing certain or all product areas. In this regard, it is vital that each partner clearly understand that conflicts can arise unnecessarily if respective territorial limits are not respected. The management contract, whether according full management authority to the foreign partners or dividing it with local partners, must not in any event be tantamount to a cession of effective voting control to foreign interests.

7.2.6 Overview of past experience with local/foreign associations

Experience with foreign/local associations in financial institutions in the past two decades has been mixed, with the number of failures relative to partnership expectations probably exceeding the number of successful joint ventures. Some associations have proved to be notably successful and profitable. When they are not, the reasons can generally be found in the factors listed below:

- failure of the potential partners to understand in detail their respective interests and objectives in forming an association;
- lack of a fundamental mutual understanding between the partners the role, powers and responsibilities of management;
- similar misunderstanding with respect to product areas to be developed and the tactics required to develop them;
- structural and organisational cultural factors in local institutions which resist the introduction of administrative techniques from abroad, product diversification, or other innovations;
- failure of the partners to recognise in advance the compatibility and limitations of synergistic interests;
- excessive expectations as to what contribution each partner could make to business development.

There has also been a case of outright fraud which caused significant losses to the foreign investor, as well as one in which the owners of the investment bank in which a foreign bank had recently made an investment proceeded to sell their entire financial group to other interests.

The factors enumerated above suggest that future partners in a Brazilian financial venture must think through carefully their respective interests and have clear strategic, tactical and synergistic objectives: and all this must be openly and successfully communicated between the partners. This orientation seems simplistic but is clearly more essential than market/competition studies, feasibility analyses, due diligence, acquisition audits, and other analytical techniques commonly employed.

NOTES

1. Data compiled by Américo Csengeri Netto.
2. Ibid.
3. As reported by the Bolsa Mercantil e de Futuros.
4. Expansion of table originally contributed by the author to '*Profile of Banking and Finance in Brazil*', published by Coopers & Lybrand in May 1986.
5. Material based on consulting report directed by the author with Coopers & Lybrand. Said report was prepared for a major international financial institution, which has approved its presentation in this work.

Part III
Financial Market Sectors

8 The Money Market

The Brazilian money market has developed rapidly since the early 1970s. In part this development can be attributed to the strenuous efforts of public sector and private sector agencies to promote the 'open market'. During the latter half of the 1970s especially, the Ministry of Finance operated in a most intelligent way in sponsoring legislation aimed at financial market development. Nevertheless problems appeared, and progress was hampered. At times prices surged ahead of projected inflation rates, yielding investors negative real returns in some money market assets. Persistent inflation placed a premium on shortening the maturities of money market instruments, as a defence tactic. Parallel shortenings of wages contracts and other patterns of price adjustment soon followed, magnifying tendencies towards market disequilibrium.

In this chapter we consider the money market in Brazil by first taking an overview of the economic environment. Here we consider the important parity relationships between interest rates, inflation, and exchange rate adjustments. Three integrated markets are considered in relation to one another (money market, gold market, black market for dollars). Considerable attention is given to the role of the Central Bank in the money market. The application of monetary correction is analysed, and the various money market instruments are considered in connection with their changing roles. Final sections focus on the futures market and foreign exchange market.

8.1 INTRODUCTION

8.1.1 Understanding the money market

The money market in Brazil has developed into a complex financial mechanism. Like money markets in other countries, it provides opportunities for liquidity adjustment at low cost. Unlike money markets in many other countries, it poses problems that are fairly unique to the Brazilian financial scene.

Special risks in the Brazilian money market stem from the following: (1) a high and changing rate of inflation; (2) possibility that at times a negative real return will be earned on some (non-indexed) money market assets; (3) the availability of indexed and non-indexed assets; (4) abrupt changes in government policy that affect returns on money market assets; and (5) limitations on residents in the use of external financial markets and foreign currency assets to hedge risks in the Brazilian financial markets.

At times in the past the Central Bank has appeared to lack the undisputed role of lender of last resort and ultimate credit control agency. In other sections of this book we have described the complex relationships operating between the Central Bank and other financial and policy-making agents (Finance Ministry, Banco do Brasil). Improvements made between 1986 and 1988 in the way in which the Central Bank and other agencies control credit include:

1. Separation of the fiscal budget from the monetary budget. Related to this was creation of a new office of National Treasury Secretary, responsible for formulation of the fiscal budget.
2. Tighter operation of the 'movement accounts' so that the Banco do Brasil can no longer independently inject credit into the financial system.
3. Tighter management of the special credit windows that in the past permitted uncontrolled flows of credit to coffee producers and other sectors.
4. Inclusion of fiscal expenditures (including transfers) in the fiscal budget. Until 1987 these were included only in the monetary budget. Now they are subject to tighter budgetary controls.[1]
5. Daily transfer of national treasury reserves from Banco do Brasil to the Central Bank. These funds come from the tax collections of the federal government, and from other receipts.

The pace of inflation can influence the extent to which money market participants are willing to extend (or shorten) maturities at which they transact. For example, between 1986 and 1987 the pace of inflation was accelerating. This was due to the price freeze maintained during most of 1986, but relaxed and eventually broken in 1987. The resulting acceleration in inflation caused money market participants to shorten their transaction maturities. This results from the uncertainties they faced when (1) interest rate levels shift rapidly on a monthly basis; (2) the Central Bank adopts a flexible monetary policy; and (3) substantial capital losses can be experienced if there are negative real interest rates. Consequently, in mid-1987, there were substantial shifts of funds between assets earning the overnight rate and 30-day rates of interest. In June–July 1987 these shifts involved funds going from savings accounts (receiving interest based on overnight rates of interest but accumulated for 30 days or longer) to gold, dollars, stocks and money market assets based on overnight rates of interest.

During the period 1986–8 the money market has focused its attention on the reference interest rate at the shortest maturity – the overnight rate. This overnight rate is payable on government securities and other money market assets. In the three-year period referred to above it has been virtually impossible to establish sizeable transactions volume or loan contracts at longer-term maturities, because of the apprehensions of market participants. These apprehensions may be traced to uncertainties of government policy, inflation, changes in indexation. Commitments at longer term are risky. But the LBC/LFT overnight rate is financed every day by the Central Bank, and the risk is low.

The concentration of the money market into the single maturity (overnight rate) has reduced flexibility and operational choices for market participants.[2] This problem has been recognised by the Central Bank. In the first half of 1988 the Central Bank undertook on several occasions to sell OTN in the open market. This was intended to 'develop the money market' at longer maturities (six months in this case). This effort met with limited success. In two cases the Central Bank was able to accomplish open market sales by offering repurchase agreements, therefore not locking in the market participants.

This strategy of offering repurchase agreements to investors in Treasury securities was announced by the Central Bank, and implemented aggressively in June–July 1988, with the objective of extending maturities at which investors would make commitments, and increasing the volume of trading. At this time the Central Bank was providing repurchase facilities at 83 day maturities.[3]

8.1.2 Important parity relationships

The Brazilian money market development has been profoundly affected by four factors: (1) alternating waves of higher and lower inflation; (2) application of monetary correction to encourage domestic saving and promote the market for government securities; (3) the role of the government in achieving financial intermediation, thereby influencing mobilisation of domestic financial resources; and (4) the ability of money market participants to acquire assets denominated in different 'currencies'. These currencies include the following:

1. financial assets protected by monetary correction;
2. financial assets not protected by monetary correction;
3. gold or financial assets backed by gold;
4. black market dollars.

The preceding suggests that Brazilian money market development has been an extremely complex process. This is very close to the truth.

Not all would agree that these four factors (that have profoundly affected money market development) have worked at maximum efficiency. Whereas the government and financial institutions controlled by the government have played an important role in intermediating and mobilising capital funds, some would argue that this has produced undesired results. In effect, government financing and mobilisation of capital has tended to 'crowd out' allocations of capital that otherwise might flow to private sector uses. This can be observed from Table 8.1. The largest share of funds was allocated to federal and state government securities (47 per cent combined). The large share going to savings deposits should be examined with skepticism, since savings deposits in part are specified by Central Bank regulations to certain end-allocations. In effect, the only category of any magnitude freely available to private sector allocation is term deposits (15 per cent of total).

To understand this money market we must state the principal operating rules which follow from the preceding. These operating rules we shall call 'parity relationships'. The parity relationships are nothing more than fundamental relationships concerning how financial market variables behave under conditions of price level and interest rate uncertainty. The principal operating rules can be expressed as follows:

1. The nominal interest rate is a function of price level changes. In Brazil, given higher inflation, there will be correspondingly higher nominal interest rates.
2. The exchange rate adjustment is a function of price level change. In this connection, Brazil has wisely followed the gradual or 'crawling peg' model.
3. For domestic investors, the real interest rate can be determined by adjusting the nominal rate for price level changes.

Table 8.1   Percentage shares of non-monetary financial assets

	December 1987	May 1988
(1) Savings deposits	36.2	37.6
(2) Term deposits	15.6	15.1
(3) Letras de Cambio	1.3	0.9
(4) Real estate securities	0.0	0.0
(5) Federal government securities*	39.9	39.8
(6) Securities of state governments*	7.0	6.6
(7) Total	100.0	100.0

* Excludes obligations of Central Bank.
Source: Andima, *Retrospectiva 1988*, January–June 1988, Assessoria Tecnica, p. 17.

4. For foreign investors, the real interest rate can be determined by adjusting the nominal interest rate for price level changes, and for exchange rate changes.

According to these parity relationships, the National Monetary Council is obliged to allow a level of monetary correction on financial assets equal to or above the price level change, if money market investors are to be expected to hold these financial assets. In addition, in the corporate sector Brazilian affiliates of foreign companies may be expected to shift their short-term borrowing between domestic (Brazilian) and foreign sources based upon the relation between interest rates (domestic and foreign) and the expected pace of exchange rate adjustment. Brazil uses (since 1983–4) a flexible exchange rate system which tends to keep the pace of exchange rate adjustment fairly closely in line with the recent (and expected) domestic inflation rate. But there are leads and lags between the two.

The Brazilian financial systen is a relatively closed one, but there are international linkages and the Central Bank must keep the incentives dampened for irregular flows of funds. In this connection the parity relationships play an important role.

8.1.3   Three integrated markets

The above discussion of parity relationships suggests that a complex financial market mechanism is in operation in Brazil. This market mechanism is closely monitored and regulated by the Central Bank, so that money market interest rates can be 'adjusted' to the rate of inflation, thereby yielding positive or negative real rates of interest. Further the system is largely a closed one where the foreign exchange rates are set by the monetary authorities conditioned in large part by the pace at which domestic prices are rising. Given a closed foreign exchange market, participants are free to trade cruzados for dollars at price levels consonant with the guidelines established by the Central Bank. In short, the Central Bank is free to have the cruzado/ dollar rate of exchange decline, running ahead of or behind the rate of domestic inflation. Nevertheless the general practice is to keep these two variables (inflation and cruzado depreciation) fairly closely related to one another. At times the need to maintain balance of payments equilibrium can reduce policy alternatives available to the Central Bank.[4]

The Central Bank regulates the gold market so that the cruzado price premium on gold is in line with the basic (international) market. The Central Bank is always ready to accumulate gold, and inevitably companies that sell gold in the market find the Central Bank on the other side of the market. This seems to translate into a price premium based on the cruzado/dollar exchange rate (16–25 per cent in 1987). Gold trading is free inside Brazil, but export is not permitted. Gold trading is facilitated by several specialised market systems, including Andima (SINO), and the futures exchanges. These are described in later sections. Companies often accumulate gold as a hedge against currency depreciation and inflation. Dealings in gold can be expected to influence the black market for dollars.[5]

To understand the role of the Central Bank in stabilising the money market, we must first consider its role in three integrated market sectors:

1. Free market in gold. This is a real commodity market, based on a high level of domestic production. The price of gold in Brazil is an important barometer of confidence in the financial market system, the cruzado, and government policy. In Brazil the cruzado price of gold can fluctuate widely, since there are no official linkages between the domestic and international gold markets.
2. Black market in dollars. This can be an important market for those that want to hedge against inflation, especially at times when financial market conditions become less stable. The premium on black market dollars can be considerably larger than the premium for gold. For example in the period April–May 1988 the premium

on gold was 18–20 per cent, while the premium on black market dollars was 32–36 per cent.[6] However by mid-July 1988 the premiums on gold and dollars respectively were 39 per cent and 44 per cent.[7]

3. Regulated money market. There are several different aspects to Central Bank regulation of the money market, which are discussed in considerable detail in the following section. This regulation includes Central Bank control of real interest rate levels, Central Bank management of nominal interest rate levels on various financial assets, and Central Bank open market operations which aim at regulating credit conditions and overall money market liquidity.

The Central Bank must be concerned with the functioning of all three of the above described markets. The following basic guidelines have generally been considered by the Central Bank in this process.

1. The Central Bank cannot let the domestic (cruzado) gold price deviate too much from the international (dollar) price (calculated at the official parity) or this will reflect adversely on the currency rate. An excessive premium in terms of the cruzado price would imply an overvalued cruzado on the foreign exchange market.

2. Dealings in gold indirectly influence the black market for dollars. The Central Bank must deal in gold to prevent an excessive premium from developing. An excessive premium on dollars (in terms of cruzados) would imply an overvalued cruzado on the foreign exchange market. Also this could trigger speculative dealings that could exacerbate the situation.

3. A regulated money market based on incentives the Central Bank wants to have operate to attract money flows to sectors of the financial markets considered to be in need of liquidity. Funds flow relatively freely between money market assets, savings deposits, the stock market, the market for gold assets, and the black market for dollars. The 'free flow' is desirable, and facilitates adjustments in the allocation of loanable funds. In addition, these flows can add to or reinforce the pressures the Central Bank is injecting into the money market.

4. The Central Bank cannot allow the premium on gold to be too high, or it will lead to accelarated imports, and delayed exports. This will make it more difficult to manage the foreign exchange position of Brazil.

5. In Brazil as in other countries the corporate sector plays an important role in the money market. Companies can buy gold as an inflation and currency hedge. Therefore, the Central Bank must balance the incentives between holding gold and money market assets most carefully. Failure to do so could result in large shifts of corporate liquidity to gold and other inflation hedges, causing a tightening and illiquidity in the money market.

8.2   ROLE OF CENTRAL BANK IN MONEY MARKET

8.2.1   Outstanding government debt

In this discussion the government securities market refers to debt obligations issued by the federal government and the Central Bank. This includes several types of securities, namely Treasury bills (LTN), Treasury bonds (OTN), Central Bank bills (LBC), and the Treasury financing bill (LFT) introduced in January 1988. Amounts of these securities outstanding are indicated in Table 8.2.

Total federal government debt grew from CZ$3991 billion in December 1987 to CZ$12 294 billion in June 1988 (Table 8.2). These amounts are roughly equivalent to US$50 billion, or 18 per cent of Brazilian GDP. This excludes Central Bank bills. At these same dates the amounts of Central Bank bills outstanding and held by the public were CZ$1633 billion and CZ$1847 billion, respectively. To understand the data on government debt, we must distinguish clearly between that issued by the Central Bank and that issued by the federal government (National Treasury). This is further complicated by the federal government selling debt securities directly to the Central Bank, which may in turn sell part of these to the public.

A matrix of federal government and Central Bank debt issued, and the amounts held respectively by the Central Bank and the public, is presented in Table 8.3. This provides a somewhat clearer picture of the respective roles played by the federal government and Central Bank in the money market. As can be seen, federal government issues outstanding at June 1988 was CZ$12 294 billion, consisting of CZ$5567 billion LFT, and CZ$6727 billion OTN. A major part of these securities (CZ$6543 billion) was held by the Central Bank. In addition, Central Bank issued securities outstanding at June 1988 totalled CZ$1847 billion. In effect, Central Bank sale of its own securities absorbs market liquidity. By contrast, Central Bank pur-

Table 8.2 Domestic Federal Government and Central Bank debt (CZ$ billion)

Month	LFT		LBC	LTN		OTN		Total		
	Central Bank Portfolio	Held by Banks & Others	Held by Banks & Others	Central Bank Portfolio	Held by Banks & Others	Central Bank Portfolio	Held by Banks & Others	Central Bank Portfolio	Held by Banks & Others	Total[1]
Dec. 1986	–	–	203	328	8	420	149	748	359	1 107
Dec. 1987	–	–	1 633	646	41	2 711	592	3 357	2 267	3 991
Mar. 1988	1 319	698	1 773	–	–	3 786	868	5 105	3 339	6 671
June 1988	2 502	3 065	1 847	–	–	4 041	2 686	6 544	7 599	12 294

[1] From 1987, calculation of the total was changed by the Central Bank, by excluding the LBC from the Federal Public debt.
Sources: Andima, *Carta Andima*, April 1988, p. 14; *Retrospectiva 1988*, Jan.–June 1988, p. 1.

Table 8.3   Matrix of Federal Government and Central Bank debt, June 1988 (CZ$ billion)

Issuer		Investor		
		Central Bank	*Public*	*Total*
Federal	LFT	2 502	3 065	5 567
Government	OTN	4 041	2 686	6 727
Central Bank	LBC	—	1 847	1 847
TOTAL		6 543	7 598	14 141

Source: Table 8.2.

chase of federal government securities tends to add to liquidity. Sale of federal government securities to the public largely may be interpreted as shifting purchasing power from the private sector to the public sector.

The dynamics of the composition of government securities is reflected by the data in Table 8.2. Here we can see that LFT were only first issued in 1988. Beginning in 1988 all LTN had been retired or purchased by the Central Bank. Also, the Central Bank is expected to discontinue issuance of LBC.

A number of policy and technical factors interact to control the relative amounts of these government securities that are held by the public (outside the Central Bank), and held in the portfolio of the Central Bank. These include: (1) Central Bank credit control and funding requirements; (2) Treasury financing requirements; and (3) the ability and willingness of the institutional and individual investor to hold these securities.[8]

Central Bank requirements

The Central Bank needs funds for its specific operations. In the past these have included agricultural priority loans, export finance, and sectoral financing programmes. Interest rates on existing debt are included in this, which means that liquidity management and the consequent level of interest rates play a role. This requirement does not necessarily reflect open market operations designed to control liquidity of the financial system. In addition, the Central Bank manages its own portfolio, including holdings of OTN and LTN. In 1986–88 the Central Bank was issuing LBC for liquidity management and to influence overall conditions in the money market.

Treasury requirements

The Fiscal Budget was revised in 1987, and the new office of National Treasury Secretary was created. With these changes the Fiscal Budget includes transfers (subsidies and fiscal incentives for state enterprises and development banks). Effective 1 January 1988, a complete budgetary unification was carried out. The government fiscal budget now includes all government sponsored development operations. At the time of writing plans were being made to index the federal budget, to take effect in 1989.

The government cannot grant loans at lower cost than those involved in the fiscal budget. The Central Bank is prohibited from supplying resources to government credit operations and expanding public debt beyond what is provided for in Congress. Central Bank operations in the government securities market are restricted to the management of its own portfolio, and issue-redemption of LBCs. Management of the public debt and government credit programs has been transferred to the Minister of Finance.

Investor requirements

Banks and other financial institutions have been subject to various regulations concerning their investments in government securities. At times bank holdings of government securities were mandated. Pension funds have been subject to specific limitations on their portfolio holdings of various types of investments, with government securities treated as a residual category. Individual investors have displayed shifting attitudes toward government securities. For example, in May 1987 five different new issues of OTN were offered to the public, with maturities ranging between six and 24 months.[9] The Central Bank purchased all of the securities offered in these five issues. The non-acceptance of the public was due to the price freeze and the related suspension of application of monetary correction to OTN (in the period March 1986 to March 1987). This was a very costly change in the rules for investors holding OTN.

8.2.2 Market for new issues of public debt securities

Until 1975 individuals wanting to invest in government securities had to go to the Banco do Brasil which operated as an agent of the government in issuing new securities. Treasury bills had been intro- duced to the market five years earlier. Over the past decade and a half the market for public debt securities has developed and reflects many important improvements. The Central Bank auctions government securities on a regular basis. In 1987–8 there were weekly auctions of LBC with the auction on Tuesday and settlement on Wednesday.[10] LBC were first issued in 1986 during the period of the Cruzado Plan.

Shift from LBC To OTN

In July 1987 there was a shift from using the LBC as the indexor, to using the OTN. In August 1987 the LBC rate of return was the lowest rate in the money market. The LBC is an average rate. As such the overnight rate on LBC is a reference or indicator rate of interest. In this regard it plays a role similar to that of the New York prime rate or London base rate. LBCs were issued for original maturities of 182 or 273 days with a Wednesday redemption, and a new issue each week. Issued for 1000 cruzados, the LBC accumulates value each day. There is no explicit monetary correction on LBCs.

During 1987 two problems developed in the Central Bank issuance of LBC. First, the market found it difficult to interpret the changes in amount of LBC issued from one period to another. Was the change in volume intended to finance the Treasury need, or to control market liquidity? Second, there was a technical problem in using the LBC both as an indexor of inflation, and as a means of regulating credit and market liquidity. This dual function of LBC, as indexor and instrument of monetary policy, represented a conflict.[11] Since the Central Bank could neither control inflation nor predict its rate, investors would earn varying amounts of overnight interest on LBCs, which could be above or below the inflation rate for that time period.

On 1 July 1987 this system was revised. From that date onward the OTN became the indexor. This freed the LBC to be utilised as a means of influencing market liquidity via Central Bank open market operations and repurchase agreements with investors in the market. A more active monetary policy could be implemented, giving the Central Bank the opportunity to regulate the rate on LBCs above or below the inflation rate.[12]

In 1988 the LFT was introduced, with regular sales of this security in the government securities market. LFT were being used to substitute for LBC. Like LBC, the LFT must be financed daily by the Cental Bank. The Central Bank must give funds to the market every day to finance its needs. At the beginning of 1988 the market had become oversold, as the Central Bank was trying to implement a more flexible (and at times tighter) policy. The open market did not have the capacity at the end of the day to close its position and therefore the Central Bank would have to give funds to the market. In this respect the Central Bank found that trying to be flexible in its policy was most difficult. During most of calendar 1988 it could be said that monetary policy was in accord with the liquidity needs of the system, not the inflation needs.

In mid-1988 the government and the Central Bank were attempting to make the government securities market more flexible. New securities appeared in 1988, including the LFT, the OTN Cambial (to give Brazilian exporters an exchange rate hedging facility), and OTN Fiscal at three month maturity. Also plans were under way to auction LTN, with the competitive auction results determining the interest rate. Finally, the Central Bank was offering repurchase facilities to induce money market participants to deal in longer maturity OTN.

Executive Act no. 2376

Beginning on 25 November 1987 several important changes were introduced to the government securities market. These were included in Executive Act no. 2376. First, a change was initiated in the relationship between the National Treasury and Central Bank. This measure required that the internal securities debt of the federal government could be increased only to cover deficits in the General Budget of the federal government through legislative authority.[13]

Second, this Executive Act created the Treasury Financing Bill (LFT). This instrument has the purpose of supplying the resources required for coverage of the budget deficit, or for credit operations involving anticipated revenues with the states and municipalities, within the limits defined by the Congress.

Issue of LFT commenced on 1 January 1988, with the volume limited to the amount specified in the Federal Budget. The LFT substitutes for the LBC. LFT possesses most of the characteristics of LBC, with the exception that the maturity term is unlimited, and therefore can be extended by the authorities as issued based upon current market conditions. It is expected that earnings on LFT will keep up with the negotiated overnight rate. Creation of LFT is directly related to the task of obtaining resources for the National Treasury.

The Central Bank possesses its own securities portfolio to make use of in overall credit control, and in the conduct of open market operations. As the LBC reaches maturity they will be replaced by LFT.

Finally, with respect to Executive Act No. 2376, the OTN may be issued with authorisation of the Minister of Finance. In such cases creditors will have an option at redemption between readjustment of its value according to indexing based on the rates of change in the consumer price index (defined by IBGE, the national agency responsible for data collection), or based on the earnings of the LFT. Aside from this, interest earnings on the OTN remain at a level of 6 per cent a year over monetary correction.

8.2.3 Central Bank open market operations

General nature of operations

Through its open market operations the Central Bank plays a crucially important role. In this connection the following three Central Bank activities are closely interrelated:

1. To project the inflation rate. This is required to anticipate the nominal interest rate required on money market paper. The nominal rate must cover the inflation rate, but also provide for a real return if investors are to be attracted to hold money market paper.
2. To control market liquidity. This is accomplished via a 24 dealer institutional system, through which liquidity is added to the market or subtracted. These open market operations are the focus of this section.
3. To set overnight rates. This is carried with a view toward offering a controlled real return to investors. This situation was to be changed late in 1988 when the LTN auctions take place. LTN auctions allow the market to determine the interest rate.

Item (3) above is a controversial point. As indicated already, federal and state government securities make up respectively 39.4 per cent and 6.6 per cent of total non-monetary financial assets.

The market for public debt securities includes the 'market' and 'extramarket'. In the 'market' non-governmental entities buy and sell, changing their holdings of government securities. In the 'extra-market', government entities (government enterprises, government banks, and state banks) change the amount of ownership they hold in government securities. These changes reflect the desire to accomplish short-term liquidity shifts and the need to make adjustments by buying or selling government securities.

With respect to the 'extramarket', every public sector company has an account with the Central Bank, which is used for settlement of transactions in government securities. In this 'extramarket' the largest 20 state enterprises generally are responsible for 80 per cent of money movements (BNDES, Petrobras, CVRD). In addition, state enterprise export-import transactions influence money market liquidity. For example, Petrobras can make foreign purchases and/or sales which in the international clearings and settlements affect liquidity of the domestic financial market. These transactions are quite large.

With respect to the 'market', there are 24 authorised dealers, through which the Central Bank conducts operations. These include commercial banks, investment banks, and securities brokers. The Central Bank trading desk carries out its transactions in government securities through these authorised dealers.

There are approximately 800 financial institutions of various types operating in the money market, including banks, financial intermediaries, investment funds, and various types of financial firms and specialised investors. In the period 1987–8 the 'extramarket' approximately equalled the 'market' in trading volume. Two decades ago the 'extramarket' was much larger.

In its daily operations the Central Bank must develop an operating strategy. Given this strategy, the Central Bank trading desk makes a daily 'go-around', keeping in close touch with the market. The trading desk operates with approximately 10 traders. Five deal with public sector institutions, and five deal with private sector institutions (Bradesco, Itau). The public sector traders deal with Banco do Brasil, Petrobras, Eletrobrás, and Nuclebrás, among others. There are approximately 500 public sector companies, all of which maintain deposit accounts at the Central Bank for settlement of money market transactions and payments. Transactions through these accounts and changes in the level of these deposits are closely monitored by the Central Bank. Most important, the Central Bank monitors the effects of transactions through these deposit accounts on market liquidity, so that it can stabilize the market (defensive open market operations).

Clearings and settlements of transactions in public sector securities (including debt issues of states) are handled through SELIC (Sistema

Especial de Liquidação e Custodia), a special system for custody and settlements. This is a computerised control system for securities custody and payments. It is managed by a unit of the Central Bank.

Market operations

Central Bank open market operations are conducted in the 'market' and 'extramarket'. At the same time, these operations can be carried out in the primary market as well as in the secondary market. In the 'extramarket' the Central Bank deals for the account of the large state enterprises. In 1988 the state banks, Caixa Economica Federal (CEF), and Banco do Brasil became classified as 'market'. Therefore they carry out their own operations in the open market, adding considerable weight to the transactions carried out competitively.

In any month open market operations can represent a relatively small percentage of the domestic public debt. For example, in May 1987 the CZ\$36 300 million in transactions represented slightly more than 1.5 per cent of domestic public debt outstanding (including LBC).

Repurchase agreements

Closely tied in with the general scope of open market operations are Central Bank repurchase-resale agreements. In the case of repurchases–resales the Central Bank is operating in the market *vis-à-vis* corporate, bank, and other investors. As can be noted in Table 8.4, repurchase–resale agreements are carried out in a range of instruments, including OTN, LBC, state and local government securities, and bank certificates of deposit (CDB). Repurchases and resales affect the level of money market liquidity, and also add to market volume and the degree of market liquidity available in each type of instrument.

In the period referred to in Table 8.4 the volume of repurchase activity conducted in LBC was substantial, exceeding all other categories. Repurchases in state and local government securities and CDBs also were high in volume, indicating a willingness on the part of the Central Bank to liquify these market sectors as well. In the case of all four instruments, most of the volume of repurchase–resale agreements was carried for one-day maturity.

Major participants are in the first instance commercial banks, investment banks, and securities firms. Close behind in volume of transactions in this market are non-financial corporations. Only in

Table 8.4   Central Bank repurchase–resale agreements with the money market, 3 August 1987 (million cruzados)

| | Repurchases | | | |
Maturity	OTN	LBC	State & Local	CDB
1 day	29 561	752 979	187 458	160 831
2–60 days	1 121	7 560	4 712	2 875
Over 60 days	–	17	18	197
Other	114	2 112	594	5 207
TOTAL	CZ30 796	CZ762 668	CZ192 782	CZ169 110
(Millions				
US$)[1]	(616)	(15 253)	(3 856)	(3 382)

| | Resales | | | |
	OTN	LBC	State & Local	CDB
1 day	15 433	201 654	126 640	32 152
2–60 days	860	150	1	118
Over 60 days	–	–	–	–
Other	–	–	600	3
Total	CZ16 293	CZ201 804	CZ127 241	CZ32 273
(Millions				
US$)[1]	(326)	(4 036)	(2 545)	(645)

[1] Estimated at the exchange rate of 50 cruzados per US dollar.
Source: Central Bank of Brazil.

the case of CDBs do non-financial corporations account for the largest part of market activity.

8.2.4   Operation of SELIC–CETIP

The decade of the 1970s witnessed a major expansion of the market for government securities.[14] To permit the market mechanisms of registration, clearing, and settlement of securities transactions to keep pace with this expansion the Central Bank and Andima agreed to implement a system for this purpose. In 1974 these two agencies jointly established a tele-processing system to be used by the open market for registration and control of transactions in public debt securities. This new system provided more efficient, cost effective, and more secure dealings.

Beginning in 1978 the system provided for electronic trading and custody of LTN, eliminating the need to issue checks to settle transactions in public securities. In 1980 this system was applied to government bonds and other securities (state and local government securities). At this point SELIC was initiated.

The Special System for Settlement and Custody (SELIC)[15] consists of processing, by use of computers, the buying and selling operations of public debt securities conducted in the open market. This system permits the transfer of securities on the day in which the transaction is carried out. Funds settlements take place on the following day. With this system, the principal risks (falsification of documents, and use of checks without funds) are removed. Settlements are effected with simple debits and credits to the accounts of the financial institutions and their clients, eliminating need for transfers of cheques drawn on bank accounts and physical securities. The custody of public securities is under the total control of the Central Bank, and is delegated exclusively to the commercial banks. Securities brokers provide the necessary information concerning purchases and sales of securities to the respective banks involved in paying/receiving funds, and in clearing securities ownership transfers.

The excellent results obtained with SELIC with respect to public debt securities led to the consideration of establishing a similar facility for private sector debt issues (including bank certificates of deposit, 'letras de cambio', and interbank deposits). As a result the Center for Custody of Private Securities (CETIP)[16] was established, to provide an identical mechanism for the clearing, settlement, and custody of transactions in debt securities issued by financial institutions. In the period 1986–8 the CETIP system was expanded to include computerised trading of shares traded over-the -counter, gold and debentures. These facilities are described in the following section, which discusses the role and activities of Andima.

SIMA, SND and SINO

In the period 1986–8 Andima established computerised trading facilities for shares traded over-the-counter, debentures and gold. These trading facilities operate through CETIP, and were put into place based on a perceived need for more efficient and secure operations in the open market. The three facilities are described very briefly in Table 8.5.

SIMA came into being in 1986, at a time when (1) the stock exchanges were buoyant, and (2) it was recognised that increased opportunity should be given to expanding the capitalisation of

Table 8.5 New facilities for computer transactions in shares, debentures and gold

(a) SIMA	Sistema Integrado de Mercado Aberto	1986	Provides information and transaction facility for trading over-the-counter shares. Shares are registered for trading, encompassing registration of trades and custody of securities.
(b) SND	Sistema Nacional de Debentures	1988	Provides facility for trading debentures which are registered in the system. Computerised trading provides for negotiation, custody, financial settlements and provision of information.
(c) SINO	Sistema Nacional de Ouro	1988	Provides facility for trading gold. Gold is deposited with an institution, and buyers and sellers carry out electronically administered trading, settlement and changes in ownership.

Source: Andima.

smaller companies whose shares are traded mainly on the over-the-counter market. SIMA follows the pattern of the NASDAQ system in New York, which has allowed for a substantial increase in trading of over-the-counter securities. SIMA permits low-cost trading, provides more information, and can lead to the opening of capital of small-and medium-size companies in Brazil. The system electronically completes purchases and sales, administers dividends, and facilitates settlements and payments through custodian banks. It provides for automated negotiation, financial settlement, and custody of the shares registered to be traded.

SND came into being in 1988, at a time when companies in Brazil were finding it difficult to finance operations by issue of debentures. The debenture market has been slow in growing, due to several types of problems discussed in the following chapter. SND should provide a low cost, secure , and efficient facility for trading of debentures, thereby making them more liquid and more attractive to investors. Only standardised-type debentures can be traded in the system. In this respect debentures must conform to Resolution 1401, Article 2 with respect to their maturity, interval between interest payments, and timing of monetary correction.

SINO came into being in 1988, at a time when inflation was accelerating and the premium on parallel market dollars was rising to the 40–50 per cent range. Trading in gold (at sight and at futures) on the futures markets in Brazil was expanding. Consequently a new trading market facility had become of much greater importance. Given the fact that Brazil is the worlds fifth largest producer of gold, introduction of an electronic trading, settlement, and custody system provides important savings in transaction and holding costs. Participants in the market include commercial banks, investment banks, 'corretoras', 'distribuidoras', the exchanges on which gold can be traded, and special clients. Gold is deposited in a depository affiliated with the SINO system. The custody operation is of a simple form, by computer. Changes in holdings are made automatically by electronic signal, with no need physically to transport gold and disrupt its security position in the depository.

8.2.5 Andima

Andima is the National Association of Open Market Institutions. This organisation has an operational and headquarters office in Rio, and also operates an office in São Paulo. As a private association, it enjoys the support of over 310 member banks, financial institutions, and brokers and dealears that operate actively in the open market (almost synonymous with money market).

Objectives

With the surge of trading in the open market in the 1970s a group of financial institutions decided to create an entity destined to give the market an improved technical structure and logistical capacity. Andima is operated much like a private sector institution, without profit objectives. It provides services that benefit the following groups: (1) bank and non-bank financial institutions trading and investing in the open market; (2) individual investors who can carry out investment transactions at lower cost, and with more complete information; and (3) industrial companies seeking to open their capital, and finance their growth requirements. The objectives of Andima are as follows:

1. To develop relations among institutions which operate in the open market.
2. To bring the legitimate interests of the market to the attention of public officials.

3. To stimulate study and research of a technical nature, concerning the functioning of the open market.
4. To provide the services required for the use of institutions in the open market.
5. To maintain an interchange of knowledge with other entities that have similiar interests, national and international.
6. To organise, co-ordinate, and present programmes concerning the technical operation of the open market.
7. To edit and publish books, journals, and other studies compatible with the broad objectives of Andima.
8. To maintain an efficient documentation sector relating to the topics to be consulted concerning the open market.
9. To administer and operate SIMA and the other market trading facilities, needed to assure an efficient functioning of the open market.

Services

Money market dealing institutions obtain the following general services from Andima:

1. Daily information concerning interest rates, and overnight rates on various types of money market paper.
2. Information on daily trading volume, by types of paper.
3. Operation of an automatic computer trading facility, by which money market trading is facilitated.

Publications

Andima publishes and disseminates much information on money market matters. These publications include (1) *Carta Andima*, a monthly report which includes considerable statistical information concerning the open market (Table 8.6); (2) daily and weekly releases of information covering volume of transactions, interest rates and market developments; (3) *Retrospectiva*, published twice-yearly covering developments in the financial markets, fiscal policy, statistics on public debt, changes in the monetary base, price indexes, interest rates and exchange rates; (4) *INFO*, a computerised on-line information system which permits market participants to obtain information in a few seconds; (5) periodic summaries of open market legislation; and (6) *Jornal do Mercado*, a system of teleprocessed information provided through CETIP terminals.

Table 8.6   Information provided by Andima for members.[1]

---

1. Indicators of liquidity.
    Bank reserves, rediscounts, free reserves.
2. Interest rates.
    Overnight financing rates, financing rates in the Central Bank 'go around'. Reference rates on federal and state debt issues.
3. Estimated factors influencing money market liquidity and bank reserves.
    Cruzado amounts to be transferred to and from special government and social accounts and funds, tax payment dates, government securities issues.
4. Overnight rate on LBC, inflation and real interest rate.
5. National Treasury Bonds.
    Public offering, maturity of OTN, value of OTN in the market.
6. National Treasury Bills.
    Prices and yields on primary offerings of LTN. Trading volume.
7. Letras do Banco Central: LBC (Obligations of Central Bank).
    Primary offering, price and yield, reference rates on LBC, open market operations by Central Bank.
8. Domestic public debt.
    Central Bank transactions in market and extramarket, total debt by type security, Central Bank holdings as percentage total, average maturity of debt, state and local debt.
9. Other information relating to the market, including price indices, monetary base, means of payments, exchange rates, investments, and other market sectors.

---

[1]Provided in *Carta Andima* monthly, and more frequently in daily and weekly information releases.

8.3   FINANCIAL INSTITUTIONS IN THE MONEY MARKET

8.3.1   Regulation of financial institution operations

The Central Bank regulates the operations and liabilities of banks and other financial institutions concerning ownership of debt securities in the open market. In connection with this, it has issued various resolutions and circulars. The Central Bank has a mix of objectives and reasons in supervising operations in the open market. These range from fear of excessive leverage on the part of banks and securities firms, to the need to ensure that strong dealer institutions operate in the market, and to concern that the market may become overly dependent on one or another group of institutions for its support and liquidity. In addition to the above considerations, there are the questions of appropriate level of risk assumption for deposit-taking institutions, and desire to promote the development of a dynamic and flexible money market system.

Prominent in the regulation applied by the Central Bank are limits on leverage, and minimum capital requirements. On 30 January 1986 Resolution No. 1088 was issued by the CMN, giving the Central Bank authority to regulate the obligations of financial institutions in the market for fixed-income securities.[17] According to regulations annexed to Resolution 1088, several types of market operations were considered to fall under the intended jurisdiction.[18] These include obligations to repurchase with maturity at a future date, and obligations to buy or sell in the future.

Repurchase transactions and trading in financial futures have been growing rapidly, adding to the depth of the money market. While the Central Bank welcomes this, it also recognises certain risks in excessive growth, and in high concentrations of exposure to changes in market conditions. For these reasons there have been numerous regulatory changes in this area since 1986.

Operations subject to Resolution 1088 (and related regulations) cover future and repurchase transactions (excluding outright spot) in the following securities which are registered in the Sistema Especial de Liquidação e Custódia (SELIC) or in the Central de Custódia e de Liquidação Financeiro de Títulos (CETIP): OTN, LTN, securities of states and localities, bank certificates of deposit, debentures, 'letras de cambio', 'letras imobiliárias' (debt supported by claims on real estate), and other securities which will be authorised by the Central Bank. Central Bank Circular No. 1270 (29 December 1987) added the newly authorised LFT to this list of covered securities.[19] Financial institutions covered by Resolution No 1088 include commercial banks, investment banks, 'sociedades corretoras' and 'sociedades destribuidoras'.

At the time of writing the latest set of regulations concerning limits on leverage were included in Circular 1319, issued on 8 June 1988. Two sets of leverage limits were specified in Circular 1319. The first applies to institutions with capital of at least 100 000 OTN, and the second to institutions with capital of at least 50 000 OTN.[20] With respect to the first group, the overall limit on leverage was set at 30 times capital. In addition, separate limits applied as follows: holdings of OTN two times capital; holdings of state and local securities 10 times capital; and private debt securities three times capital. In addition, LBC, LTN, and LFT could be used freely within the overall limits. Institutions in the first group can negotiate with counterparties of any type (individuals, institutions).

With respect to the second group with smaller capital, the overall limit on leverage was set at 15 times capital. In addition, separate limits applied as follows: holdings of OTN two times capital; holdings of state and local securities and private debt securities two times capital. Also LBC, LTN, and LFT could be used freely within the overall limit. Institutions in the second group can negotiate only with other financial institutions (banks, 'corretoras', 'distribuidoras').

Since 1986 several revisions have been made in the above areas. On 15 June 1987 Resolution 1339 put into operation new capital requirements for investment banks. At the same time new capital requirements were established for consumer finance companies, which differed according to their location, by state; and new capital requirements for leasing companies.[21] Also this resolution established new capital requirements for savings and loan associations, which varied according to their location, by state.[22] Resolution 1409 of 29 October 1987 established four categories of 'sociedades corretoras' and 'distribuidoras', according to the complexity of their activities. This resolution established new capital requirements which varied according to their category and location.[23]

8.3.2 Certificado depósito interfinanceiro

Resolution No. 1102 of 28 February 1986 permits operations between financial institutions in which they exchange obligations. Since this date the Central Bank has released various revisions to this resolution.

The interbank market for funds has grown to include non-bank financial institutions as well as banks. Therefore the term 'mercado interfinanceiro' is used in lieu of interbank market. In Brazil, this is the closest approximation in the financial markets to the New York centered federal funds market. In the 'mercado interfinanceiro' banks and financial institutions with cash deficits and surpluses exchange liquid resources and claims for short term periods, ranging from one day to 30–60 days.[24] The rates of interest in this market were initially prefixed, but have shifted towards post-fixed rates based on the OTN Fiscal, or the rate of remuneration of the LBC/LFT. In 1988 interfinancial deposits with maturity of one day carried prefixed rates, but there was little opportunity to make commitments

Table 8.7   Deposit placing and deposit receiving institutions in the
Mercado Interfinanceiro, 31 May 1988

Institution	Deposit placing %	Deposit receiving %
Commercial banks	29.45	73.36
Investment banks	15.18	16.32
Soc. corretoras	0.67	—
Soc. distribuidoras	2.05	—
Development banks & savings banks	3.31	1.93
Consumer finance companies	7.29	8.03
Savings & loan	40.56	0.01
Leasing	1.49	0.35
TOTAL	100.00	100.00

Source: Andima, *Depositos Interfinanceiros – Legislação Vigente*, 6 June 1988, p. 2.

at long maturities for prefixed rates. Interfinancial deposits with terms of 14–30 days were contracted with interest rates post fixed. The volume of these operations varies in accord with the cash needs of the financial system. The largest concentration of transactions in this market is in prefixed deposits with terms of one day.

Using information provided by CETIP, at 31 May 1988 the daily balance of operations in interfinancial deposits was CZ$400 466 million, or US$2.503 billion. This amount was distributed among deposit taking and deposit receiving institutions as indicated in Table 8.7 above.

As we can note from the table, commercial banks were the largest takers of resources in the market (73.36 per cent). Also, according to information provided by CETIP, the Banco do Brasil exercises considerable weight in the market, both as a taker and supplier of funds. In this regard Banco do Brasil operates as an informal regulator of the market.

The major deposit-placing institutions are the savings and loan associations (40.56 per cent), which on a daily basis obtain large amounts of savings deposits. These funds can be loaned into the market on a very short term basis until longer term loans can be arranged. Commercial banks and investment banks rank second and third as suppliers of deposit funds in this market.

Conditions in the money market over the period December

1987–August 1988 changed considerably, and this is reflected in the various types of data that describe operation of the market. Basically, the money market has experienced a tightening, reflecting an over-sold position. This oversold position is described in another section of this chapter. The tight money market has affected the mercado interfinanceiro as follows: First, real interest rates have increased markedly. Rates on one day CDIs prefixed advanced from 14.39 per cent in December 1987, to 29.63 per cent in August 1988. Second, the volume of CDIs more than doubled, from CZ$177.9 billion in December 1987 to CZ$400.4 billion in May 1988. Third, the volume of within-group placements of CDI increased as a share of total market transactions, reflecting the increased need of even the larger financial conglomerates to give some priority to facilitating the financial requirements of cash short members of the conglomerate. On 9 August 1988 Andima reported previous day CDI volume as CZ$502 billion intra-group and CZ$360 billion extra-group.

8.4   MONETARY CORRECTION AND INTEREST RATES

8.4.1   Monetary correction

We have discussed this topic length in Chapter 2. However we must consider monetary correction specifically in relation to its role in the money market.

Given the high inflation in Brazil, financial assets are subject to indexation.[25] That is, they are adjusted in value periodically to compensate for loss in real value due to inflation. For example, beginning on 1 July 1987 the value of OTN was adjusted periodically by an amount equivalent to the officially measured rate of inflation. Similarly, financial asset values are subject to monetary correction. Again, in the case of OTN, asset values rise each month based on the rate of inflation plus real interest.

Not all assets are treated in the same way as OTN. In the case of OTN, gains in value vary from month to month, but closely approximate the rate of inflation plus 6 per cent annually. Other financial assets may do better or worse depending on (1) maturity of instrument, that is, overnight rate or 30–60 day rate; and (2) monetary policy stance. In 1987 the Central Bank adopted a more flexible policy so that interest rates established by the Central Bank can be higher or lower than the inflation rate.

The relation between the interest rate and inflation rate is very important to the financial markets and real economic activity in Brazil. For example, when the interest rate is allowed to fall below the inflation rate there is a tendency for stock market trading volume to increase and for stock prices to move up more rapidly. This reflects a financial disequilibrium. Also, under conditions of low interest rates relative to inflation rates, companies are induced to hold inventories, causing shortages in the retail system. Again this reflects a financial disequilibrium where companies are speculating on their own inventory positions.

Vital to the indexation of interest rates, and the monetary correction of financial assets is the use of an appropriate price index. The General Price Index (GPI) compiled by the Getulio Vargas Foundation was used for a long period up to 1985. This compounds the National Wholesale Price Index (weight of 6/10), Consumer Price Index (Rio de Janeiro–Weight of 3/10), and the Rio de Janeiro City Building Cost Index (weight of 1/10).

In 1979 Finance Minister Delfim Netto had adopted a national consumer price index (NCPI) prepared by the Brazilian Institute for Geography and Economics (IBGE). This Institute has long played the role of the primary government-sponsored organisation for national economic statistics gathering and preparation. The NCPI is heavily weighted with food prices, reflecting the market basket of goods purchased by households with incomes of five minimum wages or less. It is believed that Delfim Netto thought he could control wages (indexed) better if adjusted to consumer prices.

In 1985 the GPI provided by Getulio Vargas Foundation was running higher than the national index. At that time IBGE developed a broad market basket index based on purchases of households with incomes of up to 30 times minimum wages. This index (IPCA) became the reference for all indexation in 1985. However it was soon found that the IPCA did not adequately reflect lower income levels. Therefore in 1986 indexation was shifted to the CPI, and effective in June 1987 wages became tied to the NCPI.[26] As noted above, as of July 1987 the OTN became the indexor of the Brazilian economy. Monthly changes in OTN were made based on the CPI.[27] Savings accounts earn OTN plus one-half per cent of the LBC flat rate, whichever is higher. From this date LBC average rates became based on a more flexible Central Bank policy.

8.4.2 Interest rates

To understand interest rates and interest rate movements we must keep in mind that Brazil has experienced alternating waves of accelerating and declining inflation. To provide protection to investors and lenders, government securities have been monetarily corrected. Therefore we must distinguish between monetary correction paid on a debt instrument and interest paid over or above monetary correction.

The monetary correction paid on a debt instrument for a given period of time may be equal to, above, or under the actual inflation rate for that time period. If monetary correction exactly equals the inflation rate, any interest paid over monetary correction can be identified as real interest. If monetary correction falls below the inflation rate, interest paid over monetary correction exceeds the real interest rate.

As noted in the previous section, the government, on several occasions, has changed the price index used for monetary correction. At least two distinct objectives may be at work when the government (Central Bank) focuses its attention on inflation, monetary correction, and interest paid over monetary correction. One is to establish an indexor that closely matches the inflation rate. The second is to influence the real rate of interest earned on debt securities, so as to control market liquidity and the pattern of financial fund flows.

In 1988, the OTN Fiscal served as the indexor in Brazil (Table 8.8). Investors could be fairly confident that the Central Bank would fix daily and monthly accumulations on OTN that would conform closely to the observed inflation rate. In addition, they could earn 6 per cent (annual) over monetary correction. Reported changes in the inflation rate would quickly reflect themselves in the daily accumulations on OTN Fiscal. An interesting money market game would be to forecast price index changes and invest accordingly in OTN, OTN futures, or other instruments.

In 1988 the LBC fiscal provided the basic overnight rate for operations in the money market. Overnight rates as of 22 July 1988 are presented in Table 8.9. The institutional market reflects the money market in a comprehensive way. All types of institutions are involved in trading open market paper at rates within the ranges depicted in this table.

In effect, it could be argued that in 1988 there was a dual indexor system. First the OTN Fiscal was given monetary correction which

Table 8.8   Leading money market interest rates and their significance, 1988

Interest Rate	Significance
1. OTN fiscal	Basic reference or indexor for Central Bank and money market.
2. LBC fiscal	Basis for overnight rate in the money market.
3. Savings rate (poupanca)	Basic cost of funds for banking system.
4. Mercado interfinanceiro (CDI)	Cost of funds for banks and institutions operating in the interbank and inter financial institution market.

Table 8.9   Interest rates: institutional market (per cent per month) 22 July 1988

	Maximum	Median	Minimum
Overnight LBC, Andima	37.38	37.32	37.29
Overnight OTN, Andima	37.51	37.50	37.43
OTE*	—	37.47	—

* State Treasury Obligations.
Source: Andima and *Gazeta Mercantil*.

Table 8.10   Projected returns on selected instruments, 9 August 1988 (monthly)

Application	Projected monthly return %
LBC/LFT	25.79
LBC Fiscal	25.79
OTN Fiscal	20.50
OTN BM&F (Sept.)*	22.22
Dollar BMSP (Nov.)*	24.00
Gold BMSP (Oct.)*	20.10

* Futures Contracts, traded at Bolsa Mercantil E Futuros, and Bolsa Mercadorias, São Paulo.
Source: Andima, *Resenha Diaria*, 9 August 1988.

protected the capital investment of holders of OTN from inflation. But this did not protect the holder from variations in real return that took place in the market. Second, the LBC/LFT interest rate on overnight was subject to daily adjustment, giving the holder a current return in agreement with changing market conditions.

If we turn to Table 8.10 we can see the difference in position of the institution holding OTN and LBC/LFT. On 9 August 1988 the investor with OTN has a projected monthly return of 20.5 per cent whereas the investor with LBC/LFT has a projected monthly return of 25.79 per cent. In this period of high interest rates and high inflation in 1988 Central Bank efforts to apply a flexible policy resulted in higher returns on LBC/LFT. But this situation could be reversed under different conditions, with LBC/LFT providing investor returns lower than those available on OTN.

In 1986–8 the money market became focused on the overnight rate, reflected by the LBC fiscal (Table 8.8). This shortening of time perspective reflected and followed the failure of the Cruzado Plan and the resulting surge in inflation. Market participants became unwilling to commit themselves in the market for terms longer than overnight or several days, fearing that a change in the inflation rate could cause severe losses. As a result, in 1986–8 the money market made use of the overnight rate to make judgments and decisions for lending and investment. This has reduced the flexibility of money market participants including banks, corporations, and financial institutions. One problem presented by the almost universal use of the overnight rate is the inability to trade and arbitrage funds along the yield curve. This is a fundamental constraint for money market participants.

A third important interest rate in the financial markets is the rate paid on savings deposits, or 'poupancas' (Table 8.8). This rate indicates a basic cost of funds for the banking system.

A fourth important interest rate is that paid on interbank certificates of deposits (CDIs). The 'mercado interfinanceiro' is one of the most important components of the money market, and rates applicable for the period July 18–22 1988 are presented in Table 8.11. In 1988 daily trading volume in this market ranged between $1.5 billion and $2.3 billion (Table 8.12). Table 8.12 provides comparative trading volume data for CDIs, SELIC (government securities), and CETIP (private debt).

In Table 8.11 rates are presented for the 'mercado interfinanceiro'.

Table 8.11 Short-term interest rates, mercado interfinanceiro, per cent per month, (1988)

Market sector	July 18		July 19		July 20		July 21		July 22	
	Days	Rate	Days	Rate	Days	Rate	Days	Rate	Days	Rate
CDI* monthly rate										
Maximum		31.80/31.85		–		–		–		37.25/37.30
Middle		31.75/31.80								37.20/37.20
Minimum		31.70/31.75								37.15/37.20
DI monthly CETIP		31.56		32.50		37.24		37.10		–
CDI pre fixed	60	950/1000	–	–	30	1100/–	–	–	–	–
	63	950/1000	62	970/1000	60	1000/–	60	1050/1100	60	1050/1100
CDI post–fixed	–	–	14	3.5/4.0	–	–	–	–	–	–
	30	8.0/9.0	30	8.0/8.5	30	8.3/8.5	46	8.0/8.2	30	7.5/8.0
(per year	–	–	45	8.7/9.0	–	–	60	9.8/10.0	41	–/7.7
plus OTN)	60	10.0/10.3	–	–	61	9.4/9.6	–	–	60	9.10/9.50
	63	10.0/10.3	–	–	90.	10.5/11.5	90	10.5/11.0	–	–

* Interbank Certicates of Deposit (CDI), bid/ask.)
Source: Andima, *Gazeta Mercantil*.

Table 8.12   Daily trading volume, mercado interfinanceiro and other
sectors, August 1988

| Market sector | Daily trading volume | |
	CZ$ bill.	US$ bill.
CDI	741	2.8
LBC/LFT	5 477	21.1
SELIC	16 607	63.8
CETIP	2 109	8.4

Source: Andima, *Resenha Diaria*, 9 August 1988.

The daily rates align themselves closely with the analogous rates on
OTN fiscal and LBC fiscal. Post-fixed and Prefixed CDI rates operate
at maturities of 14–90 days. However the volume at these longer
maturities is quite low, especially with respect to prefixed CDIs which
can leave the participants very much exposed to changes in the
market. Because of this market risk, rates on prefixed CDIs often are
quite high, as can be noted in the table.

Post-fixed CDIs carry rates over the monetary correction applicable to OTN. For example, on 18 July 1988 the 30-day maturity
carried rates of 8–9 per cent over OTN. As can be seen in Table 8.11,
the 'yield curve' reflected in the CDIs was quite steep, most especially on 20 July, on which day the overnight rate moved from 32
per cent to 37 per cent, and where the 90-day maturity carried rates
of 10.5–11.0 per cent over OTN.

8.5   MONEY MARKET INSTRUMENTS

In most countries with well-developed financial markets the government securities market has tended to become a central core of the
money and capital markets. This central core provides a homo-
geneous base of low-risk paper, and affords banks and securities firms
an opportunity to deal in and underwrite these issues on a scale that is
profitable to them.

In this section we take an overview of the money market considering the volume of transactions in government and non-government
instruments. Also, we examine the development of a futures market
in Brazil, considering the opportunities it offers for money market
development.

Table 8.13   Average maturities of federal government securities, 1986–8.

Date	LTN	OTN	LFT	Total
Dec. 1986	76 days	12 mo, 1 day	—	8 mo, 12 days
Dec. 1987	41 days	13 mo, 13 days	—	11 mo, 10 days
Mar. 1988	13 days[1]	11 mo, 23 days	5 mo, 29 days	10 mo, 00 days
June 1988	—	10 mo, 10 days	4 mo, 12 days	7 mo, 18 days

[1] Applies to Feb. 1988.
Source: Andima, *Carta Andima*, April 1988, p. 14; *Retrospectiva 1988*, Jan–June 1988, p. 6.

8.5.1   Government and non-government instruments

OTN

Treasury bonds have been issued since 1964, with varying maturities. Formerly they were designated as ORTN (readjustable bonds). This was changed in 1986 because of the Cruzado Plan philosophy of de-indexing. In 1987 bonds with maturities extending to five years were outstanding. Average maturities of government securities including OTN are indicated below (Table 8.13). OTN receive monetary correction plus 6 per cent real interest. In the past the market for OTN was based on bank purchases to satisfy reserve requirements. In 1987–8 the bulk of OTN was held in the portfolios of the Central Bank and public sector entities. Private sector investors became disinterested in OTN with the de-indexation of the Cruzado Plan. During 1988 the Central Bank took the initiative to increase investor interest in OTN by offering repurchase facilities to cover transactions in OTN up to 83-day maturities. A small amount of daily trading was taking place in OTN at mid-1987 (US$625 million).

LTN

Treasury bills were first issued in 1970. In the past maturities of Treasury bills were 63 days, 91 days, and 182 days. LTN were not issued in 1987, but the government intends to issue LTN in 1988 with 35-day maturity. In the past bank purchases of LTN were based on the need to satisfy part of the reserve requirement while earning income on the bills. At April–May 1987 all LTN outstanding was held by the Central Bank. In April–May 1987 new issues of LTN totalled CZ$370 billion, equivalent at that time to approximately US$8.5 billion.

LBC

Central Bank bills were issued beginning in 1986. These carried
maturities of 182 days and 273 days, and were sold at weekly auction.
In the period April–May 1987 new issues totalled CZ$150 billion,
equivalent to approximately US$3.7 billion. In the secondary market
various institutions have demonstrated an interest in buying or selling
certain issues. Doubtless, sophisticated investors are always searching for opportunities to position themselves for profitable dealings in
this market. SELIC provides a market for LBCs at the Central Bank
and the volume of trading is substantial. In June 1987 daily trading in
LBC was in excess of CZ$400 billion, equivalent to US$10 billion.
Over the period January–June 1988 LBC declined in importance
from 66.7 per cent to 24.3 per cent of government and Central Bank
securities held by the public.[29]

LFT

On 1 January 1988 the first issue of LFT appeared. In general LFT
possess characteristics similar to LBC. LFT are intended to replace
LBC. The advantage of LFT over LBC is that they can be issued at
varying maturities, subject to determination at time of issue. This
provides flexibility to the government and Central Bank, so that
when conditions become appropriate to issue longer maturity instruments the maturity can be lengthened. Over the period January–June
1988 LFT increased in importance from 9.0 per cent to 40.3 per cent of
federal government and Central Bank securities held by the public.

Certificates of deposit (CDB)

Bank certificates of deposit are issued by commercial, investment,
and public sector banks, with maturities of up to three months. These
are negotiable and actively traded. The volume of daily trading in
certificates of deposit is provided by Andima, and in June 1987
trading exceeded CZ$100 billion (US$2500 million). Trading is facilitated through the Andima-operated CETIP system. In addition to
the negotiable CDBs, Letras de Cambio and CDIs are traded on the
CETIP system.

   Until 1982 CDBs were issued with monetary correction plus interest
prefixed. In 1982 a second format was introduced and CDBs were
issued with monetary correction plus interest post-fixed.[30] The negotiable variety CDB receives interest post-fixed, in the form of
monetary correction plus interest.

Bills of exchange – letras de cambio (LC)

This instrument has been in use for a long period of time. The market for this paper developed rapidly in the 1960s due to the need to find a mechanism for avoiding the usury restriction on interest (12 per cent limit). The credit and finance companies that accepted bills drawn on them by business firms guaranteed payment of the bills accepted, earning an acceptance commission. Given the acceptance of the credit and finance companies, these bills became negotiable on the stock exchange.[31] Operations of credit and finance companies grew rapidly in the 1960s based in large part on the profitability of the LC market. Credit and finance companies are regulated by the Central Bank with respect to minimum capital, and balance sheet configurations. The volume of this paper outstanding relative to financial assets in general declined from 1.3 per cent to 0.9 per cent over the period December 1987–May 1988 (Table 8.1).

Interbank deposits – certificado deposito interfinanceiro

In this market banks provide overnight financing to one another and to other institutions. The Central Bank has encouraged banks and other financial institutions to carry out such interfinancial operations in lieu of using the discount window at the Central Bank. To carry out interbank lending banks issue very short-term CDIs. Smaller banks have greater need to borrow in this market. Large banks with substantial branch sources of funds (Bradesco, Itau) do not have this need, and can be lenders in this market.

8.5.2 Futures contracts

Futures exchanges are playing a more important role in the money market. They provide participants with the opportunity to hedge interest rate and other risks, and provide a market in which trading profits may be generated. During the mid-1980s two new futures exchanges were organized in Brazil. The Brazilian Futures Exchange (BBF) or Bolsa Brasileira de Futuros was organised in 1984, and operates in Rio de Janeiro. The Mercantile Futures Exchange (BM&F) or Bolsa Mercantil e de Futuros was organised in 1986 and operates in São Paulo. In addition there is an older exchange, Bolsa de Mercadorias de São Paulo, which was organised in 1917. Table 10–17 provides some comparative information concerning these exchanges.

Bolsa de Mercadorias de São Paulo

This exchange is the oldest of its type in Brazil. In 1987 it ranked second in overall trading volume among the three futures exchanges in Brazil (Table 10.17). The gold futures contract is the most active. In addition to the gold contract, this exchange provides opportunities for trading futures contracts in various agricultural commodities, foreign currencies, and the IBV Stock Index.

Bolsa Brasileira de Futuros

The BBF began operations in 1984. Since then the IBV Stock Index has become the most actively traded contract. The IBV Stock Index future is based on twelve 'blue-chip' stocks traded on the Rio de Janeiro Stock Exchange. This contract is designated as the IBV Blue Chip, and has a 90 per cent correlation with the Rio stock market. A second important futures contract is based on the OTN. The BBF issues futures contracts in several other areas including Central Bank bills (LBC), foreign currencies and gold.

Bolsa Mercantil e de Futuros (BM&F)

The BM&F began operation in January 1986, and since then has experienced rapid growth. In 1988 three types of financial futures contracts were traded, including the IBOVESPA (stock index) futures contract, OTN Nominal which provides hedgers with protection against interest rate and inflation rate changes, and a futures contract for bank certificates of deposit (CDBs). There are two different interest rate contracts for CDBs, a CDB prefixed and a CDB post-fixed. In 1987 the volume of contracts negotiated in CDBs was larger than in OTN. The BM&F and the other futures exchanges are discussed in more detail in Chapter 10.

8.5.3 Short-term mutual funds

In 1986 Central Bank Resolution 1199 provided for the creation of short-term mutual funds.[32] As a result investors have a choice between short-term funds, fixed-income funds, and share-mutual funds. In this section we discuss short-term funds and make some comparisons with fixed-income funds.

Investments of short-term funds are governed by regulations issued by the Central Bank. On 14 January 1988 the Central Bank issued Circular No. 1279 which established maximum and minimum percentages for funds allocation in the portfolios of short-term funds. These are as follows:[33]

1. Minimum of 50 per cent in debt paper with maximum maturity of 28 days, with at least 40 per cent in LFT and or LBC, and 10 per cent maximum in other paper.
2. Minimum of 30 per cent in LFT and or LBC.
3. Maximum of 10 per cent in CDB and/or 'letras de cambio' accepted by consumer finance companies, with maturity equal or greater than 90 days, registered in CETIP.
4. Maximum of 10 per cent in public debt issues of federal, state and municipal governments.

Short-term funds may be administered by commercial banks, investment banks, 'sociedades corretora' and 'sociedades distribuidora'. As can be noted from the above only a very small portion of the portfolio can be invested in private securities.[34]

In the period 1986–8 money flows directed towards short-term funds grew rapidly. By May 1988 these funds had invested capital amounting to CZ$727 690 million, or US$4548 million. The success of these funds can be attributed to (1) the interest of fund managers in building a larger base of stable fee income in a period of slack or declining loan demand; (2) the desire for liquidity on the part of investors; and (3) the availability of an investment medium generating income that remained largely free of income tax liability.

It should be understood that the attraction of short-term funds early in 1988 was not based mainly on their past performance, since in 1987 they earned a negative real return. A comparison of nominal and real returns on short-term funds, other types of funds, and alternative investments can be examined in Table 8.14. Clearly, savings accounts and CDBs post-fixed were the only type of investments yielding positive real returns in 1987.

Investors in short-term funds include corporations as well as individuals. Both types of investors have a need for liquidity. This is provided by short-term funds since the investor can advance and withdraw funds on a day-by-day basis. There is no minimum holding period as in the case of fixed-income funds (minimum holding period of 30 days). Given the rapid changes that can take place in the money market, the liquidity afforded by short-term funds is desirable for investors that wish to avoid interest rate and inflation risks. The cost is the somewhat lower return that may be earned on short-term as opposed to fixed-income funds.

Table 8.14   Comparison of nominal and real returns to investor on three types of mutual funds and seven alternative investments, 1987

Investment	Nominal return	Real return
Savings account	427.01	13.10
Overnight – LBC	253.10	(2.76)
IBV – Rio de Janeiro[1]	75.06	(62.43)
IBOVESPA[2]	34.87	(71.06)
Gold	329.23	(7.88)
CDB 60 day postfixed	394.69	6.17
CDB 60 day prefixed	350.53	(3.31)
Mutual funds		
Short-term	356.24	(2.09)
Fixed-income	359.39	(1.41)
Share-fund	112.43	(54.41)

Source: Andima, *Fundos de Aplicações de Curto Prazo – Legislação Vigente*, Assessoria Tecnica, 1988, p. 3.
[1] Stock Index, Rio de Janeiro Stock Exchange.
[2] Stock Index, São Paulo Stock Exchange.
Note: Bracketed numbers indicate negative return.

Two types of short-term funds are available: nominative and bearer. The bearer form is also referred to as 'Fundo Ao Portador'. In this case there is no registration of the identity of the investor for taxation purposes, and the investor is in an informal sense free of taxation, except for the taxes paid by fund managers in the form of the financial instruments tax. As of writing (August 1988) the applicable rates of the IFO are illustrated in Table 8.15.

The motivation of the government in providing an opportunity for tax-immune investment in short term funds is based on several considerations. First, this could help to retain investment funds in the domestic financial market rather than overseas markets, an important consideration in the further development of the money and capital market. Second, this would enhance the flexibility and efficiency of mobilising domestic capital. Third, the revenue loss would be minimal (and perhaps even negative), and government finance would be facilitated.[35] There is taxation on the instrument. Also government debt paper enjoys a broader market. In effect the short-term funds draw liquid resources from many sectors (formal, informal), which facilitates the financing of government budget needs.

Table 8.15   Financial Instruments Tax (IFO)

When held 28 days or less	When held more than 28 days *(Effective until 31 Aug. 1988)*
3% tax on income above monetary correction.	Capital gains above monetary correction: 35% tax on nominative shares; 45% tax on bearer shares.

(Effective from 1 Sept. 1988)

Held 1–7 days – 7% tax on income
 above monetary correction.
Held 8–15 days – 5% tax on income Same as above.
 above monetary correction.
Held 16–28 days – 3% tax on income
 above monetary correction.

Source: Jornal do Brasil, 'Aliquota do Over Muda em Setembro', 8 Aug. 1988, p. 14.

8.6   FOREIGN EXCHANGE MARKET

Increasingly around the world foreign exchange market activities are becoming more integrated with money market operations. This trading is not restricted to open financial systems, such as those centred in London, New York, and Zurich. As we describe below, even in the case of financial systems that are more closed to international influence such as Brazil, there is a tendency for increased integration of foreign exchange and money market operations.

Activity in foreign exchange trading tends to be limited in Brazil because of Central Bank controls. In Brazil the market is controlled so that bank positions in foreign exchange can be carried, subject to Central Bank limits. These limits are $1.5 million in a bought position, and $7.5 million in a sold position. Interbank trading facilitates bank compliance with these regulations. If trading activity brings a bank's position beyond the level allowed by regulation, the bank must cover its excess, or sell in the last instance. Based on balance of payments data for Brazil, transactions in the market must be in the range of $50–60 billion yearly. Half of this goes through Banco do Brasil, which enjoys a favoured position in the market. This favoured position is in part related to the special role assigned Banco do Brasil in financing foreign trade.

The foreign exchange market in Brazil has several important areas of operation:

1. Traditional foreign exchange dealing, subject to the exchange control.
2. Futures market trading, where standard contracts are involved.
3. International hedging market, with tailor-made deals.

8.6.1   Traditional foreign exchange

The basis of foreign exchange trading is foreign trade transactions, plus a small admixture of capital inflows and profit remittances. Regulation plays a significant role. Every day the rate is fixed by the Central Bank, and all transactions are approved by the Central Bank. This is administered in a unique way, with an inspector coming every day to review transactions. The Central Bank is plugged into the same computer system as the banks, and can more easily monitor the market.

In Brazil domestic foreign exchange activity involves buying and selling dollars against cruzados, based on underlying real trans-actions. In non- Brazilian foreign exchange markets the delivery date is two days later. In Brazil, cruzados must be paid one day prior to dollar payments overseas. This reduces the credit risk. Since the bank receives funds a day earlier, it can apply the funds in the local money market, gaining on the float.

In the case of an importer requiring cruzado financing, high interest rates apply. Foreign banks may not generally have the same capa-bility as Brazilian- based banks on the import finance side. But foreign banks do enjoy a competitive position on the export side of the transaction.

By agreement with the Central Bank of Brazil, trade lines of credit can be arranged with foreign banks. An assigned amount is estab-lished between the foreign bank and the Central Bank. If foreign banks were to lose the one day advance payment of cruzados against dollar deals, they would suffer a large loss in earnings. A bank can make about as much on the foreign exchange spread as on the money provided by the day early settlement of cruzado funds for dollars. At mid-year 1987 it was possible to earn 1/2 per cent a day nominal interest on funds.

As much as 90 per cent of the foreign exchange market involves dollars, suggesting that non-dollar currency trading might be at very small amounts and carried out in relatively inefficient markets. Outright spot transactions are dominant, with smaller outright forward trading. Swap trading is in small amounts.

The foreign exchange market should provide a hedging mechanism whereby foreign trade firms can reduce risk. Over the past few years the types of hedging instruments and their availability have become more limited in Brazil. In contrast, the need to hedge against risks of currency rate changes and shifts in government policy has increased. Early in 1988 the then existing 'devaluation clause' OTN issue matured (OTN Cambial), further narrowing the scope of hedging.[36] What remained included (1) investing in fixed assets; (2) foreign exchange futures market; (3) gold; (4) Central Bank deposit schemes for exporters; and (5) foreign currency loan prepayments.

On 27 July 1988 the government auctioned exchange rate protected OTN. This issue is denoted OTN Cambial, to contrast with OTN Fiscal the more typical issue of monetary correction paper. The OTN Cambial was auctioned to provide a return equivalent to 4.5 per cent yearly over foreign exchange rate correction.[37] This issue had a three month maturity. Exporters can be relieved of the need to bear a heavy finance cost in acquiring OTN Cambial, since an informal option market developed. According to one market observer the commission charged on this informal market was small.[38]

The success of the auction of OTN Cambial is not difficult to understand. Liquidity considerations of companies, conditions in the money market, limited foreign exchange market size, ineligibility for official hedges, and the imperfections in available mechanisms make it difficult for many companies in Brazil to find satisfactory alternative solutions. The export hedge is the most heavily used of options and, as reported in May 1988, some US$2.2 billion of export proceeds were on deposit with the monetary authorities.[39] At the same time the OTN Cambial was being auctioned, a proposal for a new hedging instrument was being made, called the Bonus Cambial. This proposal was made by the BM&F, and involved issuing securities 'ao portador', with interest rates based on the floating LIBOR.[40]

8.6.2 Futures market

The futures market for foreign currencies is still quite small, and a few banks are trying to develop a more fluid market. Factors influencing the development potential of futures market trading in currencies include (1) the large volume of floating rate debt owed to banks; (2) the small portion of external debt denominated in European currencies (US$10–15 billion); (3) the decline in the value of the dollar *vis-à-vis* other currencies.

The basic commodities traded in the futures market include:

$/DM $/Franc $/Gold $/Yen $/Cruzado

These commodities are traded in standard contracts, 4–6 per commodity with set maturities. Participants in these markets include the foreign banks that also fulfill the role of market maker, large private companies in Brazil (using currency and gold hedges), companies with external debt (hedge European currency debt), and multinational companies (hedge dollar debt for the local subsidiary). Computer screens facilitate participants maintaining contact with the market on a current basis. The range of products include futures contracts in the standard format, and currency and interest swaps. Margin calls are in cruzados with interest charged at current levels (26 per cent monthly interest in 1987). All settlements take place in cruzados.

It should be noted that this market generally permits participants to avoid any possible violation of exchange controls. Participants obtain protection against risk. There is no international movement of funds, and therefore no contravention of exchange control rules.

8.6.3   International hedging market

In contrast to the futures market, an international hedging market develops tailor-made instruments. As wilt the futures market, one objective is to generate currency and interest swaps. Foreign banks operating in Brazil have been especially interested in developing this market. This is because they have a substantial dollar book in the form of loans (mostly floating rate) to Brazilian borrowers. Therefore they are in a position to use this as a basis for creating futures positions for clients.

In 1987 the Central Bank of Brazil was split on the issue of supporting an active programme of debt/equity swaps. A negative attitude was based on wanting to retain control, to be able to approve each individual deal on the specific merits of that transaction. By year-end 1987 those in the Central Bank favouring an active programme of swaps had won the debate. Early in 1988 the government initiated a comprehensive programme of monthly auctions. These monthly auctions give rise to an increased need for tailored currency and interest rate swaps.

NOTES

1. Effective in 1989 budget indexation could become a reality in Brazil. This would make the indexation and monetary correction process more complete and all-encompassing. Also, it could provide greater reality for the budgetary process.
2. Money market participants are precluded from engaging in time arbitrage, and this inability to ride the yield curve is a serious constraint on money market activities and profit generation.
3. Angela Bittencourt, 'Leilão de OTN na Quinta-feira', *Gazeta Mercantil*, 24 June 1988, p. 18.
4. The Central Bank is compelled to facilitate a depreciation of the cruzado.
5. Given an international parity between dollars and gold, arbitragé requires that the cruzado price of gold find a level in accord with the cruzado price of dollars.
6. *Gazeta Mercantil*, International Weekly Edition, 9 May 1988, p. 11. In April 1988 OTN Cambial issued earlier matured, reducing the alternatives for exporters and others wanting to hedge exchange risks. In July 1988 a new OTN Cambial was issued for this purpose.
7. *Gazeta Mercantil*, 21 July 1988, p. 19. It is more difficult to control gold purchases than dollar purchases. If the Central Bank pays less for gold, it becomes difficult to avoid selling to other buyers.
8. The authors are indebted to Bruno Mauricio Ribeiro, Chefe de Divisão, Departamento Econômico, Banco Central, for helpful comments and information in this and following areas of discussion.
9. The five issues had maturities of 6 months, 9 months, 10 months, and two at 24 months. *Carta Andima*, May–June 1987, p. 25, Table 2.1.
10. The SELIC system is computerised so that there is no 'physical delivery of securities' but an electronic input to change the recorded ownership of securities that remain 'warehoused' in the system.
11. *Carta Andima*, May–June 1987, p. 33.
12. In practice LBC carry no risk and therefore offer a lower return to the investor.
13. Central Bank of Brazil, *Brazil Economic Program*, vol. 16, March 1988, pp. 64–5.
14. This description is adapted from *Open Investidor*, 1985, pp. 55–8.
15. Sistema Especial de Liquidação e Custódia is the Portuguese title for SELIC.
16. Central de Custódia e Liquidação Financeira de Títulos is the Portuguese title for CETIP.
17. Comissão Nacional de Bolsa de Valores, *Legislação Sobre Mercado de Capitais*, Rio de Janeiro, 1986, pp. 503–17.
18. Andima, *Operações Compromissadas – Legislação Vigente*, Assessoria Técnica, 9 June 1988, pp. 2–3.

19. Andima, *Operações Compromissadas*, p. 3.
20. Ibid., pp. 3–4.
21. Ibid., pp. 10–11.
22. Ibid., pp. 11–12.
23. Ibid., p. 12.
24. Andima, *Depositos Interfinanceiros, Legislacao Vigente*, 6 June 1988, p. 1.
25. It should be noted that, in addition to the monetary correction of financial assets, indexation rules applied to wages, rents, prices of public utility services, and other areas. In addition, at times price controls are utilised in an effort to decelerate inflation.
26. The difference between CPI and NCPI is due to a change in the period of time used for data collection. In the former it was the first to thirtieth day of the month. In the latter case it was shifted to the middle of one month (fifteenth day) to the middle of the following month. This change in the CPI was carried out to eliminate the last 15 days' (February 1986) residual inflation after adoption of the Cruzado Plan.
27. In this sense, the OTN value increases each month in a manner similar to that of a price index, with the difference that an additional one-half per cent value increase is added to provide a 6 per cent real (over monetary correction) return.
28. Antonio Carlos Lemgruber, *Uma Análise Quantitativa do Sistema Financeiro no Brasil*, IBMEC, Rio de Janeiro, 1978, p. 52.
29. Andima, *Retrospectiva 1988*, Jan–June 1988, p. 5.
30. *Open Investidor*, Open S.A., Rio de Janeiro, 1985, p. 184.
31. An interesting account of the early development of this financing mechanism can be found in Mario Henrique Simonsen, 'Inflation and the Money and Capital Markets of Brazil', in H. Ellis (ed.), *The Economy of Brazil* (University of California Press, 1969) pp. 146–50.
32. This Resolution was issued on 10 October 1986.
33. Andima, *Fundos de Aplicações de Curto Prazo – Legislação Vigente*, Assessoria Tecnica, 1988, pp. 5–6.
34. Jo Galazi, 'As Muitas Opções de Lucros', *Bolsa*, July 1988, p. 11.
35. This is based on the assumption that these funds would flow alternately into the underground economy or overseas financial markets.
36. During 1988 considerable controversy followed proposals to issue new readjustable government securities to provide exporters with an additional hedging instrument. In mid-1988 OTN Cambial were authorised for this purpose, and the first auction took place on 27 July 1988.
37. Angela Bittencourt, 'Leilão Eletronico dá Certo: OTN Sai a 4.5%', *Gazeta Mercantil*, 28 July 1988, p. 20.
38. Angela Bittencourt, 'A Venda do Direito de Compra', *Gazeta Mercantil*, 28 July 1988, p. 20.
39. Banco de Boston, *Newsletter Brazil*, 2 May 1988, p. 4.
40. Nelson Carrer Junion, 'Para Proteger Importador BM&F Defende a Criação de Bônus Com Lastro Ouro', *Gazeta Mercantil*, 28 July 1988, p. 22.

9 The Capital Market: Normalisation and Development of Financial Intermediaries

One can view the development of Brazilian capital markets as encompassing four specific but related developments. In a broad sense all four are tied together, and in various ways contributed to the deepening of the financial markets. These four specific developments include:

1. Normalisation
    Legislation of 1964–5
    Legislation of 1976–7
2. Development of the stock market
3. Promotion of capital market institutions
    Fiscal incentive funds
    Pension funds
    Mutual funds
4. Growth of venture capital activities
    Debt conversion programme
    Privatisation programme
    Encouragement of special venture capital vehicles

We discuss items 1 and 3 primarily in this chapter. Item 2 is discussed in the following chapter. In part we have outlined the activities of short-term mutual funds in Chapter 8. Venture capital activities are touched on in Chapters 12 and 13, and considered in more detail in Chapter 14.

This chapter focuses on the efforts of the government of Brazil to promote development of the capital market, and the related development of basic types of financial intermediaries. We designate the efforts of the government to promote development of the capital market as 'normalisation'. This normalisation process includes two time periods (1964–5 and 1976–7) when the most significant capital market and financial institution legislation was enacted.

Most significant to the financial deepening process is the growth of financial intermediaries that invest in various types of capital market and shorter term financial instruments. Brazil is still in the early stages of building a diversified base of financial intermediaries. The pension funds now have a fairly large base of operations, but the insurance companies still play a relatively small role in the capital market.

9.1 OVERVIEW OF CAPITAL MARKET

Much has been accomplished in Brazil over the past two decades in the way of capital market development. Yet much remains to be accomplished. In this brief section we describe the current status of the capital market. In this way we can appreciate to what extent the many components of the capital market (institutions, instruments) have been developed. Also we can better appreciate the discussion which follows concerning the role of the government in promoting capital market development, efforts to promote stock market efficiency, the development of financial intermediaries, and the historical perspective.

9.1.1 Legal and regulatory basis

A useful starting-point in this brief overview is the legal and regulatory basis for the capital market. In 1976 two important laws were enacted which built on earlier capital market laws. These include Law 6404 which provides for the proper governance and operation of public corporations, defines the status of shareholders and provides for the protection of shareholders, provides for registration and issuance of securities, and requires that full and complete disclosure be provided to the public concerning company financial performance. The second, Law 6385, created the National Securities Commission (Comissao de Valores Mobiliarios) or CVM, gave the Commission authority to regulate the securities markets, gave it jurisdiction over public companies, and judicial powers to prosecute companies and enforce the securities laws and regulations of its several governing bodies.

The governing bodies that are responsible for regulation of the capital market also include the National Monetary Council (Conselho Monetário Nacional) or CMN, and the Central Bank. The Central Bank regulates banks and financial firms, conducts open market operations, supervises dealings in open market paper, and has responsibility for managing foreign exchange transactions. Also, the Central Bank has the responsibility for enforcing CMN Resolutions.

The CMN has wide authority to regulate the financial system. This includes power to adjust the money supply based on current economic conditions, to coordinate monetary and fiscal policy, and to generally supervise financial institutions and the mobilisation of capital. With the Central Bank the CMN establishes guidelines for the portfolio composition of mutual funds and other financial institutions.

The CMN has a special status and composition. It is the place where different interests of the national economy meet together. Membership includes Ministers of State, bankers, chief executives of state enterprises, and representatives of industry. This means that a wide range of interests can together determine what policy actions must be followed from the monetary side of the economy.

9.1.2 Client companies of the capital market

Approximately 1000 open companies use the facilities of the stock exchanges and over-the-counter market. This includes new issues of shares and debentures, as well as trading of existing shares. Open companies are publicly owned, with their shares traded on the stock exchanges. Many share issues traded on the Bolsa are preferred since the law governing companies permits up to two-thirds of capital to be issued as preferred stock. Tax incentives have been provided to foster a more active and liquid market for the shares of open capital companies. Also investors who enjoy profits from the sale of stock exchange listed securities are exempt from capital gains taxation.

In addition to the 1000 open companies, close to 3000 other companies obtain capital through special fiscal incentive funds such as FINOR, FINAM, FISET, and FUNRES. In the past these fiscal funds channelled capital to enterprises in special regions of Brazil (north-east, Amazon) which the government had designated as requiring additional capital investment. In this process these fiscal funds acquired investments in hundreds of enterprises. The government has adopted the policy of divesting its ownership in these enterprises. One approach is to provide tax incentives for corporate taxpayers to invest in the fiscal incentive funds of FINOR and other such entities.

At present tax incentives have been provided for corporate investors. For example, in the case of FINOR the corporate investor receives a 'certificate of investment' in FINOR. FINOR auctions its holdings of equity and the corporate investor pays (in the auction) for shares of any of the several companies owned by FINOR with the certificates of investment. The certificates are traded over the counter, and are the 'currency' of the auction. Shares of companies funded by FINOR and other fiscal incentive funds generally cannot be traded on the stock exchanges (since they are not open companies properly registered with the Exchange). Therefore these special auctions provide a 'third market' through which the funded company shares can be exchanged.

9.1.3   Main capital market instruments

Using a narrow definition of the capital market to include corporate shares and debentures, federal government securities, state and local government securities, and housing securities, the US dollar value of outstanding securities approximates $113 billion. This is approximately 38 per cent of Brazilian GDP. As can be noted, three of the five sectors included in Table 9.1 are largely undeveloped.

The market for company debentures faces difficulties related to changing levels of inflation, and a narrow institutional market. In general bankers do not support development of the debenture market, since these financial assets compete directly with bank loans. A large part of the debt of state and local governments is external, denominated in US dollars. Therefore it does not appear in any listing of domestic capital market instruments. The housing finance field suffers from weak institutional and regulatory support.

9.1.4   Stock exchanges and market intermediaries

There are nine stock exchanges in operation in Brazil. The two largest are the Rio (41.7 per cent of share value) and São Paulo (55.6 per cent of value) exchanges. In addition, Brazil has three active futures and commodities exchanges. These futures and commodities exchanges provide opportunities to trade futures contracts in gold, coffee, financial futures, and other commodities.

Brokerage firms ('corretoras') and securities dealerships ('distri-buidoras') perform similar functions, in such areas as underwriting shares, organising underwriting groups, purchasing and selling se-

Table 9.1   Main capital market instruments, 1988 (billions of US dollars)

	$	%
Company shares	38.0	33.6
Company debentures	0.4	0.4
Federal government securities[1]	69.4	61.4
State and local government securities	5.1	4.5
Housing securities	0.1	0.1
TOTAL	113.0	100.0
Total relative to GDP	38%	

[1] Includes Central Bank bills.
Source: Rio Stock Exchange, Central Bank, author's estimates.

curities for their own account, and organising and administering mutual funds. Brokerage firms can own seats on stock and commodities exchanges, and lead-manage underwriting groups. Securities dealerships can carry on these latter functions under contract with a brokerage firm.

Close to 265 brokerage firms operate in Brazil, and at least half of these headquarter their business in Rio or São Paulo. Almost 90 of the 'corretoras' are affiliated with large financial conglomerates, and a small number have foreign ownership. Of the more than 400 securities dealerships operating in Brazil, over 140 are related to conglomerates. More than half of the 'distribuidoras' are independent entities, and a small number (approximately 3 per cent of the total) have foreign shareholders or are affiliated with official institutions.

There are 41 investment banks that carry on some of the functions of the brokerage firms and securities dealers. These functions include underwriting and ownership of shares and other securities, performing sale–leaseback transactions, providing medium- and long-term loans, and administering mutual funds. Investment banks are becoming more important as financial sophistication increases. In 1988 foreign investors were indicating greater interest in this vehicle to enter the diversified financial industry in Brazil.

9.1.5   Institutional investors

Since the mid-1960s Brazil has sought to develop financial institutions that would accomplish a deepening of the capital market. In the brief descriptions which follow we consider eight categories or types of institutional investors. For the most part these are private sector oriented. Only in the case of the special government funds is there a prominent government role. For the most part these institutions allocate a large share of their resources to the capital market. However in some cases they acquire capital market type assets, but do not operate in an 'open' capital market. They operate on what might be termed a 'private placement' basis. This is particularly the case with respect to the special government funds, and the Fund of Social Participation.

1. Mutual funds. Approximately 136 mutual funds operate in Brazil. They invest most of their resources in capital market assets.
2. Fiscal funds. These investment funds originated under Decree Law 157, with the main objective of promoting the development of the stock market.
3. Investment companies. Created originally under Decree Law 1401, these funds now operate under Resolution 1289 (discussed elsewhere). They invest mainly in shares and debentures. Only nine of these investment companies exist at present compared with 16 in 1980. Under Resolution 1289 a new types of investment fund was created to channel foreign funds into Brazil.
4. Private pension funds. Two types of funds operate, closed and open funds. These funds are closely regulated by the government in the manner in which they allocate funds to the capital market.
5. Insurance companies. Close to a hundred insurance companies operate in Brazil. They are regulated in a manner very close to that applicable to the open pension funds.
6. Special government funds. Includes FINOR, FINAM, FISET, and others, that have invested in the securities of companies operating in special regions of Brazil.
7. Fund of Social Participation. This fund obtains cash for investment from retirement programmes for private sector and public sector employees. Its resources are administered by the National Bank for Economic and Social Development.
8. Investment clubs. These clubs are sponsored by the stock exchanges. They provide an incentive for individual investors to participate in securities investment.

9.1.6 Other institutional investors

Brazil has developed several other types of institutional investors that allocate at least part of their funds to the capital market. These have been described in Chapter 7, and include PAIT Funds, investment holding companies, and the National Development Fund.

9.2 ROLE OF GOVERNMENT IN PROMOTING CAPITAL MARKET

9.2.1 Financial deepening and the capital market

Since the mid-1960s much progress has been made in the development of Brazil's capital market. In part, this can be attributed to the efforts of government authorities to promote the capital market by building a sound legal base. In addition, government policy has been used in the development of the market. Policy action has taken the form of fiscal incentives, portfolio regulation, and use of alternative capital market technologies.

At least four distinct financial technologies can be utilised by a nation in mobilizing capital. These include self-finance, taxation, foreign aid, and the use of financial intermediaries operating in the capital market.[1] At any one point in time a given nation may be employing several of these technologies. Over time, as a nation develops, greater efficiency in capital mobilisation may be gained from the use of different technologies. Countries select from these technologies according to the opportunities presented, domestic economic conditions and need. Brazil has used all four of these technologies, varying the proportions of each.

Self-finance involves altering relative prices to benefit a particular investing sector, and imposes involuntary saving on other sectors. Self-finance is applied through price controls, inflation, or combinations of the two. Clearly, self-finance can cause distortions and inefficient resource allocation. Foreign funds may be used to add to the financial resources of a nation, but result in a debt service burden in later years. Taxation uses the power of the sovereign state to obtain savings from various economic sectors, with part of these funds channelled to the government or to specific investing sectors. In Brazil taxation has been used to a limited extent, owing to difficulties with the federal fiscal system. The financial intermediation technology requires the development of financial institutions, or financial assets held voluntarily by investors. The financial intermediation system is to be preferred from an efficiency basis.

Beginning in the mid-1960s Brazil set out to make use of the financial intermediation technology. The government turned to capital market reform as one of its major economic and social objectives.[2] The period immediately prior to the mid-1960s had been characterised by stagnation and decay in the financial markets, despite the high rate of real economic growth and industrial expansion achieved in Brazil.[3] According to Roe, Brazil's economic difficulties in the fifteen-year period leading up to the mid-1960s largely resulted from lack of four financial institutions: (1) an efficient tax revenue mechanism: (2) a modern securities market: (3) access to foreign funds: and (4) well-developed financial intermediaries.[4] In the decade and a half leading up to 1964 Brazil had achieved high economic growth, but faced increasing distortions and financing pressures. Negative real interest rates led to financial repression for depositors and investors. The interest rate structure became highly compartmentalised with growing disparities between rates paid by borrowers and those received by depositors. Corporate financial structures became excessively dependent on borrowed capital. Finance companies diverted financial savings from investment to consumer finance, and private financial institutions exhibited competitive weakness.[5]

9.2.2 First round of government measures

In 1964–5 Brazil created the legal basis for capital market development, by the enactment of two important laws. The operational framework that resulted set the stage for further important progress, and for a second round of statutory measures in 1976. The two laws are Law No. 4594 of 31 December 1964. This law created the National Monetary Council and provided a framework for the operation of banking and credit institutions; and Law No. 4728 of 14 July 1965. This law provided for regulation of the capital market and the creation of new institutions and market incentives.

The National Monetary Council (CMN) stands at the top of the financial regulatory structure, and co-ordinates the activities of Central Bank, National Securities Commission (CVM), and National Housing Bank (until it was abolished in 1987). The Central Bank implements CMN decisions, controls credit, and supervises financial institutions. These supervisory functions have been shared with the National Securities Commission, and other government agencies.

Law No. 4728 was the first attempt to provide a comprehensive and detailed set of guidelines for the development of the capital market in Brazil. The following stand out as important features of this law.

1. Since at this time there was no Securities Commission, Law 4728 provided for the CMN to regulate and the Central Bank to supervise operation of the financial markets. The Central Bank was authorised to establish and supervise the stock exchanges, financial institutions, and brokerage companies. In addition, the Central Bank was given authority to register securities for trading on the stock exchanges, to register new issues of bonds and stocks to be distributed in the capital market, and supervise disclosure by issuing companies.

2. This law provided that the CMN establish minimum capital requirements for brokerage companies, regulate their activities, establish rules for the operation of the stock exchanges, and regulate stock brokerage commissions, fees, and margin requirements.[6]

3. In addition Law No. 4728 established guidelines concerning access to the financial markets. Accordingly, bonds and securities may be issued on the financial markets only by means of the distribution system provided for in Law No. 4728. From 1965 on it was required that registration with the Central Bank precede the public issue of securities. Rules regarding information to be provided with the registration application are to be established by the National Monetary Council. Where inadequate diclosure or fraud is involved, the Central Bank could prohibit or suspend the distribution of securities.[7]

4. Law No. 4728 further provides for regulated access to the financial markets by companies with foreign capital. The law provides that in periods of imbalance in external payments, the CMN and Central Bank may limit recourse to the financial system of Brazil in the case of companies having access to the international financial markets.[8]

5. Provisions were made for more flexible issue of bonds and debentures. This includes permitting issue of bonds with monetary correction clauses, and issue of debentures convertible into shares.

6. Law No. 4728 sought to create an institutional market for bonds and securities. Investment funds could be created with authorisation of the Central Bank. These were to be regulated in terms of minimum diversification, and rules for administration of the stock portfolio.

7. Finally, Law No. 4728 provided an attractive tax environment for investors. The National Monetary Commission was given the task

of establishing conditions under which, for regulatory purposes, a company is considered to be publicly held. Also an incentive was offered investors holding shares in open companies where the tax withheld on dividend income was reduced to 25 per cent for publicly held companies, and 40 per cent for other companies. In addition, incentives were provided for debenture financing. Interest income and discount on debentures was to be taxed at a rate of 15 per cent and deducted at source.

The Capital Market Law (Law No. 4728) provided an important and much needed stimulus to the development of the Brazilian financial markets. It organised, codified and consolidated into a more orderly system the law governing the capital market. Prior to this there had been a multitude of laws, decrees, and regulations, often inconsistent with one another, that had been applicable to the capital market. In some cases these regulations impeded development. One important benefit of the capital market law was a provision for allowing authorized but unissued shares. This facilitated subsequent development of the issue of convertible debentures, where unissued shares must be available. Another benefit was the authorization of monetary correction on loans with more than one-year terms.[9] Prior to passage of the Capital Market Law lenders could not index loans to the price level or foreign currency. Moreover, they could not charge interest in excess of 12 per cent annual rate. This caused serious distortions in the development of the Brazilian financial markets.[10]

Equally important, Law No. 4728 brought new institutions to the capital market. Prominent among these were the investment banks. Under this law investment banks were authorised to carry on direct lending, purchase of shares, and issuance of guarantees. Also these institutions are empowered to engage in financial intermediation, underwriting of shares and bonds, stock brokerage, and management of mutual funds.

While the Capital Market Law provided for creation of new institutions, it also considered the need to modernise existing ones. It succeeded in breaking what was at that time a traditional monopoly of brokerage and securities trading activities. A number of new brokerage companies were organised, and brokerage activities were made available to firms linked to financial companies.

Perhaps the most important contribution of the Capital Market Law was its emphasis on registration and disclosure of information by companies whose securities are traded on the stock exchanges. No new issues could be forthcoming until the issue was registered with the Central Bank. Firms were required to submit financial statements, through a financial institution or a registered independent accountant. Securities could be refused for registration if the Central Bank judge that the financial data was not accurate, or did not correspond with real conditions.

By passage of Law No. 4728 the government defined the 'basic institutional structure through which financial development could take place'.[11] The Law created the *possibilities* of an improved capital market. We now turn to the events of 1966–75, to examine how well these possibilities were in fact developed.

9.2.3 Developments in 1966–75

As noted above, the period 1964–5 witnessed a structural reform in which the legal basis was established for further development of the Brazilian capital market. Our purpose now is to consider how this structure was implemented in the period 1966–75. We focus on the period ending in 1975, since a new set of structural reforms was initiated in 1976. Discussion of this second round of capital market legislation is reserved for a later section of this chapter. In our discussion of the period 1966–75 we focus on the following:

1. Measures aimed at development of the open capital company.
2. Fiscal fund system and Decree Law No. 157.
3. Stock market boom and crisis of 1971.
4. Foreign investment funds and Decree Law No. 1401.
5. Introduction of investment banks as a new capital market institution.

In order to encourage the democratisation of capital the government created a special category of company, the 'open capital corporation'.[12] To qualify as an open capital company a significant proportion of the company shares must be held by the public. If the company qualifies both the shareholders and corporation receive special tax treatment.[13] An early measure in this direction taken by the Castelo Branco government was the creation of a Fund for the Democratisation of Capital of Corporations (FUNDECE). In fact FUNDECE served more effectively as an agent of recapitalisation than of democratisation.[14] Under the programme shares were to be sold to the public. But obstacles including high underwriting costs and lack of wide market interest resulted in shares issues being subscribed by existing shareholders, without any widening of ownership. Shortly after, Law No. 4506 (1964) exempted companies from a special surtax on distributed profits if they took a series of measures to enhance the negotiability and distribution of their shares.[15] The Capital Market Law of 1965 superseded the legislation of a year earlier, and the Central Bank issued new guidelines concerning implementation of the new open capital company concept.[16] Basically the Central Bank guidelines emphasised development of a trading market. Ultimately a derivative outcome of these guidelines was renewed emphasis on protection of minority shareholder rights and more balanced application of shareholder control of open companies.

The new legislation provided for the creation of investment banks, that would provide medium- and long-term credits to companies. In addition these institutions would carry out securities activities and manage investment funds. Over the years the investment banks have played a more important role in the development of the capital market.

In the period 1965–6 anti-inflation policies had generated a near crisis in company finances. The government had hoped that the equities market would develop, given the fiscal incentives available under the evolving open capital company programme, and provide alternative sources of funds for firms facing tight liquidity conditions. Unfortunately the high interest rate structure associated with the credit restraint yielded a disappointing stock market performance. Early in 1967 Mario Henrique Simonsen, a financial advisor to the government and leading supporter of capital market development, reported that strong fiscal incentives were necessary if the stock market was to function effectively as a source of capital funds for the corporate sector. Not long after the government adopted the 'forced savings' fiscal incentive. Taxpayers would enjoy fiscal incentives if they purchased securities.

In effect, Decree Law No 157 was a new approach that went beyond marginal incentives aimed at encouraging wider share ownership and more active trading of shares. Taxpayers were allowed to use part of their income tax liabilities to buy shares of Fiscal Funds.[17] This was a new approach, recognising that for a time the capital market would have to be force-fed with tax subsidies. The financial intermediation approach was desirable, but required the infusion of rapidly growing institutions to become effective. Under Decree Law 157 substantial sums were channelled into Fiscal Fund entities that in turn invested in the equities market.

A major stock market boom ensued in 1967–9, with an increasing amount of new stock issues, purchased with 157 funds. The 157 system created a large pool of savings that otherwise would have gone partly to satisfy tax liabilities. Fiscal Funds were managed by investment banks (newly created under the Capital Market Law of 1965), finance companies and brokerage firms. Fiscal Fund portfolios could consist of shares and convertible debentures only. Companies receiving the financing generated by 157 Fund investments were granted fiscal incentives related to taxable income.[18]

The 157 Fund system provided many contributions in the way of capital market development:[19]

1. It created a financial intermediary group, that at one point was the largest institutional investor group in the capital market.
2. stimulated new share issues on the stock market.
3. led to greater interest in secondary trading of shares and securities.
4. provided opportunities for underwriting of new issues in the capital market in large volume, providing opportunities for development of prosperous intermediary institutions.

The impact of the fiscal incentives programme can be observed in the stock exchanges. Stock prices began to rise, reflecting an annual compound growth of over 138 per cent in the period 1967–71. In this period trading activity (in real terms) increased 63 times.[20] New share issues increased at an annual rate of 53 per cent, and the number of companies with shares traded in the stock exchange rose from 70 in 1964 to 226 in 1970. This snowballed into a speculative wave. In 1970–1 a high point of speculative activity was reached. In 1971 trading volume reached $5 billion, or 10 per cent of GNP.[21] The stock market boom ended at mid-year 1971, and a violent fall ensued. Not until 1985 did trading volume again reach the level of 1971 as a percentage of national income.

Over the period 1971–4 the stock market experienced lean years. Investors shifted their funds away from the stock exchanges, and the government attempted to support the market with new fiscal incentives and by channeling institutional money to the market. Insurance companies were required to direct part of their reserves to investments in shares and debentures issued by publicly held companies. These efforts were not fruitful.

The financial institution framework was enlarged in 1975 with the enactment of Decree Law No. 1401. This provided for the creation of investment companies to serve as a vehicle for investments in the stock market by foreign investors. These institutions enjoyed modest success in attracting foreign investment funds. By 1980 sixteen investment companies had been established under DL 1401, with resources representing close to one per cent of the funds held by institutional investors in the securities market.[22]

9.2.4 Second round of measures

A second stage of capital market reform came in 1976. By this time several problems had become evident in the development of the Brazilian capital market. These included:

1. The absence of an agency specifically given the task of supervising the securities markets, open companies, and stock exchanges.
2. The need to restore investor confidence, badly shaken in the crisis of 1971. Closely related to this was the need to restore credibility in the securities firms and intermediary companies that linked investors with the securities market.
3. Limited representation of institutional investors in the capital market.
4. Need for a more detailed and uniform system of disclosure and financial reporting of company performance.

In 1976 two laws were created to speed up the restructuring of capital market institutions. Law No. 6385 created the National Securities Commission, and Law No. 6404 provided for an improved system of corporate disclosure and protection of shareholders.

Law No. 6385 of 7 December 1976 has become a cornerstone of the capital market edifice. In addition to creating the National Securities Commission, it establishes a system of detailed surveillance over capital market activities and the various institutions that participate in the different sectors of the market. The major provisions of this law are as follows:

1. It specifies duties of the National Monetary Council and Securities Commission.

2. It provides for creation of the National Securities Commission, specifies its area of jurisdiction, and extends broad powers to the CVM with respect to examination of accounting records, obtaining information, applying penalties, and suspending trading of securities.
3. It extends to the CVM broad power to register securities issues prior to their distribution, and to register securities for trading on the capital markets.
4. It gives the CVM authority to issue regulations applicable to publicly held companies concerning disclosures, and transactions in company shares.
5. It extends to the CVM jurisdiction over activities related to the administration of portfolios and custody of securities, including establishing rules to be observed by portfolio administrators.
6. It gives the CVM authority to register chartered accounting firms and independent accountants. This authority extends over institutions, corporations, and companies which are a part of the securities brokerage and distribution system.

The Securities Commission has issued numerous instructions concerning legal and accounting matters, the means by which companies may publicise securities issues, procedures for registration of securities with the CVM for trading, formulas for the provision of financial information by open companies, method of applying monetary correction, and procedures and methods for operation of foreign investment funds in Brazil.

9.2.5 The Corporation Law

The second legislative cornerstone of the capital market established in 1976 was The Corporation Law (Law No. 6404). This law provided an institutional framework that would further the development of the stock market, provide the corporate manager with the legal and financial requirements for the modernisation of Brazilian companies, and afford a regulatory system that would give investors greater confidence in capital market efficiency. Much emphasis is given to objective valuation of shares, public ownership, investor protection, and corporate governance. Law No. 6404 gives detailed attention to the following areas:

1. Disclosure and financial statements.
2. Shareholder protection.
3. Share and debenture issues.
4. Corporate governance.

Even with these reforms the authorities neglected to homogenise these measures among the different agencies and institutions that deal with the capital market. These include the Ministry of Finance, the National Securities Commission, National Association of Accountants, National Association of Auditors, and the banking association (FEBRABAN). Each of the above has a different approach toward making transparent the financial position and status of a company. This continues to present a problem in Brazil, and to be dealt with effectively would require a multi-agency analysis and review of financial reporting, with recommendations able to balance off the specific needs and interests of these various interest groups.

Disclosure

Optimal allocation of capital in the financial market requires adequate disclosure and dissemination of information. Optimal allocation implies that securities prices and yields reflect the productive efficiency of capital adjusted for risk. Compulsory disclosure assures more efficient allocation of capital, and protects the investor.

The task of a regulatory body such as the CVM should include the selection of information to be disclosed by corporations. In addition this agency should have the power to issue detailed instructions concerning how and under what conditions disclosures may be made.

The Corporation Law is most explicit in its requirement that the board of directors prepare financial accounts and statements, and Law No. 6404 provides details about information to be included in these statements.[23] Responsibilities are assigned in the Law, by indicating which parties shall be responsible for maintaining and disclosing this information, and by indicating company liability for losses to interested parties from any irregularities or errors found in the disclosure.[24]

The Corporation Law focuses on the role of the general meeting in deciding on all matters relating to company objectives, and the authority of the general meeting to review the annual accounts drawn up by company officers and to accept or reject financial statements presented by them. Minutes of the general meeting provide a means of disclosure. Annual general meetings have the purpose of receiving, discussing and voting on financial statements, deciding on the allocation of net profits, electing officers and audit committee members, and approving the monetary adjustment to capital. Documents which must be made available to shareholders at least one month before the date of the annual general meeting include the management report on company affairs for the last financial year, copies of the accounts and financial statements, and opinion of the independent auditors.

The Audit Committee plays a key role in the disclosure process. Specific standards apply for eligibility to serve on the Audit Committee. These include Brazilian residence, university degree or three years of prior service on an audit committee or company office. The Audit Committee has the following areas of responsibility: (1) to give opinion on any proposals for changes in capital, issue of securities, dividend distributions or merger; (2) to report any error, fraud or criminal act discovered; (3) to call the annual general meeting should the administrative bodies delay doing so; (4) to examine the trial balance sheet and other financial statements at least every three months; and (5) to examine the accounts and financial statements for the financial year and give an opinion on them.

Under Law No. 6404 the board of directors has responsibility for preparing the following financial accounts and statements: (1) balance sheet showing assets and liabilities; (2) annual profit and loss statement; (3) a statement of the results of the financial year; and (4) a statement of the origin and investment of funds. In addition, this section of the law specifies numerous details of information required for disclosure.[25]

Shareholder protection

An effectively operating capital market must provide adequate protection to individual investors. Large financial institutions have the resources and knowledge of market operations to be able to protect their interests as investors. However this is not generally true of individual investors. Therefore it is important that the regulatory environment and legal structure consider the needs of individual investors.

Concern for shareholder protection is well reflected in The Corporation Law. The Corporation Law provides for publicly owned companies to contract with a financial institution authorised by the National Securities Commission to serve as custodian of its share register books, share transfer books, and the issue of its share certificates.[26] Companies are prohibited from trading in their own

shares except in cases of ordinary redemption, refund, or amortisation operations.

Shareholders are further protected by the requirement that capital
subscriptions be fully paid up by all shareholders. The Corporation
Law enforces this provision by stating that shareholders shall be
considered in arrears when they fail to fully pay for shares. In such
cases they may be required to pay interest and penalties.[27] Once a
shareholder is deemed to be in arrears, the company may bring
proceedings, or order that the shares be sold on a stock exchange for
the account of the shareholders.

Finally, the Corporation Law explicitly states the inherent rights of
shareholders.[28] These include the right to participate in corporate
profits, to participate in the assets in case of liquidation, to supervise
the management of the business, and first refusal in subscription of
shares.

Share and debenture issues

The Corporation Law has well-defined rules for the issue of shares,
changes in capital, and the status of different types of shares (ordinary, preferred). These rules cover the prescribed means of payment
for shares issued; liability of subscribing shareholders; the relationship of different types of share issues to one another; requirements
pertaining to the physical issue and format of share certificates; limits
or restrictions on the ownership and trading of shares; and procedures for redemption, amortisation or refund.[29] Further, shareholders are given protection through various provisions designed to
preserve the capital position of the company.[30]

Law No. 6404 provides for the establishment and development of a
market for debentures. Investor safeguards are included, and the
general meeting has the exclusive competence to decide whether to
issue debentures. Other details shall be considered at the general
meeting such as amount of the issue, number and par value of
debentures, interest payments, and method of placement. Investor
protection is provided by restrictions on the issue of debentures by
companies. These restrictions relate to total company capital, but the
Securities Commission may establish other limits.

A debenture holders' trustee must be appointed, and specific
requirements screen those eligible to serve as trustee.[31] The CVM has
authority for controlling the activities of the trustee of debenture
issues offered to the public, or traded on the capital market. The

trustee must report annually to the debenture holders on matters pertinent to their interests.

Corporate governance

Ultimately the owners of the company should have a determination of corporate policy. Generally this is provided for by giving the shareholders the right to elect the board of directors at annual general meetings. Law No. 6404 provides that the management of a company shall be entrusted either to its administrative council and its board of directors, or only to the board of directors.[32] Open companies are required to have an administrative council. The responsibilities of these administrative bodies may not be delegated to another body.[33] The Corporation Law provides that the administrative council consist of at least three members, elected at a general meeting and subject to removal by a general meeting. The administrative council possesses broad authority to establish the company business strategy. In this connection it elects and discharges company directors and prescribes their duties, supervises the performance of directors, authorises the transfer of fixed assets, and selects and discharges independent auditors.

Officers of open companies are required to make public their investment in the company, options to purchase shares, and interests *in affiliated* companies. Also, officers may be requested by the shareholders to disclose to the general meeting their transactions in company securities and stock purchase options.

9.3 DEVELOPMENT OF SELECTED FINANCIAL INTERMEDIARIES

9.3.1 Introduction

In an earlier section of this chapter we noted that Brazil adopted a new approach to the development of the domestic economy and more specifically to the deepening of the capital market. Beginning in the 1960s, the government adopted a series of measures designed to promote the development of financial intermediaries. This approach was continued in the following decade, and reinforced in particular in the period 1974–9.[34]

Objectives

While we could assert that the many measures enacted by the government in this period (1964–79) aimed at promoting the development of institutional investors that would facilitate and spur the national rate of savings, many other related objectives lie behind the various laws and regulations issued by the government. Perhaps one of the more important was the need to mobilise financial resources for economic and social development purposes in a way that would also support the stronger capitalisation of private domestic enterprises. In effect, this implied a 'rebalancing' of the relative capital strength of private domestic enterprises relative to foreign-owned firms and state enterprises.[35]

By the early 1970s it had become quite evident that state enterprises and foreign-owned firms enjoyed substantial financing advantages that left private domestic enterprises in a relatively weaker competitive position. In the 1960s this was made apparent when foreign multinationals engaged in a wave of take-overs of private domestic enterprises that some observers believed threatened to disenfranchise the domestic business sector and which others believed would permanently cripple the competitive status of the domestically-owned industrial sector. State enterprises had long enjoyed ready access to low cost capital channelled through government-owned banks and credit institutions, and as a result of the credit subsidy programmes of the Banco do Brasil.

A rebalancing of relative capital strength was considered to offer the potential advantages of (1) relieving the federal government budget from the burden of subsidized credit; (2) freeing monetary policy to focus more on general credit controls; and (3) allowing market-determined interest rates to allocate capital.

Within this context, we can understand that one important objective underlying the development of financial institutions was the strengthening of the market for corporate shares and debentures. A strengthening of this capital market sector would provide a more ready market through which private sector enterprises could expand their long-term capital position. In addition, domestic enterprises would benefit from having an alternative to bank loans, and in this way inject greater competitive pressures into the financial market sectors providing industrial companies with capital funds.

Finally, we should remember that Brazil, by its basic character, is a high growth–high investment economy. To maintain the high level of investment required for satisfactory growth, Brazil requires a large amount of aggregate saving (domestic and foreign). By providing a wider variety of financial institutions it was understood that the flow of savings could expand more rapidly. In short, a more effective mobilisation of domestic funds would take place in Brazil, meaning larger savings flows channelled more efficiently to the capital scarce sectors. An important derivative benefit would be potentially less dependence on external sources of finance. Since the onset of the global debt crisis in 1982, this consideration ranks much higher in importance. However this does not mean that Brazil has closed the door in its efforts to utilise foreign source capital. As we note in Chapters 12 and 14 new and innovative investment vehicles are being created to liquidate Brazil's external debt and at the same time mobilise financial resources for domestic investment.

Overview of major type intermediaries

The major financial intermediaries operating on the capital market and their securities investments are identified in Table 9.2. In 1986 these seven institutional groups held combined resources of CZ$214 695 million, or US$15 630 million. This is equivalent to one-third of Brazilian gross saving investment in that year, and approximately one-third of the total Brazilian stock market capitalisation. Brazil's capital market intermediaries may have a long way to go to be able to play the role of intermediating a major share of capital funds each year, but they have become a significant factor, and now have a wide base of operations upon which they can build and extend themselves.

The closed-pension funds rank first in total resources. They are followed by the mutual funds. The Fund of Social Participation ranks third. This fund is supported by a compulsory savings programme that finances the retirement of covered workers. Insurance companies rank fourth as capital market investors.

The seven types of institutions display widely differing allocations of investment resources. The closed-pension funds have the largest amount of investment in the securities markets, but this represents only 40 per cent of their total resources. Similarly the mutual funds rank second in the amount invested in the securities markets, with 57 per cent of funds in this area. Open pension funds have the smallest

Table 9.2 Major capital market financial intermediaries, 1986 (million cruzados)

	Open pension funds	Closed pension funds	Insurance cos.	Mutual funds	Investfunds foreign capital	Investment clubs	Fund of social participation	Total
Shares	1 460	47 973	4 822	31 331	388	3 182	14 250	
Debentures		1 554		1 728			137	
Total securities	1 460	49 527	4 822	32 059	388	3 182	14 387	105 825
Total resources held	5 424	123 899	12 356	55 929	522	3 182	14 387	214 695
Per cent of total	2.4	57.7	5.6	26.0	0.2	1.5	6.6	100.0
Per cent of total invested in shares and debentures	27.0	40.3	39.2	57.4	74.3	100.0	100.0	
Total resources held in US dollars[1]	393.0	8 978.2	895.3	4 052.9	37.7	231.0	1 042.5	15 630.6

* Calculated at the rate of CZ$ 13.8 per US dollar.
Source: CVM, *Relatório Anual 1986*. pp. 32–7.

percentage allocation of resources in the securities markets. As is noted below, the pension funds are regulated in a detailed manner concerning the asset allocation of their portfolios.

9.3.2 Pension funds

In this section we consider the activities of closed private pension funds and open private pension funds.[36] These two types of institutions are discussed in the same section since the CMN regulations governing portfolio investments apply to both in a similar manner, and because these both represent investors with the need to invest in the capital market on a long-term basis.

Since the enactment in 1977 of Law No. 6435, which provided detailed rules for the creation and operation of private pension funds, these institutions have experienced rapid growth in assets. They passed the longer-established insurance companies in total asset holdings very quickly, and by 1980 their resources were more than two times those of insurance companies. By 1987 closed pension funds had CZ$299 billion of funds under their management (approximately $7.3 billion), and at the same time open pension funds had CZ$30 billion of funds (approximately $0.7 billion). On a real basis closed pension funds have been growing at a rate of 10–12 per cent annually. About half of this growth is from income on investments, and one-half new money from contributions of employers and employees.[37]

Organisation

The private pension system in Brazil extends back in time for several decades. But not until the coming into effect of Law No. 6435 of July 1977 was there comprehensive federal support and supervision of the private pension plans. Prior to 1977 the open pension plans were more popular, in number of plans and in resources at their disposal. Since 1977 the closed pension plans have grown rapidly, and now dominate this sector. At mid-year 1988 there were 200 closed and 114 open pension entities operating in Brazil, with the closed entities accounting for over 92 per cent of total private pension plan resources. Of the 200 closed pension funds, 91 were sponsored by firms in the private sector, and 109 by public sector enterprises (Table 9.3). Close to 800 sponsoring firms were contributing to the closed private pension entities in 1988, of which 539 or 68 per cent were in the private sector, and 256 firms or 32 per cent were in the public sector.

Closed pension organisations are administered by the Minister of Health and Education. Technically they are not of a corporate form, but are non-profit foundations. By contrast, the open pension organisations are administered by the National Securities Commission (CVM), and since they conform to the Sociedade Anonima (S.A.) form of organisation can be regarded as having profit objectives relative to their operation.

Closed pension organisations are established by companies that wish to provide pension benefits for their employees. Therefore the beneficiaries of a given closed pension organisation are employees of one company, or group of companies that are closely affiliated. By contrast, open pension organisations do not necessarily have such common bond employment aspects. And their plans can be offered to individuals from a wide range of employment and professional connections.[38] Since the largest companies in Brazil tend to be in the public sector (state enterprises), we shall observe that the largest part of closed pension assets are in funds established in the public sector. For example, in 1988 only 12 per cent of pension assets were in pension organisations in private sector companies, while 88 per cent of pension assets were in pension organisations in public sector companies (Table 9.3). From this we should remember that these are all private pension entities ('entidades de previdência privada'). In addition, there is the social security ('previdência social') program administered by the federal government. Some comparisons are made between the private pension and social security programs in a later section of this chapter.

Pension fund management in Brazil must deal effectively with inflation. A large part of the assets that closed pension entities invest in (over 80 per cent) are subject to monetary correction. Each month these entities make adjustments for monetary correction, to their applicable assets and liabilities. The objective is to protect ultimate beneficiaries from inflation. We return to this question in a later part of this section, concerning portfolio management.

Benefits and beneficiaries

In 1988 closed pension funds had 1.7 million covered participants, compared with 0.3 million for open funds. Between 1980 and 1988 covered participants of closed pension funds increased from 1.0 million to 1.7 million, or 70 per cent (Table 9.3). In the same period those retired receiving benefits increased from 42 000 to 100 000.

Table 9.3 Basic structure of closed private pension entities, sponsoring firms, distribution of reserves, and participants

Sector	Pension fund entities No.	%	Sponsoring firms No.	%	Distribution of reserves[1] CZ$million	%	Participants[2] No.	%
Private	91	46	539	68	177 801	12	527 764	31
Firms	74	37	295	37				
Banks	17	9	224	31				
Public	109	55	256	32	1 294 142	88	1 180 838	69
Federal banks	7	4	9	1				
Service cos.	8	4	9	1				
Mixed economy cos.[3]	26	13	120	15				
State banks	28	14	64	8				
Mixed economy cos.[3]	40	20	54	7				
TOTAL	200	100	793	100	1 471 943	100	1 708 602	100

[1] As of 30 April 1988.
[2] As of 31 Dec. 1987.
[3] Involving mixed ownership of share participations, by government and by private sector shareholders.
Source: ABRAPP, 'Sistema Fechado de Previdência Privada', *Consolidado Estatístico*, May 1988, p. 01.

In Brazil eligibility to retire and receive pension benefits is based on years of service with the sponsor company. Benefits received are based on actuarially determined limits. These in turn relate to the average remuneration of the employee in the final twelve month period of employment, and the benefits conceded by social security.[39]

Basically benefits of covered workers at retirement will attain a total amount, part paid by the private pension fund and part paid by the government social security programme, as measured in number of units of minimum wages. The smaller the social security component as a percentage of the total, the higher the retirement benefits from the pension programme. For example, a worker entitled to receive 50 times minimum wages of retirement benefits (fairly substantial benefits) would be paid approximately three-fourths of this by the private pension plan and the remainder by social security.

In this regard, the private pension system in Brazil works as a complement *vis-à-vis* the social security system. Employees covered by the private pension programme can enjoy a considerable increase in retirement income over what they receive from the social security programme. This is fortunate since the social security system has experienced considerable difficulties in the decade of the 1980s in maintaining the purchasing power value of benefits paid to those retired and covered by the social security programme.

Type of plans offered

Until 1987 the closed pension organisations offered only one type of plan, the defined benefit plan. In this case there are defined liabilities of the company that sponsors the plan. An actuarial system is used to estimate the total reserves needed to capitalise the fund. Contributions come from two sources, the sponsor company and the employees.

In late 1987 a second type of plan came into being that provided financial advantages to sponsoring companies. This is the defined contribution plan. In this case the actuarial calculations do not seek to arrive at a total liability for the sponsor company, but calculate three types of contributions that are required to satisfy the goals of the pension programme. These contributions include (1) employer contributions, (2) employee contributions, and (3) income generated by financial results. Under the defined contribution plans sponsor companies can find the cost (annual contribution) somewhat lower than in the case of the defined benefit plan.

Regulation of portfolios

Pension funds have grown to become the largest institutions in the securities market.[40] They play an important role in the new issues market, are the most active, and help the market to absorb large flotations of new issues. Their role in secondary share trading represents about 15 per cent of market volume. Closed funds pay full tax on capital gains, and on interest and dividend income. This affects relative returns, the cost to the sponsor company of providing pension benefits, overall fund growth, and the relative attractiveness of alternative investment outlets. Portfolio strategy can also be affected by the tax status of closed funds, and we return to this question as we consider the portfolio regulations imposed by the National Monetary Council (CMN).

Shortly after the enactment of Law No. 6435, which provided for the creation of private pension funds, the National Monetary Council issued Resolution 460.[41] This resolution is considered to be one of the most important steps in the development of Brazilian financial inter-mediaries. Resolution 460 established maximum and minimum limits on the amounts of different groups of assets that could be held in the investment portfolios of pension funds. Under Resolution 460 a minimum of 10 per cent of the portfolio of closed pension funds was to be invested in federal government securities, and a minimum 15 per cent for open funds. Further, this resolution established a range (20 to 40 per cent of the portfolio) to be allocated to shares and debentures.[42] Further, Resolution 460 established concentration lim-its. For example, no more than 2 per cent of the portfolio could be invested in the shares of any one company, no more than 4 per cent in the debt of any one company, no more than 10 per cent of the portfolio in the shares of any one mutual fund, and no more than 10 per cent in the deposits of any single financial institution.[43]

In the period 1978–82 the CMN issued three additional Resol-utions that modified these pension funds investment guidelines.[44] In 1987 CMN Resolutions 1362 and 1363 were issued, providing de-tailed revisions concerning the composition of pension fund and insurance company invested reserves. These revisions are summar-ised as follows:

Closed Pension Funds[45]

A   General portfolio allocations
  1. Obligations of the National Development Fund – 30 per cent minimum
  2. Shares of open companies – 25 per cent minimum
  3. Loans and financings – 17 per cent maximum
  4. Real estate – 20 per cent maximum
  5. Remaining resources invested in securities of the federal government, state governments, 'letras do Banco Central'; securities of the municipal governments, obligations of Ele-trobrás, securities or debt issued by the National Bank for Economic and Social Development (BNDES); mortgage debt and notes, shares of mutual funds, and other forms of invest-ment authorised by the Central Bank or Securities Com-mission.
B   Concentration limits
  1. Shares issued by any one company cannot exceed 4 per cent of fund resources. Pension fund investment in shares of a company

are limited to 8 per cent of the voting capital or 20 per cent of total capital of the company.
2. Debentures issued by any one borrower cannot exceed 4 per cent of pension fund resources.
3. Investment in the shares of any one mutual fund cannot exceed 10 per cent of pension fund resources.
4. Investment in the securities issued by any one financial institution, state government or municipality, cannot exceed 10 per cent of fund resources.

Open Pension Funds and Insurance Companies[46]

A General portfolio allocations
1. Obligations of the National Development Fund – 50 per cent maximum
2. Shares of open companies – 25 per cent minimum
3. Real estate
   40 per cent maximum for open pension funds
   25 per cent maximum for insurance companies
4. Following categories (separately or taken together) – 40 per cent maximum
   (a) debt securities of municipalities, Eletrobrás, securities or debt issued for the National Bank for Economic and Social Development (BNDES);
   (b) term deposits, debentures, 'letras de cambio' accepted by credit societies, financings and investments, mortgage debt and notes;
   (c) investments in fixed income mutual funds;
   (d) loans and participations approved by the National Private Insurance Council (CNSP), limited to 10 per cent of technical reserves;
   (e) direct credits approved by the Superintendency of Private Insurance (SUSEP), limited to 10 per cent of technical RESERVES.
B Concentration limits
1. Shares issued by any one company cannot exceed 10 per cent of total funds invested in shares and mutual funds. Investment in the shares of any one company cannot exceed 10 per cent of the voting capital or 20 per cent of the total capital of that company.
2. Debentures issued by any one borrower cannot exceed 4 per cent of the resources referred to in line 4 above.

3. Investment in the shares of any one mutual fund cannot exceed 10 per cent of the funds invested in shares and mutual funds.
4. The total resources invested in securities of any one firm, of firms under its control directly or indirectly, cannot exceed 10 per cent of total invested resources.

Portfolio structure in 1987–8

The portfolio structure of closed private pension funds is presented in Table 9.4. This represents the portfolio as of May 1987 and May 1988. The May 1988 portfolio structure reflects the maximum and minimum limits embodied in the July 1987 CMN Resolutions 1362 and 1363.

Pension funds must have a high degree of inflation protection built into their investment portfolios. Holdings of shares and real property investments may at times provide some inflation protection, if these asset categories realise appreciation in value that equals or surpasses the rate of inflation. At times investments in shares and real property may offer this type of protection, since their price levels may be expected to rise along with inflation. Government securities and other forms of debt securities are subject to monetary correction, and therefore can provide protection against inflation.

From the point of view of the pension funds, the stock market is speculative and volatile. As a result, their investments in shares tend to be close to the minimum prescribed by applicable regulations. As can be noted in Table 9.4, in the 12 months from May 1987 to May 1988 investment in shares increased from 18.5 per cent to 28.7 per cent of resources. This reflects a strong upswing in the stock market in the early months of 1988, as well as the regulatory changes of July 1987 which increased the minimum allocation to share investments.

The largest pension funds conduct block trades in shares with other investors (corporations and banks). Pension funds buy almost all of the debentures issued in the primary market, and their return on debentures includes provision for monetary correction and interest.

Investments in shares takes three forms: outright purchases in the sight market, purchases in the term market, and purchase of options. At May 1988 the distribution of share investments was as follows:

Purchase at sight	CZ$394 778 million
Purchase at term	971 million
Purchase of options	14 729 million

Table 9.4   Portfolio of closed pension funds, May 1987, May 1988

Type loan or investment	31 May 1987 Cruzado	Per cent	31 May 1988 Cruzado	Per cent
National development Fund	36 558	15.6	229 348	16.0
Shares	43 417	18.5	410 478	28.7
Loans & financings	22 061	9.4	94 041	6.6
Real estate	12 306	5.2	59 552	4.2
Straight	9 755	4.2	34 489	2.4
Term deposits in banks	35 285	15.0	181 387	12.7
Real estate	37 535	15.9	210 672	14.7
LTN & OTN	15 286	6.5	60 756	4.2
State government securities	15 982	6.7	77 332	5.4
Debentures	1 968	0.8	9 503	0.7
Loans to Participants	15 688	6.7	86 755	6.1
Other loans & investments	11 688	4.9	70 432	4.9
TOTAL RESOURCES	235 468	100.0	1 430 704	100.0

Note: Amounts are in millions of cruzados.
Source: ABRAPP, 'Sistema Pechado de Previdência Privada', *Consolidado Estatístico*, May 1988, Mapa A.

The use of the term and options market sectors reflects a fairly sophisticated approach to investing in the share market by closed pension funds.

Closed pension funds also make limited use of mutual funds in their investments in shares and fixed income securities. At May 1988 their portfolio investments in share mutual funds were CZ$4490 million, and in fixed income mutual funds were CZ$7789 million. These come to a total of 0.83 per cent of overall portfolios at that time. These investments enable closed funds to benefit from the portfolio management skills and increased diversification offered by the mutual funds.

As of May 1988 the largest asset holdings in the portfolios of closed pension funds were shares (28.7 per cent), investments in real estate (14.7 per cent), holdings of obligations of the National Development Fund (16.0 per cent), term deposits (12.7 per cent) and loans (6.7 per cent).

Investments in real estate represented 14.7 per cent of closed pension fund resources at May 1988. This compares with a maximum limit of 20.0 per cent of resources as prescribed in Resolution 1362. In recent years closed pension funds have exhibited much interest in diversified investments in real estate including financing of commercial property. Investment in commercial real estate offers favorable opportunities for maximum return, diversification, and safety, and compatability with the broader needs of the community.[47] Shopping centre investments in particular are a preferred outlet for institutional investors, in part because this represents a high growth sector offering an investment channel for many years into the future. Also, shopping centre offer a potentially high real return to pension fund investors.[48]

The information in Table 9.4 suggests a relatively broad diversification of the portfolios of closed pension funds. This reflects the following policies and conditions:

1. Inability of funds to focus on only a few broad capital market sectors to carry out their investing, owing in part to the relatively small size and capacity of many capital market sectors.
2. Policy of the government to promote the development of various capital market sectors by applying minimum and maximum percentage portfolio allocations.
3. The Brazilian capital market enjoys a wide range of sectors and instruments that afford investors and regulatory bodies some flexibility in responding to changes in economic conditions.
4. Given the detailed portfolio allocations designated by the government, the government has the responsibility to provide a framework within which pension fund managers can achieve the actuarial results required under the terms of the various pension programs in operation.[49]
5. The degree of latitude that is available to pension fund managers leaves them in the position of being subject to the prudent man rule.[50]

The portfolio structure of open private pension funds is presented in Table 9.5. The largest holdings in the portfolio include certificates of deposits in banks (27.42 per cent), shares (14.51 per cent), LTN (12.87 per cent) and OTN (9.05 per cent). It is worth noting that there are noticeable differences in the composition of the portfolios of closed as contrasted with open pension funds:

Table 9.5   Portfolio of open private pension funds, March 1987

Type asset holding	Cruzado (million)	Per cent of funds
LTN	656	12.87
CDB	1 398	27.42
OTN	465	9.05
RDB	266	5.22
State of government securities	178	3.49
Municipal government securities	–	–
Convertible debentures	7	0.13
Straight debentures	39	0.77
Obligations of eletrobras	53	1.04
Letras de cambio	37	0.73
Letras imobiliarias	–	–
Securities linked to resales	275	5.40
Mutual funds	8	0.16
Shares	740	14.51
Other	979	19.19
TOTAL	5 101	100.00

Source: Banco Central.

1. Term deposits play a more important role in the case of open pension funds.
2. Federal government securities (LTN and OTN) play a much more important role in the portfolios of open pension funds.
3. Real estate investments play an important role in the portfolios of closed funds, but not in the case of open funds.
4. Obligations of the National Development Fund play an important role in the portfolio of closed pension funds, but not in the case of open funds.

These comparisons reflect a more liquid position in the case of open pension funds in 1987 (term deposits and federal government securities make up close to 54 per cent of open pension fund portfolios). Closed pension funds do not possess this type of liquidity, since covered employees are not likely to be in a position to need or want to liquidate their pension fund reserves.

Table 9.6   Resources of insurance companies, 1982–6 (million cruzados)

Year	Shares & debentures (A)	Per cent change	Total reserves (B)	Per cent change	Shares & debentures as percentage total (A/B)
1982	44.7	–	203.5	–	21.9
1983	120.8	170.2	521.7	156.4	23.2
1984	574.1	375.2	1 739.6	233.4	33.0
1985	2 797.7	387.3	6 772.1	289.3	41.3
1986*	4 822.1	72.4	12 356.0	82.5	39.0

* Preliminary data.
Source: CVM, *Relatório Anual 1986*, p. 35.

9.3.3   Insurance companies

Like the pension funds, insurance companies are regulated by the CMN in connection with their portfolio activities. There are many links between the insurance companies and the financial system of Brazil. These operate through the investment of technical reserves, the conglomerate form of organisation, the financing of insurance premiums, and the application of credit insurance. Insurance companies are subject to CMN and Central Bank regulation of their portfolio investments, as well as National Private Insurance Council and Superintendence of Private Insurance (SUSEP) with respect to their basic insurance operations.

The insurance companies have exhibited an extremely high growth in resources (Table 9.6), and in 1986 ranked fourth among capital market institutions in total assets. Their reserves (for insurance contracts outstanding) increased by 82 per cent in 1985–6. In 1986 share and debenture investments accounted for two-fifths of total resources.

At year-end 1987 insurance companies held CZ$52 billion in portfolio investments (equivalent at prevailing exchange rates to US$0.5 billion). The largest asset categories were real estate (over 33 per cent), term deposits in banks (over 28 per cent), shares (16 per cent) and federal government securities (12 per cent). Insurance company portfolios possess a high degree of liquidity based on their government securities and term deposits (Table 9.7). These two categories account for over 40 per cent of their overall portfolios.

Table 9.7   Investment portfolios of insurance companies, year end 1987

Asset category	Per cent of portfolio
OTN & LTN	4.27
LBC	8.19
State government securities	5.04
Shares	16.04
Debentures	2.18
CDB & RDB	28.77
Quotas in investment funds	0.17
Real estate	33.90
Letras de Cambio	0.39
Obligations of eletrobras	0.56
Shares & debentures of closed capital cos.	0.42
Other	0.07
TOTAL	100.00

Source: Central Bank and CVM.

9.3.4   Mutual funds

The government has made great efforts to develop and open the Brazilian share market. It has had limited success in this direction. However mutual funds and fiscal funds offer considerable potential for further opening of the capital market in Brazil. These institutions began their history in 1967 when Decree Law No. 157 came into being, providing for tax credits for investors acquiring investments in these funds. Fiscal Funds 157 grew rapidly in the period 1968–71, in large part as a result of fiscal incentives for purchase of shares in the stock market. A stock market boom culminated in the 'crisis of 1971'. In that year these funds accounted for 4.2 per cent of financial assets, making them the largest capital market investor in Brazil. In the next four years these funds declined in importance as investors became uninterested in share investments. By 1977 they had regained some of their status, accounting in that year for 1.2 per cent of financial assets in Brazil. The distribution of their share investments is indicated in Table 9.8. As can be noted, the Mutual Funds and Fiscal Funds (Funds 157) invest primarily in non-financial national enter-

Table 9.8   Composition of shareholdings of selected investor groups

Type of investor	State enterprises	Foreign enterprises	National enterprises Financial private	Non-financial private	Total
Private investors	63.3	5.1	11.1	20.5	100
Funds 157	0.7	18.0	–	81.3	100
Mutual funds	2.4	11.9	0.7	85.0	100
Pension & other funds	59.0	1.5	22.7	16.8	100

Source: Banco Mundial, *Brasil: Analise dos Sistemas Financeiros*, IBMEC, 1985, p. 194.

prises operating in the private sector, whereas the private investor and pension funds invest primarily in state enterprises.

In the period 1982–6 mutual funds experienced strong growth, with the number of funds increasing from 58 to 225. Capital invested in these funds increased 1700-fold, and in 1986 their capital exceeded US$4.0 billion. Large mutual funds dominate the sector. Three types of funds operate: those investing primarily in fixed income securities, those investing in shares, and those investing in short-term investments. Table 9.9 reflects the portfolio composition of fixed-income and share-mutual funds in 1985–6 (the portfolio investments of short-term funds is discussed in Chapter 8). In 1986 funds investing in shares held twice the resources of funds investing in fixed-income securities. However this situation was somewhat reversed a year earlier when fixed income funds held larger resources. In large part, the change is due to the sharp upswing in share values early in 1986, related to the favourable receiption at that time to the Cruzado Plan, and the inflow of new investment money attracted by the prospect of high returns. Early in 1988 (February) fixed-income funds moved ahead of share-mutual funds in total resources, and a few months later this condition persisted (Table 9.10).

9.3.5   Fund of Social Participation (FSP)

The Fund of Social Participation (FSP) is a component of the Fund of Participation – PIS-PASEP. Operated in a manner similar to mutual funds, FPS is administered by the National Bank for Economic and

Table 9.9   Portfolio structure of mutual funds, 1985–6

Asset or security holding	1985* Value	%	1986* Value	%
SHARE FUNDS				
Shares	16 601.7	92.4	31 208.3	82.2
Convertible debentures	255.8	1.4	116.2	0.3
Straight debentures	3.7	0.1	5.1	0.1
OTN & LTN/LBC	1 067.4	5.9	6 510.9	17.2
OTE & OTM[1]	0.1	–	33.3	0.1
Other	40.0	0.2	23.3	0.1
Total capital	17 968.7	100.0	37 897.1	100.0
FIXED INCOME FUNDS				
Shares	49.6	0.2	123.3	0.7
Convertible debentures	949.8	4.5	693.4	3.9
Straight debentures	643.1	3.0	913.1	5.1
OTN & LTN/LBC	18 426.1	87.6	6 136.5	34.0
OTE & OTM	45.9	0.2	96.9	0.5
Other	939.4	4.5	10 068.9	55.8
Total capital	21 053.9	100.0	18 032.1	100.0
TOTAL MUTUAL FUNDS				
Shares	16 651.3	42.7	31 331.6	56.0
Convertible debentures	1 205.6	3.1	809.6	1.5
Straight debentures	646.8	1.7	918.2	1.6
OTN & LTN/LBC	19 493.5	49.9	12 647.4	22.6
OTE & OTM	46.0	0.1	130.2	0.2
Other	979.4	2.5	10 092.2	18.1
Total capital	39 022.6	100.0	55 929.2	100.0
Share mutual funds as % total		46.0		67.7
Fixed income funds as % total		54.0		32.3

[1] Obligations of States and Municipalities.
Source: CVM, *Relatório Anual 1986*, p. 33.
Value Amounts are in Cr. $billion.

Social Development (BNDES). FPS channels its resources, by preference, into shares and debentures of open companies. The resources of FPS applied to the securities market represent about 96 per cent of its capital funds.[51] FPS ranks third among capital market investors in the securities market.

The basic source of funds is the Programa de Integração Social (PIS) and the Programa de Formação do Petrimonio do Servidor Publico (PASEP), both initiated in 1970. These funds have as one objective to provide for the retirement needs of covered workers in

Table 9.10   Investments in mutual funds, 1988

Type of fund	12 Feb. 1988			31 May 1988		
	No. of funds	Cruzados (million)	US dollars (million)	No. of funds	Cruzados (million)	US dollars (million)
Share funds	142	142 324	890	117	123 200	770
Fixed income funds	89	203 654	1 270	89	167 510	1 047
Short-term funds	64	977 608	6 110	63	727 690	4 548
TOTAL	295	1 323 586	8 270	269	1 018 400	6 365

Note: US dollar amounts obtained by using exchange rate of CZ$ 160 per US dollar.
Sources: *Jornal de Brasilia*, 9 July 1988, p. 6; and *Bolsa*, July 1988, p. 9.

the public and private sectors. Over two-thirds of salaried workers are covered by this programme. Contributions are subject to monetary correction plus 3 per cent interest yearly. The funds for PIS are derived from charges (0.5 per cent rate) imposed on the sales of firms, plus a transfer from the National Treasury, and a 5 per cent impost on the profit of companies. The funds for PASEP are derived from a transfer of 2 per cent of the operational receipts at each level of government. These resources are channelled into the National Bank for Economic and Social Development (BNDES), for longer-term investments in infrastructure, agriculture and industry. The activities of BNDES are discussed in greater detail in another chapter (chapter 11).

FPS is a fairly active investor in the securities markets (Table 9.11). In 1986 purchases and sales of shares were CZ$225 million and CZ$417 million, respectively. Also, FPS subscribed to public offerings of shares (CZ$51.5 million in 1986).

9.3.6   Investment funds: foreign capital

In the past these institutions have played only a limited role in the capital market. It remains to be seen whether their relative importance will increase, given the new incentives being offered via the privatisation and debt swaps being authorised by the government in 1988.

In 1986 only nine institutions were operational, and these held total resources of CZ$521 million (US$37.7 million) (Table 9.12). In

Table 9.11 Fund of social participation (FPS) activities in the securities markets, 1984–6

Type activity	1984	1985	1986
Value of share portfolio	761.2	4 948.8	14 249.7
Value of debenture portfolio	62.3	132.6	137.2
Resources in securities markets	823.5	5 081.4	14 386.9
Purchase of shares on exchange	27.2	191.4	225.3
Sales of shares on exchange	14.0	107.2	417.8
Total of exchange operations	41.2	298.6	643.1
Public subscription of shares	5.6	29.9	51.5
Direct purchase of new shares issued	20.8	84.5	236.6
Total of operations in the primary market	26.4	114.4	288.1

Note: Position at 30 June 1986.
Source: CVM, *Relatório Anual 1986*, p. 36.

Table 9.12 Growth in portfolios of foreign capital investment funds, 1982–6

Year	No. of foreign capital companies	Capital funds Total CZ$ million	Total US$ million	Per cent growth	Value of portfolio of shares and debentures*	Portfolio of shares and debentures as per cent of total
1982	13	4.4	17.4	–	4.0	90.9
1983	11	16.4	16.8	–3.1	15.1	92.1
1984	10	74.4	23.4	38.9	67.1	90.2
1985	9	322.4	30.7	31.5	280.8	87.1
1986	9	521.9	37.7	22.7	388.1	74.4

* CZ$ millions.
Source: CVM, *Relatório Anual 1986*, p. 37.

US dollar terms, these institutions have enjoyed a successful investment performance, with annual growth of 38 per cent, 31 per cent and 22 per cent in the period 1983–6. Generally, these institutions allocate a relatively high percentage of resources to share and debenture investments (Table 9.12).

9.3.7 Investment clubs

Investment clubs are organised under the auspices of the various stock exchanges, and they are subject to supervision of the Bolsas. General regulations concerning the proportions of resources that may be invested in specific categories of capital market assets are issued by the CMN. Investment clubs generally invest a high proportion of their total resources in shares and debentures.

Basic data concerning investment clubs in Brazil can be found in Chapter 10. While investment clubs as a group rank as one of the smallest in capital market resources, they play an important role in bringing many individual investors into the securities markets. Also, investment clubs play an important role in providing a large number of 'players' in the securities market (2900 in 1986). This tends to add to market liquidity.

At September 1986 the resources of investment clubs could be valued at US$231 million. This represents approximately US$2650 per participant, significantly higher than average per capita income in Brazil. During the first half of 1986 there was a 200 per cent increase in the value of investment club resources. This reflects a substantial gain in stock market share valuation related to the confidence that was evident in the early stages of the Cruzado Plan.

During 1987 investment clubs fell out of favour, as the stock market turned down. The number of investment clubs declined, as did the number of individual members. Additional details concerning these developments are provided in Chapter 10.

9.4 REGIONAL AND SECTORAL FISCAL INCENTIVE FUNDS

9.4.1 General objectives

Beginning in the late 1950s, the government of Brazil established several regional and sectoral development funds.[52] These funds have as their general objective promotion of the economic and social development of their respective regions and sectors. Table 9.13 identifies three fiscal incentive funds. Over the years these funds accumulated a large number of investment participations in companies, which were to be divested at periodic auctions conducted on the Brazilian stock exchanges. These funds were assigned to the CVM in

Table 9.13 Selected regional and sectoral fiscal funds

Fund	Acronym	Bank administrator
Fundo de Investimentos do Nordeste	FINOR	Banco do Nordeste do Brazil, S.A.
Fundo de Investimentos da Amazonia	FINAM	Banco da Amazonia, S.A.
Fundo de Investimentos Sectorais	FISET	Banco do Brazil, S.A.

relation to the periodic auctions held on the stock exchanges. In 1987 these funds held share investments in almost 3000 Brazilian companies.

Financial and fiscal incentives are granted to industrial agricultural, tourist, reforestation and infrastructure projects considered as priority in the development and integration of the region or sector with the national economy. Since there are many common features among the above listed fiscal incentive funds and their related development programmes, the following discussion is limited to consideration of SUDENE, the regional development agency affiliated with FINOR and created to promote development of the Northeast Region.[53]

Among its many objectives, Sudene must propose guidelines for development of the north-east, supervise and co-ordinate projects under federal auspices, carry out projects related to development of the north-east, administer financial and fiscal incentives and co-ordinate technical assistance programmes. The administrative body of Sudene has its headquarters in Recife.

Companies setting up operations within the Sudene area may participate in the following financial and fiscal incentives:

1. Financial support from the North-east Investments Fund (FINOR).
2. Import duty and industrial products tax exemption.
3. Income tax exemption or deduction.
4. Reinvestment of 50 per cent of income tax.
5. BNB and BNDES financing or guarantees.
6. State and municipal incentives.

With the aim of promoting economic development, the federal government created FINOR, which operates within the Sudene programme. FINOR provides financial support to enterprises already established or to be established within the region. This financial support is provided through the purchase of shares and debentures. FINOR support may be up to 50 per cent of the total investment.

9.4.2 Capital market-related activities

Individuals and companies investing in the north-east may benefit from the following fiscal incentives. Individuals may deduct from their income tax due 45 per cent of the amount they apply in the purchase of stock belonging to industrial or agricultural companies considered by Sudene to be of importance to economic development of the Northeast, or in the purchase of FINOR quotas.

Companies may benefit from fiscal incentives by indicating in their income tax declarations the option of investing in FINOR up to 25 per cent of income tax due. These funds are applied by FINOR in the purchase of stocks and debentures issued by companies whose projects are to be supported by SUDENE. The investing company receives an investment certificate representing its participation in FINOR through the fiscal incentive. The bearer of these investment certificates is assured easy exchange for shares of the company of his choice among the components of the FINOR stock portfolio. Special periodic auctions are held at various stock exchanges. These quotas can then be utilised by (1) taking the quotas and using them as money at the periodic auctions held to dispose of shares of companies financed by FINOR and other fiscal funds; these quotas are in the form of certificates of investment ('certificado de investimentos'); (2) trading these certificates in an over-the-counter market, which operates parallel to the stock exchange auctions; the over-the-counter trading of these quotas is extra-legal. It is quite apparent that a formalisation of the market for these certificates would provide greater transparency to this capital market activity and perhaps at the same time facilitate the development of a more efficient market for shares of smaller companies.

The interest in investing in shares of smaller companies is indicated by the fact that, at one auction held early in 1988, approximately 65 blocks of shares (in the same number of companies) were auctioned with a value of over US$7.8 million.[54]

NOTES

1. J. Gurley & E. Shaw, 'Financial Structure and Economic Development', *Economic Development and Cultural Change*, 1967, pp. 257–9.
2. David M. Trubek, *Law, Planning and the Development of the Brazilian Capital Market: A Study of Law in Economic Change*, bulletin of New York University, Graduate School of Business Administration, April 1971, pp. 11 and 20–2.
3. The period 1947–64 is described in Trubek, pp. 15–19.
4. Mark Roe, 'Finance Rules and the Indexation of Brazilian Government Bonds', *Vanderbilt Journal of Transnational Law*, 1979, p. 10.
5. Jorge del Canto, 'Impact of Inflation on Capital Markets in Argentina and Brazil', in N. Bruck, *Capital Markets Under Inflation*, Inter-American Development Bank, 1982, pp. 181–3.
6. Law No. 4728, Articles 5–7.
7. Law No. 4728, Articles 16–17, 19–21.
8. Law No. 4728, Articles 22–4.
9. Law No. 4728, Article 27.
10. One of these distortions was the development of the 'letra de câmbio', which often substituted for bank credit. This market developed as a means of circumventing the Brazilian usury law which prohibited interest in excess of 12 per cent. With inflation, the 'letra' market grew rapidly. This bill of exchange is issued by a company and guaranteed by a 'financeira' which sells the paper to the public. The borrower pays only the legal interest rate. But the paper is sold at a discount, which brings the borrowing cost over 12 per cent. In 1964 'letras de cambio' were bringing rates of interest including the discount of 4 per cent per month. For a time these instruments became popular investment vehicles for Brazilian wealth holders.
11. Trubek, p. 28.
12. This was given the name 'sociedade anônima de capital aberto', or SA.
13. Principal tax benefits included (1) ability of taxpayer to deduct part of purchase price of new share issues from tax liability; (2) dividend distribution of open companies taxed at lower rates than other corporate distributions; (3) open companies which distribute profits enjoy special tax benefits (exemption from corporate surtax and deductibility of portion of dividend payment from gross income).
14. FUNDECE was created according to Decree Law No. 54105 of 6 August 1964. FUNDECE aimed at relieving the corporate sector from a working capital shortage brought on by a government-enforced anti-inflation credit squeeze.
15. Trubek, pp. 37–8.
16. Central Bank Resolution 16 of 1965.
17. Roberto Teixeira da Costa, 'The Brazilian Experience in the Development of a Capital Market', paper given at International Investment Conference, Istanbul, Turkey, May 1987, p. 12.
18. Roberto Teixeira da Costa, p. 13. The incentive for companies allowed them to deduct from taxable income the amount paid in dividends, up to a limit of 6 per cent of nominal value of shares.

19. This was particularly the case for investment banks which assumed a dominant role in the distribution and management of 157 Funds.
20. Roberto Teixeira da Costa, 'Capital Market in Brazil: Analysis of Performance and Outlook', in N. Bruck, *Capital Markets Under Inflation*, Inter-American Development Bank, 1982, p. 46.
21. CVM, *O Mercado de Valores Mobiliários no Brasil*, July 1986, p. 4.
22. Horacio de Mendonca Netto, 'Regulamentacoes das Aplicacoes das Fundações de Seguridade', *Rev. Brasileira de Mercado Capitais*, May–August 1981, p. 246.
23. Law No. 6404, Chapter XV, Article 176.
24. Law No. 6404, Articles 100–2.
25. Law No. 6404, Article 176.
26. Law No. 6404, Article 27.
27. Law No. 6404, Article 106.
28. Law No. 6404, Article 109.
29. Law No. 6404, Articles 5–8, 10–14, 44–5.
30. These cover the use of net profits (Article 192), allocations to legal reserves (Article 193), uses of reserve funds (Article 193), restrictions on reduction in capital (Article 173), and rules governing payment of dividends (Articles 201, 202, 203).
31. Law No. 6404, Article 66.
32. Law No. 6404, Article 138.
33. Law No. 6404, Article 139.
34. The period in which the more important measures were taken to promote financial institution growth coincided with the years in which Professor Mario Henrique Simonsen occupied the position of Minister of Finance. Horacio de Mendonca Netto, 'Regulamentação das Apleiações das Fundações de Seguridade', *Rev. Brasileira do Mercado de Capitais*, May–August 1980, p. 244.
35. Horacio de Mendonca Netto, pp. 243–5.
36. The closed pension funds are joined in an organisation which functions as an industry association. This organisation monitors trends and legislation likely to affect the operations of these institutions. The association is designated as ABRAPP (Associação Brasileira das Entidades Fechadas de Previdência Privada).
37. This information was provided by ABRAPP during interviews at their office in São Paulo, August 1988.
38. Closed pension funds are managed by the sponsor firm and provide benefits to covered employees. Open pension funds are managed by banks, securities companies, and special investment management firms.
39. ABRAPP, *Manual Bâsico Para Implantação de uma EFPP*, no date, p. 9.
40. In 1984 the total portfolio value of closed and open pension funds in Brazil was US$2.6 billion, indicating a three-year growth (in dollars) of 270 per cent. See Coopers & Lybrand, *Profile of Banking and Finance in Brazil*, 1986, p. 36.
41. Resolution 460 of 23 February 1978.
42. Included in this was the requirement that 75 per cent of such allocation be in the securities issued by national private companies.

43. Comissão Nacional de Bolsas de Valores, *Legislacao Sobre Mercado de Capitais*, 1986, pp. 339–40.
44. These were Resolution 472 of 25 April 1978. Resolution 707 of 27 October 1981, and Resolution 729 of 24 March 1982.
45. CMN Resolution No. 1362 of 30 July 1987.
46. CMN Resolution 1363 of 30 July 1987.
47. *Jornal ABRAPP*, 'De Olho Nos Imóveis', June 1988, p. 4.
48. *Jornal ABRAPP*, 'O Brilho dos Shoppings', April 1988, pp. 9–10. In 1987 there were 30 major shopping centres in Brazil, as compared with 23 000 in the United States. But this differential is projected to decline rapidly with the construction and financing of new centres in Brazil. Returns on this investment are 9–10 per cent under less favourable conditions, but 20 per cent in a more favourable economic climate.
49. Netto, p. 245.
50. Netto attributed a remark to the President of the CVM when Resolution 460 was issued in 1978. According to Netto, the President of CVM considered Resolution 460 as requiring the application of the prudent man rule in Brazil in pension fund management.
51. CVM, *Relatório Anual 1986*, p. 34.
52. SUDENE-BNB, *Fiscal and Financial Incentives for Investment in Northeast Brazil*, Recife, July 1987, p. 11.
53. The north-east Region includes over 18 per cent of Brazil's land area, encompassing nine states and other territories. In 1980 its population exceeded 35 million. In 1985 its Gross Internal Product was US$34.2 billion.
54. This auction was conducted in Porto Alegre for FINOR. FINOR conducts 8–10 auctions yearly, and has been disposing of its share holdings in this manner for almost ten years.

10 The Stock Exchanges

10.1 DEVELOPMENT AND STRUCTURE

10.1.1 Early development and organisation

The stock exchanges in Brazil date back approximately a hundred years. For example, the Rio and São Paulo Stock Exchanges were organised in 1845 and 1890, respectively. In total, Brazil has nine stock exchanges which operate as non-profit associations. Close to 95 per cent of trading takes place on the two largest exchanges in Rio and São Paulo. For that reason the focus of this chapter is on these two dominant market places.

In 1965 Law No. 4728 was enacted, providing for regulation of the capital market, and assuring a more orderly and better-regulated stock exchange market trading system. The stock exchanges came under the jurisdiction of the Central Bank with Law No. 4728. Within two years the Central Bank had issued various Resolutions governing the organisation and functioning of the Brazilian stock exchanges. These Resolutions covered such matters as proper settlement of transactions, provision of premises for the purpose of trading securities, and establishment of a system for determining prices at which shares would be traded. In 1976 Law No. 6385 brought the Brazilian stock exchanges under the jurisdiction of the newly established National Securities Commission (CVM).

The ten-year period following creation of the Securities Commission was one of rapid development and change for the stock exchanges. In this period new types of market trading were introduced, including covered call options and futures trading. Advanced communications technology was brought into operation. The São Paulo stock exchange (Bovespa) introduced its private telephone operations system. The Rio stock exchange introduced a system of computerised access to trading information, analysis of portfolios and historical data. This computer terminal system involves the use of 850 desk computers in the offices of stock brokers and investment banks.

The organisational structure of the stock exchanges in Brazil calls for decision by the board of directors. Each stock exchange has its own independent board of directors. The main duties of these boards are: to establish general policy for the stock exchange; to establish internal regulations and rules; to authorise, prohibit or suspend trading and quotations of any securities; to pass on application of new members (brokerage firms); to impose sanctions on members; and to propose budgets. Generally, the board of directors is elected by the stock exchange community, which includes listed companies, brokerage houses, private investors, and institutional investors.

10.1.2 Types of market trading

Stock trading takes place on the floor of the exchange, by operators representing brokerage houses and member firms authorised to be represented on the trading floor.[1] Customers give buy and sell orders to their brokerage house, which carries these out on the day's trading session. Securities are assigned to trading posts and trading is continuous. Prices of shares traded are determined by an open auction process. Electronic equipment transmits current information concerning, trades, prices and sales volume.

Brokers charge buyers and sellers commission fees, which are on a sliding scale related to the value of the trade. Registration fees are assessed on forward transactions, call and put transactions, and futures transactions. Several types of trading can take place on the Rio and São Paulo exchanges, including (1) cash market; (2) forward market; (3) futures; and (4) options. The cash market provides for physical settlement of the purchase and sale of stocks on the third business day after the trading session, with the financial settlement taking place on the fifth business day. In addition, beginning 4 August 1986 day-trade operations can take place on the stock market. This involves a purchase and sale of the same stock on the same trading session, by the same brokerage house and on behalf of the same investor. This permits quick realisation of gains and assumption of losses.

The forward market provides for purchase and sale of shares at a fixed price for settlement on a predetermined future date, in the form of a contract between the two parties. Forward transactions generally are arranged for settlement in 30, 60, 90, 120, 150 and 180 days. An important strategy involves the financing, where the investor can purchase shares in the cash market, and in the same trading session sell them forward for the period in which financing is needed. A profit can result in a difference between the cash and forward prices (equivalent to interest in the transaction). Forward transactions have grown in importance, representing 11 per cent of total trading volume on the Rio and São Paulo Stock Exchanges (Table 10.1).

Table 10.1   Transactions on the stock exchanges, 1987

Stock exchange	Type transaction	Share volume (000s)	Value of transactions CZ$ million
Sao Paulo	Sight	15 022 055	161 519
	Term	1 556 670	12 056
	Options	7 532 457	47 329
	Exercise*	230 914	12 259
Rio de Janeiro	Sight	5 842 069	83 749
	Term	226 152	4 019
	Future	14 009	1 929
	Options	5 509 193	53 405
	Exercise*	72 741	9 285
Minas Gerais/ Espirito Santo/ Brasilia	Sight	604 546	6 303
	Term	15 360	118
Extremo Sul	Sight	256 193	2 013
	Term	6 349	92
Santos	Sight	5 344	45
Bahia/Sergipe/ Alag.	Sight	7 819	250
Regional	Sight	930 114	1 482
Pernambuco/ Paraiba	Sight	55 963	36
Parana	Sight	13 350 219	802
	Term	1 061	9
TOTAL		51 239 238	396 706

* Exercise of options.
Source: Comissao Nacional de Bolsas de Valores, *Relatório 1987*, p. 31.

In the forward market participants can give or take money, with the interest rate linked to money market rates but 2–3 per cent higher. The holder of a large stock position can borrow in futures, equivalent to a repurchase transaction. Some companies operate in the 'mercado a termo' with the shares of other companies, and they are quite sophisticated in this use of the market.

The futures market involves trading standard amounts (generally 100 000 shares), with settlement on a certain date established by the exchange. These standardised contracts differ from the forward or term market where contracts are tailor-made in each case. Table 10.1

reflects the importance of futures trading on the Rio de Janeiro stock exchange.

In the options market an investor pays a premium in cash for the right to purchase or sell an established number of securities, at a prefixed price, and at any time during the period of the contract. In Brazil it is possible to trade in covered call transactions, uncovered call transactions, and put transactions. The volume of trading in options and the exercise of options, is reflected in Table 10.1.

10.1.3 Services provided

The stock exchanges in Brazil provide a range of services to the financial system, companies, and investors. These include (1) settlement and custody of securities; (2) communication of information; (3) automation of trading; (4) stock index; and (5) investment clubs.

Settlement and custody

Physical settlement of cash transactions occurs on the third business day after the trading session. Financial settlements take place on the fifth business day. If both buyer and seller are users of a single exchange's depository services, the securities transfer takes place within that exchange's depository services. The largest stock exchanges provide security custody services in a number of cities throughout Brazil, which facilitates these transfers. Investor safety and the quality of the depository services are assured by appropriate auditing and computerised procedures.

Settlement operates through the following steps:

1. Order. An order to buy or sell is initiated by the investor, and is carried out by brokerage houses on the trading floor of the Exchange.
2. Trading notification. The participating brokerage houses advise one another, the investors, and the exchange through a computerised system.
3. Physical settlement. The exchanges operate a depository department and a clearing department. The brokerage houses surrender and take possession of traded securities for the transaction, all of this monitored and processed through the above departments. All transactions are microfilmed.
4. Financial settlement. The brokerage houses provide and take

funds necessary for the transaction, and make financial transfers through the clearing department.

Communication of information

During the daily trading session simultaneous market information can be obtained by use of a video terminal system. Terminals are installed at financial institutions, brokerage houses, institutional investors and the offices of the stock exchanges which are located in all major cities throughout Brazil. Data transmitted through this system includes trading, market prices, volume, and historical information on listed companies. The major stock exchanges publish a daily bulletin which has a large circulation among investors and other interested parties.

The daily newspapers in Brazil carry considerable information concerning investment on the stock exchanges. Moreover the daily press generates analytical and evaluative articles concerning the possible impact of economic trends and government policies on investments.

Automation

Automation of trading is supported by extensive mainframe and smaller computers. Mainframe computers are utilised at the stock exchanges for recording trading floor transactions, custody and physical settlement of securities, control of forward contracts, and control of brokerage house financial position. Minicomputers are used for internal administration at the brokerage houses and at the stock exchanges to receive updated information on floor trading, and to permit various stock exchange departments to carry out basic administrative functions.

The large exchanges each operate video terminal networks with approximately 800 terminals in each system. These provide real-time floor trading information to the market. A private telephone system connects each of the major exchanges with several thousand brokerage houses, securities distributors, banks, investors and other interested users throughout Brazil. This provides an uninterrupted service for distributing investment information to capital market participants.

Stock index

Each of the major stock exchanges provides its own stock exchange index. This provides a measure of changes in the average price of listed stocks. Stock indexes provide a basis of comparison for investors in Brazil and in other countries, seeking an indication of how the market performed compared with other stock market sectors.

The Bovespa Index reflects changes in average prices on the São Paulo Stock Exchange. It represents the current cruzado value of a stock portfolio composed of the stocks that jointly represent 80 per cent of the volume of cash transactions during the twelve-month period prior to its creation.[2]

The participation of each stock in the portfolio is directly related to the performance of the security in the cash market in terms of number of transactions and total value. To ensure that the index remains representative over time, the composition of the index is evaluated every four months (based on the immediately preceding 12 months activity) and changes are made in each stock's relative weight. The old portfolio is then considered to have been liquidated, and the proceeds invested in a new portfolio weighted according to the latest four-month survey. During the four months in which the portfolio is active, the hypothetical number of shares is constant and may only be adjusted in the case of stock dividends, stock bonuses, or stock subscription by the companies.

Investment clubs

During the 1980s the stock exchanges encouraged the formation of investment clubs. This recognises the importance of the investor in the stock market, and has the purpose of encouraging participation of small and medium investors. These clubs consist of groups of individual investors (minimum of 10 and maximum of 150), associated for the exclusive purpose of maintaining a common portfolio of diversified stocks. Club members own quotas in the fund, with no holder permitted to own more than 40 per cent of the total equity capital.

Investment clubs have grown impressively in the 1980s (Table 10.2). The number of clubs reached a high of 1604 in 1986, with over 49 000 individual members. The stock exchanges provide material encouragement to investment clubs by providing custody of securities, computer facilities and ready access to institutional support (brokerage houses, investment banks and securities distributors). In 1987 the São Paulo Stock Exchange reported the operation of 1127 clubs, with over 26 000 members and US$27 million in equity capital.[3]

Table 10.2   Development of investment clubs, 1982–7

Investment club activity	1982	1983	1984	1985	1986	1987
No. of clubs	41	139	578	1 476	1 604	1 127
No. of members	957	4 107	16 910	49 127	49 476	26 728
Capital (CZ$million)	0.1	3.9	67.3	946	1 565	2 433

Source: Bovespa, *Perfil 1987*, p. 19.

10.2   INVESTOR PARTICIPATION

10.2.1   Asset preferences

Investor participation plays a vital role in influencing conditions and trends in the stock market. The degree of participation of different investor groups varies from one period of time to another. In general four investor groups have dominated stock exchange trading on the Rio and São Paulo Exchanges. The participation of these groups on the Bovespa is indicated in Table 10.3.

While these investor groups have averaged the levels of participation reflected in Table 10.3, their share of trading in the market has varied, and in some cases the degree of variation has been substantial. This can be seen in the table, which reflects the participation of Bovespa investors over the period 1982–6. As shown by the data, individual investors exhibited the lowest variability in participation in stock market trading, with a coefficient of variation of 0.081.[4] Institutional investors exhibited the highest variability in participation in stock market trading, with a coefficient of variation of 0.309.

It is not difficult to understand and explain the wide difference in variability of participation between institutional and individual investors. Institutional investors are more oriented to employing investment strategies of positioning themselves and trading more actively at times when they foresee economic trends and government policy providing favourable opportunities. By contrast, individual investors are less likely to employ these approaches. It is not surprising that banks and securities distributors are close behind institutional investors in exhibiting high variability of participation in the stock market. Not unlike other financial institutions, banks and securities distributors are searching for opportunities to trade more actively to generate profits. Finally, we should note that public and

Table 10.3   Average participation and variability of participation in
Bovespa, by type of investor, 1982–6, half-year periods

Investor group	Share of trading %	Standard deviation	Coefficient of variation
Individuals	39.1	3.16	.081
Public & private companies	29.4	3.71	.126
Institutional	13.6	4.19	.309
Banks & securities distributors	10.0	2.11	.211
Other	7.9	2.13	.269
TOTAL	100.0		

Source: Bovespa.

private companies rank second in *level* of participation, but *third* in variability of participation. In this respect we must consider the company as a fairly sophisticated investor in the shares of other companies. Also some large industrial companies make use of the strategy of selling and buying back shares held, a type of repurchase transaction which at times affords opportunity for profitable trading in the stock market. Furthermore in Brazil there are many small companies that were created for the purpose of trading shares. With no tax on capital gains they can operate with a favourable 'after tax' return. Also holding companies engage in share transactions.

10.2.2   Individual investors

The number of individual investors in Brazil can be estimated at 1.5 million, although indirect participation through investment clubs and various investment funds could bring this total to 2 million.[5] This does not include investment in share mutual funds, where it was reported that over 7 million investors had participated in the first half of 1988.[6] Share-mutual funds have been popular in Brazil since they offer investors the advantages of liquidity, ease of administration (receipt of dividends and subscription to new shares), security of the funds capital, transparency (disclosure on a daily basis), and diversification.

The 1.5 million to 2 million is an impressive number if we consider that alternative investments in real estate and other types of assets can be attractive under conditions of monetary instability. Brazil faces obstacles in widening ownership of stocks, since investors have experienced many market losses in the past. As a result they lack confidence in the market. We should remember that the potential number of individual investors also is severely limited by the distribution of income in Brazil. In 1985 for example, a high percentage (14.4 per cent) of income was reportedly received by the top 1 per cent of income recipients.[7] Also, during the mid-1980s there has been a downtrend in the manufacturing labour share relative to value added, reinforcing the limited scope of potential stock ownership in Brazil.

The government has provided various tax incentives to encourage individual investors to participate in stock market investing. These measures include the following:

1. No capital gains tax is payable by individual or other investors on gains from the sale of shares.
2. Fiscal incentives have been offered in the past, to encourage individual investors to participate in the stock market via special fiscal funds.
3. No tax is levied on share trading.[8]
4. Until 1985 there was a substantially lower withholding income tax on corporate dividends in the case of open companies as compared with closed companies. This differential was narrowed in 1985.

In addition, the government mandates that at least 25 per cent of earnings be passed on as dividends. In part this is aimed at making share ownership more attractive to individuals.

10.2.3 Institutional investors

Since the decade of the 1960s the government of Brazil has sought to promote the development of financial intermediaries. Various considerations are involved in this effort including the general need to improve the mobilisation of capital, to expand the market for shares and to create a market for corporate debentures. Varying degrees of success have been achieved in these areas. Perhaps the greatest success has been in expanding the market for shares.

Institutional and other share ownership is reflected in Table 10.4, for year-end 1986 and 1987. Eleven different classes of participants are identified. The first ten (mostly financial institutions) account for 12–13 per cent of share ownership. The 'other' category includes individuals and companies. In short, Table 10.4 indicates that financial

Table 10.4   Distribution of share portfolios among investor groups, 1986–7 (millions of US dollars)

	1986	1987
Closed pension funds	2 921	1 398
Open pension funds	67	34
Insurance companies	313	—
Foreign currency funds[1]	17	20
Equity mutual funds	1 736	465
Fixed income mutual funds	2	—
Investment banks	211	17
Commercial banks	12	4
Consumer finance companies	8	1
State development banks	4	0
Others	35 699	14 881
TOTAL	40 990	16 820

[1] The present figure is about $180 million.
Sources: Central Bank of Brazil; São Paulo Stock Exchange.

institution ownership of shares has become important (12–13 per cent of aggregate value), but has some distance to go to attain the level of institutional participation operating in some of the industrial countries.

The most important institutional investors in the market for shares has been the private pension funds, followed by the mutual funds. This is reflected in Tables 10.4 and 10.5. In Table 10.5 we see that private pension funds held US$9.2 billion and $9.9 billion in their investment portfolios, in 1986 and 1987. From 1986 to 1987 the composition of their portfolios changed, with the percentage devoted to shares and debentures declining from one-third to 19 per cent. In the same period mutual funds experienced a decline in their total investment portfolios, reflecting a shift of investor funds to alternative investments. This reflected stock market weakness in 1987. By year-end 1987 mutual fund share and debenture investments were less than one-third of the level a year earlier.

As is noted in other chapters of this volume, pension fund asset allocations are subject to regulation of the National Monetary Council (CMN), and their share investments generally are set at a minimum percentage of overall resources. In the case of mutual funds investing in stock, the major part of their resources is allocated to share investments. Foreign capital investment companies account for

Table 10.5 Institutional investors: main investments, 1986, 1987

Type Asset	Foreign Capital Investment Companies (1)	Mutual Funds (2)	Pension Funds (3)
	(1986)		
Stocks & debentures	17.4	1 911.1	3 131.6
Bills of exchange	—	0.4	—
Fixed term deposits	—	5.4	1 297.3
Federal government securities	1.2	397.2	1 521.3
Other	—	0.9	3 237.4
TOTAL	18.6	2 315.0	9 187.6
	(1987)		
Shares & debentures	26.2	614.2	1 893.7
Bills of exchange	—	—	24.4
Fixed term deposits	—	2.4	1 599.0
Federal government securities	11.2	126.5	895.9
Other	—	65.2	5 548.0
TOTAL	37.4	828.3	9 961.0

Note: Amounts are in millions of US dollars; dollar amounts are obtained by translating at average rate of exchange for period.
Sources: *Profile of the São Paulo Stock Exchange*, 1986, p. 36; Bovespa, *Perfil 1987*, p. 34.

only a small part of institutional investment in shares. This question is taken up in a later section of this chapter.

Pension funds are the main institutional investor in the Brazilian securities market, accounting for at least 15 per cent of the volume of share trading. During the 1980s closed pension funds have been dominant investors in the markets for shares and debentures. This is reflected in the data in Table 10.6. From the point of view of pension funds the stock market is highly speculative and volatile. Therefore pension funds generally limit their investments to what is designated as the minimum according to National Monetary Council (CMN) regulations. The largest pension funds carry on block trading with other investors (banks, corporations, individuals). Closed pension funds pay full tax on interest and dividend income. Pension funds dominate in the new issues market for debentures. Most debentures are convertible.

Table 10.6   Participation of investor groups in trading on the São Paulo stock exchange (per centage of transactions) 1987–8

		April–May 1987		
	Cash	Forward	Options	Total
Individual	33.7	34.8	61.2	43.1
Institutional	14.9	13.4	1.9	10.3
Companies (private and state owned)	30.4	45.6	15.7	26.7
Banks, securities distributors	11.5	2.4	12.5	11.1
Other	9.5	3.8	8.7	8.8
TOTAL	100.0	100.0	100.0	100.0
		April–May 1988		
Individual	21.3	23.5	38.6	23.7
Institutional	13.8	7.5	8.4	12.8
Companies (private and state owned)	23.7	40.3	17.6	23.3
Banks, securities distributors	25.4	17.9	18.5	15.9
Other	16.0	10.8	16.9	24.3
TOTAL	100.0	100.0	100.0	100.0

Source: Bovespa, *Informe Técnico*, May 1987, p. 3 and May 1988, p. 3.

10.2.4   Firms, private and state-owned

As noted above large industrial companies, smaller companies or-ganised primarily to trade in the stock market, and holding companies are fairly important participants in the stock market. As a group they rank second in level of participation, and third in variability of participation. Their second rank in level of participation is on the basis of total transactions. To obtain a clearer picture of their partici-pation we can consider the information in Table 10.6, which indicates the participation of companies in three types of market transactions (cash, forward, options).

Two comments are in order relative to company participation. First, they participate extensively in the forward or term market, representing 40–45 per cent of trading. This reflects their ability to employ idle cash in stock exchange investments in shares and in repurchase transactions. A company can employ idle cash in pur-chasing shares, and subsequently obtain short-term liquidity through a repurchase transaction. The counterparty can be another corporation wishing to inject liquidity into the market via a repurchase transaction.

Second, companies operate to a moderate extent in options trading. This may reflect the desire of a small number of company financial officers to employ this device to 'insure' its share portfolio against market declines. Individual investors appear to be the dominant group in options transactions (61.2 per cent in 1987 and 38.6 per cent in 1988).

10.3 PUBLIC COMPANIES

The concept of an open capital company was created in Law No. 4506, enacted in 1964. The objective was to establish fiscal incentives for promoting the distribution of shares among the public. In the following year Law No. 4728 (The Capital Market Law) served as the basis for establishing open capital companies. At present, open capital companies have their shares traded on the public markets (stock exchanges). Therefore they have satisfied the registration requirements of the stock exchange and the CVM.

In 1987 there were close to a thousand public companies in Brazil (Table 10.7). Public companies open their capital to the public, and are registered with the National Securities Commission. Approximately two-thirds (645) of the public companies have registered their shares for trading on the stock exchanges (Table 10.7). In 1987 the Bovespa had admitted 590 of these companies to have their shares traded on that stock exchange. Shares of most large companies are traded on both the Rio and São Paulo exchanges.

Each year additional companies are 'going public'. For example, in 1986–7 42 and 7 companies respectively opened their capital by issuing stocks, and three companies issued debentures. It is possible for a company that has opened its capital subsequently to have its securities admitted for trading on one or more of the stock exchanges in Brazil. Therefore, as can be noted in Table 10.7, in 1986 68 companies were admitted for trading at Bovespa, a larger number than is indicated opened their capital in that year.

Over the period 1982–7 the number of companies whose securities are traded on the exchanges increased from 607 to 645. This suggests that the stock market is experiencing an expansion in shares listed for trading. As we shall note in the following section, the stock market in Brazil is experiencing strong growth.

It is possible to obtain an understanding of this stock market

The Stock Exchanges

Table 10.7   General summary of public companies

Description	1982	1983	1984	1985	1986	1987
Number of public companies	1 134	1 153	981	996	1 020	999
Number of companies traded on the stock exchanges	607	592	601	611	652	645
Number of companies traded on the São Paulo stock exchange (Bovespa)	493	506	522	541	592	590
Number of companies in Brazil which opened their capital by:						
issuing stocks	14	8	20	30	42	7
issuing debentures	71	34	14	9	1	2
Number of companies registered at Bovespa	5	2	14	14	25	3
Companies admitted for trading at Bovespa	14	23	32	33	68	13

Source: Securities Commission (CVM).

expansion by examining the aggregate value or market capitalisation of companies traded on the stock exchange. For this purpose we can consider the data in Table 10.8. Over the period 1982–8 the market capitalisation of shares of all companies registered at the São Paulo stock exchange exhibited a strong increase. In 1982–6 total capitalisation increased from US$10.2 billion to US$40.9 billion. It declined in 1987, but increased again in 1988 to US$30.1 billion (May 1988). This is an impressive performance, especially considering that in this period the Brazilian economy was experiencing an external debt crisis, and strong recessionary influences. As we note in the following section, this sharp increase in market capitalisation was accompanied by equally impressive gains in stock exchange trading volume.

In 1987 the aggregate corporate capital of companies traded on the São Paulo stock exchange was distributed as follows: private domestic companies – 46 per cent; state owned enterprises – 49 per cent; and foreign controlled companies – 5 per cent.[9]

10.4   ANALYSIS OF MARKET TRANSACTIONS

10.4.1   Secondary trading

The secondary market for shares is where securities are exchanged among investors. From the economic point of view, a transaction on the stock exchange does not add to or diminish the resources available for financing business firms. Nevertheless efficient organisation of the secondary market is extremely important. This is because it is a

Table 10.8   Market capitalisation of companies registered at Bovespa

Period	Companies	Market capitalisation (US$000)*
1982	493	10 260 545
1983	506	15 099 730
1984	522	28 994 180
1985	541	42 768 464
1986	592	40 988 455
1987	590	12 790 000
1988 May	580	30 133 000
1988 June	580	26 534 000

* Converted at the exhange rate at the end of each year or period.
Source: Bovespa and *Gazeta Mercantil*.

base upon which the primary market is able to operate, where firms are able to obtain additional financial resources. A fundamental factor in the decision of the investor when buying newly offered shares is the proper pricing of the issue so that there can be expectation of reasonable profit at a future date.

The secondary market is divided in two components, the secondary market operating on the stock exchanges, and the secondary market operating over-the-counter (not on the stock exchange).[10] The over-the-counter market operates principally through telephone connections between buyers, sellers and securities firms. As in other countries, in Brazil this market provides the opportunity for transactions in the securities of new enterprises and smaller companies. Its ability to operate successfully in Brazil is linked to the success of the stock exchanges.

On the stock exchanges, the securities of companies are traded after they have been registered with the National Securities Commission and the stock exchange. To negotiate on the stock exchange investors give their buy or sell orders to securities brokers, who in turn execute these orders on the trading floor in a competitive auction market.

Since there are nine separate stock exchanges in Brazil, it is necessary to link these together with an on-line computer terminal system. This system of nine stock exchanges provides a national market for securities.

Share trading on the Brazilian stock market has grown both in nominal and real terms (Table 10.9). As can be noted in the table,

Table 10.9   Share transactions on Brazilian stock market, nominal and price adjusted amounts (CZ$million)

Year	Nominal value	Value corrected for change in general price level
1975	22	92 153
1976	23	69 168
1977	33	75 616
1978	45	74 966
1979	68	76 581
1980	147	108 957
1981	151	57 385
1982	393	75 384
1983	1 571	117 264
1984	10 248	242 374
1985	79 314	587 721
1986	259 601	1 277 240
1987	252 002	252 002

Source: Comissão Nacional de Bolsas de Valores, *Relatório Anual 1987*, Rio de Janeiro, p. 43.

share trading corrected for changes in the general price level increased from CZ$92 billion in 1975 to CZ$587 billion in 1985, and to CZ$1277 billion in 1986, a twelve-fold expansion in real terms. In 1987 there was a substantial decline (in real terms of 80 per cent) to CZ$252 billion. A somewhat better perspective can be obtained if we analyse share trading in the secondary market over the longer period 1964–86. Here we are considering stock exchange trading volume as a percentage of national income (Table 10.10). In this analysis at least five different phases of trading activity can be observed. The first was one of limited development (1964–7). Legislation was coming into effect, providing for fiscal incentives and foreign investment funds, and did tend to influence the second phase (1967–71). This second phase involved a stock market boom, reaching a peak and a crisis in 1971. The crisis of 1971 is well remembered in Brazil. The lesson it provided is to avoid excess incentives when the market base is too narrow.

A three-year decline followed, during which many investors avoided the stock market. There was still not a sufficiently large institutional base to support stock market development, but this was coming. In 1976 legislation came into being, creating the CVM and providing for companies regulation in areas of financial management,

Table 10.10   Stock exchange trading as per centage of national income, 1964–86

Year	(1)		(2)	
1964	0.40			
1965	0.48	Limited		
1966	0.24	development		
1967	0.31			
1968	0.34			
1969	1.52	Boom		
1970	2.17			
1971	9.14	Crisis		
1972	4.89			
1973	3.51	Decline		
1974	1.83			
1975	2.54		2.41	
1976	1.72		1.54	
1977	1.49	Plateau	1.40	Plateau
1978	1.42		1.27	
1979	1.39		1.14	
1980	2.13		1.17	
1981			0.61	
1982			0.82	Decline
1983			1.33	&
1984			2.65	boom
1985			5.63	
1986			7.05	

Sources: (1) Raymond W. Goldsmith, *Brasil 1850–1984: Desenvolvimento Financeiro Sob um Século de Inflação* (São Paulo: Harper & Row, 1986) p. 422.
(2) Comissão Nacional de Bolsas de Valores, *Relatório Anual 1986*, p. 47.

shareholder protection and disclosure of financial performance. In 1977 legislation was drafted to provide for orderly development of private pension funds. In this period the stock market was on a fairly stable plateau, waiting for the new institutional investor groups to expand their resource base.

Beginning in 1981–2 there was a decline in the stock market, related to monetary instability and the external debt crisis. However, since 1982, the stock market has enjoyed a fairly buoyant period in terms of trading volume. In 1984–6 this reached levels equivalent to 2.65 per cent, 5.63 per cent, and 7.05 per cent of national income.

Table 10.11   New securities issues registered

Year	Shares	Debentures
1978	35 173	1 690
1979	36 956	4 839
1980	41 783	19 780
1981	15 295	94 086
1982	25 107	93 921
1983	16 879	47 159
1984	35 318	20 111
1985	36 145	8 030
1986	80 383	9 280
1987	23 192	1 410

Note: Amounts in CZ$ million, valued with an OTN basis: December 1987 equal 522.99.
Source: Comissão Nacional de Bolsas de Valores, *Relatório 1987*, p. 32.

10.4.2   New issues

The new issues market for shares is dependent on the secondary market. Only by making detailed comparisons with outstanding share issues can a company 'price' its own shares in the market. The new issues market in Brazil is fairly volatile, as can be observed from Table 10.11. On a year-to-year basis new share and debenture issues can vary by a wide margin.

Considering the data in Table 10.11 in closer detail, we can see that new share issues reached a high in 1986 when close to $1.2 billion was distributed. The following year, 1987, witnessed a marked reduction in new share issues as the stock market declined and companies were less inclined to issue shares on a higher cost of capital basis. Generally new share issues have exceeded new debenture issues in most years. There were three exceptions, in the years 1981–83 when record levels of new debenture issues were forthcoming. The factors that motivated this expansion of debenture issues are associated with the fixing of monetary correction and exchange rate adjustments by the government in 1980. These policy measures stimulated a large issue of debentures, and raised interest rates to a level that made it possible for debenture issues to surpass share issues by a wide margin.[11]

We next consider some international comparisons of share and debenture issues. This provides us with a better understanding of how far Brazil has moved in developing its capital market, and how much additional financial deepening may be possible. However, before closing this discussion, we must observe that the volatility of the new issues market poses a serious problem for the economy, and raises the question of how effective capital mobilisation can be. These difficulties require appropriate remedies, as follows:

1. Government policies are subject to periodic shifting, where the rules change rapidly. The government must adopt a more long-term approach to financial market development.
2. The constitutional system must provide better rules, whereby the economic environment and structure becomes more permanent in nature.
3. A larger and more diversified base of financial intermediaries is needed. This suggests additional efforts at institution building in the sectors including insurance companies and real estate finance.

International comparisons

International comparisons of new issues provide additional insights into the effectiveness of the Brazilian capital market in mobilising capital. Rodrigues provides comparative data for the period 1970–83, including Brazil and 18 more developed countries. On a global basis, new debenture issues declined over the period 1970–83 relative to national income (Table 10.12). In the three sub-periods reflected, debentures issues declined from 0.86 per cent of national income, to 0.77 per cent, and to 0.58 per cent for all 19 countries. However, in the same period the Brazilian capital market was growing rapidly, responding to the reformed legal structure and evolving financial institutions described in the previous chapter. Debenture issues rose from 0.02 per cent to 0.45 per cent of national income. It should be noted that, if we consider countries such as Greece, Holland, and Finland, Brazilian new debenture issues compare favourably.

The Rodrigues study also includes data on debenture issues of financial institutions in the 18 more developed nations. Brazil is excluded because of lack of activity in this area. The average debenture/national income figures obtained were 2.03 per cent for 1970–3, 2.60 per cent for 1974–9, and 3.16 per cent for 1980–3.[12] We should note that these figures trend up, which is opposite to the trend for debenture issues of non-financial corporations. Also these figures exceed the percentage for non-financial corporations by a wide margin. In short, the capital mobilisation capacity of the more developed countries is being amplified in a stong way by the

Table 10.12 Comparisons of new debenture issues of non-financial companies, Brazil and selected countries, as percentage of national income

Country	1970–3	1974–9	1980–3
Brazil	0.02	0.02	0.45
US	1.91	1.59	1.40
Switzerland	1.63	1.98	1.44
Japan	1.99	2.60	2.50
Spain	2.15	1.77	1.28
Greece	0.29	0.07	—
Denmark	0.04	0.02	0.05
Finland	0.28	0.03	—
All Countries*	0.86	0.77	0.58

* All nineteen countries, including Brazil and eighteen more developed countries.
Source: Domingos de Gouveia Rodrigues, 'O Porte dos Mercados de Acoes e Debentures: Brasil Versus Paises Industrializados', *Rbmec*, 1985, p. 53.

debenture-issuing activities of financial institutions, and this trend was upward over the years analysed by Rodrigues. The implications are fairly clear: while Brazil needs to have a government economic policy mix that facilitates a higher level of debenture financing by non-financial corporations, it also might consider policies which permit certain financial institutions to issue debentures for the purpose of enhancing the capital mobilisation process.

The data on new share issues must be examined before we comment on any international comparisons. There are some inconsistencies in the basis on which new share issues are reported. Some data relate to all capital expansions for all companies. Other data consider only the publicly offered shares. Finally, in many cases the expansion of capital is considered to include stock dividends and shares issued in mergers and acquisitions.[13] In Table 10.13 we have two different estimates of share issues for Brazil. One considers increases in capital by all subscriptions of capital in corporations, and another considers only publicly offered shares issued by companies registered on the stock exchanges.

These two measures provide a very different picture. In the case of Brazil we have the first measure yielding 4.75 per cent of national income in 1970–3, 2.41 per cent in 1974–9 and 1.52 per cent in 1980–3. The second measure (more conservative and probably more realistic) yields 0.43 per cent, 0.11 per cent, and 0.18 per cent in the

Table 10.13   Comparison of new share issues, Brazil and selected countries, as percentage of national income

Country	1970–3	1974–9	1980–3
Brazil	0.43	0.11	0.18
US	1.01	0.57	1.20
UK	0.47	0.66	0.60
Switzerland	2.57	1.74	0.78
Japan	1.38	0.72	0.74
Greece	0.38	0.30	0.14
Spain	2.82	1.87	0.95
Holland	0.11	0.15	0.13
Finland	3.74	2.69	1.36
All Countries*	1.50	1.01	0.89
Brazil**	4.75	2.41	1.52

* All twenty countries, including Brazil and nineteen more developed countries.
** More inclusive estimate of share issues.
Source: As Table 10.12, p. 57.

same time periods. The more conservative measure leaves Brazilian new share issues ahead of Holland and abreast of Greece.

While Table 10.13 does not reflect yearly data, we should note that in 1971 new share issues in Brazil reached the level of 1.10 per cent of national income. This placed Brazil at the middle of the range of countries in that year. Admittedly this was a record year in the Brazilian experience. The demand for shares in Brazil depends on the breadth (number of individual investors and variety of financial institution investors) and depth (size of financial institution investors) of the market. Efforts by the stock exchange to expand the number of individual investors via investment clubs and other measures have enjoyed only modest success. Government encouragement and promotion of financial institutions also has enjoyed some success. Nevertheless the statistics in previous tables reflect the need for further widening and deepening of the Brazilian share market.

10.4.3   Most actively traded shares

The extent of stock market development is reflected in many ways. One indicator of market development is the extent to which share trading is concentrated among different issues. In the case of Brazil,

Table 10.14   Most actively traded shares, 1986–7

Company share	1986	Per cent National Market Volume Per Issue	Cumulative
1. Petrobras		20.50	20.50
2. Vale do Rio Doce		14.39	34.89
3. Sharp		4.99	39.88
4. Paranapanema		4.58	44.46
5. Mendes Junior		2.35	46.81
6. Banco do Brasil		2.13	48.94
7. Varig		1.61	50.55
8. Agroceres		1.48	52.03
9. Belgo Mineiea		1.38	53.41
10. Sid. Informatica		1.36	54.77
	1987		
1. Petrobras		30.30	30.30
2. Vale do Rio Doce		12.64	42.94
3. Paranapanema		5.70	48.64
4. Banco do Brasil		3.36	52.00
5. Copene		1.99	53.99
6. Samitri*		1.29	54.28
7. Agroceres		1.29	55.57
8. Brahma		1.04	56.61
9. Sharp		0.94	57.55
10. Petrobras*		0.85	58.40

* Ordinary shares, all others are preferred shares.
Sources: Comissão Nacional de Bolsas de Valores, *Relatório Anual 1986*, p. 48; *Relatório Anual 1987*, p. 44.

share trading is fairly concentrated, with the most actively traded issue (Petrobras) accounting for over 20 per cent of total national market volume in 1986 and 30 per cent in 1987 (Table 10.14). Many of the ten most actively traded shares included in the table are not private sector companies, but are either primarily state controlled (Petrobras, Vale do Rio Doce, Banco do Brasil), or foreign affiliates (Sharp).

Data included in Table 10.15 suggest that, in recent years (1977–86), there has been a moderate reduction in the extent to which share trading is concentrated among a small number of company issues. This is especially evident if we consider the column representing the percentage of trading in the five most traded issues. Here there is reflected a decline from 63.7 per cent in 1977 to 54.0 per cent in 1987.

Table 10.15   Percentage of total share trading of most traded shares

	5 most traded	10 most traded	50 most traded	100 most traded
1977	63.7	68.1	88.8	94.9
1980	30.9	38.6	66.2	81.1
1983	42.3	49.5	73.4	85.3
1984	50.5	57.7	78.5	88.2
1985	54.4	61.2	80.8	89.1
1986	46.8	54.8	73.7	83.6
1987	54.0	59.1	79.5	88.4

Source: Comissão Nacional de Bolsas de Valores, *Relatório Anual 1987*, pp. 45–6.

10.4.4   Sectoral share of stock market trading

Taken together the Rio and São Paulo stock exchanges account for over 95 per cent of total stock exchange trading in Brazil. While these two exchanges share the spotlight as the largest, dominant part of share trading, there are some differences between these two exchanges that should be mentioned. They differ basically in their sectoral shares of stock market trading. This is evident from inspection of the data in Table 10.16, which contains data on the share of total market trading in each of eleven selected industry sectors. These sectors were chosen on the basis of their market shares of trading being different.

The following appear to be the broader differences in industry and sectoral shares. First, selected government owned companies play a more important role in trading on the Rio stock exchange (petrochemicals, state banks, iron and minerals). Second, trading in the shares of private sector banks plays a more important role in São Paulo. Third, some higher technology manufacturing sectors are traded more actively in São Paulo (electronics and telecom, metallurgy, vehicles and auto parts). Fourth, São Paulo has attracted share trading in a number of traditional manufacturing sectors (food and beverages, plastic and leather, textiles).

Many Brazilian companies have several types of stock trading on the exchanges. These include various types of ordinary and preferred stock. To some extent these different issues of the same company can focus their trading on one of several stock exchanges. Also in some cases Brazilian companies will have a high proportion of their share

Table 10.16   Comparison of sectoral shares of stock market trading on Rio de Janeiro and São Paulo exchanges (selected sectors): percentage of total market trading

Sector	São Paulo	Rio de Janeiro
State banks	1.59	5.03
Private banks	2.24	0.42
Food & beverages	7.77	2.43
Plastic & leather	2.55	0.52
Electronic & telecom	7.12	2.62
Engineering construction	1.82	4.19
Metallurgy	9.58	4.80
Petrochemicals	31.35	13.32
Iron & minerals	6.76	51.07
Textiles	4.39	1.40
Vehicles and auto parts	4.24	1.08

Source: Comissão Nacional de Bolsas de Valores, *Relatório Anual 1986*, pp. 205–6.

trading focused on a market other than Rio and São Paulo. This is true of Banco Nacional (9 per cent traded on Minas Gerais Stock Exchange), Mesbla (30 per cent on Minas Gerais) and Mendes Junior (14 per cent on Minas Gerais).

10.5   INTERNATIONAL LINKAGES

10.5.1   Foreign portfolio investment

Foreign portfolio investment in stocks of listed companies can be made in Brazil through investment companies especially created for this purpose. These investment companies maintain a diversified portfolio of Brazilian securities. According to Decree Law No. 1401 of 7 May 1975 a minimum of 50 per cent of the total resources received from foreign investors shall be represented by shares or debentures issued by listed private sector companies controlled by Brazilian shareholders. The remaining funds shall be applied to federal government securities or shares of companies listed on the Brazilian stock exchanges.[17]

At present several types of foreign portfolio investment are authorised in Brazil under Decree Law No. 1986 of 28 December 1982. Based on this law, the National Monetary Council enacted Resolution 1289 on 20 March 1987 to supervise the operation of these funds. The three types of authorised funds are foreign capital investment companies, foreign capital investment fund and securities portfolios.

Foreign capital investment companies

This type of investment company must be constituted with a capital stock of at least CZ$10 million, and authorised capital of at least CZ$350 million. The management of the portfolio is carried out under contract by a Brazilian institution. A minimum of 50 per cent of the total resources must be represented by shares and convertible debentures issued by domestic corporations. The remainder may be invested in federal government bonds and bills, Central Bank bills, debentures issued by public companies, and shares issued by listed corporations. Share investments in a single company are limited to 5 per cent of the voting capital or 20 per cent of the total capital. The total investment in securities of a single company cannot exceed 10 per cent of the investment company's total resources. Capital gains of these investment companies are tax exempt, and cash dividends are subject to a 15 per cent withholding tax. A small number of foreign capital investment companies has been organised, and only a limited amount of foreign portfolio investment has been attracted to Brazil by this means.

Foreign capital investment fund

This type of fund assumes the form of an open joint ownership, and aims at achieving a diversified securities portfolio. Individuals, companies, resident or domiciled abroad can participate in this type of fund. Fund management is carried out by an investment bank, brokerage house or securities distributor. The funds equity comes from the sale of its 'quotas' abroad. These quotas may be represented by investment certificates, or maintained in deposit accounts under the owners name. The minimum value of each subscription is US$5000. A minimum of 70 per cent of the resources of this fund is invested in stocks, purchased on the stock exchanges or over the counter market. The remainder may be invested in Central Bank bills, federal government bonds, or other securities issued by public corporations.

Securities portfolio

Foreign investors can participate in a collective investment entity, provided it is managed by a Brazilian institution along with a foreign entity, and the resources are registered at the Central Bank. A foreign capital registry certificate issued by the Brazilian Central Bank is the legal means that makes possible any subsequent withdrawal of foreign resources, as well as the delivery of earnings and capital gains to the foreign owner. A minimum of 70 per cent of the portfolios resources are to be committed to share investments, and the remainder to Central Bank bills, federal government bonds, or other securities issued by public companies.

International Finance Corporation

Other portfolio investors operate in Brazil. One such investor is the International Finance Corp., an affiliate of the World Bank. In 1988 the IFC reported it had a loan portfolio in Brazil of close to $400 million. This is equivalent to 10 per cent of its world-wide portfolio. The IFC also provides equity capital, with $89 million invested in Brazil. In 1988 it could be said that the IFC was financing nearly all of the expansion projects of leading Brazilian paper and pulp producers. In mid-1988 the IFC was making plans for another $250 million in loans for ten new projects in paper, chemicals, petrochemicals, textiles, and glass ventures.[15]

10.5.2 Foreign owned companies

Over the period 1970–84 Brazil sustained a remarkable average growth rate of 6.6 per cent annually. This took place in an environment of high growth in foreign trade, and of large flows of risk capital to developing countries. To support the high growth rate in Brazil in this period, the savings rate as a percentage of gross domestic product averaged 23.5 per cent. External savings contributed on average 3.6 per cent of GDP, or 15.3 per cent of total savings. A large part of these external savings was in the form of direct foreign (business) investment. The accumulation of direct foreign investment in Brazil increased from US$2.3 billion in 1970 to US$26.2 billion in 1986.

The investment of foreign owned companies has been important to Brazil for a number of reasons:[16]

1. There is a lower remittances burden than in the case of foreign bank loans.
2. Such investment has introduced modern technology, increasing competitiveness of industry.
3. In 1986 foreign companies were responsible for 28 per cent of manufactured goods exports, contributing importantly to the Brazilian trade surpluses of the mid-1980s.
4. Foreign-owned companies represent 10 per cent of Brazils productive capital, but 25 per cent of corporate income tax revenues, 26 per cent of industrial GNP, and 35 per cent of indirect taxes of non-financial activities.

From the preceding it is clear that foreign-owned companies have made important economic contributions.

The following appear to be the more significant contributions of the activities of foreign-owned companies to the stock market and capital market in Brazil.

1. Foreign-owned companies provide an alternative means of mobilising and allocating capital in the Brazilian financial system.
2. In 1986 foreign-owned companies had a 'book value' of $26 billion. This compares favourably with the range of values of Brazilian stock market capitalisation in 1985–88 of $16–42 billion.
3. Trading of locally (Brazilian)-owned shares of foreign owned companies adds to the depth and liquidity of the Brazilian stock exchanges.
4. New direct investment inflows have been as high as $1.4 billion. This exceeds the 1986 high of Brazilian stock market new issues of $1.2 billion.

10.5.3 External debt conversions

In the preceding section we described the important role played by foreign multinational company investment in Brazil. In this section we consider the efforts made by the government of Brazil to facilitate conversions of external debt, and to stimulate new investment initiatives. Where successful, these efforts will lead to increased activity in the Brazilian capital markets, particularly the markets for company shares.

In 1987–8 the government of Brazil launched a new programme to encourage debt for equity swaps, aimed at encouraging inward business and portfolio investment. This programme is to be accomplished by means of (1) direct investments, in which case the investor selects the Brazilian company where the debt conversion is to be carried out; and (2) indirect investment through conversion funds organised for this purpose, or investment companies that provide a venture capital fund for such purposes. These investments will be carried out by the purchase of stocks through the stock exchanges or secondary market, or through new issues (increases in capital) in open or closely held companies.

Debt for equity conversions can be accomplished on a case-by-case basis, or in a formal swap auction. In the former, US-owned Banco Chase Manhattan S.A. negotiated a swap investment of $200 million in May 1988 in Autolatina, the holding company for Ford and Volkswagen in Brazil. The funds will be slated for Autolatina's expansion programme for exports. The swap will be effected under Central Bank Circular Letter 1125, which establishes that swap proposals presented before 21 July 1987 are entitled to an equity stake equal to the face value of the debt.

In March 1988 the Brazilian government initiated a monthly swap auction. The first auction was held at the Rio stock exchange, and the second (April 1988) at the São Paulo stock exchange. The government intends to alternate these monthly auctions between these two locations. In the first and second auctions a $150 million ceiling was set, although it is expected that larger monthly amounts will be authorised in future.

The swap auctions permit foreign investors to bid for the opportunity to swap Brazilian external debt (denominated in hard currency) for equity investments. In the first two swap auctions half of the authorised equity investment was set aside for the North-east, Amazon and other less developed regions of Brazil.

Several banks have presented the National Securities Commission with proposals to establish swap equity funds. For example, in May 1988, Banespa, the São Paulo state bank proposed a $50 million swap equity fund. Banespa intends to use its twelve overseas offices to provide a brokerage service between foreign investors wishing to swap their loans for investments, and Brazilian companies hoping to receive these investments to implement new projects and expand their capital base. Similarly, Banco do Brasil announced plans to set up its own swap equity fund to direct foreign money into private sector companies whose shares are traded publicly.[17]

In 1988 the government of Brazil, together with the bank creditor advisory committee, had agreed to create exit bonds for foreign creditor banks. As tentatively planned the bonds would have a 25-year maturity with a 10-year grace period. These bonds would pay 6 per cent interest yearly. Banks opting for exit bonds would free themselves of the need of more rescheduling negotiations, and from the need to provide fresh loans to Brazil. Banks would be able to swap these bonds for equity in Brazil, and for exports. Eventually these bonds could become negotiable on the secondary market for multinational companies requiring a hedge against currency rate changes.

10.6 FUTURES AND COMMODITIES EXCHANGES

10.6.1 Introduction

As of 1988 three futures and commodities exchanges were operating in Brazil. These include the Bolsa de Mercadorias de São Paulo (the oldest), the Bolsa Brasileiro de Futuros – BBF (located in Rio de Janeiro), and the Bolsa Mercantil e de Futuros – BM&F (the newest and largest). These futures exchanges are described briefly in Chapter 8, mainly in connection with their money market aspects. In the following discussion we focus on the stock market and commodities market aspects of their activities. Most of the remaining discussion focuses on the newer BM&F.

All these futures exchanges provide facilities for trading stock index futures. In the case of the BBF, the IBV Stock Index is the most actively traded contract. The Rio de Janeiro stock exchange has a large weighting of state enterprises (Banco do Brasil, Petrobras). The Bolsa de Mercadorias has an active IBV stock index, but its most active futures contract is in gold (Table 10.17). The BM&F provides facilities for trading stock index futures, the IBOVESPA Stock Index being its most active contract.

10.6.2 Bolsa Mercantil e de Futuros (BM&F)

The Bolsa Mercantil e de Futuros began operations in January 1986. In its first two years of operation it has experienced rapid growth, adding new types of trading contracts and widening the base of membership. The total number of contracts traded in 1987 was in excess of 6 million, almost two-thirds the number traded on the

Table 10.17 Comparative information: three futures and commodities exchanges in Brazil

Exchange	Year opened	Trading system	Clearing house	Futures	Options on futures	Options on cash	1987 total volume
Bolsa Brasileira de Futuros (Rio de Janeiro)	1984	Open outcry	International commodities clearing house	DMark, Yen, gold, US dollar, OTN, Certif. of deposit, IBV Stock Index,* LBC.	—	—	587 039
Bolsa de Mercadorias de São Paulo	1917	Open outcry	Caixe Nacional de Liquidacoes	Live cattle, cotton, feeder cattle, coffee, soybean, oil, gold, US dollar, cocoa, Brit. pound, DMark, Yen, Certif. of deposit, OTN, corn, frozen chicken, IBV Stock Index.	—	—	815 187
Bolsa Mercantil e de Futuros (São Paulo)	1986	Open outcry	Bolsa Mercantil e de Futuros	IBOVESPA Stock Index,* OTN, Domestic CDs, gold, US dollar, DMark, Yen, live cattle, hogs, coffee, frozen broilers, chilled broilers, soybean, tin, aluminium.	Coffee, IBOVESPA Stock Index.	Gold, local bonds, US dollar, domestic CDs.	6 087 982

* Most active contract.
Source: *Futures*, July 1988, p. 57.

London International Financial Futures Exchange (LIFFE), and nearly half the number of contracts traded on the Tokyo stock exchange (Table 10.17).[18] In 1987 the BM&F became affiliated with the São Paulo Stock Exchange, whereby the BOVESPA became a member of the BM&F, and the two exchanges share certain administrative services.

We now consider the membership structure and organisation of the BM&F, the types of contracts operating on the exchange, and the general outlook for futures and options trading in Brazil.

Membership and organisation

There are four classes of membership in the BM&F. These are (1) common members; (2) brokerage houses; (3) clearing members; and (4) institutional membership. In July 1988 there were 630 common members of the BM&F. These can be individuals or firms. Ultimately, there will be 1000 members. Common members enjoy the right to vote, to be part of the administrative council, and to enjoy reduced fees and commissions on trading activity (rebates of 25 per cent). Also they are required to deposit a lesser amount of margin (only 80 per cent of the margin deposit required by the exchange). However they do not enjoy direct access to floor trading unless they become 'corretoras' (150 corretora members in total), or 'locals' (100 local members in total). These two types of membership are described below. Included among the common members of the BM&F are commodities trading firms, major coffee exporters, agricultural co-operatives, banks and financial institutions, individuals and commodities houses.

A second type of membership includes 150 brokerage houses (Corretoras de Mercadoria) that specialise in commodities trading. These 150 commodities trading houses must be organised as companies. Individuals cannot function in this capacity, because of the need to ensure financial responsibility. The exchange has set the limit permanently at 150 for commodities brokerage houses. Each of the commodities houses may have several clerks or brokers on the trading floor. As employees of these houses they carry out the direct trading activity, interacting with other brokers. Approximately half of the commodities trading houses are Corretoras de Valores (full members of a stock exchange). The remaining commodities brokerage houses are either 'distribuidoras de valores' or commercial firms.

A third type of membership is the clearing member, of which there are 75. Each of these must be 'corretoras de valores', with membership on any of the stock exchanges in Brazil.

A fourth type of membership is the institutional member. The São Paulo Stock Exchange is the only institutional member of the BM&F.

A maximum of 250 members will ultimately be authorised to trade on the floor of the exchange. This includes the 150 brokerage houses ('corretoras de mercadoria') described above, and 100 'locals' or floor traders. In July 1988 approximately 40 of the memberships for floor traders had been issued. The BM&F was selling 5–10 of these at public auction every 2–3 months. The BM&F expects to have distributed all of the memberships for floor traders by 1990. Whereas the brokerage houses must be companies (not individuals), the floor traders are individuals who trade for their own account. A number of foreign financial institutions have shown interest in purchasing membership on the BM&F. This would provide the opportunity to develop their own futures and options trading activity in Brazil.

The BM&F is organised and managed by an administrative council and a board of directors. The administrative council has thirteen members, consisting of three indicated by the BOVESPA as an institutional member, three nominated by clearing members, three indicated by 'corretoras', three indicated by common members, and one superintendent general who is the chief executive. The administrative council establishes the major policies of the exchange, including approval of linkages with other exchanges, establishment of new futures contracts, changes in fees and governmental relations.

The board of directors consists of seven members, including the chief executive; three directors for operations, custody & settlement, and public relations; and three advisers in the fields of audit, law, and economic research.

Financial futures and stock index futures

Three types of financial futures contracts are traded on the BM&F. These include the IBOVESPA futures contract where, in mid-1988, the volume was approximately 40 000 contracts daily.[19] This is a fairly liquid contract, with a high percentage of volume oriented towards speculative trading activity.

A second financial futures contract is for OTN nominal. Here the unit of trading is 1000 OTN. This provides hedgers with protection against interest rate and inflation rate changes. There is probably more hedging activity in the trading of this contract than in the case of the IBOVESPA contract. In addition to OTN futures, there are also options to buy and options to sell OTN.

A third financial futures contract is the futures for bank certificates of deposit (CDBs). There are actually two different interest rate contracts in this area, CDB prefixed and CDB post-fixed. In 1987 the volume of contracts negotiated in CDBs was considerably larger than in OTN. In the case of prefixed, contracts are made for CDB at both 60 days and 90 days.

Contracts in gold and foreign currencies

A variety of contracts permit trading in gold on the BM&F. These include spot, futures, forward (term), call options and put options. The BM& F is probably the only exchange with a liquid market for spot gold. In August 1988 gold contracts were in excess of 10 000 contracts daily, three times the level of 1987. Brazil is a large producer of gold, and large business firms that want to hedge with gold can carry out various types of transactions for that purpose.[20] In 1988, with the acceleration of inflation in Brazil, gold trading activity increased. The gold trading contract in Brazil is equivalent to approximately $\frac{1}{12}$ of the Comex gold contract.[21]

In 1988 the BM&F offered futures contracts in three currencies (US Dollars, DMarks, and Yen). The dollar contracts have some degree of liquidity. Quotations are for US$1.00, DM10.00, and Yen 1 million.

Contracts in agricultural products

Major users of contracts in agricultural products are food processors and exporters. The exchange is working to gain permission to allow contracts of agricultural products in US dollars. In mid-1988 futures contracts were available covering live cattle, live hogs, frozen or chilled broilers and coffee.

General outlook

Growth in financial futures trading in Brazil reflects a basic need for hedging risks in these areas. This is based on a rapidly growing financial system, changing rates of inflation, and the debt conversion programme which is generating substantial pools of liquid cruzado funds in need of appropriate hedging and risk avoidance mechanisms. Continued expansion of the financial market system in Brazil and expansion of the volume of foreign debt conversions could lead to strong growth in the demand for hedging mechanisms and risk-avoidance products.

In the area of agricultural commodities, Brazil has become or is likely to become the first- or second-ranking world producer in a number of important commodities (coffee, soya, corn, cotton, cocoa, sugar, orange juice). Also Brazil has the largest live cattle herd in the world. All of this points to a gradual shifting of futures trading in these commodities to the Brazilian exchanges.

In the area of metals contracts, Brazil has been moving towards a leading producer position in various non-ferrous metals, including tin. Given the collapse of the International Tin Council price support scheme in 1985 and near bankruptcy, of the London Metals Exchange, wide opportunities are available for the Brazilian futures exchanges.

NOTES

1. Bond and debenture trading take place on the open market, and are settled through the SELIC and CETIP apparatus. This is described in detail in Chapter 8.
2. Bovespa, *Profile of the São Paulo Stock Exchange*, 1986, p. 15.
3. *Profile*, p. 19.
4. The coefficient of variation is calculated by dividing the mean participation into the standard deviation. For example, individual investors reflect a mean participation of 39.1 and a standard deviation of 3.16. This gives a coefficient of variation of 0.081.
5. These estimates were developed in discussions with officials at the various stock exchanges in Brazil.
6. Jo Galazi, 'As Muitas Opções de Lucros', *Bolsa*, July 1988, p. 7. This report indicates that between April and May 1988 the number of shareholders in share mutual funds declined from 7.0 million to 6.7 million.
7. *Folha de São Paulo*, 1 July 1987.
8. There is one exception to this. In the case of transactions on the Mercado a Termo, the financial operations tax or IOF (Imposto Sobre Operacoes Financais) applies where the term of the repurchase agreement is less than 28 days.
9. Bovespa, *Fact Sheet 1987*, p. 7.
10. Comissao Nacional de Bolsas de Valores, *Introdução Ao Mercado de Ações*, CNVB, Rio de Janeiro, 1986, pp. 88–9.
11. Domingos de Gouveia Rodrigues, 'O Porte dos Mercados de Ações e Debentures, Brasil Versus Países Industrializados', *Rbmec*, No. 33, 1985, p. 54.
12. Rodrigues, p. 55.
13. Rodrigues, pp. 54–6.
14. Rio de Janeiro Stock Exchange, *Facts and Figures 1986*.

15. *Gazeta Mercantil*, International Weekly Edition, 'More For Private Sector', 23 May 1988, p. 4.
16. Roberto Teixeira da Costa, 'Brazil's New Debt/Equity Program, Direct Investments Through Debt/Equity Swaps', workshop of the Council of the Americas, New York City, 15 April 1988.
17. *Gazeta Mercantil*, International Weekly Edition, 'Needy Area Swap Funds Ready to Go', 23 May 1988, p. 15; and *Gazeta Mercantil*, 'Banespa Joins the Race', 9 May 1988, p. 10.
18. Karen Pierog, 'International Exchanges Moving Toward Automated Trading', *Futures*, July 1988, pp. 57–62.
19. The IBOVESPA had a value for each contract of approximately US$2140 (mid-1988). This was based on taking the IBOVESPA index, multiplying by 5 cruzados per index point, which in August 1988 was approximately 80 000 points. Dividing this by 375 cruzados/$, the parallel rate on dollars, yields $2140.
20. A typical transaction would be to buy gold spot and write a call option, earning the premium which is analogous to an interest return.
21. The Comex contract is defined as 100 ounces, whereas the Brazilian contract is 250 grams each. One ounce is equivalent to 31.104 grams.

11 Industrial Finance

11.1 INTRODUCTION

The period 1974–86 is the subject of the next several sections. We focus on this period for a number of reasons. First, it is a period which follows the economic miracle of 1968–73, when economic growth was maintained at double digit levels for a number of years. Second, it is a period in which numerous external shocks beset the Brazilian economy. Third, it is a period in which the macroeconomic environment of Brazil underwent many changes. From the point of view of corporate financial activity, it was a dynamic and changing period, when inflation rates accelerated and the international terms of trade of Brazil deteriorated as basic commodity prices (exports) declined below prices of manufactured goods and equipment (imports). Aggravating these tendencies was a rapid increase in external debt, rising interest rates, a slowdown in domestic investment, and an increase in the relative role and importance of the public sector compared with the private sector. Towards the end of this period Brazil moved quickly in the direction of participative democracy, with the election in 1984 of Tancredo Neves to the Presidency. Neves was not in good health and died before he could be placed in office. His successor, President Sarney, took office. According to the Constitutional Convention that was operative in Brazil in 1987–8, there will be a presidential election in 1989.

11.2 TRENDS IN BALANCE SHEET STRUCTURE AND PROFITABILITY: NON-FINANCIAL CORPORATIONS

11.2.1 Introduction to corporate sector and information sources

The objective of these sections is to consider the principal characteristics of company finances since 1973, and to analyse the manner in which large enterprises in Brazil managed their financial position. Included in this analysis are the structure of finance and the capacity for autofinance, profitability, financial expenses, liquidity, dividend policy and investment policy.

Much of the statistical information included in the following sec-

314

tions is obtained from studies completed by Rodrigues, covering the period 1975–84.[1] This has been updated by use of statistics regularly published in *Conjuntura Econômica*.[2] In cases where other statistical sources are used, they have been cited. The Rodrigues data covering Brazilian enterprises is based on a sample of 90 of the largest firms. This includes 62 firms subject to national private ownership and control, 16 foreign controlled firms, and 12 enterprises subject to control and ownership of the government. The data from *Conjuntura Econômica* is based on the operations of the 1000 largest firms in Brazil.

The corporate sector in Brazil is unique, in that it is composed of three very large and almost equally important parts. The national private firms are larger in number, smaller in size, and dominant in the areas of traditional manufacturing (food, textiles, light manufacturing). The state enterprises are very large, with eight of the ten largest non-financial companies falling in this category. These firms operate in the public utilities and energy, telecommunications, and key mining and minerals sectors. State control has been based on the understanding that these sectors play a strategic role in the economy, and must be supported and regulated by the government. The third sector, foreign-controlled, includes a smaller number of enterprises that are capital-intensive, and bring advanced technology into Brazil. They dominate the motor vehicle sector, and are important participants in the electronics and certain consumer durables industries.

While government industrial policy is complex, detailed and ever-changing, it appears to have taken a fairly consistent approach to the respective roles of these three industrial sectors. State capitalism in Brazil should not be considered as an ideological preference, but rather a need based on pragmatic viewpoint. According to Trebat, the state functions both as regulator and owner–entrepreneur in the non-financial and financial institution sectors.[3]

The pragmatism in Brazil with respect to ownership of industry is reflected in the changing attitude towards state enterprises in the 1980s. Much interest has developed in Brazil concerning shifting ownership of some parts of the state enterprises to private national ownership. This is because of the demonstrated inability of the federal government to narrow the budget deficit to an acceptable level, and of the belief that private ownership may bring about more efficient performance. The question of privatisation is discussed in Chapter 13.

11.2.2   Macroeconomic trends and company finance

The purpose of this section is to acquaint the reader with the economic environment which prevailed in the 1970s and early 1980s. This
will give a better understanding as to why and how company finances
developed as they did in Brazil. Company finance does not operate in
a vacuum, and the macroeconomic developments described below
had perceptible influence on the ability and incentives of companies
to generate and maintain profits, borrow, cover debt charges, maintain corporate liquidity, invest and retain a satisfactory capital structure.

In a macroeconomic perspective the period from 1974 on is distinct
from earlier periods in three ways: (1) reduced rate of economic
growth; (2) accelerated inflation; and (3) change in the external
accounts of the country. Economic growth decelerated from 12 per
cent in the period 1970–3 to 7–8 per cent in 1974–6, to 6 per cent in
1977–80, to nearly zero growth and recession in 1981–4. Declining
growth reduces the amount of required financing in the corporate
sector, but also introduces problems with respect to maintaining
profitability and covering fixed financing expenses.

In the period under analysis, inflation pressures intensified. In 1974
inflation was at a level of 28 per cent per annum, but shifted up to 42
per cent in 1975–6, to 104 per cent in 1979–80, and to 220 per cent in
1983–4.[4] With this rising inflation rate companies experienced much
higher financial costs on both internal and external debt. Ultimately
this began to wear heavily on the ability of the non-financial corporate sector to undertake investment commitments.

Brazil's balance of payments also experienced considerable alterations in this period. Imports expanded sharply from 1974 onwards,
owing to higher petroleum prices and speculative activity.[5] Brazil
experienced a reversal in its international terms of trade, declining
from 95 (1977 = 100) in 1973, to 78 in 1974.[6] From 1977 to 1984 the
terms of trade deteriorated persistently, reaching 53 in 1983. This
reflects a recession in the market prices of Brazilian exports (including coffee and soya), and in international inflation in the prices of
manufactured goods (imported by Brazil).

The balance of payments was further affected adversely by external
borrowing. The borrowing became necessary to finance current account deficits. In 1974 the current account deficit was $7.1 billion,
averaging $6.1 billion in the period 1974–8. In 1979 the current
account deficit climbed to $10.7 billion, and continued to rise until

1982, when it was $16.3 billion. By savagely cutting imports over the period 1981–4 Brazil was able to reduce the current account deficit to zero. This was accompanied by a sharp curtailment of investment projects. In 1973 the external debt was $12.6 billion, but it rose rapidly over the next ten years. By the end of the period under review external debt was approaching $100 billion. By 1982 the debt service (interest and amortisation) represented 96 per cent of exports.[7] In 1982 the macroeconomic policy mix brought on a recession. Brazil considered itself to be in a situation of quasi-insolvency.

The macroeconomic trends described in the preceding several pages are reflected in the data concerning industrial fixed investment (Table 11.1). Investment in fixed capital is approved by the Council for Industrial Development (CDI), and actual releases of funds financing investment by the National Bank for Economic and Social Development (BNDES) can be interpreted as a thermometer of the government disposition to support aggregate investment.[8] This is reflected in Table 11.1 where 1975–6 represents the high point in industrial investment, measured as a percentage of industrial fixed investment to national income (1976–6.2 per cent), or as total fixed capital formation as a per cent of national income (1975–32.5 per cent). From 1977 on, CDI-approved investment declined steadily, a trend continuing until 1980. In 1981 fixed investment approved by the CDI increased in real terms (for the chemical, petroleum and pharmaceutical sectors).[9] The tendency for CDI to reduce industrial investment financing persisted with much intensity in 1983–4.

11.2.3 Balance sheet: assets

In the following sections we consider the manner in which three groups of firms carried out their financial policies. These include private national, state enterprise and foreign-owned firms. Over the period 1975–84 all three groups of firms increased their permanent assets relative to total, and all three groups reduced their investments in working capital. The reduction in percentage of assets devoted to working capital reflects the need to reduce liquidity, brought on by changes in the economic environment, particularly rising interest rates. In 1984–6 permanent assets remained fairly stable relative to total for all three groups of firms.

Considering all three groups of firms taken together, we can observe that liquid securities represent a declining share of the total (Table 11.2). This decrease in liquidity is also reflected in the smaller

Table 11.1   Industrial investment and BNDES financing

Year	Industrial fixed investment as per cent GDP	Release of loan funds by BNDES as per cent GDP	Fixed capital formation as per cent GDP
1970	2.9	0.9	25.8
1971	1.5	1.0	26.3
1972	3.6	1.2	26.4
1973	4.4	1.2	27.8
1974	4.4	1.7	30.8
1975	2.1	2.2	32.5
1976	6.2	2.1	27.8
1977	2.1	2.1	26.3
1978	1.6	2.1	25.7
1979	0.9	1.9	22.7
1980	0.5	1.4	23.2
1981	0.5	1.1	22.1
1982	0.5	1.5	22.4
1983	0.3	1.9	18.0
1984	0.3	1.7	14.0

Source: Domingos de Gouveia Rodrigues, *Empresas Não-Financeiras No Brasil: Evolução de Desempenho No Periodo 1975–84*, IBMEC, Rio de Janeiro, Feb. 1986, p. 36.

share of working capital assets in the total, which is reflected most strongly for the private national enterprises (53.2 per cent in 1975 to 38.5 per cent in 1984).

Private national firms and foreign controlled firms reflect an inverse correlation between interest rates and inventory levels, principally from 1980. The inventory behaviour of state enterprises is influenced by Petrobras, which, with the shock of cruzeiro depreciation in 1979, increased its inventories in real terms between 1978 and 1981 by 199 per cent.[10] Except for this specific situation, state enterprises reduced their inventories considerably in the period analysed.

Accounts receivable[11] remained fairly level during the early years covered by our analysis (1974–81). But this asset declined substantially from 1981 to 1984 for foreign-controlled firms, related to the higher interest rates in effect. In the period 1984–6 accounts receivable of all three groups of firms were stable or declined slightly.[12]

Brazilian companies often hold investments in other companies. In

Table 11.2 Balance sheet composition: assets

	Private national				State enterprise				Foreign controlled			
	1975	1978	1981	1984	1975	1978	1981	1984	1975	1978	1981	1984
WORKING CAPITAL	53.3	47.4	44.5	38.5	26.3	21.5	30.0	22.1	54.8	57.1	56.7	42.3
Cash	3.7	3.5	1.9	1.5	2.3	1.4	0.9	0.9	4.2	3.7	2.6	1.0
Liquid securities	7.8	6.7	4.7	4.9	5.1	1.7	1.5	1.5	9.2	7.1	8.2	6.8
Inventory	18.8	13.3	12.7	8.5	7.9	6.1	14.3	8.7	21.1	18.3	18.5	12.9
Accounts receivable	18.7	17.5	20.0	17.6	6.0	6.5	6.8	5.0	17.0	17.7	22.1	11.5
Prepaid expense	0.2	0.3	0.5	0.4	0.0	0.1	0.1	0.1	0.1	0.6	0.8	0.4
Other	4.1	4.7	4.7	5.6	5.1	5.8	6.4	6.0	3.2	6.7	4.5	9.7
LONG-TERM CLAIMS[1]	3.4	1.6	4.9	3.7	1.8	0.5	1.5	4.9	3.3	2.4	1.9	3.5
PERMANENT ASSETS	43.3	52.1	50.6	57.8	71.9	78.0	68.5	73.0	41.9	43.5	41.4	54.2
Fixed assets	50.2	58.2	50.8	52.5	70.8	89.2	72.5	73.9	53.2	62.6	60.6	61.7
Participation in other companies	7.9	14.6	16.5	25.3	6.6	9.1	5.0	12.8	9.2	9.3	9.9	22.3
Other[2]	3.4	1.0	2.4	3.4	2.0	1.2	6.1	7.5	2.7	0.9	0.9	3.0
Depreciation	−18.3	−21.7	−19.2	−23.4	−7.6	−17.6	−15.2	−21.2	−23.3	−29.3	−30.0	−32.8
TOTAL ASSETS	100.0	100.0	100.0	100.0	100.0	100.0	100.0	100.0	100.0	100.0	100.0	100.0

[1] Duplicatas to be received, issued on other companies with maturity of 12 months; loans to controlled or affiliated companies.
[2] Expenditures of funds for expenses which contribute to operating results over more than one productive cycle. These are amortised periodically.

Source: Domingos de Gouveia Rodrigues, *Empresas Não-Financeiras No Brasil: Evolução e Desempenho No Período 1975–84*, IBMEC, Rio de Janeiro, 1986, pp. 75–7.

1975 this represented 7.9 per cent of the assets of private national firms, 6.6 per cent for state enterprises, and 9.2 per cent for foreign controlled firms. From 1981 on all groups of enterprises increased these holdings by a substantial margin. In 1984 their respective investment in other companies was 23.3 per cent, 12.8 per cent, and 22.3 per cent of total assets. This represents an effort to diversify into unrelated activities, at a time when macroeconomic conditions were becoming less stable. Foreign companies diversified into sectors more dynamic offering better opportunities. In the period 1984–6 foreign companies continued to increase their investments in other companies.[13]

Considering the position of companies in fixed assets, in general there was a tendency to increase the percentage of assets in this category. For foreign-controlled firms this reflects a tendency to maintain or increase relative market position in Brazil. This is further reflected in a substantial increase in the relation of depreciation to total assets for the foreign controlled firms, which use accelerated depreciation to recover and roll over investment funds more efficiently. Since they operate in technologically more advanced areas, regulation allows them higher depreciation rates.[14] Further, they are able to rationalise technology more rapidly and reduce profit through depreciation expense. Moreover, as inflation accelerates, these permanent investments grow in proportion to total assets, through the application of monetary correction, which is mandated according to the company laws.

State enterprises have had strong investment programmes over the period of the second development plan. As can be seen in Table 11.2 their investment in fixed assets increased to 89.2 per cent of total assets (1978). This percentage denotes a greater capital intensity as compared with private national firms.

Returning to the share investments of private national firms and foreign-controlled firms in other enterprises, these increased from 7.9 per cent and 9.2 per cent in 1975 to 25.3 per cent and 22.3 per cent in 1984 of total assets. This can be interpreted as an attempt to maintain profitability and at the same time reduce risk, using a policy of diversification. For the state enterprises, investment in other enterprises rose in this period from 6.6 per cent to 12.8 per cent of assets, reflecting less emphasis on this strategy of diversification by the state-owned firms.[15]

11.2.4   Balance sheet: liabilities

As in the case of trends in asset composition, so in the case of liabilities and capital the private national and foreign-controlled firms display similarity. The state enterprises display their own distinct pattern of composition of liabilities.

Both private national and foreign-controlled firms increased the proportion of net worth. In the case of private national between 1975–84 net worth advanced from 45.2 per cent to 60.6 per cent of total funds (Table 11.3). Foreign-controlled firms were also able to accomplish a more modest increase in the proportion of net worth to total funds (50.7 per cent in 1975 to 54.4 per cent in 1984). By contrast, state enterprises experienced a reduction in the proportion of net worth, from 57.7 per cent in 1975 to 45.3 per cent in 1984. Considering the increased proportion of net worth for private national and foreign controlled firms, this reflects a shift away from long-term debt financing from banks and other sources. For example, in 1975–84 private national firms reduced their long-term loans and financing from 19.7 per cent to 12.3 per cent of funds. Similarly, foreign controlled firms reduced long-term borrowings from 12.0 per cent to 5.3 per cent of funds over the same period. This reflects an attempt to match capital structure to a new environment of higher interest rates and slower overall growth in the economy.[16]

By contrast, state enterprises increased the proportion of funds obtained from long term borrowing, from 20.3 per cent to 28.3 per cent (1975–84). This reflects (1) government policy aimed at solving the balance of payments problem via borrowed external resources; and (2) an excess of spending by these firms over resources, due to the large-scale investment projects in which they participated.

There are two possible factors explaining the reduction in long-term debt of the private national firms. One is associated with the reduction in credits provided by BNDES, and measures which reduced subsidies to firms, and the other that these firms anticipated foreign exchange rate risk and undertook to trim back their borrowings from external sources. Over the period 1984–6 all three groups of firms succeeded in increasing the proportion of net worth and reducing the proportion of long term liabilities in their balance sheets.[17]

Turning to short-term liabilities, one of the principal changes that took place was the increased use of accounts payable to suppliers in

Table 11.3   Balance sheet composition: liabilities and capital

	Private national				State enterprise				Foreign controlled			
	1975	1978	1981	1984	1975	1978	1981	1984	1975	1978	1981	1984
WORKING CAPITAL	25.4	28.5	31.4	24.4	18.2	20.1	28.6	24.3	32.8	37.3	46.3	38.4
Accounts payable	7.6	6.7	5.9	5.6	5.5	5.1	7.1	6.7	8.8	10.5	7.8	11.7
Taxes & fiscal payables	3.1	5.0	5.2	3.1	2.3	1.8	3.3	0.9	11.5	10.8	16.4	5.1
Loans & financings	6.4	8.9	10.4	6.5	5.1	7.7	9.8	10.3	6.3	8.8	12.4	9.5
other obligations	8.2	7.9	9.9	9.2	5.1	5.5	8.3	6.4	6.1	7.2	9.7	12.0
RECEIPTS FOR FUTURE DELIVERIES[1]	5.6	1.0	0.9	0.3	2.6	1.1	0.3	0.0	1.4	0.9	0.1	0.1
LONG-TERM	23.9	16.1	16.2	14.7	21.1	23.0	25.7	30.4	15.1	8.4	5.1	7.1
Loans & financings	19.7	15.6	14.0	12.3	20.3	21.1	23.6	28.3	12.0	7.6	4.7	5.3
Other	4.2	0.4	2.2	2.4	1.2	1.9	2.1	2.1	3.1	0.8	0.4	1.8
NET WORTH	45.2	54.5	51.5	60.6	57.7	55.7	45.1	45.3	50.7	53.4	48.5	54.4
Capital	21.0	19.7	11.4	11.6	33.9	21.5	12.3	7.9	26.0	21.3	16.8	12.7
Reserves	18.0	29.4	34.6	44.0	16.7	27.6	26.9	32.9	18.2	27.2	28.4	36.7
Accumulated profits	6.1	5.4	5.5	5.0	7.0	6.6	6.2	4.5	6.5	4.9	3.4	5.0
TOTAL	100.0	100.0	100.0	100.0	100.0	100.0	100.0	100.0	100.0	100.0	100.0	100.0

[1] Receipts for future services performed, in anticipation of the sale and delivery of goods that are now in the manufacturing process.
Source: As Table 11.2, pp. 79–81.

the 1980s. This became a major source of financing at short term for the foreign controlled firms. By contrast, private national firms made less use of this financing source over the period, owing to the acceleration in inflation rates and interest rates. Taxes and other fiscal payables declined in 1983–4, probably as a result of a reduction in profitability during this recession period. The decline in fiscal payables was sharpest among the foreign-controlled firms.

Short-term loans from banks increased for all three groups of enterprises. In the case of private national firms loans and financings increased from 6.4 per cent in 1975 to 10.4 per cent in 1981, and in the case of foreign-controlled firms from 6.3 per cent in 1975 to 12.4 per cent in 1981. For state enterprises loans and financings increased from 5.1 per cent in 1975 to 10.4 per cent in 1981. These short-term loans declined after 1981 for private national and foreign-controlled firms.

In the period 1984–6 the most noteworthy change in short-term liabilities was the increase in bank financings by state enterprises, which increased from 7.9 per cent of liabilities and capital to 11.2 per cent.[18]

11.2.5 Results from operations

Operating results

In previous pages we have seen that balance sheet changes reflect broad macroeconomic trends. Similarly, company performance also reflects macro-trends. The composition of company receipts shifted in the period 1975–84. Private national and foreign controlled firms experienced an increase in the proportion of non-operating to total receipts (Table 11.4). For private national firms non-operating receipts increased from 2.6 per cent to 9.0 per cent, whereas for foreign-controlled firms non-operating receipts increased from 2.1 per cent to 13.6 per cent. This was brought about by a slowdown in the expansion of sales, and a higher level of interest rates earned on non-operating assets. Firms altered their strategies and shifted investments to short-term liquid assets, expanding the base of non-operating income. State enterprises did not experience any increase in the proportion of non-operating receipts in this period, since they experienced greater financial difficulties.

On the expenses side of operations financial expenses shifted up markedly as a proportion of total expenses. State enterprises in

Table 11.4 Results from operations

	Private national				State enterprises				Foreign controlled			
	1975	1978	1981	1984	1975	1978	1981	1984	1975	1978	1981	1984
TOTAL RECEIPTS	100.0	100.0	100.0	100.0	100.0	100.0	100.0	100.0	100.0	100.0	100.0	100.0
Sales	97.4	96.1	90.2	91.0	96.4	94.4	87.7	97.8	97.9	92.0	93.9	86.4
Non-operating receipts	2.6	3.9	3.8	9.0	3.6	5.6	12.3	2.2	2.1	8.0	6.1	13.6
TOTAL EXPENSES	100.0	100.0	100.0	100.0	100.0	100.0	100.0	100.0	100.0	100.0	100.0	100.0
Cost of goods sold	75.1	73.1	73.4	62.0	75.4	79.6	70.8	61.9	71.1	70.6	63.7	67.2
Admin. expenses	5.8	6.6	6.1	5.8	4.2	9.2	5.7	5.7	4.7	5.5	5.9	6.0
Selling expense	10.1	5.4	4.9	7.7	2.2	8.9	4.1	3.0	15.0	9.2	9.1	6.4
Financial expense	4.9	5.5	10.1	10.8	7.2	7.5	8.9	29.8	3.9	4.6	10.3	17.2
Result from monetary correction	1.6	2.1	2.0	−0.6	0	−6.9	−17.3	−61.4	–	1.1	2.7	0.3
other expenses	2.5	7.4	3.5	14.3	11.0	1.7	27.8	61.0	5.4	8.9	8.2	2.9

Source: As Tables 11.2 and 11.3, pp. 83–5.

particular experienced a sharp increase in financial expenses from 7.2 per cent in 1975 to 29.8 per cent in 1984. This was associated with the 1979 maxi-devaluation of the cruzeiro, which especially affected those firms with substantial external debt.[19] The second maxi-devaluation in 1983 aggravated this problem.

Private national firms experienced the smallest increase in financial expenses as a proportion of total expenses. In their case financial expenses rose from 4.9 per cent in 1975 to 10.8 per cent in 1984. This was a result of their adapting their financial policies well to the slowing economy and to their minimising debt so as to avoid vulnerability to cyclical oscillations. We should understand further that these firms utilised subsidised credits and indirect autofinancing mechanisms through efficient administration of company finances.

During the period 1984–6 all three groups of firms experienced a substantial reduction in financial expenses. In part this was related to the artificial controls exercised over interest rates and borrowing costs during the early stages of the Cruzado Plan.[20]

The other item of importance with respect to expenses is the accounting mechanism for monetary correction. This is important for state enterprises, representing a negative percentage of total expenses in almost all of the years. According to the Law of Companies, firms must undertake monetary correction of their capital and their permanent assets. When permanent assets exceed capital, there is a credit balance of monetary correction which appears as a receipt in the accounts for operating results. The opposite takes place when there is an excess of capital over permanent assets. In the case of state enterprises, permanent assets are considerably larger than capital. The final result of this is that these enterprises are subject to a large impact on their accounts from monetary correction. For example, in 1984 we have a reduction of expenses of these firms of 61.4 per cent of total expenses as a consequence of monetary correction.[21]

Profitability

Trends in profitability over the period 1981–6 are summarised in Table 11.5. For private national firms there was little change in profit as measured by return on assets or return on capital. However the operating margin was up strongly. This reflects a sharp decline in cost of goods sold in 1981–4, and a sharp decline in financial expenses in 1984–6. In this period (1981–6) inventory and accounts receivable turnover rose strongly, reflecting more efficient use of working capi-

Table 11.5   Analysis of profitability of industrial enterprises, 1981–6

	1981	1984	1986
NATIONAL PRIVATE			
(799 firms)			
Return on assets	6.11	7.96	6.74
Return on capital	11.27	12.68	10.03
Operating margin	11.89	25.07	18.93
FOREIGN CONTROLLED			
(84 firms)			
Return on assets	4.48	6.79	6.62
Return on capital	10.35	13.74	12.27
Operating margin	5.35	12.40	11.13
STATE ENTERPRISES			
(117 firms)			
Return on assets	3.50	2.51	2.94
Return on capital	7.84	5.64	6.33
Operating margin	−18.62	3.14	8.53

Source: *Conjuntura Econômica*, March 1988, pp. 71, 75, 79.

tal. Monetary correction played a minor role in profitability trends of these firms.

Foreign-controlled firms displayed more consistent improvement in profit, reflected in all of the profit measures included in Table 11.5. Return on assets advanced from 4.48 per cent to 6.62 per cent (1981–6), and return on capital rose from 10.35 per cent to 12.27 per cent. The operating margin reflected the most favourable improvement, moving from 5.35 per cent in 1981 to 11.13 per cent in 1986. Like the national private firms, the foreign-controlled experienced a sharp decline in cost of goods sold in 1981–4, and a sharp decline in financial expenses (in the period 1983–6). Inventory turnover increased steadily throughout the 1980s, but there were no gains in efficiency in the use of assets dedicated to accounts receivable. The monetary correction factor proved to be of minimal importance for foreign-controlled firms.

As can be seen in Table 11.5, foreign-controlled firms display lower profitability than private national firms. However, from the point of view of operating efficiency, the foreign-controlled firms display higher turnover of working capital than the private national firms. Therefore we have to look elsewhere for an understanding of their lower profitability than the private national firms. One indicator is the cost of goods sold relative to sales revenues. Over the period

1981–6 this averaged 67 per cent for private national firms, and 77 per cent for foreign-controlled firms. Doubtless the higher ratio for foreign-controlled firms represents an important explanation for their lower reported profitability. In this regard we should remember that the foreign-controlled firms enjoy wide latitude for transfer pricing (in transactions with non-Brazilian affiliates). This could result in lower profit reporting, although the data available do not permit us to confirm this.

State enterprises displayed mixed profit performance. In 1981–6 return on assets and return on capital declined (Table 11.5). However the operating margin improved dramatically. A major factor was the movement in financial expenses. Financial expenses increased to 38 per cent, 54 per cent, and 62 per cent of sales revenues, over the period 1981–3.[22] This reflects the external indebtedness of these firms, and the high cost of carrying the dollar denominated debt at this period of time. By 1986 financial expenses had returned to a more normal 11 per cent of revenues, and all three measures of profitability reflected this improvement.

11.3 SOURCES AND USES OF FUNDS

11.3.1 Organisation of sources and uses data

In carrying out their financing activities enterprises constantly make decisions concerning how to manage assets (uses of funds), and how to obtain financing (sources of funds). These decisions are particularly important when we refer to long-term investment decisions. Each type of financing can be associated with a cost of capital. By balancing the decisions to invest in assets offering a certain prospective return, with decisions to finance at a certain projected cost of capital, the financial manager of the firm is seeking to maximise the value of the enterprise in the share market.

The main sources of funds for Brazilian enterprises are outlined in Table 11.6. The first category, autofinance, includes resources generated by ordinary activities and operations of the firm. These funds are distinct in that they are generated within the firm, and are not directly related to external developments. Over the period 1978–84 autofinance provided approximately two-thirds of total funds of private national firms, two-fifths of funds of state enterprises, and four-fifths of the funds of foreign controlled firms. Autofinance has as its main

Table 11.6   Schematic outline of main sources of funds of Brazilian enterprises

---

A *Autofinance*
   1 Profit
   2 Depreciation of fixed assets
   3 Amortisation of other assets
   4 Balance from exchange adjustment and monetary adjustment of debts and credits
   5 Monetary correction balance
   6 Dividends received from affiliates and controlled companies
B *External funds*
   1 Contributions from shares sold
   2 Sale of assets (book value)
C *Resources from third parties (lenders)*
   1 Loans and financings
   2 Sale of asset at profit (or loss)

Source: Rodrigues, pp. 87–93.

components profits, depreciation, balances from exchange adjustment and monetary adjustment, monetary correction and dividends from affiliates.

External funds have two basic components; sale of shares and sale of assets. Generally sale of assets provides small marginal increments to total funds. But sale of shares can play an important role as a funds provider. In some years sale of shares provided 10–12 per cent of total funds.

Resources from third parties (lenders) is the third source. Over the period covered this was more important for state enterprises than either private national or foreign-controlled firms. The largest component of resources from third parties is loans and financings (largely from banks).

The principal uses of funds include (1) making long-term investments; (2) debt operations; and (3) increasing or reducing assets at short term. There are two principal long-term assets that Brazilian firms invest in: fixed assets and participations in other companies. Taken together, these have accounted for half or more of funds uses over the period 1978–84. Debt operations can also absorb enterprise funds. Debt operations include prepayment of expenses (removing existing debt), repayment of debt obligations, and payment of dividends to investors (not strictly a debt, but an obligation to investors). The third group of activities involving uses of funds includes sale of assets (at profit or loss), and investment in working capital.

11.3.2 Trends in sources and uses

Private national enterprises

In 1978–84 the structure of finance and investment of private national enterprises reflects a strategy of adjusting to the deceleration in growth, and recession in Brazil. In conformity with this, total auto-finance increased as a percentage of sources of funds, rising from 58.8 per cent in 1978 to 76.8 per cent in 1984 (Table 11.7). Profit represented a declining share of funds sources over most of this period. Autofinance increased as a percentage of funds sources, permitting these firms to reduce their utilisation of the share market as a source of funds.

The process of improving the funding sources included a reduction in the use of resources from third parties. In 1984 this source provided only 16.64 per cent of funds (Table 11.7).

In the period 1984–6 profits of private national enterprises increased by a significant margin as compared with 1980–3. In 1984–6 profits after tax for private national firms averaged 13 per cent of revenues compared with 9 per cent in 1980–3.[23] In 1984–6 funds derived from the sale of shares in the new issues market trended up, providing a substantial inflow of funds. On a real (purchasing power) basis, new share issues in 1983–6 increased from an index value of 100 in 1983 to 209 in 1984, 261 in 1985, and 709 in 1986.[24] The distribution of these share issues by group of companies is indicated in Table 11.8. As can be seen, in 1983–6 92 per cent or more of new share issues represented sources of funds for private national enterprises. Only in 1987 did state enterprises obtain a large share of this source of funds. With respect to new debenture issues, on a real basis these declined in amount at a sharp rate over the period 1983–7, reflecting the policy of enterprises to reduce debt, especially debt contracted on a long-term basis.

On the uses of funds side one of the most significant changes was the reduction in the role of fixed assets, declining from 29.9 per cent to 9.71 per cent (1978–84). On the other hand, resources committed to participate in other companies increased, from 9.53 per cent in 1975 to 14.62 per cent in 1984. Dividend payments remained fairly stable as a percentage of funds uses over the period 1978–84. It has been noted that in the period 1978–82 private national firms maintained relatively high dividends, while profits and investment were declining, suggesting that a more conservative policy might have been called for. As we shall note below, the portion of funds used as

Table 11.7   Sources of funds of industrial companies

Year	Profit	Depreciation	Operating resources from autofinance				
			Balance from adjustment of ex-change rate changes	Balances from monetary correction	Dividends from subsidiaries and controlled firms	Other operating receipts	Total of autofinance
PRIVATE NATIONAL FIRMS							
1978	28.72	11.41	8.53	5.35	0.57	4.22	58.80
1979	26.14	12.38	10.73	7.54	0.57	6.52	63.88
1980	30.59	12.14	6.45	10.01	0.55	2.72	62.47
1981	21.08	13.10	− 0.93	23.12	1.43	6.47	64.27
1982	21.95	11.54	− 1.73	25.76	1.13	7.01	65.66
1983	16.45	10.60	1.13	34.40	1.13	2.08	67.38
1984	28.51	9.69	− 1.76	37.69	1.42	− 3.53	76.80
STATE ENTERPRISES							
1978	39.25	16.86	− 22.04	20.29	0.35	− 4.04	50.68
1979	23.00	20.61	− 45.81	46.19	0.48	− 4.55	39.91
1980	26.75	24.18	− 55.84	51.70	0.36	3.31	50.47
1981	25.66	17.35	− 62.47	58.28	0.98	− 0.10	39.70
1982	17.75	17.92	− 68.10	71.95	1.03	− 1.17	39.38
1983	20.61	26.49	−190.29	200.12	0.97	−12.72	28.89
1984	32.00	22.83	−200.22	182.14	0.72	−12.52	40.39
FOREIGN CONTROLLED FIRMS							
1978	41.37	18.58	5.72	2.82	1.72	6.52	76.72
1979	18.79	23.83	13.68	4.23	2.02	8.23	70.77
1980	39.84	20.87	8.64	4.04	1.27	10.94	85.59
1981	37.60	21.54	12.59	5.67	0.72	4.17	82.28
1982	42.43	17.85	5.16	6.08	7.63	5.22	84.37
1983	33.59	24.77	0.28	25.09	21.87	−28.37	77.23
1984	64.59	17.35	1.25	10.92	18.10	−24.49	87.73

External funds		Resources from third parties (lenders)				Total
Contributions from shares sold	Sale of assets	Financings and loans	Sale of an asset at a profit	Other	Total from third parties	Sources
PRIVATE NATIONAL FIRMS						
14.79	3.66	21.06	1.42	0.26	22.75	100
10.22	2.19	22.00	1.44	0.26	23.71	100

9.06	1.79	26.12	0.55	0.00	26.68	100
3.78	1.90	28.00	2.04	0.01	30.05	100
9.96	1.25	20.21	2.91	0.02	23.13	100
2.47	0.45	17.23	2.95	9.52	29.70	100
5.75	0.81	12.68	2.67	1.29	16.64	100

STATE ENTERPRISES

12.11	0.42	36.69	0.04	0.07	36.79	100
8.74	2.68	44.35	0.03	4.12	48.49	100
8.19	3.95	36.35	0.18	0.87	37.40	100
9.52	18.31*	28.20	4.11	0.15	32.47	100
11.78	3.14	42.52	2.79	0.40	45.71	100
32.94	0.20	34.43	2.73	0.81	37.97	100
8.14	0.18	43.46	4.19	3.64	51.29	100

FOREIGN CONTROLLED FIRMS

7.42	3.16	11.81	0.55	0.34	12.70	100
11.03	0.75	16.95	0.42	0.08	17.45	100
9.10	0.90	4.03	0.37	0.08*	4.40	100
10.35	1.41	5.29	0.50	0.17	5.98*	100
1.10	1.01	13.21	0.17	0.15	13.53	100
2.95	2.37	16.12	0.00	1.33	17.45	100
1.86	1.56	6.33	1.67	0.85	8.85	100

* Influenced by disposal of assets of Eletropaulo.
Source: As Tables 11.2 and 11.3, pp. 120–2.

Table 11.8   Issue of shares by type of enterprise

	Foreign-controlled	State enterprise	Private national
1983	—	—	100.0
1984	—	4.1	95.9
1985	0.1	2.3	97.6
1986	1.3	6.6	92.1
1987	0	44.9	55.1

Source: CVM, *Revista*, Oct.–Nov.–Dec. 1987, p. 16.

dividends by private national firms (8 per cent) is much lower than in the case of foreign-controlled firms (14–29 per cent).

Over the period 1978–84 private national firms allocated a larger percentage of funds to the reduction of long-term debt. This was part of the strategy aimed at minimising risk, and was prompted by the changes in economic conditions. A final point with respect to the uses of funds is that private national firms allocated an increasing percentage of funds to working capital. This increased from 32.02 per cent in 1978 to 46.51 per cent in 1984 (Table 11.9). In part this reflects the rising inflation rate, which necessitated use of more resources to provide circulating capital.

In the period 1984–6 private national enterprises did not distribute as large a proportion of profit in dividends as in the period 1980–3. This conservative financial policy with respect to dividends was reinforced by a reduction of long-term debt.

State enterprises

Over most of the period 1978–84 state enterprises experienced declining profitability. Consequently profit accounted for a declining percentage of funds sources. With the decline in profitability autofinance also experienced a fall-off, from 50.6 per cent in 1978 to 40.39 per cent in 1984. Opposite movements in monetary correction and adjustments for exchange rate and monetary changes more or less offset one another over the period. In contrast, profitability improved in 1984–6, with profit after tax averaging 12.3 per cent of sales revenues compared with 8.3 per cent in 1980–3.

Share participations by the National Treasury and the stock market provided between 8 and 12 per cent of funds required by state enterprises (in 1978–84), with one exception. In 1983 the government injected large amounts of resources into Acesita and Companhia Siderurgica Nacional, reflected in Table 11.7 where in that year share contributions reached the level of 32.94 per cent of funds. Over the period 1978–84 resources from third parties became a larger source than autofinance. By 1984 state enterprises were obtaining 51.29 per cent of funds from these borrowing activities.

The efforts of state enterprises to reduce long-term debt continued in 1984–6. From 1983 to 1986 the ratio of long-term debt to total resources declined from 40 per cent to 33 per cent. This was facilitated by a conservative dividend policy. In 1980–3 dividend distributions were 27.1 per cent of after tax profits, but in the period 1984–6 this fell to 2.7 per cent of profits.

Compared with private national enterprises, state enterprises made different uses of their funds. Investments in fixed assets accounted for an average 56 per cent of funds in 1978–84, much more than private national firms. Participations in other companies increased moderately. But over the period 1978–84 state enterprises

Table 11.9 Uses of funds of industrial companies

Year	Fixed assets	Participation in other companies	Prepayment of expenses	Dividend paid and to be paid	Reduction in long-term debt	Sale of asset at loss	Other uses	Working capital	Total
PRIVATE NATIONAL FIRMS									
1978	29.90	9.53	2.10	8.80	8.03	8.33	1.29	32.02	100
1979	31.15	10.92	4.94	8.54	8.49	10.53	0.99	24.44	100
1980	30.26	10.49	4.52	10.13	8.04	7.00	1.34	28.23	100
1981	25.50	8.04	4.30	7.58	8.97	14.83	1.18	29.60	100
1982	18.60	16.88	2.21	8.79	7.60	9.34	0.91	35.68	100
1983	19.50	14.58	1.61	7.30	15.22	6.66	0.47	34.67	100
1984	9.71	14.62	0.35	8.18	11.58	8.03	1.02	46.51	100
STATE ENTERPRISES									
1978	60.77	5.57	6.51	15.23	12.39	3.53	0.66	− 4.66	100
1979	61.22	4.84	11.80	10.44	18.21	6.03	3.75	−16.28	100
1980	56.19	8.07	1.33	8.91	19.92	5.05	2.11	− 1.58	100
1981	59.15	7.75	4.63	8.16	13.50	20.81*	3.68	−17.67	100
1982	70.13	6.91	7.17	7.52	12.02	13.16*	2.01	−18.92	100

Table 11.9 Uses of funds of industrial companies

Year	Fixed assets	Participation in other companies	Prepayment of expenses	Dividend paid and to be paid	Reduction in long-term debt	Sale of asset at loss	Other uses	Working capital	Total
1983	57.95	12.85	29.96	8.16	36.00	13.00	0.86	−58.77	100
1984	31.97	9.19	7.04	9.52	35.80	10.69	0.25	− 4.46	100
FOREIGN CONTROLLED FIRMS									
1978	31.93	8.91	2.53	20.77	6.91	3.41	0.12	25.42	100
1979	41.49	3.30	2.02	19.24	5.82	10.24	2.77	15.13	100
1980	40.34	3.69	1.52	14.10	8.79	4.95	0.66	25.95	100
1981	48.77	6.57	1.53	16.96	3.01	5.85	0.69	16.62	100
1982	33.57	6.91	3.22	19.66	5.47	8.66	0.65	21.86	100
1983	29.90	4.77	4.42	21.15	9.47	16.89	0.54	12.87	100
1984	23.96	19.62	1.49	29.59	3.93	6.01	0.61	15.18	100

* Influenced by high volume of loan concessions.
Source: As Tables 11.2 and 11.3, pp. 120–2.

never allocated as much funds to participations in other companies as private national firms (percentage-wise). Instead they concentrated their resources on investments in their own activities.

Dividend distributions were a larger percentage of funds uses for state enterprises than for private national firms. These distributions declined moderately over this period, responding to the decrease in profitability. Along with this, state enterprises allocated a larger percentage of funds to reducing long-term debt in 1983–4, further explaining their inability to maintain the level of dividend distributions of the late 1970s.

The need of state enterprises to improve their financial position can be seen in the case of working capital. During almost the entire period working capital represented a rising negative use of funds, reflecting cutbacks in net working capital and a declining liquidity condition. Partly for this reason state enterprises made considerable use of borrowings from third parties in later years.

Foreign controlled firms

The high level of profit enjoyed by these firms permitted them to rely on autofinance for a major portion of funds sources. Profitability of foreign controlled firms fell sharply in 1979, probably affected by the maxidevaluation. From 1979 to 1984 profits increased from 18.79 per cent to 64.59 per cent in (Table 11.7). Over the entire period profits accounted for 39.7 per cent of funds of foreign-controlled firms, compared with 24.8 per cent and 26.4 per cent for national private and state enterprises, respectively.

Depreciation constituted a more important source of funds for foreign-controlled firms than the other groups of firms. Balances from monetary correction also proved to be an effective source of funds. On average, foreign-controlled firms obtained 80.0 per cent from autofinance, compared with 65.6 per cent and 41.4 per cent for private national and state enterprises.

In spite of having declined in relative importance in the final years (1982–4) as a source of finance, the contribution from shares sold by open capital companies averaged 6.3 per cent over the period 1978–84. Foreign-controlled firms made much less use of loans and financings than private national and state enterprises, due in large part to the large role played by autofinance. From 1982 onward foreign-controlled firms turned away from the share market and relied on loans and financings to a much larger degree as sources of funds (Table 11.8).

Foreign-controlled firms made larger proportionate investments in fixed assets (averaging 35.7 per cent of funds) than private national firms.[25] However, in 1983–4, they reduced the percentage of funds used for investment in fixed assets. As they reduced their allocation of funds to fixed assets, they increased their participations in other companies (Table 11.9), allocating 19.2 per cent of funds to this purpose in 1984. With the continued high level of profits throughout the period 1978–84, foreign-controlled firms made substantial dividend distributions. These averaged 20.2 per cent over the entire period, compared with 8.5 per cent and 9.7 per cent of funds for private national and state enterprises, respectively. Foreign-controlled firms followed a policy of maintaining their liquidity, demonstrated by the high percentage of funds allocated to increases in working capital. Allocations to working capital averaged 19 per cent in the period 1978–84, reflecting a favourable financial position for these firms.

11.4 NATIONAL BANK FOR ECONOMIC AND SOCIAL DEVELOPMENT

11.4.1 Early development

The National Bank for Economic and Social Development (BNDES) was organised by the government of Brazil in 1952. Through its ownership and control of the BNDES, the government has been the most important source of long-term industrial financing. The government has used the credit allocation power of the Bank as a means of discriminating among economic sectors and borrowers. In the 1950s the Bank focused on infrastructure finance, and public enterprises took a majority of the funds provided by it. By 1965 it was recognised that a wider lending base was called for. In that year the charter of BNDES was revised and the Bank began to allocate a major part of its lending to private enterprises. By the mid-1970s over three-quarters of the bank's lending was directed towards firms in the private sector, and over the period 1975–85 BNDES has continued to give preference to private sector borrowers.

The role of BNDES has been to permit borrowers to obtain long-term financing. This is very important in a country such as Brazil, where inflationary episodes come and go, and lenders develop a strong preference for short-term lending. Commercial banks have been reluctant to provide long-term financing that is needed for economic development. Until the 1980s, the financial intermediaries in Brazil were not large enough, and lacked the resources required to play a significant role in providing long-term financing. Finally, the debenture market has faced difficulties in its development, largely related to the problem of inflation.

11.4.2 Operational role

The basic activity of BNDES has been to provide credits to finance public and private sector industrial projects. The bank obtains funds from various sources including loan repayments, the fund for national development, the merchant marine fund and foreign banks. However, its major sources of funds have been tax revenues and funds derived from public pension programmes. The bank generally has operated profitably, even though its lending is subsidised, charging interest below commercial rates of interest.

Over the past 25 years the Bank has been an essential factor in facilitating Brazil's high rate of economic growth. Together with a number of development banks owned by the state governments, the BNDES has administered financing programmes providing nearly all of the cruzeiro-denominated project financing of Brazilian financial institutions.[26] The bank has played a much broader role than that of a long-term lender. It provides working capital credits for domestic companies, financial assistance in the case of reorganisations, and stock and bond underwriting for small- and medium-size companies.

The existence of the bank has posed several basic dilemnas. One is that the government has tried to use the bank as a means of fostering development of industrial sectors, and at the same time avoid ownership of these entities. However, at times the bank has been required to take over financially troubled companies. This has led to the unintended result of public ownership, as well as public control. We return to this question in Chapter 13, which focuses on privatisation.

Another problem is that it is possible that the operations of the bank have tended to impede the development of private sector financial institutions and bond markets. Further development of these sectors is desired so that long-term finance can be provided in a more competitive environment. It has been suggested that private sector companies find the attractiveness and ready availability of BNDES financing such that few care to opt for more expensive financing from the investment banks and other financial institutions.

In addition to its basic role in providing long-term development finance, over the years BNDES has introduced a number of special lending and development financing programmes. This has included investment in private enterprise and support of industrial exports. The Bank has also supported advanced technology sectors, urban passenger transport, and programmes of improved productivity (shipping, shipbuilding). BNDES administers the FINSOCIAL programme. With funds from FINSOCIAL it has assisted key areas such as food production, low-income housing, education, and aid to small farmers.

Credits

Data on approvals for credits by the BNDES system over the twelve-year period 1975–86 is presented in Table 11.10. As can be noted from the table, in real terms bank lending has not expanded very much over this time period, although there have been substantial year-to-year changes in credits approved. As a general rule, disbursements of credits lag approvals by a fairly short time period, and the year-to-year changes in disbursements coincide closely with approvals.

As can be seen, credit approvals were on a high plateau in 1975–9, averaging 3.2 per cent of GDP. Considering that investment spending in this time period averaged no more than 24 per cent of GDP, it appears that BNDES-financed investments represented over 13 per cent of real investment. In 1980–2 there was a significant fall-off in credit approvals, reflecting federal budget tightening and the external debt crisis. Since 1983 BNDES credit approvals have been on a low plateau, representing on average 1.7 per cent of GDP.

In recent years the largest part of bank credit approvals has been for plant expansion or remodelling. In 1984–5 this accounted for 61–70 per cent of credit approvals.

Capital market activities

In addition to its role as provider of credit, the BNDES functions as an investment banker. In this regard it underwrites new securities issues, operates in the secondary market for securities, and provides various specialised financial services for enterprises. In 1986 participation in the primary stock market included 92 flotations of shares in this market with a total value of CZ$705.1 million. BNDES took part

Table 11.10   BNDES system: approvals for credits (CS$ million)

Year	Credits in current values	Credits in constant values*	Real growth	Credits as per cent GPD	
1975	35.9	83 600	—	3.57	
1976	67.7	108 020	34%	4.15	
1977	45.5	50 970	–53	1.83	High plateau
1978	153.4	123 860	143	4.26	
1979	136.0	71 840	–42	2.23	
1980	305.9	80 794	12	2.43	
1981	717.3	90 238	12	2.90	Fall off
1982	830.4	53 432	–41	1.73	
1983	2 313.8	58 493	9	1.80	
1984	7 997.9	63 091	8	2.06	
1985	21 839.4	52 904	–16	1.56	Low plateau
1986	56 676.4	56 676	7	1.55	

* Measured in CZ$ purchasing value of 1986.
Source: BNDES, *Annual Reports*, 1985, p. 8; 1986, p. 9.

in 66 per cent of the 140 share offerings and 78 per cent of the aggregate number of flotations of all types of securities registered with the national securities commission in 1986.[27]

In secondary market activities BNDES operates as manager of the Social Participation Fund (FPS), and carries out the purchase and sale of the shares making up the BNDES and BNDESPAR portfolios. In 1986 transactions of the Social Participation Fund were 256 per cent higher than the previous year, with substantial increases in the primary stock market and convertible debentures.

Another activity of BNDES in the capital market is the sale of investments made in previous years. At year-end 1986, the value of its shareholding portfolio aggregated CZ$32 billion (approximately US$1.6 billion). To recycle its resources, whenever the companies it supports can stand on their own feet, BNDESPAR proceeds to divest part or all of its holdings. In such a case, the preference is to carry out such divestments on the stock exchanges. In 1986 these divestments had an aggregate value of CZ$610 million (approximately 5 per cent of the overall portfolio).[28] We return to this topic in Chapter 13.

Decentralisation of growth

A major objective of the BNDES system is to encourage the decentralisation of economic growth. The rationale for this includes taking advantage of natural resource availability, regional comparative advantage, and local labour force endowments. Enterprises located in less well-developed regions enjoy special access to credits based on a policy of harmonising regional development with national development objectives. In 1986 several factors combined to reduce the total disbursements of BNDES to the North, North-east, and Centre-West regions. The reasons for this include the shifting of Finsocial programmes to the federal budget, the conclusion of certain projects and restrictions on investments in new projects, and expanded demand for consumer goods in the south-east which led to increased investment in that region.

Programmes supporting micro- mini- or medium-sized companies provided a means toward achieving sectoral decentralisation. These included Promicro, Proinfo, and the Small- and Medium-Sized Company programmes. The number of companies benefiting from these programmes in 1986 rose to 3427, more than double the number in the previous year. The needy regions of the north and north-east received 35 per cent of these investments.

Capital goods

The BNDES system traditionally supports the capital goods sector by loans for the installation, improvement or expansion of plant facilities, and by providing incentives for the purchase of Brazilian-made machinery and equipment. In this respect a bank subsidiary, FINAME, plays a central role. In 1986 FINAME disbursed CZ$16.5 billion, and approved operations amounting to CZ$26.4 billion.[29]

The information science sector is a priority area for the bank. In 1988 BNDES provided CZ$330 million in credits for Cobra, one of the largest Brazilian firms in this field. Bank credits permitted this company to manufacture super-minicomputers and offer its products on a leasing basis, facilitating Cobra's ability to compete with multinational rivals.

Other industrial projects supported by bank funding include Heliodinamica, the only integrated company in the Southern Hemisphere that is working in the field of solar energy for the production of silicon; and Sid Macroeletronica, which is modernising its technology base for the production of electronic devices.

11.4.3 Strategic plan, 1988–90

BNDES has been a proponent of the opening of the economy to enhance competition, promote trade and permit the inflow of new technology.[30] This is based on the following analysis, which is stated in the bank's strategic plan.

1. Financing a new cycle of Brazilian growth will have to be carried out almost in its entirety by domestic resources, owing to the restrictions on foreign flows of capital.
2. Self-financed growth signifies a radical alteration in the process of Brazilian development. This translates into maintenance of a substantial trade surplus. The long-term growth of Brazil can only be achieved in an environment of open economy, which is receptive to Brazilian merchandise exports and allows the import of required technology.
3. Public sector finance must be restrained, releasing financial resources for private sector borrowing. To avoid any crowding out of the private sector, it is necessary that the public sector generate adequate tax revenues and that state-controlled companies generate adequate internal resources.
4. Various forms of participation by private capital should be encouraged, particularly in activities that previously were considered to be the exclusive responsibility of the state. This requires a careful redefinition of the areas of activity of the state, private capital, and foreign capital.
5. The BNDES three-year strategic plan aims at a competitive integration of the Brazilian economy into the international economy. It is recognised that this presents certain risks (fluctuations in world economic activity and international interest rates).

In its efforts to effect a closer integration of the Brazilian economy into the international economy, the bank adheres to certain principles of operation that have guided it in the past. These include the operation of BNDES as an agent of change, which involves a constant striving for modernisation of the economy, and restructuring of public institutions and companies. Finally, this calls for the use of industrialisation as a basic moving force for development.

Successful industrial development requires a strong entrepreneurial class. Entrepreneurial activity is especially required in sectors such as petrochemicals, information science and capital goods production. More effective utilisation of available entrepreneurial talent may call for some restructuring in industry, similar to that taking place in Western Europe and developed countries.

In the past BNDES activities have focused on fuller utilisation of internal resources, as well as development that reduces social and regional inequalities. Therefore the bank has stated that it intends to focus in part on the development of needy regions, and social development projects that will deliver improved services to a wider range of the population.

To implement the strategic plan, the bank adopted six operational strategies:

1. Strategy for improved competition with the foreign sector. Here the bank focuses on modernisation, provision of technology, and development of industrial automation systems. This requires the use of industrial parks for the location of modern sector investments. Also required is a revised management model for certain Brazilian enterprises, especially in such fields as microelectronics, information science and capital goods. Finally, support of export activities and Latin American integration schemes must be part of this strategy.

2. Strategy for investment recovery, and participation of the public and private sectors. Here the bank supports basic input industries, as well as related infrastructure. Energy investments in particular require support, apparently because of the expectation that sectors referred to in the first strategy will tend to be energy-intensive. Further aspects of this strategy include support of modern farming and stock-breeding projects, and support of agencies that promote the transfer of economic activities to the private sector. Finally, the bank promotes more rational pricing of services provided by companies supported by bank activities.

3. Strategy for relief of poverty and removal of unequal distribution of income. Here the bank supports community projects that satisfy certain standards, supports the agricultural production of small farmers involved in land allotment programmes, and contributes to the expansion of those sectors producing essential goods that are adapted to the better distribution of income.

4. Strategy aimed at reinforcing the financial and patrimonial structure of the BNDES system. Here the bank must establish channels for obtaining resources in the capital market.[31] Further, it seeks to obtain a significant increase in the amount transferred to BNDES

of funds collected each year by Finsocial. The bank encourages the transfer to private ownership of companies controlled by the BNDES system, the disposal of its minority holdings in state controlled companies, and the disposition of non-operational assets. Further, the bank expects to expand via BNDESPAR its operations with shareholding participations and convertible debentures in high yield companies.

5. Strategy for political and institutional integration of BNDES. Here the bank must intensify the policy of social communication, and improve on its representation within the community. The bank intends to provide more complete information concerning the standards for appraisal of projects. Further, it intends to promote wider discussion of its strategic plan among the various sectors of the community, and in this way facilitate a larger role in the development of the Brazilian economic and social system.

6. Strategy for the rationalisation and modernisation within the BNDES system. Here the bank has been initiating decentralised support systems, to improve the machinery of integration of the various sectors of the system, to develop automatic information systems and more reliable system information, to establish new approaches and methodology for project analysis, and to develop a system of performance appraisal for the BNDES system. In addition, the Bank plans to implement reforms in human resources management, and undertake a reorganisation of the overall BNDES system.

NOTES

1. Domingo de Gouveia Rodrigues, *Empresas Não-Financeiras No Brazil: Evolução e Desempenho No Periodo 1975–84*, IBMEC, Rio de Janeiro, February 1986.
2. *Conjuntura Econômica*, 'Balanco da Mil Sociedades Por Ações', Fundação Getúlio Vargas, Rio de Janeiro, March 1988, pp. 65–122.
3. Thomas J. Trebat, *Brazil's State-Owned Enterprises: A Case Study of the State as Entrepreneur* (Cambridge University Press, 1983) pp. 10–11.
4. Rodrigues, p. 11.
5. Rodrigues, p. 11. In dollar values, Brazilian imports climbed from $6.2 billion in 1973 to $12.6 billion in 1974.
6. Rodrigues, pp. 12, 34.
7. Rodrigues, p. 13.
8. Rodrigues, p. 21.
9. Rodrigues, p. 22.
10. Rodrigues, p. 55.

11. Brazilian practice calls for companies selling merchandise to draw drafts on the buyer. These 'duplicatas' can be discounted with financial institutions. Therefore accounts receivable contain a somewhat different mix of claims as compared with the United States where they are primarily open account claims on other companies.
12. *Conjuntura Econômica*, March 1988, pp. 70, 74, 78.
13. *Conjuntura Econômica*, March 1988, p. 78.
14. Rodrigues, p. 58.
15. Less emphasis on diversification can be interpreted in several ways. First, state enterprises have enjoyed the support of the federal government, and therefore have less concern with diversification of risks. A second alternative interpretation is that through this period the cost of borrowed capital was increasing, while the ability of the government to provide capital funds was declining.
16. Rodrigues, pp. 62–3.
17. *Conjuntura Econômica*, pp. 71, 73, 75.
18. *Conjuntura Econômica*, p. 74.
19. Rodrigues, p. 67.
20. *Conjuntura Econômica*, pp. 71, 75, 79.
21. Rodrigues, pp. 68–9. Also it must be noted that these firms correct their debts *vis-à-vis* financial institutions, and increase their future obligations. This variable for monetary correction and exchange rate variations is of the opposite sign as monetary correction, and in the 1980s was of the same approximate percentage relative to total expenses. These firms can reflect higher profit in monetarily correcting fixed assets, but lower profit in correcting liabilities.
22. *Conjuntura Econômica*, p. 76.
23. *Conjuntura Econômica*, p. 71.
24. CVM, *Revista do Comissão de Valores Mobiliários*, vol. 5, no. 18, Oct.–Nov.–Dec. 1987, p. 15.
25. Domingos de Gouveia Rodrigues, 'Estrutura de Financiamento e Investimento das Empresas Nao-Financeiras No Brasil:1978–82', *Rbmec*, 1984, p. 274.
26. World Bank, *Brazil: Financial System Review*, 1984, p. 67. In 1978 BNDES disbursements were Cruzeiro $62.0 billion, or 40 per cent of industrial gross fixed capital formation.
27. BNDES, *Annual Report 1986*, pp. 9–10.
28. Ibid., p. 10.
29. Ibid., p. 14.
30. BNDES, *Strategic Plan 1988/90*, p. 1.
31. *Gazeta Mercantil*, 'Opcao de Financiamento', 16 June 1988. In late 1987 the BNDES obtained authorisation from the government to issue its own securities in the capital market. These have been tentatively given the name 'Letra de Desenvolvimento Economico' (LDE). It is expected that these could be issued directly to financial institutions and various other market sectors.

Part IV
Recent Developments

12 The Debt Conversion Programme

12.1 INTRODUCTION

12.1.1 Changing attitudes towards external indebtedness

The decade of the 1980s brought with it new economic problems for Brazil. In this chapter we consider these problems within the context of the debt conversion programme introduced by the government. In the following chapter we consider these problems in the context of the privatisation programme introduced in 1988.

During the decade of the 1980s Brazilian attitudes towards the economic potential of the nation, and the appropriate mix of policies related to this potential, moved through several changing phases. Among others, these included the belief (1982–3) that the external debt crisis was more a temporary liquidity problem that could be resolved when export growth resumed its natural course. Other interpretative approaches to the new realities facing Brazil included a closing down of the international linkages to achieve greater self-sufficiency and improve the international financial status of the country. This was implemented by a savage reduction in imports in 1983–4, and had the result of stifling technology inflows.

Other interpretations of Brazil's new economic potential included the belief that heterodox economic shock could reawaken Brazil's growth potential. The now-defunct Cruzado Plan of 1986 was an effort to implement this analysis. In February 1987 Brazil announced a debt moratorium, temporarily suspending payment of interest on external debt. The debt moratorium brought serious economic difficulties and catapulted Brazilian thinking with dramatic effect. Brazilian economists began to discuss the need to reopen the economy, and the possibility of reducing the role of government in internal economic activity. Efforts were made (discussed in other chapters) to reform and modernise the financial system and monetary policy. A more active monetary policy was introduced and fiscal reforms were initiated.

In 1988 the government faced several critical problems, given the overhang of substantial external debt, the depressed level of fixed investment, and the need to improve on the utilization of now scarcer financial resources. These problems were (1) the debt problem; (2) the creditworthiness problem; and (3) the efficiency problem. The debt problem had been facing Brazil since 1982. But 1988 represented a critical turning-point, for the following reasons. In 1987 creditor banks had written off large amounts of the Brazilian debt in their loan portfolios, and these institutions were in a position to bargain much harder on the restructuring of debt maturities. The market value of Brazilian external debt had fallen to its lowest level in the secondary market in 1987–8, making it even less likely that Brazil could negotiate any new credits from private international lenders (Table 12.1).

The creditworthiness problem was in part derived from the debt problem. But there were other factors making Brazil's international creditworthiness suspect. These included the recognised failure of the Cruzado Plan in 1986, the debt moratorium in the following year, the escalation of inflationary pressures in 1987–8, and political uncertainties stemming from the Constitutional Convention (1987–8).[1] In 1988 the Constitutional Convention appeared, on the surface, to be carrying Brazil towards a system which was more responsive to populist demands, whereas the underlying trend of thought in Brazil was unmistakenly 'Let's get back to being business-like in our conduct and management of the economy'.

The efficiency problem had been accumulating in Brazil for many years, but had been pushed into the background, owing to many other new problems that appeared to challenge policy makers. There are several facets to the efficiency problem in Brazil. Perhaps the most obvious is the question of the operation of large state enterprises. While many of these state enterprises enjoy sophisticated and professionally competent directors and managers, there are exceptions. Moreover they are subject to administrative supervision from government agencies seeking to align their investment with the economic plan developed in Brasilia. This non-market-oriented supervision of investment activities can lead to highly inefficient resource allocation. Finally, some enterprises operated by the various state governments find it difficult to operate on a financially viable basis. The state-owned bank of Rio de Janeiro (Banespa) for example, had to be administered by a third party to bring about needed reforms.

Table 12.1   External debt of Brazil (billions of US dollars)

1972	9.5	1978	43.5	1984	91.1
1973	12.6	1979	49.9	1985	95.8
1974	17.2	1980	53.8	1986	101.5
1975	21.1	1981	61.4	1987	107.5
1976	26.0	1982	70.2		
1977	32.0	1983	80.0		

Source: Central Bank of Brazil.

12.1.2   External debt position

Brazilian external debt grew rapidly during the ten-year period leading up to the debt crisis of 1982 (Table 12.1). In 1972 external debt was less than $10 billion, but grew rapidly with the escalation of oil prices and the need to finance petroleum imports. Between 1973 and 1976, encompassing the period of the first oil price increase, external debt had more than doubled. During the period of the second oil price increase Brazilian external debt doubled again (1976–80).

During 1973–82 two special factors operated to inflate external debt. These were the two rounds of oil price increases, and the rapid escalation of interest rates that took place in 1977–81. From 1977 to 1981 Eurodollar interest rates (3 month) increased from 6.03 per cent to 16.79 per cent. Since almost 70 per cent of the external debt was on a floating rate basis, dollar interest costs shifted up rapidly. To some extent this placed Brazil in the unfortunate position of having to borrow additional foreign exchange resources to be able to accomplish the required external transfers.

We have made some estimates of the extent to which rising oil prices and upward movements in interest rates on dollar denominated credits could have raised the amounts of dollars Brazil was required to borrow to meet scheduled external payments (Table 12.2). These estimates are conservative in the sense that the interest rates used in the calculations are Eurodollar deposit rates, without including spreads over LIBOR. Brazil was paying substantial spreads over LIBOR on dollar loans. Over the period 1973–82 the estimated increase in debt due to special factors was approximately $20.0 billion, or 34.8 per cent of the debt outstanding at year-end 1982.

The year 1982 is a watershed in international financial experience, and in relation to the Brazilian external debt situation. As can be

Table 12.2   Estimated effect of special factors in enlarging Brazil's borrowing requirements and external debt (billions of US dollars)

1. Increase in debt, 1973–82	57.6
2. Increase in debt due to higher oil price	15.4
3. Increase in debt due to higher interest rate level	4.6
4. Total increase in debt due to special factors	20.6
5. Per cent of debt increase in 1973–82 due to special factors	34.8

Notes:
(1) Line 1 obtained from Table 12.1
(2) Line 2 calculated by estimating effect of higher oil price on external financing requirement, and calculating full debt increase according to interest rates prevailing each subsequent year.
(3) Line 3 calculated by estimating effect of higher interest rates on external financing requirement, and calculating full debt increase according to interest rates prevailing each subsequent year.

noted, external debt continued to expand after 1982, but at a reduced rate. In 1982–7 there was a 53 per cent expansion in external debt. But this was too small an amount of external financing to have any strong favourable influence on the Brazilian growth rate, and the economy limped along at a slow pace during the mid-1980s.

The large external debt, and the difficulties experienced by Brazil in carrying out debt service payments, have constituted pivotal conditioning elements with regard to government policy. The importance of the debt conversion programme focuses on the potential it has to revitalise investment activity in Brazil. For a successful revitalisation of investment can bring the economy out of the slow growth phase it has experienced during much of the 1980s.

12.2   DEBT CONVERSION

12.2.1   Main issues

During the period 1982–6, which we may refer to as the 'optimistic years', it was believed and expected that Brazil's external debt could be repaid ultimately, and that any difficulties in accomplishing the yearly debt service was more a question of liquidity status than one of insolvency. In 1985–6 Brazil made payments of interest on external debt of $11–12 billion annually. But as the Cruzado Plan proved

Table 12.3   Secondary market price range of Brazilian external debt, as per cent of face value

Year	Price range
1986	74–78
1987	40–75
1988	46–60
1 July 1988*	52–53

* Approximate point at which debt agreement was signed by Brazil with banks, and at which time Brazil was entering discussions with IMF concerning economic stabilisations programme.
Source: *Gazeta Mercantil*, 'Corretoras Americanas Procuram Alternativas Para Regras Brasileiras', 1 July 1988, p. 21.

unworkable in late 1986, views began to change regarding the prospects of Brazil's fundamental solvency status. These fears crystallised early in 1987 with the debt moratorium and the precipitous fall in market value of Brazilian debt paper. From 1987 on the Brazilian external debt picture looked less optimistic.

In the secondary market for debt paper international banks had been adjusting their portfolios, buying or selling Brazilian and other debt paper. In 1986 Brazilian debt paper traded at a high percentage of face value (Table 12.3), and the price range was fairly narrow, reflecting little change in sentiment in the market concerning the ability or willingness of Brazil to make debt service payments. Late in 1986 there was a small decline in market price, based on the second half of 1986 deterioration in Brazil's trade balance. However in 1987 the market price suffered a sharp decline as rumours began to circulate in January of an expected moratorium. With the moratorium Brazilian debt paper fell to 40 per cent of face value (Table 12.3). By this time Citibank had announced its intention to write off $3 billion of its portfolio of Brazilian loan paper. In the fourth quarter of 1987 the market value of Brazilian debt rose sharply to almost 60 per cent of face value, reflecting a determined effort by the Brazilian Finance Minister to negotiate a debt settlement. By mid-1988 Brazilian debt paper was selling in a relatively narrow range of slightly over 50 per cent of face value, as the time approached for a negotiated debt agreement with the creditor banks, and as Brazil indicated that it was resuming discussions with the IMF concerning the economic policy programme.

Debt conversion has been promoted as a potential solution to the developing nation debt problem. However, until 1988 in the case of Brazil, only limited amounts of debt had been converted. This is because there are many issues which interfere with successful conversion of debt. Existing external debt can be converted into other debt, or into risk capital holdings (equity ownership of companies). Debtor country interests must be balanced with creditor needs.

The major issues that have delayed an active programme of debt conversion in the case of Brazil are the following:

1. How much debt can be permitted to be converted in any one period of time? Here there are practical problems of capital market capacity. The value of Brazilian stock exchange listed shares ranged between $25 billion and $40 billion in 1986–8. This represents between 22 per cent and 36 per cent of the total external debt.
2. What format can best be used to achieve conversion? Here there are questions of control, maintenance of social policy objectives, and the ability to attract investors. Alternatives suggested range from special mutual funds to auctions conducted by government agencies.
3. What discount can be utilised in conversion? Here there is the question of the government giving formal recognition to the discounted value of external debt. The government has sought to avoid this, not only because it is a source of embarrassment, but also because it enables purchasers of this debt to gain control of Brazilian productive assets at lower prices.
4. What effect will conversions have on economic activity? Here there is the problem of slower growth associated with low levels of investment activity in the mid 1980s. Can conversions elicit larger amounts of investment activity and energise the economy?
5. Effect on efficiency and technology level? Here there is the problem of the local economy needing continued injections of entrepreneurial activity and new technology. Without these, the overall level of efficiency of the industrial sector may decline. How can conversions be utilised to improve efficiency level?
6. Can foreign ownership and control be permitted? Here the question is the degree and extent of foreign ownership and control. Brazil already has a large foreign multinational presence. Moreover foreign- controlled enterprises represent the more modern, more efficient, and more technologically advanced sectors of

Brazilian industry. How can a proper balance be achieved between maintaining domestic ownership and control while attracting foreign technology and enterprise?

12.2.2   Conversions until 1988

The conversion of external debt into risk capital has a legal basis going back to 1965,[2] but not until the secondary market gained substantial size in 1982 were large transactions feasible.[3] Here we must distinguish between formal conversions (registered with the Central Bank) and informal conversions (not registered and therefore difficult to estimate amounts). Formal conversions have been estimated at $160 million in 1978, $207 million in 1979, and then declining for several years (Table 12.4) In 1983 formal conversions surged to $452 million, and to $700 million the following year. Again they declined for several years. In 1987 they surged to $745 million, and to an estimated $2.5 billion in 1988. The high level in 1988 is explained in the following section of this chapter. Informal conversions were estimated at $800 million in the twelve-month period ending June 1988.

Brief history of legal basis for conversions

The conversion of external debt in Brazil was provided for in Decree No. 55 762 of 17 February 1965. This has been the legal basis for debt conversions until 1988. In 1978 and 1979 the government provided incentives for conversion of debt into preferred shares of enterprises, permitting the deductibility of dividends paid to preferred shares that resulted from conversion. This authority came from Decree Laws No. 4598 of 1977 and 1654 of 1978.

Somewhat later, in 1983 and 1984, new incentives for conversion were introduced by the government. These were embodied in Decree Law No 1994 of 29 December 1982, which instituted a financial credit of up to 10 per cent for the conversion of debt contracted until 31 December 1982. From June 1984, however, there was a suspension of these credits for conversions, which was regulated by Circular No. 1125 of November 1984.[4] Central Bank Circular No. 1125 declared that only the original creditor could be a candidate for investment through swaps and only that creditor's investment would be registered at face value. The Central Bank recognised that Brazi-

Table 12.4   Investment: inflows and conversions of external credits (millions US dollars)

	1978	%	1979	%	1980	%	1981	%	1982	%
Investment	1 320.5	100.0	2 233.6	100.0	1 634.4	100.0	1 905.4	100.0	1 513.1	100.0
Income	1 104.1	83.6	1 750.4	85.9	1 515.9	92.3	1 795.3	94.2	1 280.1	84.6
Goods	55.5	4.3	80.8	4.0	79.2	4.8	107.9	5.7	89.8	5.9
Conversions	159.9	12.1	207.4	10.1	39.3	2.4	1.8	0.1	143.2	9.5

	1983	%	1984	%	1985	%	1986	%	1987	%
Investment	1 019.0	100.0	1 235.7	100.0	1 066.6	100.0	631.9	100.0	1 150.0	100.0
Income	452.2	44.4	362.3	29.3	366.8	36.3	330.5	52.4	350.0	30.4
Goods	114.8	11.3	127.8	10.4	98.5	9.2	81.1	12.8	100.0	8.7
Conversions	452.0	44.3	745.6	60.3	581.3	54.5	220.0	34.5	700.0	60.9

Source: *Conjuntura Economica*, March 1988, p. 61.

lian debt was being negotiated abroad at a discount, and thereafter refused to allow third parties to register investments at the bank at face value on the grounds that the investor was gaining from a system that offered no advantages to Brazil.[5]

New regulations came again in 1987, when requests for conversions presented until 20 July 1987 were to be processed in accord with the rules of Circular 1125 of 1984. With this, requests presented for conversion after this date were to become subject to new rules to be established for conversion. New rules which were issued in February 1988 (Resolution 1460) are outlined in the following section.

Balancing interests of investors and debtor country

Foreign investors are attracted to Brazil where opportunities exist for profitable investment with a minimum of regulatory problems. Brazil seeks to attract foreign investment where this activity generates employment, income, new technology and a competitive industrial base. How can debt conversion be chanelled into foreign investment offering Brazil a favourable form of investment, investment in priority sectors, and the development of an acceptable mechanism for investment?

The data in Table 12.4 reflect foreign investment in Brazil over the period 1978–87. In addition it reflects the extent to which investment was supported by reinvested income, goods and products provided, and funds directed through debt conversion. At year-end 1987 the accumulation of foreign business investment in Brazil was $27 billion or one-quarter of the external debt outstanding. Clearly, there could be substantial support of business investment in Brazil for many years to come via conversions of debt into active business investment.

The sub-periods 1978–82 and 1983–7 differ markedly in several respects. These differences are summarised as follows:[6]

1978–82

1. Level of foreign investment averaged $1.7 billion annually.
2. Reinvested income provided 85–95 per cent of total investment.
3. Conversions provided less than 10 per cent of total in-

1983–7

1. Level of foreign investment averaged $1.1 billion annually.
2. Reinvested income provided only 30–45 per cent of investment.
3. Conversions provided over half of total investment.

vestment.
4. Goods provided 5 per cent of
   total investment.

4. Goods provided 10 per cent of
   total investment.

It is clear that, since 1982, debt conversions have been an important support to foreign investment in Brazil. The implication is very clear that adoption of a debt conversion programme that in any way would reduce the scope of debt conversion into foreign investment could pose a threat to the level of foreign investment activity in Brazil.

Balancing interests of debtor country and creditors

Creditor banks have an interest in investing the funds realised from conversion, and in this way recovering part of the loss in value resulting from sale of debt at a discount in the secondary market.[7] This requires that a conversion be authorised where the creditor can exchange funds realised from conversion for an investment in the debtor country, and not eliminate the gain from this investment.

Debtor country interests in debt conversions can be exceedingly complex. Whereas conversions encourage new investment and reduce the need for local government subsidies, foreign investors can obtain significant subsidies while the nation's industry is being denationalised. Converting external debt could result in an increase in internal debt, a costly exercise for an economy already heavily burdened with a large domestic debt structure. Other difficulties faced by a debtor such as Brazil in the case of debt conversions is the expansion of monetary base, possible superpositioning of foreign investors, and possible pressures on the parallel market for dollars. We consider implications for the parallel market in the following section.

It is not surprising to see that, in 1987–8, many innovations were introduced to give the Central Bank greater flexibility in controlling liquidity in Brazil. This includes a shift to a flexible monetary policy, greater separation of the Central Bank from the federal budget and Banco do Brasil financing, and introduction of new and longer-dated government securities. With respect to the positioning of foreign investors, this can be a political question with little empirical content. As long as markets remain competitive, suppliers (foreign and domestic) will enjoy little or no special positioning benefits.

An important consideration for the debtor country is whether conversion can function as an investment for capitalising the firm. If a creditor (international bank) transforms debt paper into cruzados, the resulting funds may be invested in firms other than the debtor firm. In this way, conversion can function as an instrument for capitalising enterprises. Given the insufficiency of domestic savings in Brazil over the period 1982–7, the release of new capital resources to firms in need of capital represents a key potential benefit from the conversion programme.

12.2.3 Resolution 1460

If it were possible to visit Brazil at mid-year 1987 and interview bankers, academicians, and members of the financial community, one might find them describing the Brazilian economy at a point of 'stop' in the so-called stop–go process. In effect Brazil could be considered at a watershed with regard to the debt conversion situation. Until 1987 creditor banks and financial market participants could engage in refinancing arrangements, arbitrage of assets, buying weak assets and converting them into stronger assets, acquiring investments in companies to be sold at a later time, and securitising assets for sale to others.

But, since the government had not fully committed itself to an ambitious programme of formalised debt/equity swaps, most banks and financial institutions were marking time. New regulations were needed, and soon to come. Until year-end 1987, Brazil had avoided opening up opportunities for debt conversion because of (1) political fears of takeover by foreign investors; (2) higher potential cost of carrying foreign equity as compared with foreign debt; and (3) the possibility of reducing basis for obtaining new money, since conversions could relieve some banks (those fully repaid) of pressure to make new loans.

Early in 1988 the National Monetary Council (CMN) established standard guidelines for debt/equity swaps when it approved Resolution 1460 (February 1988). Resolution 1460 simplified the swap process by removing any requirement for securitisation. The major provisions of Resolution 1460 are as follows:

1. Funds invested may be repatriated only after a 12-year investment period.
2. Dividends resulting from a swap investment may be remitted freely. However, they are subject to the usual withholding tax.
3. Swaps are not permitted where the potential investor has a guaranty of fixed remuneration on the proposed investment. In effect a fixed return contradicts the concept of risk investment.

4. Swaps will be prohibited when they result in transfer of control of a company from Brazilian residents to individuals, or groups resident abroad. This does not prevent foreign investors from increasing capital invested in existing foreign controlled enterprises, or from creating new foreign controlled enterprises.
5. Swaps will not be permitted if participants have remitted capital or any form of capital gain abroad in the three years prior to the swap proposal, unless the transferred funds are reinvested in Brazil.
6. Profits from swap investments cannot be used for 12 years, unless for reinvestment in Brazil.

Swaps can be carried out by auction in the case of that part of the external debt already due. In this case, in 1988, $25 billion was already due for payment to creditors and the local currency equivalent had been deposited with the Central Bank by borrowers.

Circular Letter 1302 deals with this part of the debt. The first auction was held on 29 March 1988 at the Rio de Janeiro stock exchange, with a ceiling of $150 million to be swapped. The Central Bank is responsible for setting the maximum amount to be converted. Half of this must be swapped into the high priority areas of the northern and north-eastern regions. The other half is for swaps in non-priority areas and to build up swap mutual funds. The auctions alternate every month between the Rio and São Paulo Stock Exchanges. At the first three swap auctions in 1988 the discounts on debt paper swapped were as indicated in Table 12. 5 .

Circular Letter 1303 deals with that part of the external debt coming due for payment in the future. Of this, $32.4 billion is from the public sector and $10.0 billion from the private sector. Circular Letter 1303 states that the $42.4 billion may be swapped through direct negotiation between the foreign creditor and the borrower, at a discount that need not be revealed to the Central Bank. The investment is registered with the Central Bank at the amount determined by using the average rate of discount established at the most recent swap auction. In April 1988 the Central Bank estimated it had received close to $2 billion in proposals for swaps through direct negotiation.[8] In the case of this part of the debt, there is no ceiling on the total amount that can be swapped.

While the Central Bank has set no limits on the amount of maturing debt that may be converted, the following limitations apply:

Table 12.5   Monthly swap auctions: discounts on debt

Date of swap auction	Discounts on swap (%)	
	swaps for free investment	Swaps for investment in needy areas (North-east)
March 1988	27	10.5
April 1988	32	15.0
May 1988	22	0.5

Source: *Gazeta Mercantil*, 16 June 1988, p. 23.

1. Loans taken by Brazilian banks for relending to local companies under the terms of Resolution 63.
2. Loans taken by borrowers looking for funds to repay maturing debts.
3. Loans taken out by leasing companies under terms of Circular Letter 600.

The type of debt to be converted is important. Private sector debt may be swapped for equity in either the private or public sector. But swaps for public sector debt may only fund public sector projects or companies. In either case, privatisation can take place.

In 1988 many investments were announced under debt conversion programmes. In June Lloyds Bank of the United Kingdom announced a $55 million conversion for investment in a newly created investment department and a personal bank. These funds were destined for investment in Banco Multiplic, 50 per cent owned by Lloyds, permitting Multiplic to launch new financial products and special services (opening capital of companies, fixed income funds, and underwriting).[9] Also, Bank of America announced conversion of $50 million into investments and also assumed control of Multibanco Internacional de Investimentos. American banks depend on authorisation of the Federal Reserve Board for investments with value in excess of $15 million. This limitation is not applicable to European banks undertaking equity investments in Brazil.

12.2.4   Swap mutual funds

In 1988 the Central Bank and the National Securities Commission defined the basic guidelines for swap mutual funds. Swap funds can raise capital from two sources. First, foreign creditors may purchase shares in the fund by converting their loans at scheduled auctions on the stock exchanges. Second, fund managers may convert their own loans into a portfolio of stock held by the swap fund.

The swap funds face certain restrictions on their portfolio activities. Investments in any single company cannot exceed 5 per cent of that company's voting capital, or 20 per cent of the total equity of that company. Further restrictions will apply to swap funds aimed exclusively at investing in companies located in the Northern and North-eastern regions. In this case 70 per cent of each fund's portfolio must be invested in private-sector companies whose shares are publicly traded, or in other firms that meet CVM requirements. The remaining 30 per cent can be invested in government securities or in open market operations.

In May 1988 a number of swap funds had been proposed and approved. Others were in various stages of planning and organisation. For example, Banco Nacional do Norte (Banorte), a private sector commercial bank based in the north-eastern state of Pernambuco was authorised by CVM to form a $150 million swap fund. Foreign investors to be represented by Banorte were interested in the textile, chemicals, mining, pulp and paper, and tourism sectors. A similar fund was to be formed by Banco da Amazonica S.A. (Basa), a government-owned commercial bank in the state of Para.

PNC International Bank, the holding company that manages the global assets of PNC Financial Corp. of Pittsburgh, Pennsylvania, a consortium of 28 US banks, indicated plans to convert $70 million of debt into investments. PNC participated in the first swap auction in Rio (March 1988). The equity won at that auction was to be invested to restructure and expand the capital base of PNC Comércio e Participações Ltda., a fund operating since 1973. While PNC had not, as of mid-1988, established a special swap fund, plans were under way to prepare a prospectus outlining the type of investments anticipated in Brazil.[10]

A number of variations have developed from the swap mutual fund initiative. One is the fund with a special focus. One such fund was organised to make high-risk investments.[11]

12.2.5 Informal conversion activity

Informal swap activity has been taking place in Brazil for many years. With the introduction of a formal programme, and the clarification of the legal framework, formal and informal conversions accelerated.

Figure 12.1   Informal conversion of external debt.

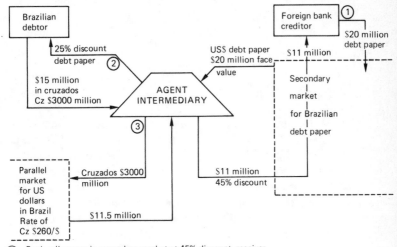

1. Bank sells paper in secondary market at 45% discount, receives $11 million from agent.
2. Agent sells paper to Brazilian debtor for cruzados, at 25% discount. Official rate is Cz $200/$. Agent receives Cz $3000 million.
3. Agent sells cruzados in parallel market for Cz $260/$, a 30% premium on dollars, receiving $11.5 million for the cruzados.

Note: This type of operation, referred to as 'bicicleteiros' in the Brazilian press, was effectively curtailed by action of the Central Bank at the end of June 1988.

Formal conversions grew rapidly in amount in 1988, for good reason. Financial market participants could generate considerable profit by undertaking such transactions. Investors could purchase cruzados indirectly in the debt conversion market much more cheaply, and have a lower cost basis (in dollars) for the investment. Intermediary agents (including securities brokers, investment banks, and other financial companies) could generate quick profits for arranging such transactions.

Informal swaps also were advantageous, even though the investor might not obtain Central Bank registration. Domestic (Brazilian) investors ordinarily would not need to register, and those seeking only short-term arbitrage profits would not wish to be bothered with any form of registration.

Figure 12.1 reflects the transaction relationships that might take place in an informal conversion, where the agent intermediary is seeking no more than arbitrage profit. There are two important points to be drawn from this illustration. First, in the case of a pure arbitrage transaction (as indicated in the figure) funds do not flow into increased capitalisation of a Brazilian enterprise, and investment activity derives no stimulus. In short, there are no basic economic benefits for the debtor country from this type conversion. In effect, the arbitrageur–intermediary is utilising a questionable device to reap a profit. The profit is possible because of the varying discounts along the successive steps included in the conversion. For the informal conversion to provide lasting benefits to the debtor country it would be necessary to block the possibility of the third part of the series of transactions, that is, cut off conversions from the parallel market.

In June 1988 the Central Bank instituted controls over informal conversions via Circular No. 1326 (28 June 1988), with the intent of ensuring that such conversions would be channelled into domestic investment. The Central Bank stated that it did not wish to interfere with the free application of cruzado proceeds from debt conversions, but to make certain that these cruzados would be utilised within Brazil.[12] The controls were aimed at the actions of the 'bicicleteiros' who were benefiting from informal conversion operations. The 'bicicleteiros' were the agents who purchased externally-held debt paper at a discount, exchanged this for cruzados in Brazil, and exchanged the cruzados into dollars in the parallel market, using the proceeds to purchase more external debt paper. The Central Bank controls required that cruzado proceeds from informal conversions be paid into bank accounts, with the obligation on the banks to notify the Central Bank of the deposits.[13] Information to be provided to the Central Bank includes identity of original creditor, nature of payment (amortisation, interest, or both), value of funds transfer in foreign and local currency, discount obtained in percent, date of payment in local currency, name of recipient of local currency, bank of deposit and destination of resources.[14]

12.3 FUTURE PROSPECTS

In its first year the formal debt conversion programme has given indications of success. The success achieved lies in at least four areas: (1) the reduction in external debt outstanding; (2) the activation of capital for investment in new industrial sectors and regions; (3) the mobilisation and reallocation of capital; and (4) the capitalisation of Brazilian enterprises with a larger equity base.

These contributions from the debt conversion programme can bring about a further development of financial institutions and a deepening of the capital markets in Brazil. Also they can improve the qualitative aspects of the financial system. The qualitative aspects that can be improved upon from debt conversions include (1) stronger capital base for enterprises; (2) greater volume of activity in the capital markets; (3) a widening of the industrial technology base in Brazil to make enterprises more competitive; and (4) creation of more diversified activities for capital market participants. As is commented on in the concluding chapter of this volume, debt conversion activity is expanding the base of venture capital activities in Brazil. In this process, more diversified capital market participants will appear on the scene, offering domestic and foreign enterprises and investors a greater variety of venture capital services.

NOTES

1. The Constitutional Convention gave foreign investors and lenders many reasons for concern. These include proposals for differentiating between the treatment of nationally- and foreign-owned firms, amnesty for small firm debtors, an interest rate ceiling, and other populist measures.
2. Conversion was provided for in Article 50 of Decree No. 55 762 of 17 February 1965, which has served as a legal basis for debt conversions.
3. Yves Leon Winandy, 'Conversão Formal Deve Atingir US$1.02 Bilhão no Semestre', *Gazeta Mercantil*, 16 June 1988, p. 23.
4. Antonio Carlos Monteiro, 'A Conversão da Dívida Externa Como Instrumento de Capitalização de Empresas', *Conjuntura Economica*, March 1988, p. 60.
5. *Gazeta Mercantil*, International Weekly Edition, 23 April 1988, p. iv.
6. Antonio Carlos Monteiro, 'Converção de Créditos em Investimento-O Caso Brasileiro', *Conjuntura Econômica*, April 1988, pp. 93–4.
7. Monteiro, April 1988, p. 94.
8. *Gazeta Mercantil*, International Weekly Edition, 25 April 1988, p. ii.
9. Nilton Horita, 'Lloyds Investe no Banco US$55 Milhões de Dívida', *Jornal do Brasil*, 28 June 1988, p. 11.
10. *Gazeta Mercantil*, International Weekly Edition, 'PNC Prepares Fund', 25 April 1988, p. v.
11. *Gazeta Mercantil*, International Weekly Edition, 'Swapping Close to the Edge', 25 April 1988, p. 2.
12. *Gazeta Mercantil*, 'BC Regulamenta Operações Informais', 1 July 1988, p. 21.
13. *Jornal do Brasil*, 'BC Baixa Normas de Controle Para a Conversão Informal', 1 July 1988, p. 14.
14. There would be some difference in the information to be provided if (1) recipient is the original creditor, or (2) recipient is not the original creditor. In the case of the recipient not being the original creditor, documents relative to the transfer or sale of the credit would be required as well.

13 The Privatisation Programme

Brazil has experienced a unique development of its economy. In the process the state has expanded its sphere of activities, by regulation, by defining certain sectors of industry as of central national interest, and by financing industrial development. A first approach to understanding the privatisation programme in Brazil is to say that the economy appears ready to reverse much of what has been done in the way of expanding the role of the state in economic activity. But this is an oversimplification.

The programme of privatisation has a general purpose of reforming the public sector, and returning activities and responsibilities to the private sector. This reform consists of modernising the State: rationalising its decision processes, method of organisation, and sources of funds. At the level of state enterprises this involves adopting an entrepreneurial approach in planning, operation and control.

Privatisation then includes restructuring, deactivation or transfer to the private sector firms in which state control can no longer be justified. In this process the state must remove itself from sectors and activities which can be developed efficiently by free motivation, without loss of economic initiative. An ultimate objective of privatisation is to make possible self-sustained economic growth, oriented towards retirement of the enormous internal and external debt accumulated over a long period of time.[1]

13.1 MAIN ISSUES

A number of issues arise in the development of a privatisation programme. These include:

1. What to privatise? In 1987 privatisation had been confined largely to reprivatisation of companies formerly in the private sector. By 1988 government officials, bankers, and businessmen in Brazil expected that a tentative list of perhaps 100 companies in the public sector could be privatised. But this would not include the

giant public sector companies such as Petrobrás, Siderbrás and Eletrobrás. Although it was expected that small pieces of these holding company systems might be spun off, at mid-year 1988 approximately 6 per cent of the net worth of government-owned corporations was available for privatisation. Since the net worth of all state enterprises at that time was $42 billion, privatisation could at that time encompass sales of ownership with book value of $2.5 billion.

2. How to do it? Perhaps the ideal way to privatise is through a secondary offering, where a large underwriting group distributes the shares widely to many institutional and individual investors. This would follow the pattern in the United Kingdom. A second-best alternative would be an increase in capital through issue of shares in the primary market. However, this might not be required in all cases. The third-best choice (mainly in use until 1988) would be to sell the company in a stock exchange auction to the highest bidding management group. This does not help to develop the capital market as in the first two cases, but permits early divestment of companies and speeds up the privatisation programme. The first and second approaches were introduced in 1988.

3. How quickly? This is partly answered in the preceding point. A major rationale for privatisation in the Brazilian case is the understanding that the private sector can finance and operate enterprises more efficiently. Private sector status is identified in part with gaining the ability to compete in a changing and competitive world market system. Given the slowdown in investment and economic growth in Brazil in the mid-1980s, the answer must be 'as soon as possible'.

4. How to retain appropriate social control? The Brazilian economic model is one in which the government has pursued a complex of social and economic goals in each of its separate policy measures. In the case of privatisation of public sector enterprises, there was an original set of reasons for their being included in the public sector. A social–economic interest was important to the community. How can government retain 'control' without ownership? Three possibilities exist. One is to enact legislative authority for control, but this seems to be going in two directions at the same time – privatisation and new regulation. A second is to retain control through Golden Shares held by the government. These would give the government a privileged vote on certain matters (one cannot change company by-laws without this vote). A third

approach is to rely on the invisible hand of the market place.

The preceding suggests that many questions have had to be answered before Brazil could move towards a privatisation programme. According to critics, the following represent serious questions that still must be answered if a privatisation programme is going to prove workable and contribute in a positive way to economic progress.[2]

1. Does the capital market possess the capacity to mobilise sufficient resources for the needs of investors?
2. If managers of firms are unable to deal with the existing debt of the enterprise, will they be better able after privatisation?
3. Can a fair price be established for the sale of control shares?
4. Is there possible abuse of monopolistic position after the government withdraws as an owner? Will there be a guarantee of essential services?
5. Could the new issues market for securities of private sector firms become restricted, owing to the predominance of issues involving privatisation?
6. To what extent will denationalisation interfere with industrial development?

Most of these questions are addressed in full or in part in the following discussion.

13.2 FIRST STEPS TOWARD PRIVATISATION

In this section we consider two auction programmes that, on the surface, appear to involve a process of reprivatisation. This involves the sale of ownership interests in companies formerly acquired by government agencies. The manner in which these interests were acquired varied, but largely fall into two categories. The first represents financing of enterprises under government programmes aimed at achieving specified objectives. For example, some years ago several special funds were created to help finance industrial development in needy areas (for example, Finam – Fundo de Investimentos da Amazonia and Finor – Fundo de Investimentos do Nordeste). In their financing role, they acquired participations in many private-sector enterprises. The second represents companies acquired by government agencies as a result of their falling into financial difficulties. These difficulties could have resulted from the firms assuming excessive debt, or changes in economic conditions. The BNDES and other government financing institutions acquired participations in companies that they financed, as well as ownership of companies that suffered financial reversals.

13.2.1 Two types of auctions

The National Securities Commission is responsible for supervising activities of the stock exchanges in Brazil. This includes supervising auctions conducted on the exchanges for the purpose of divesting participations in companies acquired as described above. The most formal programme that has been in operation for approximately ten years involves the sale of companies from the portfolios of regional development funds (Finor, Finam, Fidece, Fispec). Ownership in approximately 3000 companies was acquired by these regional funds, largely through provision of fiscal incentives. The CVM has arranged to sell these interests by auctions on all nine Brazilian stock exchanges.

The companies involved are essentially private sector-oriented, and in this sense a privatisation is not taking place. Rather the sale is a form of divestment by the government – a reprivatisation. The shares of many of these companies were not registered with the CVM or with the stock exchanges, so their shares are auctioned in what amounts to a private placement (a limited number of bidders submit their offers). In such cases there may be no further trading in these shares on the stock exchanges, unless the company has its capital opened. In that case shares of the company are registered with the CVM and stock exchange, and offered to the public. For example, Copene, a petrochemical company, was auctioned, and then afterwards went public. After this Copene became a very large and successful company.

A second type of auction, also conducted on the stock exchanges, provides for the sale of ownership in companies acquired by the National Bank for Economic and Social Development (BNDES). In many cases these were companies that became financially weak, and there were limited alternatives to the BNDES taking control of these firms.

The unit of BNDES that carries out the preparatory work for auction of companies is BNDESPAR, which in part operates much like an investment banking unit. BNDESPAR was organised in 1982 by merging several specialised financing units of BNDES.[3] Whereas the auctions carried out by BNDESPAR are similar to those involving disposition of companies held by the regional development funds, there are some differences. First, in some cases the companies reprivatised by BNDES are quite large. Therefore there can be a simultaneous auction and opening of capital. This is a preferred approach, since it facilitates an expansion of the share market. Second, auction is one of several alternatives utilised by BNDES. At least four alternatives have been utilised:

1. Companies to be extinguished. This can be a marginal company that cannot be saved, except with large subsidy loans. In one such case a pig-iron producer was extinguished, with the assets offered for sale.
2. Stockmarket sale. In the case of a company with good profitability, it is possible to open the capital of the company when or shortly after it is auctioned. Many divestments by BNDES have followed this pattern.
3. Change ownership. The federal government created a large network of centres for food distribution and supply, termed CEASAs. These were to be 'privatised' by sale to the state governments such as Minas Gerais and São Paulo.
4. Typical auction. In this more typical case a majority of the company stock is held by BNDESPAR, and is auctioned to the highest bidder. An example would be Caraiba Metais, where, in 1988, 67 per cent of the voting stock was offered for auction. Caraiba is the only producer of copper in Brazil, and to preserve the interests of smaller companies (buyers from Caraiba Metais), there was a sale of non-voting stock to these consumers. This carries the power to decide how to divide up to 20 per cent of the production of Caraiba, since these smaller companies require an assured supply of copper in their operations.[4]

The Caraiba privatisation was one of the largest undertaken by BNDES. An initial step in preparing the sale was to split the enterprise into two units, a mining company and a copper-processing company. The processing unit was offered for sale in the auction. In 1988 the government was studying the feasibility of continued operation of the mining unit, and the social implications of its closing down.[5]

BNDES has completed a number of other large privatisations, including USIMINAS (formerly owned by SIDERBRAS), Mafersa (state owned since 1964), Cimetal Siderurgia, and Aracruz Cellulose.

In the case of Aracruz, in May 1988 BNDES sold 26.2 per cent of the voting shares for CZ$18.7 billion (equivalent to US$133.5 million) to the Safra financial conglomerate.[6] In the case of both USIMINAS and Aracruz, a similar process of privatisation was followed with control shares separated into several groups, and a pulverisation of the capital reflected in the preference shares.[7]

13.2.2 BNDESPAR activities

BNDESPAR has gained much experience in preparing companies for privatisation. The process of auctioning a holding may take three to four months. Considerable effort is made to conduct the auction in an open, competitive manner, where all parties and interests have the opportunity to participate fully. In this period there is first an announcement that the company will be offered, published in the newspapers. Candidates interested in buying the company to be auctioned must be Brazilian (foreign capital is accepted up to a limit of 24 per cent of the company capital). Candidates submit information and BNDESPAR must check the candidates for adequacy of resources and managerial experience. The newspapers are given information concerning candidates interested in bidding for the company. A prospectus is issued, which in most cases is quite long and detailed. The prospectus contains audited financial statements. A minimum bid price is obtained from an independent auditor, and is advertised.

At the auction the buyer must be prepared to pay 30 per cent of the value of the acquisition. BNDES will finance (if necessary) up to 70 per cent of the value, at 12 per cent interest, up to ten years' term. Also, in cases where 5–10 per cent of the shares are offered to employees (to open the capital of the company), the employees can also finance 70 per cent of the purchase with BNDES.

In several cases BNDES has received considerably more than the minimum bid price. In the case of Celpag (purchased by the Votorantim Group in May 1988), Votorantim paid 2200 cruzados (per lot of 1000 shares) when the minimum price was established at 1156.95 cruzados. In the auction of Sibra (a ferromanganese producer) in April 1988, the buyer paid 2050 cruzados (per ordinary share) when the minimum price was set at 500 cruzados.[8]

BNDESPAR has developed the capability to carry out a wide range of investment banking activities, including the preparation of companies for sale in public auctions (akin to private placement), opening the capital of companies, and mergers and acquisitions. BNDESPAR has undertaken these services for other companies, such as Banco do Brasil, Petrobras, and others. In 1988 it was in the process of developing privatisation services for other sectors, including harbour facilities, water services and transport.

13.3 INTERMINISTERIAL COUNCIL FOR PRIVATISATION

With the signing of Decree No. 91 991 by President Sarney (28 November 1985) the government of Brazil initiated a formal privatisation programme. The major provisions of this Decree are:[9]

1. The government indicated that enterprises under its direct control would be included in the programme, and that privatisation would include opening of their capital to wider ownership.
2. The President would determine the firms to be included in the programme of privatisation. The ministers would propose to the President which enterprises to include.
3. Firms that will not have their share ownership transferred to private control include those whose activities are directly linked with national security; those assigned to a legal status of monopoly; and those responsible for operation of the economic infrastructure or production of strategically important inputs, or under state control to maintain viable development of the private sector.
4. Establishment of an Interministerial Council for Privatisation with authority to shape the process of privatisation. The Council will be made up of the Minister of Planning, who serves as president, Ministers of Finance, Industry and Commerce, and Ministers who have enterprises to be included in the privatisation programme. The Council is assigned broad authority to initiate conditions and criteria for privatisation, subject to general requirements of broad disclosure of activities, use of market facilities (including stock exchanges), use of external auditors, and requirement that control be restricted to Brazilian residents or firms.

By 1987 the government, through the Interministerial Council, had established a portfolio of 65 state enterprises to be privatised. These represented 28 per cent of state enterprises operating in the productive sector, and 5 per cent of the assets of productive state enterprises.[10]

Decree No. 95 886 was issued on 29 March 1988. The 1988 decree differed from the decree of 1985 in the following respects. The earlier decree focused only on privatisation. In 1988 the approach was broadened to include deregulation and destatisation as well. Also the title of the Council was modified to reflect this broader approach. Effective from 1988 the title became Conselho Federal de Desestatização.

At mid-year 1988 the Council was preparing to issue a resolution outlining its plan to accomplish privatisation, destatisation and deregulation. A pre-released text of this resolution indicates the following key approaches:[11]

1. A wide range of methods can be used to implement the programme, including opening the capital of companies, sale of share participations, merger, augmenting capital through sale of shares in the primary market, or dissolution.
2. The Council plans to use standard procedures in the privatisation of firms, including reorganising of capital structure, publicising minimum prices for sale of companies, and public disclosure of privatisation operations.
3. Privatisations will conform to the public interest, with the objective of obtaining the best dissemination of share participations. Execution of privatisation in the way of transfer of ownership control of the enterprise will follow one of several approaches including transfer of all or part of the capital shares, transforming ordinary shares into preference shares, subscription of shares of direct creditors, and other.
4. Destatisation will include closing down or reducing some economic activities of the federal public sector, transfer to the private sector of public services which can be executed indirectly, extinction of components or units of the federal government which conduct economic activities, deactivation or divestiture of assets not necessary in carrying out essential functions of controlled entities or controlled firms, and dissolution of enterprises under direct or indirect control of the federal government.
5. Deregulation projects will include proposals to free and debureaucratise economic activities in the areas of federal, state, and municipal government. The Executive Secretary of the Council will promote and activate the work of various units and organs of the government, to identify segments of the economy in which it is possible to implement measures of reducing bureaucratic control and regulation of economic activities.

6. The Executive Secretary of the Council or its organs will make use of professional or specialist firms relative to the following work: technical studies, consultation, financial intermediaries, independent auditors, auctions and distribution of share participations.

13.4 MODELS OF PRIVATISATION

It is clear that the model of privatisation employed must fit the needs of the case at hand. Essentially this depends on the characteristics of the firm to be privatised. Various alternatives are possible. Moreira outlines seven models, and an eighth alternative (deactivation and liquidation).[12] In this section we describe the seven models, and then discuss their applicability to specific cases of privatisation taking place in 1988.

13.4.1 Seven models

The seven models can be summarised as follows:

1. Transfer of all share capital. All control shares are sold to a single private group of investors. Generally, smaller enterprises can be privatised in this way, and there may be several groups with sufficient capital to bid for such entities.
2. Transfer of a controlling block of shares. A sufficient quantity of ordinary shares (with voting rights) are sold to a group, giving it a majority control among shareholders. There tends to be two different patterns of capital structure among firms in Brazil, and the percentage of capital stock owned relative to the total will differ. One situation or pattern is for all shares to have voting rights; and a second is for one-third of shares to have voting rights and the remainder to be without voting rights. In this way, in the first pattern ownership of 51 per cent of the capital stock is required for control, and in the second 17 per cent (51 per cent of 33.3 per cent).
3. Pulverisation of capital. In contrast to the pattern of privatisation where all shares are transferred to a single private group which owns and manages, it may be possible to separate management control from ownership. To achieve this pulverisation of capital, share participations may be sold to diverse segments of investors so that the managers do not have control of a majority of the

voting shares. An illustration of pulverisation is included in the description of privatisation in the iron and steel sector.

4. Transfer of control to administrators. Generally this process is associated with a situation where the enterprise is in financial difficulty, or where there is disinvestment by the controlling group in a subsidiary firm.

5. Sale of discontinued operations. There are situations where the firm has not initiated operational activities. Either the project is not physically ready, or economic or financial factors have prevented commencing operations. In such cases a reformulation, redefinition or restructuring of the enterprise may be necessary, along with other measures. A private group can assume continuation of the project or operations, with the opportunity to make future additions to capital, giving it eventual full control.

6. Privatisation of administration. There may be cases where it is not feasible to transfer share control. In the meantime, efficient administration can be provided by a private sector group.

7. Opening capital: gradual privatisation. This involves opening the capital of the firm, and utilising the share market to create opportunities for selling controlling share participations.

13.4.2 Electric energy sector

In 1988 interest was developing in Brazil in privatisation of the electric energy sector. If Brazil is to resume its high growth, the demand for electric power will grow correspondingly. Privatisation would enable the capital markets to assume a greater share of the financing of the required expansion in electric energy capacity.

Figure 13.1 outlines the prospects for privatisation in the electric power sector (circa 1988), based on discussions with various government officials and private investors. Considering that until 1988 the stock market has had no more than $1.2 billion of new issues in a given year, the possibility of privatisation where large electric generating plants are involved is doubtful. However the government is hoping for privatisation of entities with small generating plants, or entities distributing electric power. In the latter case these entities must be operating profitably, or have prospects of profitability in one or two years.

Figure 13.1 Electric power sector: privatisation model

Generation of power	Small plant	Can privatise	In the case of smaller plants generating electric power, there is possibility of private sector investment and ownership. Required investment is not large.
	Medium plant	Possible privatisation	In these two cases the private sector cannot be expected to finance these substantial projects. In the north-east there may be a $1 billion project. This is too large for private sector and the capital market.
	Large plant	Difficult to privatise	

Distribution of power	Two criteria will determine if privatisation will take place. (1) Profitability. If utility can generate attractive rate of profit (12 per cent per year) it will be of interest to private sector investor. (2) Project will be profitable in 2–3 years. This is required for private sector investment interest.

13.4.3 Iron and steel sector

In 1988 the government sold 67 per cent of the ordinary capital of COFAVI, Companhia Ferro e Aço de Vitoria. The sale took place at an auction conducted at the Rio de Janeiro Stock Exchange on 23 September 1988. The privatisation follows a strategy of Siderbrás to transfer ownership in certain aspects of its business to the private sector. Siderbrás is one of the largest government-owned state enterprises.

Siderbrás contracted with Bndespar Participações S.A. to act as agent in the privatisation of Cofavi, assuming temporary control of the company. Application for pre-qualification of interested buyers took place on 19 August 1988, and these potential buyers had until 12 September 1988 to complete the financial aspects of qualifying to submit a bid. Candidates bidding for Cofavi had to satisfy the requirement of residence, and demonstrate their financial and managerial capabilities. Foreign minority participation was permitted up to a maximum of 24 per cent of the shares sold (16 per cent of the total voting capital). Distribution of share ownership is reflected in Table 13.1(a).

Siderbrás and Bndespar were committed to sell shares equivalent

Table 13.1   Cofavi
(a) Ownership distribution of capital

Class of Shares	Percentage of total capital	Distribution of capital (%)			
		Siderbras	*Bndespar*	*Other*	*Total*
Ordinary	96.71	27.19	72.80	00.01	100.00
Preference					
Class A	3.10	90.76	9.24	—	100.00
Class B	0.19	—	—	100.00	100.00
TOTAL	100.00				

(b) Growth in sales (tons)

	1984	*1985*	*1986*	*1987*
Internal market	104.6	109.3	153.8	178.9
External market	62.8	86.1	42.2	77.5
TOTAL	167.4	195.4	196.0	256.4

(c) Balance sheet at 30 April 1988

	US $ million	*Per cent*
Assets	127.3	100.0
Current	24.3	19.1
Long-term claims	3.5	2.7
Fixed assets	99.5	78.2
Liabilities	127.3	100.0
Current	15.2	11.9
Long-term debt[1]	23.6	18.5
Net worth	88.5	69.6

[1] Of the long-term debt, $31.3 million are loans of BNDES. The first amortisation payment on these loans took place on 15 November 1988. Source: BNDESPAR.

to 10 per cent of voting capital to employees in a secondary distribution. The price was set at 50 per cent of the auction price. The shares remaining after the auction and distributed to employees were to be sold on the stock exchanges to further widen (pulverise capital) ownership of the company.

Cofavi experienced strong growth in sales over the period 1984–7 (Table 13.1(b)). Shortly prior to the privatisation auction its balance sheet total was $127.3 million (Table 13.1(c)). In the case of the Cofavi privatisation, a pulverisation of capital was accomplished. The sale was made in two parts. The first involved an auction of 67 per cent of the shares to a control group with the price set in the auction. The second (pulverisation of capital) involved sale of 33 per cent of the shares, with 10 per cent to employees at 50 per cent of the auction price, and 23 per cent to the public at 70 per cent of the auction price. Sale to the public was carried out by securities distributors.

13.4.4 Copper sector

In 1988 the government offered to sell 67 per cent of the capital of Caraiba Metais S.A. The sale took place at an auction conducted at the Rio de Janeiro Stock Exchange. Caraiba Metais is the only copper producing company in Brazil, and came under control of BNDES in connection with a large debt obligation that could not be serviced.

The auction was prepared by BNDESPAR Participacoes S.A.. Foreign ownership is limited to no more than 16 per cent of the capital with direct vote. To widen ownership of the company (pulverise capital) a second distribution of Preference Class E shares (Table 13.2(a)) was scheduled for 14 November 1988. Prior opportunity to purchase these shares was designated for 116 consumers (companies) that purchase copper from Caraiba, with final sale of all Preference Class E shares by 24 November 1988. Caraiba enjoyed strong sales growth over the period 1983–8 (Table 13.2(b)). In 1988 its assets totalled $439.7 million (Table 13.2(c)).

13.5 PRIVATISATION AND THE CAPITAL MARKET

An important objective related to the privatisation programme is 'widening of the capital market'. As noted above, where privatisation can be carried out through primary or secondary share distributions, or where the capital of privatised enterprises can be opened to public trading on the stock exchanges, there can be strong positive effects on the capital market. Therefore an important reason for support of privatisation is the belief that in some circles in Brazil these positive effects will be quite strong.

The following discussion considers implications for the capital market where (1) domestic investors participate; (2) foreign investors are able to participate; and (3) specific mechanisms operate to benefit development of the capital market.

Table 13.2   Caraiba Metais
(a) Ownership distribution of capital

Class of shares	Percentage of total capital	Distribution of Capital (%)			
		Bndespar	Finor & others	State of Bahia	Total
Ordinary	96.94	99.99	0.01	—	100.00
Preferred A	0.01	0.86	99.14	—	100.00
Preferred C	0.08	—	100.00	—	100.00
Preferred D	0.47	—	—	100.00	100.00
Preferred E	2.50	100.00	—	—	100.00
	100.00				

(b) Growth in sales (tons)

1983	1984	1985	1986	1987	1988 (prel)
55 074	621 000	93 880	115 990	186 969	160 000

(c) Balance sheet at 31 Jan. 1988

	US $ million	Per cent
Assets	439.7	100
Current	175.4	40
Long-term claims	3.8	1
Fixed assets	26.5	59
Liabilities	439.7	100
Current	93.4	21
Long-term debt[1]	170.3	39
Net worth	176.7	40

[1] Of the long-term debt, $134.6 million are loans of BNDES. The first amortisation payment on these loans takes place in August 1989.
Source: BNDESPAR.

13.5.1   Domestic investor participation

At least two distinct viewpoints can be found concerning the possible effects of privatisation when domestic investors participate. The first is moderately negative and expresses the view that privatisation will absorb private savings and depress prices of financial assets (particularly share prices on the leading stock exchanges). This is a complex issue and requires judgments concerning the pattern of flows of funds in Brazil, and the possible role of the Central Bank in providing credit funds for such purposes.

A more positive view considers the possible effects on public sector deficits. An interesting point about privatisation is that it affords the opportunity to reduce the public sector deficit both in the short run and the long run. In the short run the proceeds from privatisation can supplement current revenues, and in the long run there will be less government debt on which interest must be paid.[13] There is probably little argument with the proposition that more effective control over public sector deficits and growth of the federal government debt will improve the qualitative tone of the capital market.

13.5.2 Foreign investor participation

In the original privatisation decree issued in 1985 there were strong prohibitions against foreign capital participation. Nevertheless subsequent laws do not include any strong restrictions, and foreign participation can be evaluated on a case-by-case basis.

Foreign participation can avoid the difficulty of a shortage of savings in the capital market. In this case the Central Bank would have to monetise the inflow of capital, expanding internal credit. There may be limits to how far this process could operate without introducing inflationary pressures. Where privatisation can be participated in by foreign investors, accompanied by new investment in plant facilities, and where import of equipment will relieve domestic supply inelasticities, inflation pressures may be minimal. However, there is the question of the widening of capital market effects. Will foreign participation lead to wider participation in the capital market by domestic savers? A possible approach to this question might involve mandated but lagged opening of capital to employees and public investors, should foreign investors become control shareholders.

13.5.3 Specific mechanisms

Mechanisms that could be utilised in privatisation that would promote development of the capital market include the following:
1. Two-stage privatisations. The Aracruz Cellulose privatisation is an example. In the first stage ordinary shares were sold to the Safra Bank. In the second stage there was a public offering of 40

per cent of the preferred shares held by BNDES (pulverisation of capital).

2. Private placement funds. These can invest in capital market assets in Brazil. They have been organised since year-end 1987, and registered with CVM. These are sold to investors outside Brazil (United States, Europe) without public offering; and placed with a small number of investors. One of these was BatteryMarch, managed by Banco Bozano Simonsen.

3. Swap funds, organised for conversion and investment at the monthly stock exchange auctions for debt conversion. There are two types, the general fund which can invest anywhere in Brazil, and the fund for needy areas (Amazon and North-east). These funds will eventually invest in companies that were privatised, as well as in other companies.

4. Brazil Fund. Offered for sale and listed on the New York stock exchange in 1988. This type of fund can invest in privatised assets as well as existing share issues.

In addition, government authorities involved in privatisation have indicated a desire to conduct privatisations in a manner that facilitates a widening of the share market and an expansion in shares listed and traded on the stock exchanges.

13.6 CO-ORDINATING PRIVATISATION AND DEBT CONVERSION

Until 1987 there was little or no relation between privatisation and debt conversion activities. Debt conversions focused primarily on minority participations and incremental investments by foreign companies. As of 1988 there developed a possibility of overlap between the two, where debt conversion could provide the opportunity to obtain cruzados inexpensively for investment in privatised assets. Nevertheless, in 1988, most of the debt conversion funds were not going into privatisation-linked investments but to purchase minority interests or expand capital of existing subsidiary companies in Brazil by foreign investors.[14]

It could be argued that the government should accept a linkage between the conversion programme and the privatisation programme. There exist various state enterprises where the government could offer minority participations and many others which could be sold to domestic or foreign investors. It is a question either of opening the capital or of selling the assets. If the assets of enterprises to be privatised are sold and if the capital of enterprises is opened, this will add to the participation of the private sector. Among other advantages, there will be a control of the public deficit.[15]

This argument continues with the suggestion that it is necessary to reduce the public deficit and reduce the public debt. This can be accomplished via three approaches. These are to reduce spending, increase taxes, or couple together the conversion and privatisation programmes. Spending reductions are difficult for several reasons. One is that state and local governments are important spending units and beyond the control of the federal government.[16] Increased taxes are not a solution because of the revenue sharing system (decentralisation programme) instituted in the 1980s. The federal government would have to raise taxes by Cz\$2 to net Cz\$1 after revenue sharing. This leaves a joint programme of conversion and privatisation.

Conversion is one method of reducing the public debt, but it is not enough on its own. It must be reinforced by privatisation. If we suppose that in the process of privatisation the government pays off debt equivalent to 1 per cent of national income (with private savings generated through sale of assets), and also pays off additional debt equivalent to 1 per cent of national income with funds from conversion, the debt will be reduced by an amount equal to 2 per cent of national income. If the public deficit is held to the same 2 per cent of national income, the public debt will be held fixed at the same level. It is exactly this reinforcement of debt conversion with privatisation that could permit Brazil to keep the expansion of public debt at zero per cent, or at least ensure that it grows less rapidly than national income.

There is one additional benefit to be derived from linking conversion and privatisation programmes. This is related to the liquidity effects of debt conversion. Part of the conversion funds will go to privatisation, and that part which does not will free private capital, which, in turn, can be used for privatisation.

NOTES

1. David Casimiro Moreira, 'O Grande Desafio', *Privatização, Mercado de Capitais, E Democracia* (Rio de Janeiro: Codimec, 1988) p. 323.

2. Walter L. Ness, 'Privatização: A Hora Chegar?' *Mercados Financeiros*, IBMEC, Rio de Janeiro, November 1987, p. 18.
3. These included FIBASE, which financed the steel and copper sectors, EMBRAMEC, which financed equipment suppliers, and IBRASA, which financed consumer goods firms.
4. In the case of Caraiba, eight companies buy over 50 per cent of its production of refined copper, but there are approximately 140 companies that must purchase copper from Caraiba, many of which are quite small.
5. Ronaldo Lupa, 'Caraiba da Prejuizo de US$1 Bilhao ao BNDES', *Jornal do Brasil*, 4 July 1988, p. 12.
6. *Gazeta Mercantil*, International Weekly Edition, 16 May 1988, p. 7.
7. *Jornal do Brasil*, 'Usiminas Será Privatizada Pela Brasilpar', 7 July 1988, p. 19.
8. *Exame*, 'O Arauto da Privatização', 15 June 1988, p. 27.
9. Decree No. 91 991 of 28 November 1985, as published in *Privatização, Mercado de Capitais, E Democracia*, pp. 352–6.
10. David Casimiro Moreira, 'O Grande Desafio', *Privatizacao, Mercado de Capitais, E Democracia*, p. 334.
11. *Folha de São Paulo*, 'A Integra do Projeto de Desestatizacao Preparado Pelo Governo', 10 June 1988.
12. Moreira, pp. 336–42.
13. This point is implicit in Mario Henrique Simonsen, 'Em Caso de Dívida, Venda os Ativos', *Privatização, Mercado de Capitais, E Democracia*, pp. 271–2.
14. Ethan B. Kapstein, 'Brazil: Continued State Dominance', in R. Vernon (ed.), *The Promise of Privatization*, Council on Foreign Relations, 1988, p. 143. Here reference is made to the Federal Reserve Board in Washington DC easing the restriction on US bank equity investment in non-financial enterprises.
15. Mario Henrique Simonsen, pp. 271–2.
16. For example, state governments become responsible for the debts and expenditures of the corporate entities they create (tourist hotels, state banks). State banks often issue CDBs to meet their payroll expenses, where in some cases these expenses amount to over 80 per cent of operating revenues.

14 Venture Capital Activities

Brazilian capital market development has been built on four basic pillars: (1) a normalisation of the capital markets through the introduction of legislation and regulations that provide a stable legal structure; (2) development of a broader and more active stock market; (3) creation of financial institutions that mobilise capital and intermediate investment funds; and (4) development and encouragement of venture capital activities. We have discussed the first and third of these in Chapter 9, which focuses on the capital market. Development of the stock market has been considered in Chapters 9–10. In this chapter we focus on the development of venture capital activities.

Venture capital activities can be considered to include the mobilisation of capital for relatively high-risk investments, and the development of specialised institutions geared to channel funds into risky investments. In previous chapters we described the role of investment banks, which can operate as underwriters of new securities issues, investment fund managers, and long-term lenders. Since they first appeared on the scene in the mid-1960s they have come to play a vital role in promoting venture capital activities in Brazil. Nevertheless, as we describe below, the venture capital industry is a relative newcomer to the scene.

14.1 EMERGENCE OF VENTURE CAPITAL INDUSTRY

The Brazilian experience in developing venture capital activities is relatively recent. Venture capital companies were first given special status by Resolution 1184 of 4 September 1986. Previous to this, financial services companies operated in the venture capital field, but did not enjoy any particular fiscal or other benefits. For example, in 1972 Brasilpar Comercio e Participações S.A. was organised as a venture capital company and operated successfully for over fifteen years.

Beginning in 1986 under Resolution 1184 venture capital companies could invest their own resources in securities issued by small and medium-size Brazilian companies. Where possible they bring other investors into financing the project. Venture capital companies generally concentrate their activities in the industrial sector, and according to Regulation 1184 are not permitted to invest in financial institutions.

The regulations which apply to venture capital companies provide the following incentives:[1]

1. Dividends received by the venture capital company from the investee company are tax deductible for the dividend paying company.
2. Dividends received and capital gains originating from divestment or liquidation of participations are tax exempt for the venture capital company.
3. With respect to the stockholders of venture capital companies, the proceeds received and the capital gains originated by the liquidation or sale of the participation company are taxable at the rate of 23 per cent.[2]

Venture capital activity in Brazil may be expected to enjoy successful growth for several reasons. First, there is a strong entrepreneurial culture, and when economic conditions are favourable many new companies are organised. Second, the securities law provides a favourable environment (Law No. 6404 of 1976). This law covers all types of investment instruments that can be used by venture capitalists (preferred stock, cumulative and non-cumulative preferred, convertible preferred, subordinated and convertible debentures). Third, technology can be transferred to Brazil on a favourable basis from mature economies, and without the risks associated with new technology. Fourth, a fairly active stock market operates in Brazil. Finally, the large size and rapid development of the economy of Brazil provides interesting investment opportunities.

The venture capital industry was given two stimuli in 1988 with the adoption of a formal debt conversion programme and a privatisation programme. While these are discussed in detail in the previous two chapters, their specific relationship to venture capital activities was not made explicit. The debt conversion programme can be expected to promote venture capital activities in several ways:

1. Creation of special debt conversion funds to facilitate risk capital investment in Brazil. These are discussed in a following section.
2. Liquifying of capital for investment in industrial projects. In this case investors provide funds used to extinguish external debt. In this way capital tied up in difficult-to-service external debt can be 'released' by attracting an alternative investor willing to take the risks associated with an equity participation.
3. Debt conversions can stimulate higher levels of foreign investment in Brazil. One study reported that, in the period 1983–7, conversions provided between 34 per cent and 61 per cent of funds invested in Brazil by foreign investors.[3]

The privatisation programme can be expected to promote venture capital activities in several ways:

1. By providing profitable opportunities for investment banker activities in preparing state-owned enterprises and investors for the sale or auction of participations in these state enterprises.
2. By mobilising resources into venture capital channels.
3. By providing a clear signal to capital market participants that the government supports risk capital investment.

14.2 SPECIAL FUNDS FOR RISK INVESTMENT

Venture capital activities focus on channelling funds into risky investments. One means of achieving this is to establish specialised investment vehicles, capable of assuming and diversifying risks for participating investors. In the 1980s several specialised funds have been created for this purpose. These funds are compared in the Table 14.1 with respect to their number, major fund sources, and investment objectives.

A number of debt conversion funds have been organised since early 1988, when Resolution 1460 came into operation (Table 14.1, line I). The National Securities Commission and the Central Bank have defined the basic guidelines to create swap funds aimed at purchasing shares in companies located in the less developed Northern and Northeastern regions. In this case a minimum 70 per cent of each funds portfolio must be invested in private sector companies whose shares are publicly traded. The remaining 30 per cent can be invested in government securities or open market paper. In addition, these swap funds must follow the following limits: the value of shares

Table 14.1 Brazilian investment and venture capital funds, 1988

	Type Fund	Applicable legislation and regulation	Number of funds organised and operating	Source of funds and amount invested (millions)	Investment objectives
I	Debt conversion fund	Resolution 1460, 1 Feb. 1988	Organised, 54 operating, 8	Debt conversion	Channel funds released from debt conversion into venture capital
II	foreign investment companies	Circular 1339, 26 July 1988	1	Debt conversion, other foreign and local $85	Permanent type investments
III	Foreign capital investment funds	Resolution 1289 20 March 1987	15	Foreign investor $512	Diversified securities portfolio
IV	Managed porfolio of bonds & securities[1] (Brazil Fund)	Resolution 1289,	1 in United States	Foreign investor $150	Long-term appreciation through securities portfolio
V	Mutual funds			Domestic	
	1 shares	Resolution 1280, 20 Mar. 1987	142	$890	Share investments
	2 Fixed income	Resolution 1286, 20 Mar. 1987	89	$1 270	Fixed income investments
	3 Short-term	Resolution 1199, 10 Oct. 1986	64	$6 110	Liquidity & anonymity

[1] Information refers to Brazil Fund, launched March 1988, with shares distributed to US investors.
Source: Author's compilation of materials regarding legislation and regulations issued concerning investment funds in Brazil.

cannot exceed 5 per cent of the voting capital or 20 per cent of total equity in a company. Swap funds obtain capital by the conversion of loans of fund managers into a portfolio of stock held by the swap fund, and by conversion of loans by foreign creditors at scheduled auctions.[4]

Foreign capital investment funds enjoyed brief success, and fifteen of these were operating in 1988 (Table 14.1, line III). These funds were authorised and created under Resolution 1289. Resolution 1289 also provides for the creation of another type of investment fund – the Managed Portfolio of Bonds and Securities. One such fund was established early in 1988 and distributed in the United States (Brazil Fund). Brazil Fund (Table 14.1, line IV) is also subject to US securities laws and regulations including the Investment Company Act of 1940.[5]

A number of mutual funds have been organised in Brazil, specialising in shares, fixed income securities, or short-term investments (Table 14.1, line V). Whereas only the share mutual funds represent venture capital type activities, all three types of mutual funds are described, since they compete with one another for investor capital. Moreover investors readily shift funds from one type of mutual fund to another, depending on general economic conditions and changes in government regulation of their permitted portfolio allocations.

A final type of fund is the Foreign Investment Company, authorised under Circular 1339 (1988). At the time of writing only one such fund had been organised (Table 14.1, line II): Equitypar Companhia de Participações. This fund may only invest in the primary share market and not in the secondary market, unless it takes a minimum of 5 per cent of the capital of the company. Investee companies use funds for expansion, modernisation or financial restructuring. Participations of Equitypar will be more permanent, and the portfolios of foreign investment companies generally are expected to be less volatile than in the case of debt conversion funds.

Equitypar is a Brazilian portfolio company whose purpose is to invest in a select number of medium and large industrial or commercial companies. It is managed by BSF – Brasilpar Serviços Financeiros Ltda., a financial services company with experience in managing industrial and venture capital investment funds in Brazil.

In order to provide a more diversified capital base for Equitypar, a two-tranche capital offering was made (Table 14.2). The capitalisation of Equitypar at July 1988 was as follows: first Tranche – Banque Paribas $42.0 million, Banque Sudameris $10.0 million, First National Bank of Chicago $10.0 million, Morgan Grenfell & Co. Ltd. $10.0 million, Banco del Gottardo $5.0 million, Banque Internation-

Table 14.2   Two-tranche capital offering of Equitypar

Tranche	Total Capital ($)	Minimum subscription ($)	Source of funds
1	80 million	5–10 million	External debt conversion
2	20 million	2 million	Direct foreign investment and domestic funds
TOTAL	100 million		

ale à Luxembourg $3.0 million. The second tranche included Banco Financeiro e Industrial de Investimento S.A. $3.0 million and Brasilpar Comércio de Participações S.A. $2.5 million. Also it was reported that the International Finance Corporation was considering a participation in Equitypar as a minority stockholder.[6] Investors must agree to maintain their capital investments in Brazil for a 12-year period. The investment strategy to be followed by Equitypar includes minority participations in dynamic and reasonably well managed companies. The average maturity of investments will be geared to attain an annual turnover of approximately 12 per cent. Equitypar aims at financing around 20 projects with an average investment amount of $5 million, with not more than 20 per cent of the portfolio in any one project, or more than 30 per cent in any one sector.

14.3   CONCLUSION

Brazil has succeeded in stimulating the development of a growing number and variety of investment funds. All of these funds operate in the venture capital field, or are closely related to and have close association with it.

The combination of debt conversion and privatisation programmes with a growing number of venture capital funds injects a dynamic factor into the capital market that has no precedent. Complex interactions are possible between these elements. For example, debt conversions are providing liquid capital for swap funds, which seek to make venture capital investments. In addition, private placement funds have been attracting creditor banks, and other foreign investor funds. The various types of mutual funds provide temporary resting-places at which capital funds can be temporarily 'parked' while risk investments are analysed. Privatisation auctions stimulate the mobilisation of capital resources. Moreover privatisations and debt conversions create a supply of and a demand for liquid capital.

While it is exciting to see venture capital activities multiply in amount and types, it is still too early to judge how beneficial these will be in promoting further development of the capital market. Nevertheless the prospects are promising.

NOTES

1. Decree Law 2284 created incentives for venture capital companies in Brazil, and Resolution 1184 covers the tax matters relating to venture capital investors.
2. Roberto Teixeira da Costa, 'The Venture Capital Industry in Brazil', report given at international conference in Sao Paulo, June 1988, p. 2.
3. Antonio Carlos Monteiro, 'A Conversão da Dívida Externa Como Instrumento de Capitalização de Empresas', *Conjuntura Econômica*, March 1988, p. 61.
4. *Gazeta Mercantil*, International Weekly Edition, Special Section on Debt Conversion, 25 April 1988, pp. i, ii.
5. The First Boston Corp. & Merrill Lynch Capital Markets, *Prospectus – The Brazil Fund Inc.*, 31 March 1988, p. 5.
6. *Gazeta Mercantil*, Supplement Titled Conversão da Dívida, 'Equitypar Estuda Como Investir', 16 April 1988, p. 10.

Index

Acesita 332
ANDIMA *see* National
    Association of Open Market
    Dealers
Aracruz Cellulose 368, 378
Austral Plan 74
autofinance 328–9
Autolatina 306

balance sheet 314–15
    assets 317–18
    liabilities 321–2
Banco Bozano Simonsen 379
Banco Chase Manhattan 306
Banco de Amazonia 143, 360
Banco de Brasilia 143
Banco de Roraima 143
Banco del Gottardo 386
Banco do Brasil 3, 37, 56, 74, 76,
    78, 106, 141–2, 205, 215, 300,
    306
    CACEX 142
Banco do Nordeste do Brasil 143
Banco Financeiro e Industriel de
    Investimento 387
Banco Meridional 144
Banco Multiplic ' 358
Banco Nacional ·302
Banco Nacional de Credito
    Cooperativo 144
Banco Nacional do Norte 360
bancos de negocios 159, 178
Banespa 306, 348
Bank of America 358
banking reform 103
banking system
    competition 107
    conglomerates 106, 108
    deposit growth 126
    evolution 119–20
    foreign participation 118–19
    number of banks 107
    point system 114–15
    structure 107

banks
    activities permitted 137
    classification 140
    conglomerate 104, 148
    definition 139
    investment 105
    minimum net worth 117–18
    multiple 104, 108
    number 145
    prohibited activities 140–1
    type 145
Banque Internationale à
    Luxembourg 386
Banque Paribas 386
Banque Sudameris 386
Battery March 379
bill of exchange 152, 225
black market (dollars) 196, 197
block trading 289
BNDESPAR 145, 339, 343, 367,
    369–70
Bolsa 237, 273
Bolsa Brasileira de Futuros
    (BBF) 225, 226, 307
Bolsa de Mercadorias de São
    Paulo 225, 226, 307
Bolsa Mercantil e de Futuros 225,
    226, 307
Bovespa Index 284
Bradesco 186, 205
Brasilpar Comercio e Participações
    S.A. 382, 387
Brasilpar Servicos Financeiras
    Ltda. 386
Brazil Fund 379, 386
Brazilian Reinsurance
    Institute 173
Brazilian Statistics Institute
    (IBGE) 121, 217
Bresser Plan 94
brokerage firms 158–9
    minimum capital 167
budget
    deficit 20–1, 31

389

budget *cont.*
  deficit equilibrium   28
  fiscal   77, 192, 201
  monetary   192
  unification   201

Caixa Economica Federal   *see*
    Federal Savings Bank
capital   126–9
capital market
  BNDES   338–9
  Capital Market Law   244
  conflicting objectives   254–5
  corporation law   249–53
  development 1966–75   245–6
  first round of laws   242–3
  fiscal funds   247
  institutions   239–40, 255–73
  instruments   238
  investment banks   244, 246
  investment companies   248
  open companies   237–8, 245
  privatisation   376–7
  registration of securities   243, 245
  second round of laws   248–9
  stock exchanges   238
  tax measures   244
capitalisation companies   172
Caraiba Metais   368, 376
Castelo Branco   245
CEASA   368
Center for Custody of Private
    Securities   *see* CETIP
Central Bank
  and government debt   198
  and money market   197
  created   75, 107
  credit control   192
  gold price   197
  movement account   192
  open market operations   200–1,
    202, 204–6
  regulation of money
    market   212–13
certificates of deposit   224
CETIP   207–8, 213
Cobra   340
Cofavi   374
Comissão de Valores Mobiliarios

  (CVM)   *see* Securities
    Commission
commercial banks
  activities   146
  cheque clearing and float   147
  leverage limit   147
  number and type   145
  owned by government   141–3
commodities exchange   158
Companhia Ferro e Aco de
    Vitoria   374
Companhia Siderurgica
    Nacional   332
company finance
  balance sheet   314–22
  macroeconomy   316–17
  operating results   323–5
Conjuntura Econômica   315
Conselho Federal de
    Desestatização   371
Conselho Monetario Nacional   *see*
    National Monetary Council
constitution   5, 79, 103, 104
  convention   314, 348
consumer finance companies   152
consumption function   26
Copene   367
corporate finance   176
corporate governance   253
corporate sector
  and monetary correction   325
  composition   315
  profitability   325
  sources and uses of funds   327–9
  state enterprises   315
Corretores de Mercadoria   309
Corretores de Valores   309
Council for Industrial Development
    (CDI)   317
crawling peg   91, 194
credit co-operatives   151–2
crowding out   194
Cruzado Plan   55, 65, 66, 69, 73,
    90, 93, 220, 325
currency futures   311

debenture trustee   252–3
debentures   209
debt conversion   350–3

before 1988 353
bicicleterios 362
debtor and creditor 355
direct negotiation 358
informal 360–1
legal basis 353–4
monthly swaps 358
parallel market 362
policy issues 352
source of capital 357
swap funds 358–9
debt–equity swaps 305–6
debt moratorium 347
debt restructuring 348
defined benefit plan 260
defined contribution plan 260
Delfim Netto 65, 89, 217
deregulation 371
destatisation 371
devaluation 90, 93
development banking 144–5
disclosure 250–1
distribuidora 105, 158–9
  minimum capital 167

elections 5
Eletrobras 174, 205, 365
employment 4
entrepreneurial activity 341–2
Equitypar Companhia de
  Participações 386
escalator clause 13, 17, 78
exit bonds 307
exports 3
external debt 7–8, 34, 41, 72
  amount 349
  creditworthiness 348
  debt crisis 94–5
  moratorium 8
  oil shock 349
  secondary market 348, 351
external crisis 97

factoring companies 174
Federal Savings Bank (Caixa
  Economica Federal) 149
FINAME 340
financial deepening 236, 241–2
financial futures 310

financial innovations 40, 70, 79–80
  and interest rates 81
financial institutions
  capital 126–9
  capital market 239, 253–7
  distinctive features 133–7
  foreign ownership 103, 131, 155
  fund allocations 255–7
  profit 129–31
  real estate 265
  savings 149–52
  specialisation 136
  stock market 287–8
financial instruments tax 228–9
financial intermediation 241–2
financial repression 242
financial sector
  diversification 124–6
  importance 121–3
financial services 175–7
FINOR 274–5
First National Bank of
  Chicago 386
fiscal funds 238, 240, 246, 247
fiscal incentives 275
Ford 306
foreign business
  investment 304–5, 355–6
foreign capital investment
  companies 303
foreign-controlled firms 317, 320,
  326, 335, 336
foreign exchange market
  Banco do Brasil 229
  futures market 231
  trading limits 229
Fund for Democratisation of
  Capital (FUNDECE) 245
Fund of Social Participation 240,
  269–70, 339
Fundo ao Portador 228
Fundo de Investimentos da
  Amazonia 366
Fundo de Investimentos do
  Nordeste 366
futures contracts 225–6, 232
futures exchanges 158

Getulio Vargas Foundation 217

gold futures 311
gold market 196, 210
Golden Shares 365
government securities 78, 80,
   223–5
   amount outstanding 198
   authorised dealers 204, 205
   clearing and custody 208
   expansion 207–8
   extramarket 204–5
   new issues 201–4
   open market operations 200,
      201
   OTN Cambial 203
growth
   industrial output 88
   real 6, 88–9

hedging instruments 231, 232
Heliodinamica 340
heterodox shock 347
high-powered money 77

IBRACON (Brazilian Institute of
   Accountancy) 133
income policies 56–7
indexation 216
industrial production 3
inflation
   and accounting 18–19
   and finance 134–5
   inertial 66–7, 68
   tax 19, 73, 75
insurance companies 172–3, 240,
   262–3, 267–8
Insurance Superintendent 108,
   121
interbank market 214–16
interest rate 218–20
   and central bank 197
   and monetary correction 195,
      216–18
   ceiling 15–16, 64, 79
   earned on OTN 204
   inflation rate 204
   market risk 222
   nominal and real 29, 194, 197,
      204, 218
   overnight rate 193, 202, 203,

204, 218, 220
   parity relation 194–5
Interministerial Council for
   Privatisation 370
International Finance Corp.
   (IFC) 304, 387
International Monetary Fund
   (IMF) 20, 25
investment 4
investment banks 107, 148–9,
   238–9
investment certificates 275
investment clubs 240, 273, 284
Investment Company Act of
   1940 386
investment holding companies 171
invisible hand 366
Itau 205

Job Tenure Guarantee Fund
   (FGTS) 149
joint venture 186–7

land area 3
lease and leaseback 136
leasing company 105, 155–6
legal environment 235, 242–53
   banking law 106
   capital market law 106, 236–7
   company law 107
   complementary bank law 119
   Manual of Rules and
      Instructions 133
   normalisation 235
   stock exchange law 279
letra de cambio 152, 225
LIBOR 96
LIFFE 309
Lloyds Bank 358

Mafersa 368
maxi-devaluation 91, 325, 335
Mendes Junior 302
mercado a termo 281
mercado de balção 156
mercado interfinanceiro 214–15,
   220
merchant banking 176
Mesbla 302

Mexican moratorium 97
monetary correction 10, 11, 12,
    23, 25, 43, 48, 216–22
  and inflation 218
  dual indexor 218
money demand 82–3
money illusion 22–9, 31, 46, 74
money market
  ANDIMA 210–11
  bills of exchange 225
  central bank activities 196–7
  certificates of deposit 224
  development 193–4
  foreign exchange market 229–32
  government debt 198
  institutions 212–14
  instruments 222–5
  interbank market 214–16
  monetary correction 216–19
  money market funds 226–7
  Morgan Grenfell 386
  movement account 75–6
  restricted to overnight 220
  risks 191–2
Multibanco Internacional de
    Investimentos 358
multibank   *see* banks, multiple
mutual funds
  capital market 268–9
  comparisons 227
  foreign currency 169–70
  portfolio rules 227
  short term 226–7, 240
  swap funds 359–60
  venture capital 386

National Association of Open
    Market Dealers
    (ANDIMA) 124, 208, 210–11
National Bank for Economic and
    Social Development
    (BNDES) 135, 144–5, 205,
    317, 336–42, 367
National Development Fund
    (FND) 174, 241
National Monetary Council
    (CMN) 56, 75, 77, 108, 195,
    242
  membership 237

National Treasury Secretary 201
Neves, Tancredo 314
new issues
  BNDES 338
  financial institutions 298
  international comparisons 297–8

oil shock 4
open capital company 245, 291,
    292
open company 237
open market 191
over the counter market 209, 293

PAEG Plan 55, 62–3
PAIT Funds 172, 241
parallel market 210
parity relationships 191
pension funds 173–4, 240, 257–8
  and social security 259
  benefits 258
  closed funds 261–2
  open funds 262–3
  organisation 257–8
  portfolio regulation 260–1
  portfolio structure 263–4
Petrobras 4, 205, 300, 318, 365
Phillips curve 69
Planning Secretariat 145
Plano Verao   *see* Summer plan
PNC Comércio e Participações
    Ltda 360
PNC International Bank 360
poupancas 220
preferred stock 237
previdência privada 258
previdência social 258
price controls 241
price freeze 69, 192
price index 217
private placement 367
  funds 379
privatisation
  copper sector 376
  electric energy 373–4
  foreign participation 378
  Interministerial Council 370
  iron and steel 374–5
  main issues 364–6

privatisation *cont.*
  methods 365
  1988 Decree 371
  pulverisation 369
  seven models 372–3
  two-stage 378
profits
  corporate 47–8
  corrected for inflation 50
  illusory 18, 47
Programa de Formação do
  Patrimonio do Servidor
  Publico (PASEP) 270
Programa de Integrações Social
  (PIS) 270
project financing 337
pulverisation of capital 369, 372

real estate investment 265
rediscount rate 76
regional development
  funds 273–4, 367
remunerated accounts 79–80
reprivatisation 366–7
repurchase agreement 193, 206–7
Resolution 63 Loans 135

Sarney, President 314
savings, external 96
savings and loans 150–1
Securities Commission 108, 115, 121
  creation 249
  powers 249
securities firms 238–9
securities dealing 177
securities portfolio 304
self-finance 241
SELIC 205–6, 207–8, 213
shareholder rights 251–2
shocks
  external 96
  supply shocks 67
Sibra 369
Sid Macroeletronica 340
Siderbras 174, 365, 374
SIMA 208–9
Simonsen, Mario Henrique 89,
  246

SINO 210
Sistema Especial de Liquidação e
  Custodia *see* SELIC
Sistema Integrado de Mercado
  Aberti *see* SIMA
Sistema Nacional de
  Debentures *see* SND
Sistema Nacional de Ouro *see*
  SINO
SND 209
Social Security System 173
Sociedade Anonima (S.A.) 258
stagnation 96
state enterprises 315, 332
stock exchanges 156–7
stock index futures 307, 310
stock market
  asset preferences 285–6
  actively traded shares 299–300
  automation 283
  boom of 1967–71 247
  calls and puts 282
  capitalisation 292–3
  company participation 290–1
  custody 282
  growth in trading 294–5
  institutional participation 288
  international links 302–3
  investment clubs 284
  new issues 296
  over the counter 293
  period 1971–9 247
  public companies 291–2
  secondary trading 292
  settlement 282
  stock index 283
  tax status 287
  trading 280–2
  trading concentration 300
  type investors 285–6
SUDENE 143, 274
Summer plan 94
Superintendent for Northeast
  Development *see* SUDENE
Superintendent of Private
  Insurance 173
swap auctions 306
swap equity funds 306
swap funds 379

tax
  direct 14
  indirect 14
  inflation *see* inflation
  inflationary 11, 34, 36, 40, 45
trade finance 176
trade surplus 98
transfer pricing 327

underwriting securities 136, 157
Unibanco 186
United Kingdom 365
Usiminas 368

Vale do Rio Doce 300
venture capital 386
venture capital activities
  debt conversion 384

privatisation 384
special funds 384–6
venture capital companies 171–2, 382–3
venture capital incentives 383
Volkswagen 306
Votorantim Group 369

wage corrections
  and income policy 56–7
  average adjustment 55, 60–1
  peak adjustment 55, 57–8
  trigger point 56
wages
  policies 92
  real 58–9, 60, 91
working capital credits 337
World Bank 25